American College of Physicians

MKSAP® 15

Medical Knowledge Self-Assessment Program®

Rheumatology

Rheumatology

Contributors

Marcy B. Bolster, MD, FACP, Book Editor[2]
Professor of Medicine
Director, Rheumatology Training Program
Medical University of South Carolina
Charleston, South Carolina

Virginia U. Collier, MD, FACP, Associate Editor[2]
Hugh R. Sharp, Jr. Chair of Medicine
Christiana Care Health System
Newark, Delaware
Professor of Medicine
Jefferson Medical College of Thomas Jefferson University
Philadelphia, Pennsylvania

Anne R. Bass, MD, FACP[2]
Associate Professor of Clinical Medicine
Weill Cornell Medical College
Rheumatology Fellowship Program Director
Hospital for Special Surgery
New York, New York

Richard D. Brasington, Jr., MD, FACP[2]
Professor of Medicine
Director, Rheumatology Training Program
Division of Rheumatology
Washington University School of Medicine
St. Louis, Missouri

Alan N. Brown, MD, FACP[2]
Associate Professor of Medicine
Medical University of South Carolina
Charleston, South Carolina

Beth Jonas, MD[2]
Director, Rheumatology Training Program
Assistant Professor of Medicine
Division of Rheumatology
University of North Carolina School of Medicine
Chapel Hill, North Carolina

Leslie S. Staudt, MD[1]
Assistant Professor of Medicine
Director, Rheumatology Training Program
University of Oklahoma Health Sciences Center
Oklahoma City, Oklahoma

Editor-in-Chief

Patrick C. Alguire, MD, FACP[1]
Director, Education and Career Development
American College of Physicians
Philadelphia, Pennsylvania

Rheumatology Reviewers

Robert D. Arbeit, MD, FACP[2]
Stewart Babbott, MD, FACP[1]
Frantz Duffoo, MD, FACP[1]
Barri J. Fessler, MD, FACP[2]
Lois J. Geist, MD, FACP[1]
Kent A. Kirchner, MD, FACP[1]
Carlos J. Lozada, MD, FACP[2]
Joseph J. Padinjarayveetil, MD[1]
Trish M. Perl, MD, MSc[2]

Rheumatology ACP Editorial Staff

Amanda Neiley, Staff Editor
Sean McKinney, Director, Self-Assessment Programs
Margaret Wells, Managing Editor
Charles Rossi, Senior Associate of Clinical Content Development
Shannon O'Sullivan, Editorial Coordinator

ACP Principal Staff

Steven E. Weinberger, MD, FACP[2]
Deputy Executive Vice President
Senior Vice President, Medical Education and Publishing

D. Theresa Kanya, MBA[1]
Vice President, Medical Education and Publishing

Sean McKinney[1]
Director, Self-Assessment Programs

Margaret Wells[1]
Managing Editor

Charles Rossi[1]
Senior Associate of Clinical Content Development

Becky Krumm[1]
Senior Staff Editor

Ellen McDonald, PhD[1]
Senior Staff Editor

Amanda Neiley[1]
Staff Editor

Katie Idell[1]
Production Administrator/Editor

Valerie Dangovetsky[1]
Program Administrator

John Murray[1]
Editorial Coordinator

Shannon O'Sullivan[1]
Editorial Coordinator

Developed by the American College of Physicians

---

1. Has no relationships with any entity producing, marketing, re-selling, or distributing health care goods or services consumed by, or used on, patients.

2. Has disclosed relationships with entities producing, marketing, re-selling, or distributing health care goods or services consumed by, or used on, patients. See below.

Conflicts of Interest

The following contributors and ACP staff members have disclosed relationships with commercial companies:

Robert D. Arbeit, MD, FACP
Employment
Paratek Pharmaceuticals

Anne R. Bass, MD, FACP
Research Grants/Contracts
Centocor

Marcy B. Bolster, MD, FACP
Research Grants/Contracts
Procter & Gamble
Speakers Bureau
Genentech, Merck, Novartis
Other
Abbott, UCB

Richard D. Brasington, Jr., MD, FACP
Speakers Bureau
Centocor, Genentech, Bristol-Myers Squibb, Biogen Idec, Abbott

Alan N. Brown, MD, FACP
Speakers Bureau
Abbott
Other
UCB, Genentech

Virginia U. Collier, MD, FACP
Stock Options/Holdings
Celgene, Pfizer, Merck, Schering-Plough, Abbott, Johnson & Johnson, Medtronic, McKesson, Amgen

Barri J. Fessler, MD, FACP
Research Grants/Contracts
Actelion
Consultantship
Gilead, Abbott Immunology
Speakers Bureau
Actelion, Gilead, Encysive Pharmaceuticals

Beth Jonas, MD
Research Grants/Contracts
Stryker Biotech, Roche, Pfizer
Other
Abbott

Carlos J. Lozada, MD, FACP
Honoraria
Wyeth, Amgen, Abbott, Bristol-Myers Squibb
Speakers Bureau
Wyeth, Amgen, Abbott, Bristol-Myers Squibb

Trish M. Perl, MD, MSc
Stock Options/Holdings
Visicu
Research Grants/Contracts
3M, Sage
Honoraria
Pfizer, Ortho-McNeil
Consultantship
VHA, IHI, Theradoc

Steven E. Weinberger, MD, FACP
Stock Options/Holdings
Abbott, GlaxoSmithKline

Acknowledgments

The American College of Physicians (ACP) gratefully acknowledges the special contributions to the development and production of the 15th edition of the Medical Knowledge Self-Assessment Program® (MKSAP 15) of Scott Thomas Hurd (Senior Systems Analyst/Developer), Ricki Jo Kauffman (Manager, Systems Development), Michael Ripca (Technical Administrator/Graphics Designer), and Lisa Torrieri (Graphic Designer). The Digital version (CD-ROM and Online components) was developed within the ACP's Interactive Product Development Department by Steven Spadt (Director), Christopher Forrest (Senior Software Developer), Ryan Hinkel (Senior Software Developer), John McKnight (Software Developer), Sean O'Donnell (Senior Software Developer), and Brian Sweigard (Senior Software Developer). Computer scoring and reporting are being performed by ACT, Inc., Iowa City, Iowa. The College also wishes to acknowledge that many other persons, too numerous to mention, have contributed to the production of this program. Without their dedicated efforts, this program would not have been possible.

Continuing Medical Education

The American College of Physicians is accredited by the Accreditation Council for Continuing Medical Education (ACCME) to provide continuing medical education for physicians.

The American College of Physicians designates this educational activity for a maximum of 166 *AMA PRA Category 1 Credits*™. Physicians should only claim credit commensurate with the extent of their participation in the activity.

AMA PRA Category 1 Credit™ is available from July 31, 2009, to July 31, 2012.

Learning Objectives

The learning objectives of MKSAP 15 are to:
- Close gaps between actual care in your practice and preferred standards of care, based on best evidence
- Diagnose disease states that are less common and sometimes overlooked and confusing
- Improve management of comorbidities that can complicate patient care
- Determine when to refer patients for surgery or care by subspecialists
- Pass the ABIM certification examination
- Pass the ABIM maintenance of certification examination

Target Audience

- General internists and primary care physicians
- Subspecialists who need to remain up-to-date in internal medicine
- Residents preparing for the certifying examination in internal medicine
- Physicians preparing for maintenance of certification in internal medicine (recertification)

How to Submit for CME Credits

To earn CME credits, complete a MKSAP 15 answer sheet. Use the enclosed, self-addressed envelope to mail your completed answer sheet(s) to the MKSAP Processing Center for scoring. Remember to provide your MKSAP 15 order and ACP ID numbers in the appropriate spaces on the answer sheet. The order and ACP ID numbers are printed on your mailing label. If you have <u>not</u> received these numbers with your MKSAP 15 purchase, you will need to acquire them to earn CME credits. E-mail ACP's customer service center at custserv@acponline.org. In the subject line, write "MKSAP 15 order/ACP ID numbers." In the body of the e-mail, make sure you include your e-mail address as well as your full name, address, city, state, ZIP code, country, and telephone number. Also identify where you have made your MKSAP 15 purchase. You will receive your MKSAP 15 order and ACP ID numbers by e-mail within 72 business hours.

Permission/Consent for Use of Figures Shown in MKSAP 15 Rheumatology Multiple-Choice Questions

Figure shown in Self-Assessment Test Item 26 is modified with permission from Yee AMF, Paget SA, eds. Expert Guide to Rheumatology. Philadelphia, PA: American College of Physicians; 2004.

Figure shown in Self-Assessment Test Item 39 is modified with permission from Moore G. Atlas of the Musculoskeletal Examination. Philadelphia, PA: American College of Physicians; 2003.

Figures shown in Self-Assessment Test Items 53 and 60 are reprinted with permission from Physician's Information and Education Resource (PIER). Philadelphia, PA: American College of Physicians. Copyright © 2009 American College of Physicians.

Disclosure Policy

It is the policy of the American College of Physicians (ACP) to ensure balance, independence, objectivity, and scientific rigor in all its educational activities. To this end, and consistent with the policies of the ACP and the Accreditation Council for Continuing Medical Education (ACCME), contributors to all ACP continuing medical education activities are required to disclose all relationships with any entity producing, marketing, re-selling, or distributing health care goods or services consumed by, or used on, patients. Contributors are required to use generic names in the discussion of therapeutic options and are required to identify any unapproved, off-label, or investigative use of commercial products or devices. Where a trade name is used, all available trade names for the same product type are also included. If trade-name products manufactured by companies with whom contributors have relationships are discussed, contributors are asked to provide evidence-based citations in support of the discussion. The information is reviewed by the committee responsible for producing this text. If necessary, adjustments to topics or contributors' roles in content development are made to balance the discussion. Further, all readers of this text are asked to evaluate the content for evidence of commercial bias so that future decisions about content and contributors can be made in light of this information.

Resolution of Conflicts

To resolve all conflicts of interest and influences of vested interests, the ACP precluded members of the content-creation committee from deciding on any content issues that involved generic or trade-name products associated with proprietary entities with which these committee members had relationships. In addition, content was based on best evidence and updated clinical care guidelines, when such evidence and guidelines were available. Contributors' disclosure information can be found with the list of contributors' names and those of ACP principal staff listed in the beginning of this book.

Educational Disclaimer

The editors and publisher of MKSAP 15 recognize that the development of new material offers many opportunities for error. Despite our best efforts, some errors may persist in print. Drug dosage schedules are, we believe, accurate and in accordance with current standards. Readers are advised, however, to ensure that the recommended dosages in MKSAP 15 concur with the information provided in the product information material. This is especially important in cases of new, infrequently used, or highly toxic drugs. Application of the information in MKSAP 15 remains the professional responsibility of the practitioner.

The primary purpose of MKSAP 15 is educational. Information presented, as well as publications, technologies, products, and/or services discussed, is intended to inform subscribers about the knowledge, techniques, and experiences of the contributors. A diversity of professional opinion exists, and the views of the contributors are their own and not those of the ACP. Inclusion of any material in the program does not constitute endorsement or recommendation by the ACP. The ACP does not warrant the safety, reliability, accuracy, completeness, or usefulness of and disclaims any and all liability for damages and claims that may result from the use of information, publications, technologies, products, and/or services discussed in this program.

Publisher's Information

Unauthorized Use of This Book Is Against the Law

MKSAP 15 ISBN: 978-1-934465-25-7
Rheumatology ISBN: 978-1-934465-30-1

Printed in the United States of America.

For order information in the U.S. or Canada call 800-523-1546, extension 2600. All other countries call 215-351-2600. Fax inquiries to 215-351-2799 or e-mail to custserv@acponline.org.

Errata and Norm Tables

Errata for MKSAP 15 will be posted at http://mksap.acponline.org/errata as new information becomes known to the editors.

MKSAP 15 Performance Interpretation Guidelines with Norm Tables, available December 31, 2010, will reflect the knowledge of physicians who have completed the self-assessment tests before the program was published. These physicians took the tests without being able to refer to the syllabus, answers, and critiques. For your convenience, the tables are available in a printable PDF file at http://mksap.acponline.org/normtables.

Table of Contents

Rheumatology

Approach to the Patient with Suspected Rheumatic Disease

The assessment of a patient with musculoskeletal symptoms of rheumatic disease should initially differentiate between inflammatory and noninflammatory features (**Table 1**). Inflammatory arthritis usually manifests as the five cardinal signs of inflammation: (1) swelling, (2) warmth, (3) erythema, (4) tenderness, and (5) loss of function. Determining the pattern of joint involvement helps refine the differential diagnosis (**Table 2**).

Localized Versus Diffuse Rheumatic Pain

Localized Rheumatic Pain

Careful questioning is necessary to identify whether the patient has joint pain or periarticular pain, and asking the patient to point to the location of the pain with one finger can be helpful. Pain that truly emanates from the hip joint typically is experienced in the groin and medial thigh. Patients who report "hip pain" may actually have pain in the buttock or in the lateral thigh. Buttock pain can represent referred lumbar spine disease, sciatica, or ischial bursitis; lateral thigh pain usually indicates trochanteric bursitis, often accompanied by iliotibial band syndrome.

Pain from a glenohumeral joint disorder will be experienced medial to the humeral head and a few centimeters below the clavicle, but periarticular pain involving the shoulder will have different locations. For example, rotator cuff tendinitis and subacromial bursitis tend to be more lateral and adjacent to the acromion. Distinguishing between problems in the shoulder and cervical spine can also be difficult. Neck pain can radiate to the trapezius region and be mistaken for a "shoulder" problem; if the shoulder range of motion is full and painless, however, this suggests a source in the cervical spine.

Different joints are variably affected by different disorders. Rheumatoid arthritis and osteoarthritis can both involve the proximal interphalangeal joints of the hands, but metacarpophalangeal joint involvement occurs in rheumatoid arthritis and not osteoarthritis. Distal interphalangeal joint involvement is characteristic of osteoarthritis but not rheumatoid arthritis. Unless a secondary condition, such as trauma, metabolic disorder, or inflammatory arthritis, has already affected the joint, osteoarthritis does not occur in the metacarpophalangeal, wrist, elbow, shoulder, and ankle joints.

Diffuse Rheumatic Pain

Patients with rheumatic disease commonly report having "pain all over." Although this symptom sometimes indicates polyarticular arthritis, more often the source of discomfort is the soft tissues around the joints. Patients with fibromyalgia, for example, typically have pain in nonarticular areas above and below the waist and on both sides of the body; elderly

TABLE 1 Features of Inflammatory Versus Noninflammatory Arthritis		
	Type of Arthritis	
Feature	**Inflammatory**	**Noninflammatory**
Physical examination findings	Joint inflammation (warmth, erythema, soft-tissue swelling, effusion)	No signs of inflammation; bony proliferation in osteoarthritis
Morning stiffness	Lasting (generally) >1 hour	Lasting <1 hour
Systemic symptoms	Low-grade fever, fatigue, rash	None
Synovial fluid	Leukocyte count >2000/µL, predominantly neutrophils	Leukocyte count <2000/µL, <50% neutrophils
Other laboratory studies	ESR and/or CRP often (but not always) elevated; anemia of chronic disease; positive rheumatoid factor or anti-CCP antibodies	Normal findings
Radiographs	Erosions, periostitis, joint-space narrowing	Joint-space narrowing, osteophytes, subchondral sclerosis

CCP = cyclic citrullinated peptide; CRP = C-reactive protein; ESR = erythrocyte sedimentation rate.

TABLE 2 Patterns of Joint Involvement in the Differential Diagnosis of Inflammatory Arthritis

Differential Diagnosis	Joint Involvement						
	Symmetric	Asymmetric	Spine	Monoarticular	Oligoarthritis	Polyarthritis	Migratory
Bacterial (non-GC) arthritis	–	++++	++	++++	+++	+	–
Crystalline arthropathies							
Gout	+	++++	+	+++	+++	+	+
Pseudogout	++	+++	–	+++	++	++	
Rheumatoid arthritis	++++	–	+++ (cervical spine only)	–	+	++++	
Psoriatic arthritis	++	+++	+	++	+++	++	
IBD	++	+++	+	++	+++	++	
Disseminated GC arthritis		++++			++++		++++
Lyme disease		++++			++++		++++
Acute rheumatic fever		++++			++	+++	++++

– = extremely unlikely; + = can occur; ++ = frequent; +++ = very common; ++++ = most common; GC = gonococcal; IBD = inflammatory bowel disease.

persons with polymyalgia rheumatica also have diffuse pain, with symptoms more localized to the neck, hips, and shoulders. Depression, somatoform pain disorder, and malingering also may manifest as diffuse musculoskeletal symptoms.

Referred Rheumatic Pain

The site of origin of the pain may be remote from the area of the symptoms. When range of motion of a joint area is limited and painful, this joint is likely the source of the pain. The cause of the pain may be elsewhere if a joint can be moved painlessly.

Frequently, symptoms of cervical radiculopathy are referred to the shoulder girdle area and can be mistaken for a shoulder problem. Shoulder pain is also a potential presentation of cholecystitis, with pain referred from the diaphragm. In the latter case, physical examination of the shoulder would show normal range of motion and would not reproduce the discomfort. Osteoarthritis of the hip may present with knee pain; in such a case, subjecting the hip to flexion and internal and external rotation by the FABERE (Flexion–Abduction–External Rotation–Extension) maneuver would demonstrate decreased range of motion and likely discomfort in the groin. Conversely, pain in the hip region may be due to osteoarthritis of the knee or to leg-length discrepancy. Osteoarthritis of the subtalar joint of the ankle can cause referred heel pain, and an abdominal aortic aneurysm can cause low back pain. Similarly, a commonly missed cause of knee pain is anserine bursitis; range of motion of the knee is full and painless, with no knee effusion, but exquisite tenderness is produced by pressing on the anserine bursa in the anteromedial knee, distal to the joint line.

KEY POINTS

- Inflammatory arthritis typically presents with the five cardinal signs of inflammation, namely, swelling, warmth, erythema, tenderness, and loss of function.
- Full, painless range of motion of a joint suggests that the patient's "joint pain" is actually referred from another anatomic area.

Arthralgia, Periarthritis, and Bursitis

Arthralgia

Arthralgia implies pain in a joint in the absence of signs of inflammation. A firm diagnosis is less likely to be established when joint pain exists in the absence of abnormal findings on physical examination.

Periarthritis

Some common inflammatory processes can affect the soft tissues surrounding, but not involving, the joint. Such conditions are described as periarthritis and are usually regional and not widespread on physical examination. No diagnostic laboratory tests can differentiate periarthritis from arthritis, so the diagnosis is made on the basis of the history and physical examination. Periarthritic disorders of the shoulder region include rotator cuff tendinitis, bicipital tendinitis, and adhesive capsulitis ("frozen shoulder"). Medial epicondylitis ("golfer's elbow") and lateral epicondylitis ("tennis elbow") are periarthritic disorders commonly seen around the elbow, and a periarthritic tendinitis of the thumb abductors and extensors (de Quervain tenosynovitis) often involves the wrist area.

Bursitis

A bursa is a connective tissue sac with a potential space that facilitates smooth movement of one tissue over another. Bursitis results when a bursa becomes inflamed (usually from trauma or an overuse syndrome) or infected. As with other forms of periarthritis, the physical examination distinguishes bursitis from involvement of an adjacent joint. Subacromial bursitis is often seen over the shoulder; differentiating this condition from rotator cuff tendinitis is difficult but not always necessary, because the treatment for these conditions is similar. Olecranon bursitis commonly manifests as swelling and pain over the posterior elbow. Aspiration of the affected bursa and analysis of the synovial fluid are indicated to evaluate for an infectious cause. Other common forms of bursitis include trochanteric bursitis (lateral hip), prepatellar bursitis ("housemaid's knee"), and anserine bursitis (proximal tibia).

Monoarticular Arthritis

Acute monoarticular inflammatory arthritis is assumed to be infectious until proved otherwise by synovial fluid analysis and culture. Synovial fluid leukocyte counts are useful in suggesting the presence of an infectious arthritis; total leukocyte counts greater than 50,000/µL are strongly suggestive of bacterial arthritis. Bacterial septic arthritis is associated with significant morbidity and mortality and may cause irreversible joint destruction within a few days. Thus, early diagnosis and treatment are critical.

In clinical practice, acute inflammatory monoarticular arthritis is usually due to gout or pseudogout. However, synovial fluid analysis should be performed to exclude an infectious cause because infectious and crystalline arthritis can coexist. The diagnosis of crystal-induced arthritis is confirmed by visualizing crystals under polarized light microscopy. Fever, peripheral blood leukocytosis, and elevated acute phase reactants all may be seen in either condition and are not useful for distinguishing crystalline from infectious monoarticular arthritis.

Fungal or mycobacterial infections or Lyme disease may also manifest as monoarticular arthritis. Culture for fungi and mycobacteria is usually not indicated in the acute setting. Lyme disease may cause large joint effusions, especially of the knee. Serologic testing for *Borrelia burgdorferi* should be performed only in patients with a definite risk of exposure, including traveling to an endemic area, obtaining a tick bite in an endemic area, or having a characteristic rash (erythema chronicum migrans).

Hemarthrosis may likewise result in monoarticular arthritis and may be caused by trauma from a fracture through the joint line into the joint space or internal derangement. An accompanying history of acute trauma or joint damage from overuse is usually suggestive of these entities. Patients with a bleeding diathesis or those being treated with anticoagulation therapy may be particularly at risk. Synovial fluid analysis does not reveal elevated leukocyte counts in these patients.

Osteoarthritis can cause monoarticular symptoms but does not cause inflammatory monoarticular arthritis, unless a secondary complication (typically infection or crystalline deposition) exists. Avascular necrosis can be associated with an acute monoarticular arthritis, but synovial fluid leukocyte counts are not as elevated as in other types of inflammatory arthritis. Corticosteroid therapy, alcoholism, vasculitis, sickle cell disease, and trauma are clinical circumstances that should raise suspicion of avascular necrosis.

Acute monoarticular arthritis is rarely the presenting symptom of rheumatoid arthritis or a connective tissue disease and therefore does not warrant routine testing for rheumatoid factor or antinuclear antibodies. However, arthritis associated with the seronegative spondyloarthropathies often does have a monoarticular presentation. Similarly, reactive arthritis, which includes the combination of arthritis, conjunctivitis, and urethritis and was formerly known as Reiter syndrome, frequently has a monoarticular presentation. In such patients, the involved joint is usually the knee or ankle, and a history of a diarrheal illness or sexually transmitted disease suggests the diagnosis. Sarcoidosis may present as monoarticular arthritis (usually of the ankle); Löfgren syndrome, a subset of sarcoidosis, manifests as arthritis, erythema nodosum, and hilar lymphadenopathy.

Chronic monoarticular arthritis, defined by symptoms persisting for more than 6 weeks, has a different differential diagnosis from that of acute monoarticular arthritis. In the chronic form, for example, crystalline arthritis and pyogenic bacterial infections are much less likely. The evaluation of all patients with chronic monoarticular arthritis should include synovial fluid analysis and radiography of the affected joint to assess for characteristic bony or soft-tissue abnormalities; synovial biopsy is indicated when routine testing does not reveal a cause. The presence of inflammatory synovial fluid from patients with chronic monoarticular arthritis suggests mycobacterial or fungal septic arthritis, Lyme disease, or a seronegative spondyloarthropathy. Noninflammatory synovial fluid suggests a structural abnormality, avascular necrosis, internal derangement, or osteoarthritis.

KEY POINTS

- Immediate synovial fluid analysis is indicated in patients with monoarticular swelling to exclude bacterial infection.
- An infectious cause of monoarthritis and crystalline arthritis can coexist.

Oligoarticular and Polyarticular Arthritis

The differential diagnosis of acute oligoarticular arthritis (involving two to four joints) and acute polyarticular arthritis (involving more than four joints) is more extensive than that of acute monoarticular arthritis. Bacterial septic arthritis rarely involves more than one joint, but all other causes of acute monoarticular arthritis also may have an oligoarticular or polyarticular presentation. The causes of acute polyarticular and oligoarticular arthritis may be determined by considering the pattern and distribution of joint involvement.

Infectious causes of acute polyarticular and oligoarticular arthritis include gonococcal arthritis; Lyme disease; endocarditis; acute rheumatic fever; and, most often, a virus. Viruses that are especially likely to cause acute polyarticular arthritis include hepatitis B and C, parvovirus B19, HIV, Epstein-Barr virus, and rubella. Noninfectious causes of polyarticular or oligoarticular arthritis include rheumatoid arthritis, systemic lupus erythematosus (SLE) and other connective tissue diseases, polyarticular gout, the arthropathies associated with seronegative spondyloarthropathies, sarcoidosis, and serum sickness. Systemic forms of vasculitis, such as Wegener granulomatosis, polyarteritis nodosa, and microscopic polyangiitis, also may be associated with polyarticular arthritis. Adult-onset Still disease, Behçet disease, relapsing polychondritis, palindromic rheumatism, familial Mediterranean fever, and Whipple disease are uncommon conditions that can manifest as an inflammatory polyarticular (or oligoarticular) arthritis.

The temporal pattern of joint involvement may help clarify the diagnosis of polyarticular and oligoarticular arthritis. Gonococcal arthritis, Lyme disease, and acute rheumatic fever often have a migratory pattern in which symptoms are present in some joints for a brief period of time, remit, and later appear in different joints. An intermittent or episodic pattern characterized by repeated episodes of inflammatory arthritis with complete resolution between attacks is typical of gout, sarcoidosis, palindromic rheumatism, and reactive arthritis; less commonly, rheumatoid and psoriatic arthritis also may manifest in this manner.

The distribution of joint involvement also helps to suggest the cause of inflammatory oligoarticular or polyarticular arthritis. Rheumatoid arthritis, viral infections, and SLE are typically associated with a symmetric joint distribution. Conversely, an asymmetric pattern is more typical of crystal-induced arthritis and the seronegative spondyloarthropathies.

Chronic polyarticular arthritis is characterized by symptoms that persist for more than 6 weeks. Infections other than hepatitis C; HIV; and, rarely, parvovirus B19 are generally not associated with chronic polyarticular arthritis. Otherwise, most of the causes of acute polyarticular arthritis also may cause chronic symptoms.

The Musculoskeletal Examination

A general screening musculoskeletal examination can help to determine the cause of a patient's musculoskeletal symptoms. Inspection and careful palpation of each joint to assess for symmetry, swelling, warmth, tenderness, and crepitation can reveal if the joints are the source of the symptoms or if there is a periarticular cause. A familiarity with normal joint range of motion is necessary to identify pathologic abnormalities in the joints.

Certain maneuvers can also elicit findings that suggest a specific cause of a joint problem. For example, watching the patient walk away, turn, and walk back can reveal gait abnormalities suggestive of a dysfunction of the hip, knee, ankle, or foot. Having the patient make a fist to see if the fingertips touch the palm can reveal limitation of range of motion of the interphalangeal joints. Inspection of the dorsum of the hands helps to assess whether interphalangeal joints are swollen, whereas inspection of the palmar side of the hands can reveal Dupuytren contracture.

Observing a patient's ability to laterally rotate the forearm and turn the palm upward (supination) can determine the presence of elbow dysfunction. Power grip and pinch grip should be checked to assess range of motion and strength of the fingers. Additionally, the metacarpophalangeal joints should be palpated to detect any synovial proliferation; synovial proliferation is often described as "boggy" or "squishy," which is easily differentiated from the hard, discrete feeling of the bony hypertrophy typical of osteoarthritis.

An inability to completely extend the elbow and fully supinate and pronate the hands raises suspicion for disease of the radioulnar joint. To test internal and external rotation and abduction of the shoulder, the examiner should ask the patient to put both hands together above the head (without elevating the scapulae), put both hands behind the head, and put both hands behind the back, with the thumb tip reaching the tip of the scapula. If a patient can perform these maneuvers without pain, shoulder joint involvement is unlikely.

Eliciting the "apprehension sign" tests for impingement of the supraspinatus tendon between the humeral head and the acromion. In this test, the patient points the arm straight ahead as the examiner presses the proximal arm down toward the floor; a look of "apprehension" on the patient's face indicates that impingement is occurring. To test for rotator cuff pathology, the patient should point the arm laterally and then pronate it, as if pouring out the contents of a beverage can (the "empty can" or Jobe test). In the presence of supraspinatus disease, pain is elicited when the patient resists abduction.

By having the patient touch the tip of the chin to the chest, look up, and then look over each shoulder, the examiner can determine if range of motion in the cervical spine is intact in flexion/extension and rotation. The resulting fingertip-to-floor distance when the patient bends forward and touches the toes without bending the knees is an index of spinal motion, which can be significantly reduced in ankylosing spondylitis. Another measure of spinal motion is the modified Schober test, in which the sacral dimples of Venus are identified with the patient standing erect; the examiner then measures upward 10 cm and downward 5 cm. The resulting 15-cm line should lengthen by at least 5 cm as the patient flexes forward; a lesser distance indicates decreased range of motion. The previously mentioned FABERE maneuver involves having the patient put the heel on the contralateral knee with the examiner then pressing down on the medial flexed knee, which places the hip into external rotation. This puts stress on the ipsilateral sacroiliac joint and tests the range of internal and external rotation of the hip. Pain elicited with the "log roll" maneuver, which involves rolling the hip into internal and external rotation while in extension in a supine position, indicates arthropathy of the hip. A patient without impairment of the hip joint should be able to straighten the knee fully (extension) and to flex it so that the heel almost touches the buttocks.

The "bulge sign" indicates the presence of excess synovial fluid within the knee joint cavity; this sign is easily demonstrated by "milking" the fluid with the hand from the medial to lateral side of the knee, followed by gently pressing on the lateral side with the fingers. A fluid wave of the viscous synovial fluid produces a bulge in the skin overlying the medial knee joint (**Figure 1**). In the ankle, look for limitations in flexion, extension, inversion, and eversion, which could indicate arthritis in the tibiotalar or subtalar joints. The feet should be observed with the patient standing to assess pronation of the midfoot, a very common cause of foot pain, and to detect pes planus. Leg-length discrepancy is demonstrated by measuring from the anterior-superior iliac spine to the distal medial malleolus on the ipsilateral side, with the patient supine, and then comparing the result with the comparable measurement for the other leg.

When systemic symptoms, such as fever or weight loss, are present, a general physical examination is necessary to detect signs of infection, malignancy, or nonarticular features of autoimmune disease.

General Approach to the Patient with Multisystem Illness

Rheumatoid Arthritis

The presence of rheumatoid factor in a patient with chronic polyarticular arthritis is suggestive but not diagnostic of rheumatoid arthritis. Anti–cyclic citrullinated peptide antibodies are more specific for rheumatoid arthritis, especially early in the disease course. The presence of subcutaneous nodules in the setting of chronic polyarticular arthritis also supports the diagnosis of rheumatoid arthritis. Rheumatoid arthritis does not affect the lower spine or the distal interphalangeal joints.

Dermatologic Lesions in Arthritis

Photosensitivity, malar, and discoid rashes are features of SLE. Gottron papules over the metacarpophalangeal and proximal interphalangeal joints, a heliotrope rash over the eyelids and periorbital region, a "shawl sign" over the upper back and shoulders, and a "V-neck sign" over the upper chest suggest the diagnosis of dermatomyositis. Dry, cracked skin over the radial surfaces of the fingers and the thenar eminence ("mechanic's hands") suggests the presence of the antisynthetase syndrome associated with polymyositis.

Psoriasis is associated with an underlying inflammatory arthritis in up to 30% of patients with skin disease; nail pitting suggests psoriatic arthritis, even in the absence of psoriatic skin lesions. Erythema marginatum is associated with acute rheumatic fever; erythema chronicum migrans is strongly associated with Lyme disease; and erythema nodosum is associated with sarcoidosis, enteropathic arthritis, and Behçet disease (**Figure 2** and **Figure 3**). Pyoderma gangrenosum may be seen with an enteropathic arthritis, Behçet disease, and

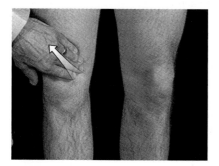
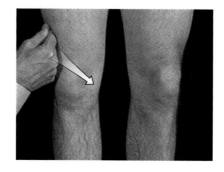
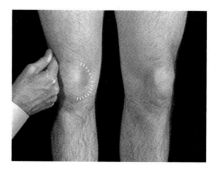

FIGURE 1.
Bulge sign.
The "bulge sign" indicates the presence of a knee effusion. First, the medial knee is stroked in a cephalad fashion (*left panel*). The lateral side of the knee is then stroked in the opposite direction (*center panel*). If an effusion is present, a "bulge" is seen medial to the patella (*right panel*).

Reprinted with permission from Lawry GV. The General Musculoskeletal Examination Study Guide. Iowa City, IA: University of Iowa; 2002.

rheumatoid arthritis and most often manifests as ulcerations on the lower extremities (**Figure 4**).

Palpable purpura and livedo reticularis suggest an underlying systemic vasculitis, and leukocytoclastic vasculitis may manifest as palpable purpura and may be associated with rheumatoid arthritis, SLE, Sjögren syndrome, or relapsing polychondritis. Keratoderma blennorrhagicum and circinate balanitis are features of reactive arthritis, whereas evanescent, salmon-colored rashes are characteristic of adult-onset Still disease (**Figure 5**).

Fever and Arthritis

Fever is often a feature of polyarticular crystalline arthropathies, SLE, systemic vasculitis, infectious arthritis, and adult-onset Still disease. Notably, fever is not a common feature of rheumatoid arthritis and, if present, should trigger a search for an infectious cause.

Inflammatory Eye Disease and Arthritis

The presence of inflammatory eye disease (conjunctivitis, scleritis, episcleritis, and anterior uveitis, all of which may manifest as a red eye) may help diagnose an underlying inflammatory arthritis. Photophobia and a painful eye are associated with scleritis and anterior uveitis but not with conjunctivitis. Conjunctivitis (and more rarely anterior uveitis or scleritis) occurs in some forms of reactive arthritis, and scleritis is a feature of rheumatoid arthritis, Wegener granulomatosis, and relapsing polychondritis. Uveitis is associated with the seronegative spondyloarthropathies and Lyme disease. SLE, sarcoidosis, and Behçet disease can affect the sclera and any part of the uveal tract.

Lung Disease and Arthritis

Bibasilar interstitial lung disease is seen in rheumatoid arthritis, systemic sclerosis, and polymyositis/dermatomyositis.

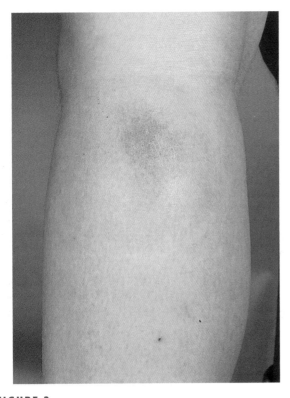

FIGURE 2.
Erythema chronicum migrans.
This condition manifests as large, expanding, erythematous annular lesions. Central clearing may develop as these lesions increase in size.

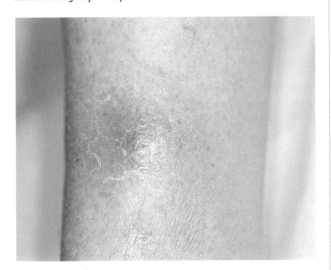

FIGURE 3.
Erythema nodosum.
This condition manifests as erythematous, tender, indurated nodules that most frequently develop over the lower extremities.

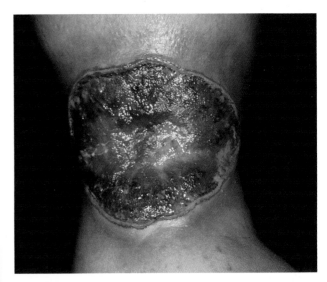

FIGURE 4.
Pyoderma gangrenosum.
This condition manifests as rapidly expanding ulcerated lesions with irregular, dusky borders.

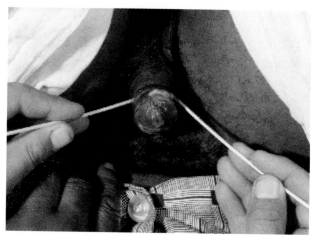

FIGURE 5.
Circinate balanitis.
In uncircumcised men, this condition manifests as moist lesions with well-demarcated borders that develop on the penis; circumcised patients with this condition develop hyperkeratotic plaques.

Reprinted with permission from Physician's Information and Education Resource (PIER). Philadelphia: American College of Physicians. Copyright 2009 American College of Physicians.

Ankylosing spondylitis is associated with upper lobe pulmonary fibrosis. Cavitary lung disease is a feature of Wegener granulomatosis. Microscopic polyangiitis and SLE are associated with pulmonary alveolar hemorrhage. Sarcoidosis can affect any part of the lung and the hilar lymph nodes.

Diarrhea and Arthritis

The onset of an inflammatory arthritis in the setting of a diarrheal illness suggests inflammatory bowel disease as the unifying diagnosis. Other forms of arthritis associated with diarrhea include reactive arthritis, Whipple disease, celiac disease, and the intestinal bypass arthritis-dermatitis syndrome.

Other Disorders Associated with Arthritis

Raynaud phenomenon in the setting of polyarticular arthritis should raise suspicion for systemic sclerosis, SLE, polymyositis/dermatomyositis, or a systemic vasculitis. Dactylitis (fusiform swelling and tenderness of a finger or toe) is associated with the seronegative spondyloarthropathies, sarcoidosis, and sickle cell anemia.

Laboratory Studies

Metabolic Survey

The testing of a patient with a suspected systemic disease always should include a complete blood count, metabolic profile, and urinalysis. Findings of anemia, leukopenia, thrombocytopenia, and abnormalities of hepatic or renal function are particularly informative because the presence of systemic abnormalities influences the differential diagnosis.

Assessment of thyroid function is also essential in the setting of diffuse pain, fatigue, or weakness.

Tests That Measure Inflammation

Erythrocyte Sedimentation Rate and C-Reactive Protein

An elevated erythrocyte sedimentation rate or C-reactive protein level does not always indicate inflammation just as normal results do not exclude it. In many patients, however, especially those with rheumatoid arthritis, these measurements fluctuate with disease activity, and the individual pattern must be established for each patient.

C3 and C4

Patients with active SLE may have hypocomplementemia, although the absence of hypocomplementemia does not exclude lupus activity. Similarly, patients vary with regard to whether these complement levels fall with flares of disease and rise with response to treatment. Hypocomplementemia also may be seen in vasculitis or immune complex–mediated disorders such as rheumatoid vasculitis or infective endocarditis. Any disease process that entails complement consumption can lead to reduction of C3 and C4 levels. Reductions can be seen in C4 levels alone or in both C3 and C4 levels. However, reduction of C3 levels in the absence of reduction of C4 levels should raise the question of a laboratory error.

CH50

CH50 (total hemolytic complement) is a test of the entire classic complement pathway. It is most useful when a complement component deficiency is suspected, as in some patients with disseminated gonococcal infection, which can occur in patients with a deficiency of the terminal component of complement, C5 through C9. CH50 is not a particularly good test for measurement of complement activation because substantial complement component consumption must occur for the CH50 value to be reduced.

Specific Serologic and Antibody Tests

Antinuclear Antibodies

The antinuclear antibody test is positive in virtually every patient with SLE and is primarily used to exclude this condition when the test is negative. A positive test result has low predictive value when the pretest probability of SLE or a related disease is low. Therefore, this test should not be used to screen indiscriminately for the presence of rheumatic disease. A positive result also may occur in the absence of a rheumatic disease in patients with Hashimoto thyroiditis, certain medication use (isoniazid, hydralazine, procainamide, and many anticonvulsants), and those who have a close relative with an autoimmune disease. Similarly, a nonspecific test such as the antinuclear antibody test might be positive at a high titer in the setting of an opportunistic infection with multiple-organ involvement, which could lead to confusion with SLE.

Anti–Double-Stranded DNA Antibodies and Anti-Smith Antibodies

High titers of antibodies to double-stranded DNA are quite specific for SLE, but a negative test does not exclude the diagnosis. Anti–double-stranded DNA levels do not increase in all patients with active disease and have limited value in monitoring disease activity. The anti-Smith antibody is another specific but insensitive test for SLE.

Antiribonucleoprotein Antibodies

The antiribonucleoprotein antibody is strongly associated with mixed connective tissue disease but also can be seen in patients with SLE and myositis.

Anti-SSA and Anti-SSB Antibodies

Anti-SSA and anti-SSB antibodies (sometimes referred to as anti-Ro and anti-La, respectively) are seen in Sjögren syndrome, but their presence is neither sufficiently sensitive nor specific to establish or exclude the diagnosis. The anti-SSA antibody is also seen in patients with SLE, especially in patients who have subacute cutaneous lupus erythematosus. Infants of mothers with a positive anti-SSA antibodies are at risk for fetal heart block and neonatal lupus syndrome.

Anti–Scl-70 and Anticentromere Antibodies

Two antibodies are associated with systemic sclerosis: anti-topoisomerase I (anti–Scl-70) and anticentromere. The anti–Scl-70 antibody is seen in approximately half of the patients with diffuse systemic sclerosis and is associated with the development of interstitial lung disease. The anticentromere antibody is associated with limited cutaneous systemic sclerosis.

ANCA, c-ANCA, and p-ANCA

Testing for the presence of ANCA helps in the diagnosis of Wegener granulomatosis and, to a lesser extent, microscopic polyarteritis. The c-ANCA correlates with antibodies to proteinase-3, and the p-ANCA correlates with antibodies to myeloperoxidase. A positive result on an ANCA test is clinically significant only if the screening immunofluorescence test is associated with specific antibodies to proteinase-3 and myeloperoxidase. A positive ANCA test result with an atypical pattern is a nonspecific finding and can occur in infections or other types of vasculitis.

Antiproteinase-3 and Antimyeloperoxidase Antibodies

Virtually all patients with active systemic Wegener granulomatosis have positive results on testing for antiproteinase-3 antibodies. However, a positive test is not sufficient to establish the diagnosis, and a biopsy is often necessary for certainty. Although controversial, measuring antiproteinase-3 antibody titers is probably not useful for following disease activity because the titers do not consistently correlate with disease activity. The presence of antimyeloperoxidase antibodies is associated with microscopic polyarteritis and some cases of Churg-Strauss syndrome.

Anti–Jo-1 Antibodies

A number of antibodies are associated with various subsets of inflammatory myopathy. The anti–Jo-1 antibody is directed toward a transfer RNA synthetase. This antibody is associated with antisynthetase disorders, including inflammatory polyarticular arthritis; interstitial lung disease; dry, cracked skin over the radial surfaces of the fingers and the thenar eminence ("mechanic's hands"); and Raynaud phenomenon in the setting of polymyositis or dermatomyositis.

KEY POINTS

- Serologic tests, such as antinuclear antibody and ANCA assays, should be ordered when the clinical findings suggest the presence of a specific disease and not to screen for autoimmune disease in general.

- A positive antinuclear antibody test has no clinical significance if not accompanied by clinical evidence of systemic lupus erythematosus or a related disease.

- Testing for c-ANCA and the antiproteinase-3 antibody is very useful in confirming a suspected clinical diagnosis of Wegener granulomatosis, but the extent to which this testing is useful for following disease activity is controversial.

Imaging Studies in Rheumatic Diseases

Radiography

Plain radiographs are adequate to assess most rheumatologic problems, but obtaining plain radiographs on initial evaluation is often unnecessary and not cost effective. Shoulder impingement in middle age, for example, can usually be diagnosed on the basis of the patient's history and physical examination. Likewise, a typical presentation of hip or knee pain with use that is relieved with rest may be sufficient to diagnose osteoarthritis; radiography, in fact, is not usually indicated in patients with suspected osteoarthritis because of the poor correlation between the degree of radiographic abnormality and the anatomic and clinical disease severity.

Plain radiographs of the hands and feet should be performed at the time of diagnosis in all patients with rheumatoid arthritis to detect erosions and joint-space narrowing. The presence of radiographic abnormalities early in the disease course is a poor prognostic sign and should lead to consideration of aggressive disease-modifying antirheumatic drug (DMARD) therapy. Shoulder radiographs help distinguish glenohumeral disease from rotator cuff pathology.

CT and MRI Scanning

CT scans can show sacroiliac joint abnormalities not visible on radiographs but are less sensitive than MRIs. CT scans more accurately image the bony cortex, but MRIs can identify bone marrow edema due to sacroiliac joint inflammation.

Bone marrow edema adjacent to the sacroiliac joints can be detected by an MRI years before plain radiographs show sacroiliitis; a definite diagnosis of ankylosing spondylitis can thus be made years before radiographs are diagnostic and effective treatment can be instituted. MRIs can also show pathologic abnormalities in the rotator cuff and knee and thus eliminate the need for arthrography. MRIs are also extremely sensitive in detecting soft-tissue infections, osteomyelitis, and avascular necrosis. Likewise, synovial proliferation and erosion not detectable on radiographs can be seen on MRIs very early in the course of rheumatoid arthritis; however, no consensus yet exists regarding how MRI should be used in this setting.

Ultrasonography

The sonograms produced by musculoskeletal ultrasonography can show pathologic abnormalities and tears in the rotator cuff, synovial proliferation (and perhaps erosions), joint effusions, and fluid collections around joints that require aspiration. However, the usefulness of ultrasonography is more dependent on the skill of the operator than is the case with radiography.

Joint Aspiration

Sampling synovial fluid is the most definitive way to determine whether or not an inflammatory process is present in a joint. Joint aspiration is particularly important in patients with monoarticular arthritis because of the potential for infection. A synovial fluid leukocyte count above 2000/μL with a predominance of neutrophils indicates inflammation. As the leukocyte count increases, with a higher percentage of neutrophils, the probability of infection increases. There is no evidence-based threshold for diagnosing septic arthritis, but a leukocyte count in excess of 50,000/μL is highly suspicious for infection. Analysis of synovial fluid with a polarized light microscope can identify the crystals of gout (monosodium urate) and pseudogout (calcium pyrophosphate). Routine measurement of protein and glucose in synovial fluid is unnecessary. Gram stain and culture should always be performed whenever there is a clinical suspicion of infection.

KEY POINTS

- Joint aspiration should always be performed in patients with monoarticular arthritis because of the potential for infection.
- A synovial fluid leukocyte count above 2000/μL indicates inflammation and a count above 50,000/μL suggests infection.

Bibliography

Bai JC, Mazure RM, Vazquez H, et al. Whipple's disease. Clin Gastroenterol Hepatol. 2004;2(10):849-60. [PMID: 15476147]

Franz JK, Krause A. Lyme disease (Lyme borreliosis). Best Pract Res Clin Rheumatol. 2003;17(2):241-64. [PMID: 12787524]

Pascual E, Jovani V. Synovial fluid analysis. Best Pract Res Clin Rheumatol. 2005;19(3):371-86. [PMID: 15939364]

Powell A, Davis P, Jones N, Russell AS. Palindromic rheumatism is a common disease: comparison of new-onset palindromic rheumatism compared to new-onset rheumatoid arthritis in a 2-year cohort of patients. J Rheumatol. 2008;35(6):992-4. [PMID: 18412310]

Principles of Therapeutics

Evaluation of Disease Progression

Outcome measures help to evaluate disease progression in patients with the rheumatic diseases. These tools also help to assess the efficacy of treatment and guide treatment decisions.

Health Assessment Questionnaire

The Health Assessment Questionnaire (HAQ) can be used to evaluate patients with rheumatoid arthritis, systemic lupus erythematosus (SLE), the seronegative spondyloarthropathies, systemic sclerosis, and fibromyalgia. This tool has been validated in monitoring the patient response to treatment and is used as a standard outcome measure in clinical trials of therapeutic agents. The HAQ does not require special training and can be used in the office setting. It is available at http://aramis.stanford.edu/downloads/2005BruceCERS14.pdf.

In the HAQ, patients answer questions that assess their functional capacity in dressing, rising, eating, walking, hygiene, reach, grip, and usual activities. These questions assess the extent of difficulty involved in performing various tasks, such as getting dressed and entering and exiting a bathtub. Answers are scored on a scale of 0 (no difficulty) to 3 (inability to do). The HAQ index is the mean of the scores from these eight domains and ranges from 0 to 3. An HAQ index greater than 1 indicates a significant degree of disability.

Disease Activity Score

The Disease Activity Score (DAS) is a validated tool for assessing patients with rheumatoid arthritis at any point in their disease course. This tool also is used in clinical trials, in studies comparing different therapeutic regimens, and in the office.

The DAS is calculated using a complex equation that involves the tender joint count, swollen joint count, a patient assessment of general health by a visual analogue scale, and the measurement of the erythrocyte sedimentation rate or C-reactive protein level. The DAS28 is a shorter, simpler version of this tool and is more practical for use in clinical practice. These tools are available online at www.das-score.nl/www.das-score.nl/index.html.

The Tight Control in Rheumatoid Arthritis (TICORA) trial demonstrated that adjusting treatment toward a DAS target produced better results in patients with rheumatoid arthritis than routine care. This finding suggests that management of rheumatoid arthritis may eventually resemble management of diabetes mellitus, in whom the hemoglobin A_{1c} level is used to adjust treatment.

KEY POINT

- The Health Assessment Questionnaire and Disease Activity Score are tools that can be used in the office to evaluate the condition of a patient with rheumatoid arthritis.

Anti-Inflammatory Agents

NSAIDs

NSAIDs relieve musculoskeletal pain, regardless of whether inflammation is the cause. Their mechanism of action is the nonspecific inhibition of the cyclooxygenase (COX)-2 enzyme, which is involved in the production of inflammatory prostaglandins. NSAIDs also are effective in treating systemic conditions, such as fever and pleuritis.

Many NSAIDs have similar efficacy, and they all have a similar toxicity profile. Stomach ulcers, perforation, and gastrointestinal bleeding develop in a small percentage of patients treated with NSAIDs; these effects are more likely to occur in patients treated with concomitant warfarin, H_2 blockers, and corticosteroids, as well as in patients with a history of ulcers and cardiovascular disease.

H_2 blockers do not protect against NSAID-induced stomach ulcerations. Concomitant use of a proton pump inhibitor reduces, but does not eliminate, the risk for serious gastrointestinal toxicity.

All traditional or nonselective NSAIDs inhibit COX-1 and COX-2 enzymes. COX-1 is responsible for the production of prostacyclin, which protects the gastric mucosa; COX-2 is an inducible form of COX primarily responsible for mediating pain and inflammation. Selective inhibition of COX-2 is believed to reduce inflammation and pain without affecting the protective effects of COX-1. Use of the selective COX-2 inhibitor celecoxib has been shown to reduce the risk of recurrent NSAID-induced bleeding as effectively as coadministration of a nonselective NSAID and a proton pump inhibitor.

However, selective COX-2 inhibition is associated with cardiovascular toxicity. The selective COX-2 inhibitors rofecoxib and valdecoxib have been removed from the market because of a significant increase in cardiovascular events believed to involve COX-2 inhibition; celecoxib is the only currently available agent that selectively inhibits COX-2 without affecting COX-1.

Studies comparing the cardiovascular risks of celecoxib and nonselective COX-2 inhibitors have produced conflicting results, but celecoxib appears to be associated with no higher risk for cardiovascular toxicity than nonselective agents. However, numerous studies have shown that several NSAIDs are associated with an increased relative risk for cardiovascular events but are not consistent in identifying which NSAIDs are associated with this risk. Therefore, all nonselective NSAIDs and celecoxib should be regarded as having some increased risk for cardiovascular disease and may not be appropriate for patients with established cardiovascular disease.

Both selective and nonselective NSAIDs reduce prostaglandin-mediated renal blood flow and may cause acute renal failure in patients with renal insufficiency. All NSAIDs except celecoxib and nonacetylated salicylates such as salsalate also inhibit platelet function and may potentially worsen asthma or inflammatory bowel disease. Patients who are allergic to aspirin may sometimes be safely treated with nonacetylated salicylates, but these agents should be used cautiously.

Corticosteroids

Corticosteroid therapy is appropriate in patients with rheumatoid arthritis who have significant limitations in their activities of daily living. These agents are particularly beneficial early in the disease course until DMARD therapy, which has a slow onset of action, becomes effective. Corticosteroids should be tapered to the lowest effective dose and discontinued when feasible.

Manifestations of corticosteroid toxicity include weight gain, cushingoid features, osteoporosis (with fracture), avascular necrosis, infection, diabetes mellitus, hypertension, cataracts, and an increase in serum cholesterol levels. Maintaining a prednisone dosage of 5 mg/d or less often decreases the toxic effects.

Bone loss occurs rapidly in the first 6 months of corticosteroid treatment. Baseline bone mineral density testing should be performed on all patients started on long-term corticosteroids. Bisphosphonates as well as vitamin D and calcium supplementation are recommended for men and postmenopausal women taking corticosteroids at a dosage of more than 5 mg/d for longer than 3 months. Bisphosphonates are category C agents in pregnancy and should be used cautiously in premenopausal women. Corticosteroids may also cause adrenal insufficiency, which can be prevented by tapering the corticosteroid dosage slowly over several months and adding supplemental corticosteroid replacement during times of stress.

- In patients using NSAIDs, concomitant use of a proton pump inhibitor reduces the risk for serious gastrointestinal toxicity.
- Use of a selective cyclooxygenase-2 inhibitor is believed to reduce inflammation and pain without affecting the protective effects of COX-1 on the gastric mucosa and platelets.
- All nonselective NSAIDs and celecoxib should be regarded as having some increased risk of cardiovascular disease and may not be appropriate for patients with established cardiovascular disease.
- Both selective and nonselective NSAIDs reduce prostaglandin-mediated renal blood flow and may cause acute renal failure in patients with renal insufficiency.
- Use of bisphosphonates and vitamin D and calcium supplementation are important to prevent bone loss in men and postmenopausal women using more than 5 mg/d of corticosteroids for longer than 3 months but should be used cautiously in premenopausal women.

Immunosuppressive Agents and Disease-Modifying Antirheumatic Drugs

In patients with rheumatoid arthritis, DMARD therapy reduces bone and cartilage damage. All patients with rheumatoid arthritis should begin DMARD therapy as soon as the diagnosis is established; patients with rheumatoid arthritis who begin DMARD therapy within the first 3 months of disease onset have an improved long-term outcome.

Combination DMARD therapy is more effective than single-agent therapy. No consensus yet exists regarding the most effective way to use DMARDs to treat rheumatoid arthritis. Patients commonly undergo 3 to 6 months of methotrexate therapy; if the clinical response is inadequate, sulfasalazine and hydroxychloroquine, or a tumor necrosis factor α (TNF-α) cyclooxygenase inhibitor, can be added.

Oral DMARDs typically take 3 months to produce a clinical response and up to 6 months for a full response. Biologic DMARDs require less time to demonstrate efficacy.

Methotrexate

Methotrexate is the DMARD of choice for most patients with rheumatoid arthritis. If methotrexate is at least partially effective, it should be continued as other agents are added.

Methotrexate therapy inhibits folic acid metabolism and may cause stomatitis, nausea, and diarrhea. Folic acid supplementation may reduce these side effects. Bone marrow suppression rarely occurs but may develop in elderly patients treated with low doses of this agent.

The most common severe adverse effect of methotrexate is hepatotoxicity, and a temporary but acute increase in liver enzyme levels may occur. The risk of hepatotoxicity is increased by alcohol consumption, pre-existing liver disease, and possibly diabetes and obesity. Methotrexate also suppresses the immune system and increases the risk for opportunistic infection. Contraindications to methotrexate therapy include liver disease, abnormal findings on liver chemistry studies, and regular alcohol consumption.

Measuring serum methotrexate levels is not helpful in monitoring therapeutic efficacy. Patients using methotrexate should undergo monthly liver chemistry studies and a complete blood count until the dosage is stable and every 4 to 8 months thereafter.

Liver biopsy is indicated in patients treated with methotrexate who have persistently elevated liver chemistry study results or decreased serum albumin levels. In patients with persistently elevated liver study results, the methotrexate dosage should be decreased or therapy discontinued.

Hydroxychloroquine

Hydroxychloroquine is most commonly used to treat rheumatoid arthritis and SLE. This agent has a slow onset of action and may require 3 to 6 months of therapy to gain full efficacy.

Hydroxychloroquine is contraindicated in patients with renal or hepatic insufficiency. Macular toxicity is a severe side effect of hydroxychloroquine therapy but is unlikely at a dosage of 6.5 mg/kg/d or less and rarely occurs before completion of 5 years of treatment. Nevertheless, referral to an ophthalmologist for a baseline examination and routine monitoring every 6 to 12 months is indicated in patients using hydroxychloroquine. Nausea and skin discoloration also occasionally occur.

Hydroxychloroquine is a category C agent in pregnancy, and conception should be avoided during its use. However, if pregnancy does occur, expert opinion considers use of this agent to be appropriate because the benefits outweigh the risks.

Sulfasalazine

Patients treated with sulfasalazine should be monitored for neutropenia and elevated aminotransferase levels every 1 to 3 months. Gastrointestinal intolerance due to nausea or abdominal pain may occur, but an enteric-coated preparation is available.

Sulfasalazine is contraindicated in patients with sulfa allergy or glucose-6-phosphate dehydrogenase deficiency but is considered safe during pregnancy (category B agent in pregnancy).

Leflunomide

Leflunomide is as effective as methotrexate in the treatment of rheumatoid arthritis. This agent should be started at a lower dose when used concomitantly with methotrexate.

The most common side effects of leflunomide include diarrhea, nausea, and hair loss. Use of a loading dose is associated with diarrhea and hepatotoxicity; this agent is more commonly begun at a dosage of 10 mg/d that, if tolerated, is increased.

Because leflunomide is teratogenic, women who plan to become pregnant must discontinue this therapy and undergo a course of cholestyramine elimination therapy. Women should attempt pregnancy only when serum leflunomide levels are less than 0.02 mg/L on two occasions at least 14 days apart.

Aminotransferase levels should be measured monthly to monitor for hepatotoxicity. If levels are persistently elevated or if the drug is not tolerated, the dosage of leflunomide should be decreased.

Azathioprine

Azathioprine is approved for the treatment of rheumatoid arthritis but is more commonly used as a corticosteroid-sparing agent in patients with SLE and systemic vasculitis.

Patients using azathioprine should undergo periodic complete blood counts and liver chemistry studies. Patients with a genetic deficiency of thiopurine methyltransferase (TPMT), the primary enzyme responsible for metabolizing azathioprine, are highly susceptible to serious azathioprine toxicity, such as pancytopenia. Therefore, although this condition is rare, genotype testing for TPMT may be warranted before initiating azathioprine therapy. Patients with this deficiency should be given lower doses of this agent than other patients. Rarely, azathioprine causes a hypersensitivity reaction characterized by fever and a severe flu-like syndrome that resolves upon withdrawal of this agent.

Cyclophosphamide

Cyclophosphamide is primarily used to treat lupus nephritis and systemic vasculitis and is an effective initial therapy for Wegener granulomatosis.

Daily oral cyclophosphamide is more potent than that administered by other routes but is associated with more severe toxicity, especially hemorrhagic cystitis, cytopenias, bladder cancer, and leukemia. Monthly intravenous administration usually prevents toxicity and has become the gold standard for the treatment of lupus nephritis.

Frequent complete blood counts and urinalyses, as well as prompt evaluation of gross hematuria, are critical in patients treated with cyclophosphamide. After several months of oral or intravenous therapy, progressive cytopenias may necessitate a dosage reduction.

Mycophenolate Mofetil

Mycophenolate mofetil was developed to prevent rejection of transplanted organs but has emerged as an off-label treatment for lupus nephritis, for which it is as effective as intermittent intravenous cyclophosphamide therapy with considerably less toxicity.

Mycophenolate mofetil has been associated with birth defects and is therefore contraindicated during pregnancy. Women of child-bearing age should use effective contraception while taking this agent.

Cyclosporine

Cyclosporine is effective in the treatment of rheumatoid arthritis. However, the cost and potential for severe renal toxicity associated with this agent even in low doses have limited its use. Monitoring of blood pressure and serum creatinine levels is essential to prevent permanent renal damage.

KEY POINTS

- Contraindications to methotrexate therapy include liver disease, abnormal findings on liver chemistry studies, and regular alcohol consumption.
- Macular toxicity is a side effect of hydroxychloroquine therapy, and referral to an ophthalmologist for a baseline examination and routine monitoring is indicated.
- Women using leflunomide who plan to become pregnant must discontinue this agent and undergo a course of cholestyramine elimination therapy before attempting pregnancy.
- Patients with thiopurine methyltransferase deficiency should receive significantly lower doses of azathioprine than other patients.
- Frequent complete blood counts and urinalyses and prompt evaluation of gross hematuria are critical in patients treated with cyclophosphamide.

Biologic Agents

Biologic agents are used to treat rheumatoid arthritis as well as other systemic autoinflammatory conditions. Therapy with more than one biologic agent does not increase efficacy and causes a definite increase in infectious toxicity and is therefore contraindicated.

Tumor Necrosis Factor α Inhibitors

TNF-α inhibitors generally are well tolerated and may be effective as early as 1 to 2 weeks after initiation of therapy, whereas oral immunosuppressive agents usually require 2 to 3 months to produce an effect. In patients with rheumatoid arthritis, all TNF-α inhibitors prevent damage of bone and cartilage more effectively than methotrexate alone. Combination therapy with methotrexate and a TNF-α inhibitor also has consistently been shown to be more effective than single-agent TNF-α inhibitor therapy. Therefore, these agents are often administered concomitantly with methotrexate.

The TNF-α inhibitors etanercept, infliximab, and adalimumab are effective in rheumatoid arthritis, and several more TNF-α inhibitors are anticipated to be released during the next few years. Etanercept is a genetically engineered human fusion protein; adalimumab is a fully human monoclonal antibody to TNF-α; and infliximab is a chimeric antibody specific for human TNF-α.

The efficacy of infliximab is believed to decrease with repeated dosing unless methotrexate is administered concomitantly; this decreased efficacy is believed to occur because the patient develops an immune response to the chimeric antibody. Approximately 1% of patients treated with infliximab develop serious infusion reactions.

TNF-α inhibitors should be used in consultation with a rheumatologist. Rarely, serious infections have occurred in patients treated with these agents. Therefore, they are not indicated for patients with indolent chronic infections, such as osteomyelitis or tuberculosis, or for anyone with significant and active common infections. Patients with a serious infection such as pneumonia should discontinue treatment with these agents until they receive appropriate therapy for the infection and demonstrate significant improvement.

Toxicity associated with the TNF-α inhibitors includes reactivation tuberculosis with fulminant extrapulmonary involvement. Purified protein derivative testing is indicated before beginning treatment with these agents, and positive results on this test warrant treatment for latent tuberculosis (see Special Issues in Patients Taking Pharmacologic Immunosuppressants).

Rare cases of multiple sclerosis or demyelinating conditions such as optic neuritis have been reported but usually remit upon discontinuation of therapy. TNF-α inhibitors also may cause or exacerbate heart failure.

TNF-α inhibitors have been associated with a drug-induced SLE syndrome. Approximately 10% of patients treated with TNF-α inhibitors develop antinuclear antibodies and anti–double-stranded DNA antibodies. There is also evidence that TNF-α inhibitors may increase the risk of cancer, particularly lymphoma, some solid cancers, and skin cancer. However, patients who are prescribed TNF-α inhibitors often have an increased risk of cancer because of their underlying disease; therefore, the causality is difficult to prove. Furthermore, associated treatments such as cyclophosphamide, methotrexate, and azathioprine also increase the risk of cancer.

Studies attempting to demonstrate a relationship between TNF-α inhibitors and lymphoma and solid-organ malignancies have yielded mixed results. In a study that used the National Data Bank for Rheumatic Diseases, the odds

ratio for developing melanoma was approximately 2.0 but did not reach statistical significance. Nevertheless, standard practice based on expert opinion is to discontinue TNF-α inhibitor therapy in patients who develop cancer, including melanomas.

Abatacept
Abatacept is a biologic agent approved for the treatment of rheumatoid arthritis that does not respond adequately to methotrexate therapy. This agent can be used as monotherapy or in combination with methotrexate.

Rituximab
Administration of rituximab, a monoclonal antibody to the B-lymphocyte surface antigen CD20, causes rapid and complete depletion of peripheral blood B cells in patients with rheumatoid arthritis. Rituximab has been approved since 1997 for the treatment of lymphoma. In 2006, it was approved for the treatment of rheumatoid arthritis that is unresponsive to one or more TNF-α inhibitors. Approximately 25% of patients treated with rituximab in phase III clinical trials showed at least 50% improvement in their condition. Studies are underway to assess the efficacy and safety of rituximab in the treatment of SLE.

The mean duration of response to rituximab is 7 months. Repeated courses of this agent can be administered, although long-term data are not available.

Anakinra
Anakinra, an interleukin-1 (IL-1) receptor antagonist, is administered daily via subcutaneous injection. Approximately 20% of patients with rheumatoid arthritis treated with this agent demonstrate a positive response. This agent also is used in patients with adult-onset Still disease.

KEY POINTS
- Combination therapy with two biologic agents is contraindicated in patients with rheumatic disease.
- Combination therapy with methotrexate and a tumor necrosis factor α inhibitor is superior to either agent alone in patients with rheumatoid arthritis.
- Tumor necrosis factor α inhibitors are not indicated for patients with indolent chronic infections or significant and active infections.
- Abatacept is approved for the treatment of rheumatoid arthritis that does not respond adequately to methotrexate therapy.
- Rituximab is approved for the treatment of rheumatoid arthritis that is unresponsive to tumor necrosis factor α inhibitor therapy.

Lifestyle Modification

Lifestyle modifications are useful adjuncts to pharmacologic therapy in numerous rheumatologic diseases. Weight loss and the use of devices such as canes and walkers are critical in the treatment of osteoarthritis. In patients with osteoarthritis and rheumatoid arthritis, modification or discontinuation of certain activities that aggravate joint symptoms and may potentially promote disease progression is important. For example, continued involvement in an occupation requiring stooping and bending may worsen symptoms of osteoarthritis of the hips or knees.

Management of Risk Factors for Cardiovascular Disease

Patients with rheumatoid arthritis and SLE have an increased incidence of cardiovascular disease. Lifestyle modifications targeted towards decreasing cardiovascular risk factors that are recommended for all patients, such as maintaining a healthy diet, engaging in moderate exercise, smoking cessation, and controlling blood pressure and lipid levels, are therefore particularly warranted in patients with rheumatoid arthritis. Smoking also has been shown to worsen the severity of rheumatoid arthritis, although there are no data showing that smoking cessation is specifically beneficial in this condition. In addition, control of lipid levels is important in patients with rheumatoid arthritis who are treated with corticosteroids, because these agents may increase lipid levels.

Control of the underlying rheumatic disease in patients with rheumatoid arthritis may improve cardiovascular outcomes. For example, methotrexate therapy has been shown to reduce cardiovascular mortality in patients with rheumatoid arthritis.

In patients with SLE and systemic sclerosis, aggressive control of hypertension and management of obesity, diabetes, and hyperlipidemia that are associated with coronary heart disease is similarly critical.

Special Issues in Patients Taking Pharmacologic Immunosuppressants

Infection prophylaxis is critical in patients who undergo long-term immunosuppressive therapy. Administration of trimethoprim-sulfamethoxazole to prevent pneumocystis pneumonia in patients taking immunosuppressants remains controversial; evidence supporting the use of this therapy in these patients is limited.

Reactivation tuberculosis is a major concern in patients treated with TNF-α inhibitors. Before initiating treatment with these agents, patients should undergo a careful assessment for latent tuberculosis, including exposure history, epidemiologic factors, chest radiography, and tuberculin skin testing or in-vitro lymphocyte activation. Patients at increased risk for this condition should undergo further evaluation for isoniazid prophylaxis. No consensus yet exists regarding how long isoniazid should be administered before starting TNF-α inhibitor therapy. Whether patients who previously have been treated for latent tuberculosis require additional treatment before starting TNF-α inhibitor therapy is uncertain.

Even when appropriate suppressive treatment is administered, there is still a risk of reactivation tuberculosis during the period of TNF-α blockade. In addition, much of the reactivation is extrapulmonary, which raises challenges in identifying reactivation tuberculosis using chest symptoms and imaging of the chest as the primary monitoring tools.

All patients undergoing immunosuppressive therapy should be considered for varicella-zoster virus vaccination more than 6 weeks before starting the immunosuppressive agent, but this vaccine is contraindicated in already immunosuppressed patients. Conversely, pneumococcal vaccination is safe in already immunosuppressed patients and is indicated for patients undergoing immunosuppressive therapy. All patients receiving immunosuppressive therapy also should undergo annual influenza virus vaccination. Generally, use of live vaccines such as vaccinia; varicella-zoster virus; measles, mumps, and rubella; or intranasal live attenuated influenza virus vaccinations should be avoided.

KEY POINTS

- A careful history of exposures to tuberculosis and tuberculin skin testing should be performed before initiating tumor necrosis factor α inhibitor therapy.
- Pneumococcal vaccination is safe in already immunosuppressed patients and is indicated for patients undergoing immunosuppressive therapy.

Complementary Medications

Glucosamine and chondroitin sulfate are classified as nutritional supplements in the United States. N-acetylglucosamine is a critical component of hyaluronan. Chondroitin sulfate is one of the hydrophilic molecules in aggrecan, the predominant proteoglycan in articular cartilage. Because degradation of the hyaluronan-aggrecan complex occurs in osteoarthritis, use of these agents is hypothesized to benefit patients with this condition.

At least two industry-sponsored trials in Europe showed that glucosamine was superior to placebo in relief of pain associated with osteoarthritis of the knee. In the Glucosamine/ chondroitin Arthritis Intervention Trial (GAIT) of patients with symptomatic osteoarthritis of the knee showed that glucosamine, chondroitin sulfate, or combination therapy with these agents was not shown to be superior to placebo. However, a post hoc subanalysis showed that combination therapy with glucosamine and chondroitin sulfate was superior to placebo in patients with moderate to severe pain.

Omega-3 fatty acids are found in oils from fish, plants, and nuts and may be beneficial in reducing cardiovascular disease risk. Several studies also have suggested that these agents may benefit patients with rheumatoid arthritis. However, these studies have not been definitive, and there currently is no sound evidence supporting the use of these agents to treat musculoskeletal conditions.

Bibliography

Clegg DO, Reda DJ, Harris CL, et al. Glucosamine, Chondroitin Sulfate, and the Two in Combination for Painful Knee Osteoarthritis. N Engl J Med, 2006;354(8):795-808. [PMID: 16495392]

Cohen SB, Emery P, Greenwald MW, et al; REFLEX Trial Group. Rituximab for rheumatoid arthritis refractory to anti-tumor necrosis factor therapy: Results of a multicenter, randomized, double-blind, placebo-controlled, phase III trial evaluating primary efficacy and safety at twenty-four weeks. Arthritis Rheum. 2006;54(9):2793-2806. [PMID: 16947627]

Ginzler EM, Dooley MA, Aranow C, et al. Mycophenolate Mofetil or Intravenous Cyclophosphamide for Lupus Nephritis. N Engl Jour Med. 2005; 353(21):2219-2228. [PMID: 16306519]

Grigor C, Capell H, Stirling A, et al. Effect of a treatment strategy of tight control for rheumatoid arthritis (the TICORA study): a single-blind randomised controlled trial. Lancet. 2004;364(9430):263-269. [PMID: 15262104]

Solomon SD, McMurray JJ, Pfeffer MA, et al; Adenoma Prevention with Celecoxib (APC) Study Investigators. Cardiovascular risk associated with celecoxib in a clinical trial for colorectal adenoma prevention. N Engl J Med. 2005;352(11):1071-1080. [PMID: 15713944]

Woessner KM, Simon RA, Stevenson DD. The safety of celecoxib in patients with aspirin-sensitive asthma. Arthritis Rheum. 2002; 46(8):2201-2206. [PMID: 12209526]

Rheumatoid Arthritis
Pathophysiology and Risk Factors

Rheumatoid arthritis is a complex disorder of unknown cause. Experts believe that this condition occurs in response to an antigenic trigger, such as an infectious agent. Some evidence suggests that smoking may increase the risk for rheumatoid arthritis.

Genetic factors comprise approximately one third of a patient's susceptibility to rheumatoid arthritis. The best understood genetic factor associated with this condition is the shared epitope, a conserved region on chromosome 6 that encodes the class II major histocompatibility locus. The presence of HLA-DRB1*0401 or HLA-DRB1*0404 is highly associated with the onset of rheumatoid arthritis.

Pathologic changes in the joint begin in the synovial lining of the diarthroidal joints. Early changes include neovascularization and thickening of the normally thin, delicate synovial membrane. Infiltration of the tissues with leukocytes and increased expression of adhesion molecules, proteolytic enzymes, cytokines, and other inflammatory mediators also occur.

Synovial macrophages act as antigen-presenting cells through HLA-DR. The most likely inciting incident in the development of rheumatoid arthritis is activation of the T cell by a putative antigen in a genetically susceptible patient. B lymphocytes produce autoantibodies, secrete proinflammatory cytokines, and can act as antigen-presenting cells in the synovium. B-cell depletion therapy recently has been shown to be beneficial in patients with rheumatoid arthritis.

Synovial proliferation leads to the development of pannus, which acts as a localized tumor that invades cartilage and bone. The rheumatoid synovium contains abundant osteoclast-like synovial macrophages, which are the primary cells involved in bone and cartilage destruction.

Numerous cytokines are involved in the pathogenesis of rheumatoid arthritis, and many may be potential targets for biologic therapies. Tumor necrosis factor α (TNF-α) plays a critical role in initiating and perpetuating the inflammatory cascade in this condition, and TNF-α inhibitor therapy can benefit patients with active disease. Interleukin-1 is a primary proinflammatory cytokine in rheumatoid arthritis; interleukin-6 and interleukin-17 also may affect this condition.

Disease Course

Established rheumatoid arthritis has a highly variable disease course. A small percentage of affected patients have mild disease with intermittent flares. However, most patients with rheumatoid arthritis have persistent inflammatory disease with periods of exacerbation accompanied by progressive joint destruction that causes increasing functional limitation.

Erosive disease, the hallmark of persistent synovitis, develops in most patients within 2 years of disease onset. Functional decline may be rapid and is related to numerous factors, including the degree of inflammatory disease, damage to the affected joints, the muscle strength and general fitness status of the patient, and psychosocial variables. Infections or cardiovascular disease may cause early mortality.

Work disability occurs within 5 years in up to 50% of patients with severe rheumatoid arthritis, but some studies suggest that this percentage is overestimated. Factors that help to determine work disability in patients with rheumatoid arthritis include disease status, the ability to commute to work, control over the work environment, ergonomic features of the workplace, and psychosocial factors.

KEY POINTS
- B-cell depletion therapy recently has been shown to have efficacy in the treatment of rheumatoid arthritis.
- Tumor necrosis factor α inhibitor therapy can benefit patients with active rheumatoid arthritis.

Epidemiology

Rheumatoid arthritis affects approximately 1% of North Americans and Europeans. Certain Native American populations such as the Pima Indians have an unusually high incidence of this condition, which suggests that rheumatoid arthritis has a genetic component.

Rheumatoid arthritis has a peak age of onset in the mid 50s but can occur in patients 18 years and older and is increasingly diagnosed in octogenarians. Women are affected more often than men (ratio of 3:1). However, after 60 years of age, the gender differential equilibrates.

Diagnosis

Clinical Manifestations

Rheumatoid arthritis is a multisystem disease characterized by a chronic inflammatory polyarthropathy (**Table 3**). This condition most often involves the small joints of the hands (wrist, metacarpophalangeal, and proximal interphalangeal joints) and feet (metacarpophalangeal joints) in a symmetric pattern (**Figure 6**). However, rheumatoid arthritis occasionally presents with an inflammatory oligo- or monoarthritis. Disease of the larger joints also is common. In early disease, inflammation may be limited to the feet, particularly the metatarsophalangeal joints, and this manifestation is often overlooked.

The key features of rheumatoid arthritis are swelling and tenderness in and around the joints. Synovial hypertrophy or joint effusion and loss of normal range of motion also may occur. Synovitis is appreciated on physical examination by the presence of soft or occasionally rubbery extra tissue around the joint margins. Joint warmth frequently is appreciated, although redness is uncommon.

Prominent morning stiffness that usually lasts more than 1 hour and nonspecific features such as malaise and fatigue, low-grade fevers, and myalgia and arthralgia characterize early rheumatoid arthritis. This prodrome may last from weeks to months before clinically evident synovitis is noted. Despite the lack of overt synovitis, articular destruction occurs during this time. Therefore, rapid diagnosis of early disease is imperative.

Nodules may be present and are frequently appreciated in the subcutaneous tissue just distal to the elbow on the extensor surface of the forearm (**Figure 7**). Nodules also may be appreciated on the extensor surface of the hand and over the Achilles tendons.

Evaluation

Rheumatoid arthritis is primarily diagnosed based on the patient's history and physical examination and is supported by serologic and imaging studies. Early disease may manifest as undifferentiated inflammatory polyarthritis that does not meet the American College of Rheumatology's classification criteria for this condition (**Table 4**). These criteria have 91% to 94% sensitivity and 89% specificity for established rheumatoid arthritis; the sensitivity of these criteria to diagnose early rheumatoid arthritis decreases to 40% to 60% with a specificity of 80% to 90%.

Rheumatoid arthritis must be distinguished from self-limited joint disorders such as viral arthritis due to parvovirus B19 and from other chronic inflammatory arthritides. Features that suggest rheumatoid arthritis include rheumatoid factor positivity, anti–cyclic citrullinated peptide (CCP) antibody positivity, and radiographic changes. However, these findings are relatively insensitive indicators in early disease.

The synovial fluid in patients with rheumatoid arthritis is inflammatory. Arthrocentesis is not essential for the diagnosis of this condition but should be performed in patients with

TABLE 3 Articular and Extra-articular Manifestations of Rheumatoid Arthritis	
Articular Manifestations	
Evidence of inflammation	Joint tenderness; joints warm but not erythematous; swelling of soft-tissue synovium and synovial fluid
Small-joint involvement	Symmetric involvement of proximal interphalangeal, metacarpophalangeal, and metatarsophalangeal joints; distal interphalangeal joints not usually involved
Functional limitation	Limited range of motion; decreased muscle strength and function around inflamed joints
Extra-articular Manifestations	
Dermatologic	Rheumatoid nodules, vasculitis, drug reactions
Ophthalmologic	Keratoconjunctivitis sicca, episcleritis, scleritis, scleromalacia perforans
Pulmonary	Basilar pulmonary fibrosis, multiple lung nodules, pleuritis, bronchiolitis obliterans organizing pneumonia
Cardiac	Pericarditis, pericardial effusion, valvular defects, conduction defects
Gastrointestinal	Xerostomia, gastritis or peptic ulcer disease from NSAIDs
Renal	Proteinuria if secondary amyloid is present; interstitial disease from NSAIDs and other treatment-related problems
Hepatic	Nodular regenerative hyperplasia, portal fibrosis
Neurologic	Cervical spine instability, peripheral nerve entrapment, mononeuritis multiplex from vasculitis
Hematologic	Lymphadenopathy, splenomegaly, leukopenia (Felty syndrome), malignancy, amyloidosis, cryoglobulinemia, large granular lymphocyte syndrome

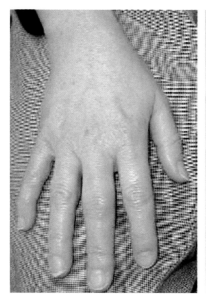 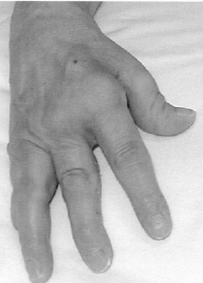 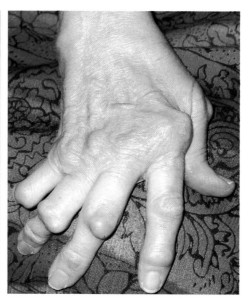

FIGURE 6.
Involvement of the hands in rheumatoid arthritis.
Early rheumatoid arthritis with mild fusiform soft-tissue swelling of the proximal interphalangeal joints (*left panel*). Moderate to severe rheumatoid arthritis with synovitis of the metacarpophalangeal joints and swan neck deformities of the second and third digits (*center panel*). Severe deforming rheumatoid arthritis with ulnar deviation, multiple rheumatoid nodules, and proximal interphalangeal joint subluxations (*right panel*).

signs and symptoms that raise suspicion for crystal-induced or infectious arthritis.

Laboratory Studies

The results of initial laboratory studies in patients with rheumatoid arthritis may be normal but can reveal thrombocytosis, leukocytosis, mild anemia (normochromic, normocytic, or microcytic), an elevated erythrocyte sedimentation rate, or an elevated C-reactive protein level.

Serologic markers for rheumatoid arthritis, including rheumatoid factor and anti-CCP antibodies, have been found in the serum of affected patients years before the onset of clinically apparent disease. Whether these antibodies are associated with a low level of subclinical inflammation or indicate susceptibility to this disease remains unclear.

Most rheumatoid factor assays detect the presence of an IgM that reacts to the Fc portion of IgG. IgG and IgA rheumatoid factors also may occur but are less common.

Approximately 75% of patients with rheumatoid arthritis are rheumatoid factor positive, but the prevalence rate of rheumatoid arthritis may be as low as 50% in early disease. Rheumatoid factor positivity is not specific for rheumatoid arthritis and frequently occurs in other autoimmune disorders and chronic infections, most notably chronic active hepatitis C virus infection.

Anti-CCP antibody assays are as insensitive for rheumatoid arthritis as rheumatoid factor assays but are more specific. Anti-CCP antibody assays may be particularly useful in patients with suspected early disease who are rheumatoid factor negative.

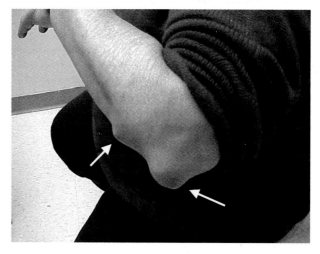

FIGURE 7.
Nodules in rheumatoid arthritis.

Reprinted with permission from Yee AMF and Paget SA, eds. Expert Guide to Rheumatology. Philadelphia: American College of Physicians; 2004.

Concomitant rheumatoid factor and anti-CCP antibody positivity are highly specific for rheumatoid arthritis.

Imaging Studies

The presence of bone erosion at presentation is a poor prognostic marker in rheumatoid arthritis (**Figure 8**). Plain radiographs may show periarticular osteopenia in early disease but are most frequently normal. Plain radiographs also may not reveal articular erosions for months or longer.

TABLE 4 Criteria for the Classification of Rheumatoid Arthritis[a]

Criterion	Definition
1. Morning stiffness	Morning stiffness in and around the joints, lasting at least 1 hour before maximal improvement
2. Arthritis of three or more joint areas	At least three joint areas simultaneously have had soft-tissue swelling or fluid (not bony overgrowth alone) observed by a physician The 14 possible areas are the right or left PIP, MCP, wrist, elbow, knee, ankle, and MTP
3. Arthritis of hand joints	At least one area swollen (as defined above) in a wrist, MCP, or PIP
4. Symmetric arthritis	Simultaneous involvement of the same joint areas (as defined in 2) on both sides of the body; bilateral involvement of PIPs, MCPs, or MTPs is acceptable without absolute symmetry
5. Rheumatoid nodules	Subcutaneous nodules over bony prominences or extensor surfaces or in juxta-articular regions observed by a physician
6. Rheumatoid factor	Demonstration of abnormal amounts of rheumatoid factor by any method for which the result has been positive in <5% of normal control subjects
7. Radiographic changes	Radiographic changes typical of rheumatoid arthritis on posteroanterior hand and wrist radiographs, which must include erosions or unequivocal bony decalcification localized in or most marked adjacent to the involved joints (osteoarthritis changes alone do not qualify)

PIP = proximal interphalangeal joint; MCP = metacarpophalangeal joint; MTP = metatarsophalangeal joint.

[a]For classification purposes, patients shall be said to have rheumatoid arthritis if they meet 4 of these 7 criteria. Criteria 1 through 4 must have been present for at least 6 weeks. Patients with two clinical diagnoses are not excluded.

Modified from Arnett FC, Edworthy SM, Bloch DA, et al. The American Rheumatism Association 1987 revised criteria for the classification of rheumatoid arthritis. Arthritis Rheum. 1988;31(3):315-324. [PMID: 3358796] Copyright 1988 American College of Rheumatology. Modified with permission from John Wiley & Sons, Inc.

MRI and ultrasonography are more sensitive imaging modalities for early erosive disease compared with radiography. However, these studies currently are not widely used because of cost and lack of high-quality performance and interpretation.

KEY POINTS

- Rheumatoid arthritis is characterized by a chronic inflammatory polyarthropathy that most often involves the small joints of the hands and feet in a symmetric pattern.
- The key features of rheumatoid arthritis are morning stiffness and symmetric swelling and tenderness in and around the small joints.
- Anti–cyclic citrullinated peptide antibody assays are more specific for rheumatoid arthritis than rheumatoid factor assays.
- Concomitant rheumatoid factor and anti–cyclic citrullinated peptide antibody positivity are highly specific for rheumatoid arthritis.
- MRI and ultrasonography are more sensitive imaging modalities for early erosive rheumatoid arthritis than radiography.

Complications and Extra-Articular Manifestations

Patients with the most severe forms of rheumatoid arthritis may have extra-articular manifestations, including ocular conditions such as scleritis; episcleritis; and peripheral ulcerative

keratitis, which can decrease vision. In addition, subcutaneous nodules; secondary Sjögren syndrome; pleuropericarditis and other lung diseases; and, rarely, rheumatoid vasculitis may occur. Patients with long-standing, aggressive rheumatoid arthritis may develop Felty syndrome, a clinical triad of rheumatoid arthritis, granulocytopenia, and splenomegaly. However, extra-articular disease in rheumatoid arthritis (particularly rheumatoid vasculitis and Felty syndrome) is increasingly less prevalent because of recent advances in the treatment of this condition.

Infection

Patients with rheumatoid arthritis are susceptible to infection due to immunosuppressive medications as well as joint damage and immobility. Infection in these patients can affect functional outcomes and morbidity and mortality. Patients with rheumatoid arthritis also are at increased risk for lymphoproliferative disorders, including acute leukemia and lymphoma.

Cervical Instability

Cervical instability at the atlantoaxial articulation is a long-term consequence of active rheumatoid arthritis and may be relatively asymptomatic until very late in the disease course. Symptoms of cervical instability at this site may include painful, limited range of motion of the neck; occipital headaches; loss of coordination; paresthesias of the hands and feet; and urinary retention or incontinence. Severe cervical instability can be associated with respiratory arrest or quadriplegia but is rare. Evaluation for this complication is indicated for any patient with aggressive or long-standing rheumatoid arthritis. Plain radiographs of the neck with

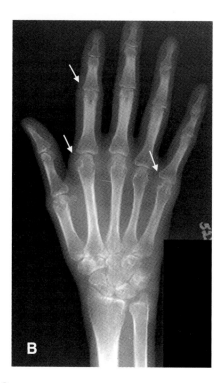

FIGURE 8.
Bone erosions.
This radiograph of the hand shows marginal erosions.

Reprinted with permission from Yee AMF and Paget SA, eds. Expert Guide to Rheumatology. Philadelphia: American College of Physicians; 2004.

flexion and extension views are usually sufficient to demonstrate translational instability; MRI can reveal the extent of the pannus and bony erosion.

Evaluation for cervical instability is particularly important in the perioperative setting, when extension of the neck for intubation may lead to cord compromise with resultant neurologic impairment. In patients who require intubation, a controlled nasal intubation with the patient upright and the neck in the neutral position is preferred.

Rheumatoid Vasculitis

Rheumatoid vasculitis is a small- and medium-vessel vasculitis usually associated with long-standing, severe erosive rheumatoid arthritis. Rheumatoid vasculitis is characterized by skin involvement that manifests as deep cutaneous ulcerations; digital ischemia; and, occasionally, necrosis. Some evidence shows that the prevalence of rheumatoid vasculitis is decreasing in patients with rheumatoid arthritis, most likely because of earlier and more widespread use of disease-modifying antirheumatic drug therapy (DMARD).

Mononeuritis multiplex is a manifestation of rheumatoid vasculitis that may manifest as a wrist or foot drop that usually does not fully resolve even with aggressive immunosuppression. Mesenteric vasculitis may lead to bowel infarction and, rarely, death.

Coronary Artery Disease

Coronary artery disease is the leading cause of death in patients with rheumatoid arthritis. Patients with rheumatoid arthritis may have traditional risk factors for this disease, and the underlying inflammatory condition in rheumatoid arthritis is an independent risk factor for multivessel coronary artery disease.

In patients with rheumatoid arthritis, aggressive treatment of the underlying inflammatory process has been shown to decrease the development of atherosclerotic disease and the associated morbidity and mortality. Management of the traditional cardiovascular risk factors, including smoking, hyperlipidemia, diabetes, hypertension, and obesity, is recommended.

KEY POINTS

- Extra-articular manifestations of rheumatoid arthritis include ocular conditions such as scleritis and episcleritis; subcutaneous nodules; secondary Sjögren syndrome; pleuropericarditis and other lung diseases; and rheumatoid vasculitis.

- Patients with rheumatoid arthritis are particularly susceptible to infection.

- Evaluation for cervical instability with plain radiographs of the neck with flexion and extension views is indicated for patients with aggressive or long-standing rheumatoid arthritis, particularly those who will undergo intubation.

- Coronary artery disease is the leading cause of death in patients with rheumatoid arthritis.

Management

Once rheumatoid arthritis is suspected, promptly confirming the diagnosis and initiating aggressive therapy is critical. Early referral to a rheumatologist to assess the disease, document prognostic factors, and recommend optimal treatment is imperative. Serial measurement of factors such as the number of swollen and tender joints and acute phase reactants also can help to evaluate disease progression and guide treatment decisions.

Nonpharmacologic modalities such as heat and joint range-of-motion exercises can help to alleviate the joint stiffness that limits many patients with rheumatoid arthritis. Referral to other providers, including physical therapists, occupational therapists, and psychologists, also may help many patients with early rheumatoid arthritis. Counseling regarding joint protection techniques, use of assistive devices, and therapeutic exercises is essential. In patients with rheumatoid arthritis with concomitant hyperlipidemia, statin agents may have an adjunctive role in controlling inflammation.

Early, aggressive disease control is essential to slow the progression of joint damage, stabilize or prevent functional limitations, and prevent the complications of long-term uncontrolled inflammation. Damage in rheumatoid arthritis is irreversible once it has occurred, even when aggressive DMARD therapy is used. Evidence shows that rapidly escalating therapy with a multidrug regimen is the most effective means of controlling disease.

Treating rheumatoid arthritis often involves adjustment of agents and dosing.

Frequent reassessment of affected patients is essential to ensure continued response to therapy and disease control and to monitor for drug toxicity. Periodic radiographs are recommended to confirm that erosive disease has not progressed despite therapy. The goal of treatment is to maintain no evidence of disease, because control of inflammation is the best predictor of radiographic and functional stability.

NSAIDs and Corticosteroids

In early rheumatoid arthritis, NSAIDs and systemic low-dose corticosteroids can help control symptoms but do not adequately prevent disease progression. Intra-articular corticosteroids are useful to control localized disease that is unresponsive to systemic therapy.

Corticosteroid-induced osteoporosis is a major concern in patients with rheumatoid arthritis. Prevention of osteoporosis using a bisphosphonate is indicated for men and postmenopausal women. Dual-energy x-ray absorptiometry scanning is recommended for patients using long-term corticosteroid therapy or those over 65 years of age.

Disease-Modifying Antirheumatic Drugs

Experts recommend that patients begin DMARD therapy within 3 months of the onset of rheumatoid arthritis. The earlier that DMARDs are instituted, the more likely that damage from this condition will be limited. The initial choice of a DMARD should be based on the severity of the inflammatory disease; the pace of disease progression; whether erosive disease is seen on radiography; and whether a patient is anti-CCP antibody positive.

Monotherapy with hydroxychloroquine or sulfasalazine or combination therapy with these agents is indicated to treat early, mild, and nonerosive disease. Hydroxychloroquine therapy alone has not been shown to retard radiographic progression of rheumatoid arthritis and therefore should be used only in patients whose disease has remained nonerosive for several years.

Use of methotrexate or leflunomide may benefit patients with early mild to moderate rheumatoid arthritis but is imperative in patients with rapid disease progression or functional limitations. In the absence of contraindications, methotrexate with or without the addition of another DMARD should be instituted immediately in patients with erosive disease documented at disease onset. The methotrexate dosage should be rapidly escalated as tolerated up to 20 to 25 mg weekly. Experts also recommend that patients using methotrexate take folic acid, 1 mg/d.

In patients with rheumatoid arthritis, combination therapy generally is more effective than monotherapy and may include use of two or three DMARDs. In some patients, combination therapy with hydroxychloroquine, sulfasalazine, and methotrexate has been shown to be more effective than monotherapy with methotrexate or sulfasalazine plus hydroxychloroquine.

Leflunomide may be added to methotrexate, but combination therapy with methotrexate and leflunomide is associated with a higher incidence of adverse hepatic events and requires careful monitoring and dose adjustments. In the absence of any appreciable response to methotrexate, leflunomide can be instituted as monotherapy or in combination with hydroxychloroquine and/or sulfasalazine. Regardless of the combination chosen, more intensive therapy is indicated if significant improvement does not occur.

Biologic Therapy

When adequate disease control is not achieved with oral DMARDs, biologic therapy should be initiated. The initial biologic therapy should be a TNF-α inhibitor. This agent generally should be added to the baseline methotrexate therapy, because the rate of radiographic progression has been shown to decrease with combination therapy. Combination therapy with methotrexate plus a TNF-α inhibitor can be used in patients with early disease who have high disease activity and poor prognostic factors (see Prognostic Factors).

Screening for tuberculosis is indicated before beginning therapy with any biologic agent, and patients who test positive for latent tuberculosis should be treated with isoniazid before beginning biologic therapy. Furthermore, periodic purified protein derivative skin testing for tuberculosis is now recommended during treatment with a TNF-α inhibitor.

The patient's preferred route of administration and cost usually determine the choice of a TNF-α inhibitor. The three currently available agents, etanercept, infliximab, and adalimumab, all have similar efficacy. Individual patients may respond better to one of these agents, but no currently available methods predict the likelihood of response to a particular agent. Many patients who do not respond to one TNF-α inhibitor have a positive response to a different agent in the same class.

Patients with an inadequate response to TNF-α inhibition can be treated with either abatacept, a T-cell costimulation inhibitor, or rituximab, an anti-CD20 monoclonal antibody. Combination therapy with biologic agents does not enhance their efficacy and poses a risk for toxicity due to infections and is therefore not recommended. Annual influenza vaccination is indicated for all patients using immunosuppressants, and pneumococcal vaccination is indicated before beginning treatment with methotrexate, leflunomide, or a biologic agent.

Surgical Therapy

Mild rheumatoid arthritis may be easily controlled with minimal therapy, but a subset of patients has an unremitting, worsening course of joint destruction and functional disability despite aggressive treatment. Surgical therapy may be indicated for patients with destructive rheumatoid arthritis that cannot be managed pharmacologically. End-stage disease of the hip or knee is frequently treated with total joint arthroplasty. Because of improvements in prosthetic design and surgical techniques, arthroplasty of the shoulder or elbow is increasingly performed. Other surgical procedures, such as synovectomy or joint arthrodesis, may be warranted in patients with persistent inflammatory disease and pain when medical management is ineffective.

KEY POINTS

- Patients with rheumatoid arthritis should be frequently monitored for drug toxicity and assessed with periodic radiographs to ensure continued response to therapy and disease control.
- Patients should begin disease-modifying antirheumatic drug therapy within 3 months of the onset of rheumatoid arthritis.
- Combination therapy with disease-modifying antirheumatic drugs typically is more effective than monotherapy in patients with rheumatoid arthritis.
- Screening for tuberculosis is indicated before beginning therapy with a biologic agent in patients with rheumatoid arthritis, and periodic purified protein derivative skin testing for tuberculosis is recommended during treatment with TNF-α inhibitors.
- Surgical therapy may be indicated for patients with destructive rheumatoid arthritis that cannot be managed pharmacologically.

Pregnancy and Rheumatoid Arthritis

Generally, women with rheumatoid arthritis have fertility rates and pregnancy outcomes comparable to those of women without this condition. Preconception counseling is essential for women with active rheumatoid arthritis who are taking DMARDs, particularly DMARDs that are known to be teratogenic (see Disease-Modifying Antirheumatic Drugs).

Approximately 75% of women with rheumatoid arthritis who become pregnant experience a spontaneous remission of symptoms that usually begins in the second trimester of pregnancy. During pregnancy, most women with rheumatoid

arthritis can therefore safely discontinue therapy for this condition. However, pregnant patients with persistent disease activity may require treatment with low-dose prednisone, which generally is believed to be safe in pregnancy. Hydroxychloroquine and sulfasalazine also can be used during pregnancy, if necessary.

There are limited data on the safety of TNF-α inhibitors in pregnancy, and therapy with these agents should be discontinued before conception. NSAIDs may be continued during the first and second trimesters of pregnancy but should be avoided in the third trimester because of the risk of premature closure of the ductus arteriosus in utero before birth.

Most pregnant women with rheumatoid arthritis experience a disease flare after delivery. DMARD therapy should be reinstituted immediately unless the woman is breast feeding. In women with highly aggressive disease, breast feeding should be discontinued so that DMARD therapy can be resumed.

KEY POINTS

- During pregnancy, most women with rheumatoid arthritis can safely discontinue therapy for this condition.
- In women with highly aggressive rheumatoid arthritis who are postpartum, breast feeding should be discontinued so that DMARD therapy can be resumed.

Prognostic Factors

Predicting disease outcome is often difficult early in the course of rheumatoid arthritis but is essential to ensure that patients with the greatest risk of a poor outcome receive earlier and more aggressive treatment. Older age, the presence of erosions at baseline, rheumatoid factor positivity, high titers of rheumatoid factor, and anti-CCP antibodies predict radiographic progression in rheumatoid arthritis. Other poor prognostic factors include female sex, cigarette smoking, extra-articular disease, functional limitations, a high number of tender and swollen joints, and an elevated erythrocyte sedimentation rate and C-reactive protein level. Patients who are *HLA-DRB1*0401* or *HLA-DRB1*0404* positive have an increased likelihood of developing more severe disease and premature mortality, and those who are homozygous have the worst outcome. Patients with a lower socioeconomic status and less formal education also usually have a poorer prognosis.

In patients with persistent polyarticular rheumatoid arthritis that is uncontrolled despite therapy, high titers of rheumatoid factor, the presence of the shared epitope, and systemic extra-articular disease are associated with premature mortality.

- Older age, the presence of erosions at baseline, rheumatoid factor positivity, high titers of rheumatoid factor, and anti–cyclic citrullinated peptide antibody positivity predict radiographic progression in rheumatoid arthritis.

- In patients with persistent polyarticular rheumatoid arthritis that is uncontrolled despite therapy, high titers of rheumatoid factor, and systemic extra-articular disease are associated with premature mortality.

Bibliography

Aletaha D, Breedveld FC, Smolen JS. The need for new classification criteria for rheumatoid arthritis. Arthritis Rheum. 2005;52(11):3333-3336. [PMID: 16255014]

Goekoop-Ruiterman YPM, de Vries-Bouwstra JK, Allaart CF, et al. Clinical and radiographic outcomes of four different treatment strategies in patients with early rheumatoid arthritis (the BeSt study): a randomized, controlled trial. Arthritis Rheum. 2005;52(11):3381-3390. [PMID: 16258899]

Goekoop-Ruiterman YP, de Vries-Bouwstra JK, Allaart CF, et al. Comparison of treatment strategies in early rheumatoid arthritis: a randomized trial. Ann Intern Med. 2007;146(6):406-415. [PMID: 17371885]

Mattey DL, Thompson W, Ollier WE, et al. Association of DRB1 shared epitope genotypes with early mortality in rheumatoid arthritis: results of eighteen years of followup from the early rheumatoid arthritis study. Arthritis Rheum. 2007;56(5):1408-1416. [PMID: 17469097]

Nishimura K, Sugiyama D, Kogata Y, et al. Meta-analysis: diagnostic accuracy of anti-cyclic citrullinated peptide antibody and rheumatoid factor for rheumatoid arthritis. Ann Intern Med. 2007;146(11):797-808. [PMID: 17548411]

Saag KG, Teng GG, Patkar NM, et al; American College of Rheumatology. American College of Rheumatology 2008 recommendations for the use of nonbiologic and biologic disease-modifying antirheumatic drugs in rheumatoid arthritis. Arthritis Rheum. 2008;59(6):762-784. [PMID: 18512708]

Osteoarthritis

Pathophysiology and Risk Factors

Osteoarthritis traditionally was believed to be caused by "wear and tear" on the joints with age. This condition is now known to be an active disease process in which the chemical composition and structural integrity of the articular cartilage deteriorates. This deterioration impairs the viscoelastic properties of articular cartilage and its ability to minimize friction between bones moving against one another.

Age is the primary risk factor for the development of osteoarthritis. Obesity is another major risk factor for this condition and is particularly associated with the development of osteoarthritis of the knee and hand. Obesity also has been shown to be an independent risk factor both for disability due to osteoarthritis and for the severity of knee pain.

Occupations that involve repetitive knee bending and physical labor, such as farming and construction work, have been associated with an increased relative risk for developing osteoarthritis of the knee. However, occupational change has not been shown to be beneficial in decreasing the clinical manifestations of osteoarthritis in this setting. Female sex and trauma are additional risk factors for the development of this condition.

Clinical Features and Classification

Osteoarthritis most commonly affects the weight-bearing joints as well as the distal and proximal interphalangeal and first carpometacarpal joints of the hand (**Figure 9**). The cardinal symptom of this condition is pain with activity that is relieved with rest; pain at rest or at night is a sign of advanced disease. Affected patients also typically experience morning stiffness that lasts for less than 30 minutes daily.

Joint swelling in patients with osteoarthritis generally is minimal. Heberden and Bouchard nodes (bony proliferation at the distal and proximal interphalangeal joints, respectively) may develop in this setting and cause pain, limited range of motion, and difficulty wearing and removing rings (**Figure 10**). Osteoarthritis of the knee usually does not present with visible swelling of the knee but may manifest with a crackling sound known as crepitus on flexion of this joint. Range of motion of the knee or hip may be reduced in patients with progressive disease, which causes difficulty when exiting an automobile.

Primary and Secondary Osteoarthritis

Primary osteoarthritis is a disease of unknown cause. This condition affects the lower cervical and lumbar spine, the acromioclavicular joint, the first carpometacarpal joint of the thumb, the proximal and distal interphalangeal joints of the hands, the hips, the knees, and the metatarsophalangeal joint of the great toe.

Secondary osteoarthritis develops because of another condition, such as trauma, previous inflammatory arthritis, or metabolic disorders such as hemochromatosis or calcium pyrophosphate deposition disease. This form of arthritis typically involves joints not usually affected by primary osteoarthritis, including the metacarpophalangeal joints, (which should specifically raise suspicion for hemochromatosis), wrist, elbow, shoulder, ankle, and second through fifth metatarsophalangeal joints.

Erosive Inflammatory Osteoarthritis

Erosive inflammatory osteoarthritis is characterized by pain and palpable swelling of the soft tissue in the proximal and distal interphalangeal joints. This condition also may be associated with disease flares during which these joints become more swollen and painful. Radiographs in patients with erosive inflammatory osteoarthritis may reveal erosions at the interface of the involved phalanges.

Diffuse Idiopathic Skeletal Hyperostosis

Diffuse idiopathic skeletal hyperostosis (DISH) is an often asymptomatic form of osteoarthritis that causes significant radiographic changes similar to those associated with degenerative spondylosis or ankylosing spondylitis (**Figure 11**). Radiographs of the spine in patients with DISH reveal flowing ossification that develops along the anterolateral aspect of

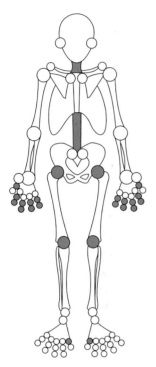

FIGURE 9.
Joints involved in osteoarthritis.

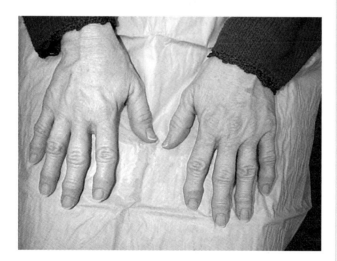

FIGURE 10.
Heberden and Bouchard nodes.
This patient with osteoarthritis has bony proliferation at the distal and proximal interphalangeal joints (Herberden and Bouchard nodes, respectively).

Modified with permission from Moore G. Atlas of the Musculoskeletal Examination. Philadelphia: American College of Physicians; 2003.

the vertebral bodies, particularly the anterior longitudinal ligament. However, neither disk-space narrowing nor syndesmophytes are visible in this setting, as they are in lumbar spondylosis or ankylosing spondylitis, respectively. Rare complications of DISH include dysphagia, cervical myelopathy, and lumbar spinal stenosis.

KEY POINTS

- Osteoarthritis most commonly affects the weight-bearing joints as well as the distal and proximal interphalangeal and first carpometacarpal joints of the hand.

- Osteoarthritis is characterized by pain with activity that is relieved with rest and morning stiffness that lasts for less than 30 minutes daily.

- Secondary osteoarthritis involves joints not typically affected by primary osteoarthritis and develops due to conditions such as trauma, previous inflammatory arthritis, or metabolic disorders such as hemochromatosis or calcium pyrophosphate deposition disease.

- Radiographs of patients with diffuse idiopathic skeletal hyperostosis and degenerative spondylosis and ankylosing spondylitis are similar except that patients with diffuse idiopathic skeletal hyperostosis do not develop disk-space narrowing or syndesmophytes.

Diagnosis

Osteoarthritis is a clinical diagnosis. Physical findings may be minimal early in the disease course. As disease progresses, joint range of motion becomes progressively limited. Whether affected joints are tender varies significantly.

Bony hypertrophy is commonly detected in the fingers, and Heberden and Bouchard nodes may be easily palpated. Osteoarthritis also may cause squaring or boxing of the carpometacarpal joint at the base of the thumb.

According to the American College of Rheumatology's clinical criteria, osteoarthritis of the knee can be diagnosed if knee pain is accompanied by at least three of the following features: age greater than 50 years, stiffness lasting less than 30 minutes, crepitus, bony tenderness, bony enlargement, and no palpable warmth. These criteria are 95% sensitive and 69% specific but have not been validated for clinical practice.

Crepitus of the knees is common in patients with osteoarthritis between the patella and the femur. Passive range of motion of the knee or hip often elicits pain at the extremes of flexion, extension, or internal and external rotation. Palpation of the knee discloses only mild tenderness. Valgus or varus angulation of the knees may be apparent when the patient stands. Patients with advanced osteoarthritis may have instability or joint laxity, which may be identified using the drawer test (**Figure 12**).

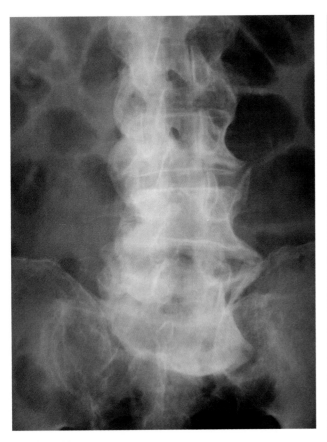

FIGURE 11.
Diffuse idiopathic skeletal hyperostosis.
Radiograph of the spine showing flowing linear calcification and ossification along the anterolateral aspects of the vertebral bodies that continues across the disk space.

Osteoarthritis of the hip can be established in patients with a history of chronic pain in the groin and medial thigh that worsens with activity and is relieved by rest. However, acute pain in the hip area suggests fracture and should be evaluated with radiography and, if needed, additional imaging studies.

Differential Diagnosis

Differentiating between osteoarthritis of the hand and rheumatoid arthritis can be difficult. Both of these conditions can present with swelling of the proximal interphalangeal joints, but osteoarthritis also may involve the distal interphalangeal joints. In addition, the bony enlargements of these joints that develop in osteoarthritis are significantly harder than the synovial proliferation that develops in rheumatoid arthritis.

Occasionally, laboratory studies may be warranted to differentiate between these conditions. Elevated levels of an acute phase reactant such as the erythrocyte sedimentation rate or C-reactive protein, or rheumatoid factor or anti–cyclic citrullinated peptide antibody positivity, would exclude osteoarthritis or suggest a concomitant condition in addition to osteoarthritis.

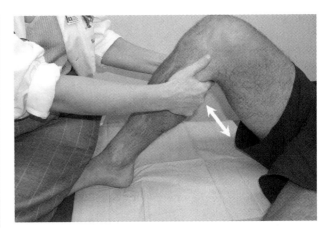

FIGURE 12.
Drawer test.
In the drawer test, the patient's knee is bent at a 90-degree angle with the physician sitting on the patient's foot to stabilize the leg. The leg is then moved forward and back, evaluating for laxity or instability of the joint.

Reprinted with permission from Moore G. Atlas of the Musculoskeletal Examination. Philadelphia: American College of Physicians; 2003.

Imaging Studies

Radiography is not needed to confirm the diagnosis of osteoarthritis in patients with a history and physical examination compatible with this condition. Clinical examination is more sensitive and specific for the diagnosis of osteoarthritis of the hand compared with radiography, and radiographs in patients with early osteoarthritis of the knee may be normal.

Radiographs in patients with osteoarthritis may show joint-space narrowing, subchondral sclerosis, and osteophyte formation. However, there is a poor correlation between radiographic evidence of osteoarthritis and symptoms. An absence of joint-space narrowing on radiography does not indicate that the cartilage is healthy and functioning normally. MRI is more sensitive for detecting abnormalities of articular cartilage compared with radiography but is rarely clinically indicated to establish a diagnosis of osteoarthritis.

KEY POINTS

- Osteoarthritis of the knee can be diagnosed if knee pain is accompanied by at least three of the following features: age greater than 50 years, stiffness lasting less than 30 minutes, crepitus, bony tenderness, bony enlargement, and no palpable warmth.

- Osteoarthritis of the hand may manifest as swelling of the proximal and distal interphalangeal joints and hard bony enlargement, whereas rheumatoid arthritis of the hand presents with only proximal interphalangeal and metacarpophalangeal joint swelling and soft synovial proliferation.

- Compared with radiography, clinical examination is more sensitive and specific for the diagnosis of osteoarthritis of the hand.

- There is a poor correlation between radiographic evidence of osteoarthritis and symptoms.

Management and Treatment

Nonpharmacologic Interventions

Weight is a significant risk factor for worsening of osteoarthritis. Weight loss is a particularly important intervention for patients with osteoarthritis of the hip and has been shown to cause a slower rate of progression of osteoarthritis of the knee in obese patients and to decrease symptoms of this condition.

Work simplification via use of assistive devices such as thick-handled kitchen utensils, specially designed rocker knives, and jar openers can help to reduce symptoms of osteoarthritis of the hands. Use of a cane or walker may be warranted in patients with osteoarthritis of the hip or knee, and instruction in the correct use of these devices is essential. For example, a patient with unilateral knee or hip pain should be instructed to hold the cane in the contralateral hand to help relieve the symptomatic side.

Physical therapy benefits most patients with osteoarthritis of the hip or knee. Quadriceps muscle strengthening in particular helps to reduce pain due to osteoarthritis of the knee and is an important intervention in patients who are considering total knee replacement.

Therapeutic knee taping in patients with osteoarthritis of the knee remains controversial. In one randomized study of patients with this condition, weekly taping effectively reduced pain compared with placebo. Valgus bracing of the knee also has been shown to effectively reduce knee pain in this setting. Studies on the usefulness of shoe insoles in osteoarthritis remain inconclusive.

Pharmacologic Therapy

Many patients with osteoarthritis achieve adequate pain relief with acetaminophen. This agent is inexpensive, effective, and relatively safe and is therefore typically the first oral analgesic agent considered in patients with osteoarthritis. However, treatment with acetaminophen can prolong the INR in patients on warfarin and can lead to hepatotoxicity.

A 1992 study showed that the efficacy of acetaminophen and NSAIDs in the treatment of osteoarthritis is comparable, but subsequent studies have demonstrated better results with NSAIDs than acetaminophen. However, the use of nonselective NSAIDs or celecoxib may be risky in some patients. Evidence shows that cyclooxygenase-2 selective and nonselective NSAIDs may be associated with cardiovascular and cerebrovascular disease. The U.S. Food and Drug Administration has concluded that use of prescription and over-the-counter traditional NSAIDs also may increase cardiovascular risk.

Cyclooxygenase-2 selective and nonselective NSAIDs also have been shown to increase the risk for gastrointestinal irritation, ulceration, bleeding, and perforation. Coadministration of a proton pump inhibitor or misoprostol can reduce the gastrointestinal toxicity of these agents. Substitution of a nonacetylated salicylate for these agents also may be warranted. In 2005, the American College of Rheumatology revised their guidelines to recommend that physicians and patients weigh the potential risks and benefits of treatment with NSAIDs, but no evidence-based guidelines yet exist to indicate which patients can safely use these agents.

The American College of Rheumatology guidelines recommend tramadol and opioid analgesics as second-line agents in the treatment of osteoarthritis. These agents are particularly useful in patients with osteoarthritis of the hip or knee who are intolerant of or who do not achieve adequate pain control using acetaminophen and/or NSAIDs. Tramadol is a nonopioid analgesic that binds to the opioid receptor but generally does not cause constipation or sedation. This agent is contraindicated in patients with a history of substance abuse and may cause seizures in patients using selective serotonin reuptake inhibitors or tricyclic antidepressants.

Propoxyphene and other narcotics may be appropriate for some patients with osteoarthritis, particularly those who are not candidates for surgical therapy. However, chronic use of these agents may lead to tolerance and require repeated escalation of doses.

Intra-articular Injection

Intra-articular corticosteroid or hyaluronan injections may be considered in patients with mono- or pauciarticular osteoarthritis in whom NSAIDs are either contraindicated or do not provide adequate pain relief.

Corticosteroids

Corticosteroid injection therapy provides rapid but temporary relief of pain due to osteoarthritis of the knee and hip. Most injectable corticosteroid preparations, including methylprednisolone and triamcinolone, are approximately equipotent.

Clinical experience shows that patients with osteoarthritis of the knee may have symptomatic relief for several months after a corticosteroid injection, but a 2005 review suggests that there is no evidence that this therapy is associated with relief lasting longer than 1 week. In patients with osteoarthritis of the hip, intra-articular corticosteroid therapy has been shown to effectively relieve pain for up to 3 months. The efficacy of this therapy in treating osteoarthritis of joints other than the knee and hip remains uncertain.

To prevent joint damage, most experts recommend that a joint should not be injected with corticosteroids more frequently than once every 3 months. Intra-articular injection of any medication is contraindicated in patients with overlying cellulitis and should not be used if the cause of the joint pain has not been definitively diagnosed. In addition, patients with signs of inflammation such as heat or redness, which are atypical for osteoarthritis, should not undergo intra-articular corticosteroid therapy until synovial fluid analysis excludes infection.

Hyaluronans

Studies have generally shown that intra-articular hyaluronan injection has comparable efficacy to NSAID therapy in patients with osteoarthritis of the knee. Hyaluronan levels in the synovial fluid are decreased in patients with osteoarthritis, but the mechanism of action of hyaluronan agents in this setting remains unclear. Three or more hyaluronan injections administered 1 week apart are indicated depending on the preparation. Patients may not experience relief until several weeks after undergoing injection, but the effects of this therapy can last for 6 months or longer.

Surgical Intervention

Referral to an orthopedic surgeon for consideration of total joint arthroplasty (replacement) of the knee or hip is warranted only when no further medical therapy is available and the patient decides that the impairment caused by his or her condition warrants this intervention. The degree of radiographic severity of osteoarthritis is not a pivotal determinant in whether this procedure is appropriate, although radiographic changes are usually severe by the time arthroplasty is considered.

Patients who are likely to live more than 10 years after undergoing joint arthroplasty should be cautioned that prosthetic implants may eventually loosen and require surgical replacement, which is a more difficult procedure than implantation. Patients with recurrent or chronic infections are at increased risk for prosthetic joint infection, which usually also requires removal of the prosthesis as well as prolonged antibiotic treatment.

KEY POINTS

- Weight loss and physical therapy benefit patients with osteoarthritis of the hip and knee.

- NSAIDs have been shown to be more effective in the treatment of osteoarthritis than acetaminophen but may increase cardiovascular risk.

- Tramadol and opioid analgesics are effective second-line agents in the treatment of osteoarthritis.

- Intra-articular corticosteroid injection therapy is warranted in patients with osteoarthritis of the knee or hip in whom NSAIDs are either contraindicated or do not provide adequate pain relief.

- Patients with signs of inflammation should not undergo intra-articular corticosteroid therapy until synovial fluid analysis excludes infection.

Bibliography

Altman R, Asch E, Bolch D, et al. Development of criteria for the classification and reporting of osteoarthritis. Classification of osteoarthritis of the knee. Diagnostic and Therapeutic Criteria Committee of the American Rheumatism Association. Arthritis Rheum. 1986;29(8):1039-1049. [PMID: 3741515]

Bellamy N, Campbell J, Robinson V, Gee T, Bourne R, Wells G. Intraarticular corticosteroid for treatment of osteoarthritis of the knee. Cochrane Database Syst Rev. 2005;(2):CD005328. [PMID: 15846755]

FDA Public Health Advisory: FDA Announces Important Changes and Additional Warnings for COX-2 Selective and Non-Selective Non-Steroidal Anti-Inflammatory Drugs (NSAIDs). U.S. Food and Drug Administration Web site. www.fda.gov/cder/drug/advisory/COX2.htm. April 7, 2005. Accessed February 10, 2009.

Felson DT, Zhang Y, Anthony JM, Naimark A, Anderson JJ. Weight loss reduces the risk for symptomatic knee osteoarthritis in women. The Framingham Study. Ann Intern Med. 1992;116(7):535-539. [PMID: 1543306]

Hinman RS, Crossley KM, McConnell J, Bennell KL. Efficacy of knee tape in the management of osteoarthritis of the knee: blinded randomized controlled trial. BMJ. 2003; 327(7407):135. [PMID: 12869456]

Lambert RG, Hutchings EJ, Grace MG, Jhangri GS, Conner-Spady B, Maksymowych WP. Steroid injection for osteoarthritis of the hip: a randomized, double-blind, placebo-controlled trial. Arthritis Rheum. 2007;56(7):2278-2287. [PMID: 17599747]

Recommendations for the medical management of osteoarthritis of the hip and knee: 2000 update. American College of Rheumatology Subcommittee on Osteoarthritis Guidelines. Arthritis Rheum. 2000;43(9):1905-1915. [PMID: 11014340]

Solomon DH, Schneeweiss S, Glynn RJ, et al. Relationship between selective cyclooxygenase-2 inhibitors and acute myocardial infarction in older adults. Circulation. 2004;109(17):2068-2073. [PMID: 15096449]

Solomon SD, McMurray JJV, Pfeffer MA, et al; Adenoma Prevention with Celecoxib (APC) Study Investigators. Cardiovascular risk associated with celecoxib in a clinical trial for colorectal adenoma prevention. N Engl J Med. 2005;352(11):1071-1080. [PMID: 15713944]

Fibromyalgia

Introduction

Fibromyalgia is characterized by chronic widespread musculoskeletal pain for at least 3 months and pain in at least 11 of 18 diffuse potential tender points (**Figure 13**). Pain and tenderness often are not limited to these tender points. Affected patients also have an increased prevalence of anxiety and major depression and almost always have fatigue, sleep disturbances, and a lowered pain threshold. A diagnosis of fibromyalgia is established in patients who meet the 1990 American College of Rheumatology classification criteria (**Table 5**). However, expert opinion now states that these tender points are arbitrary and not essential in the diagnosis of fibromyalgia.

KEY POINT

- Fibromyalgia is characterized by chronic widespread musculoskeletal pain for at least 3 months and pain in at least 11 of 18 diffuse potential tender points.

Pathophysiology

The cause of fibromyalgia is unknown but may be related to central nervous system mechanisms such as dysregulation of neurotransmitter function and central pain sensitization. Comorbid conditions such as chronic fatigue syndrome, irritable bowel syndrome, multiple chemical sensitivity, tension or migraine headaches, pelvic pain, atypical chest pain, interstitial cystitis, and temporomandibular joint pain frequently

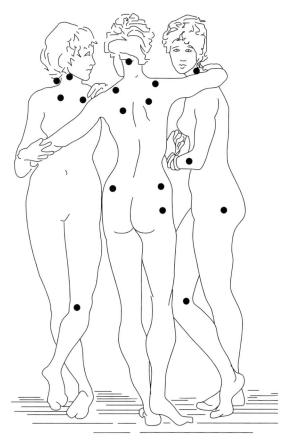

FIGURE 13.
Tender point locations for the 1990 classification criteria for fibromyalgia (The Three Graces, after Baron Jean-Baptiste Regnault, 1793, Louvre Museum, Paris).

occur in fibromyalgia, which suggests the presence of a common pathophysiologic mechanism.

Epidemiology

Fibromyalgia affects women more frequently than men but may be more severe in men. Patients with low socioeconomic status, poor functional status, and disability have a greater risk for developing this condition. The onset of fibromyalgia in women typically occurs between the ages of 20 and 50 years.

Patients with fibromyalgia often have a history of an accident, injury, or traumatic event, but a clear association between these factors and the development of fibromyalgia has not been established. Cognitive behavioral variables such as abnormal coping mechanisms also appear to play an important role in this condition.

Diagnosis and Evaluation

The differential diagnosis of fibromyalgia includes hypothyroidism, polymyalgia rheumatica (in patients older than 50 years of age), hepatitis C virus infection, sleep apnea, and restless legs syndrome. The American College of

Rheumatology criteria for fibromyalgia have no exclusions, and this condition occasionally occurs in association with autoimmune disorders such as rheumatoid arthritis, systemic lupus erythematosus, and Sjögren syndrome. In addition to hypothyroidism, other endocrinopathies such as Addison disease or hyperparathyroidism rarely present with features of fibromyalgia.

The physical examination in patients with fibromyalgia usually is normal except for widespread pain and tenderness. Diagnosis may also be established by asking patients to indicate tender spots on a diagram of a human figure.

Laboratory studies are useful only in excluding conditions that may mimic fibromyalgia and generally should include only measurement of the serum thyroid-stimulating hormone level, erythrocyte sedimentation rate, alanine and aspartate aminotransferase levels, and complete blood count. Routine testing for antinuclear antibodies or rheumatoid factor is not indicated. Patients with appropriate risk factors should be tested for hepatitis C virus antibodies. A sleep study is indicated for patients with a history of excessive daytime somnolence, abnormal snoring, nocturnal apneas, or restless legs syndrome.

KEY POINTS

- The physical examination in patients with fibromyalgia usually is normal except for widespread pain and tenderness.

- Laboratory studies in patients with fibromyalgia are useful only in excluding conditions that may mimic this disease, such as hypothyroidism, polymyalgia rheumatica, hepatitis C virus infection, sleep apnea, and restless legs syndrome.

Treatment

Treatment of fibromyalgia often involves nonpharmacologic and pharmacologic therapy. Educating patients with fibromyalgia about the nature and course of the disease is imperative. Physicians should validate patients' concerns about their condition and acknowledge their pain. Patients should be counseled that this condition is not destructive but that they should establish realistic expectations and recognize that meaningful improvement rarely occurs unless they take an active role in the treatment plan.

Nonpharmacologic Therapy

Nonpharmacologic therapy is the cornerstone of treatment of fibromyalgia and should be initiated in all affected patients. Regular aerobic exercise has been shown to be effective in this setting. High-impact aerobic exercises frequently are poorly tolerated, whereas walking and/or water aerobics are better tolerated. Cognitive behavioral therapy has been shown to be beneficial in fibromyalgia but is not always covered by insurance plans.

TABLE 5 American College of Rheumatology 1990 Criteria for Fibromyalgia
Criterion 1. History of Widespread Pain
Definition: Pain in the right and left side of the body and above and below the waist and axial skeletal pain (cervical spine or anterior chest or thoracic spine or low back). In this definition, shoulder and buttock pain is considered as pain for each involved side. Low back pain is considered lower segment pain.
Criterion 2. Pain in 11 of 18 Tender Point Sites on Digital Palpation
Definition: Pain, on digital palpation, must be present in at least 11 of 18 specified tender point sites. Digital palpation should be performed with an approximate force of 4 kg (8.8 lb). For a tender point to be considered "positive" for pain, the patient must state that the palpation was painful. "Tender" is not to be considered "painful."

Pharmacologic Therapy

Tricyclic antidepressants are the most studied pharmacologic agents in the treatment of fibromyalgia. Low-dose amitriptyline and cyclobenzaprine are the most used therapeutic agents in this setting.

Pregabalin is approved by the U.S. Food and Drug Administration for the treatment of fibromyalgia. In a randomized double-blind trial of patients with fibromyalgia, this agent was shown to significantly decrease the average severity of pain and fatigue and to improve sleep compared with placebo. However, in some patients, pregabalin was associated with only modest and transient benefits. In the FREEDOM trial, 566 patients with fibromyalgia who had a more than 50% reduction in mean pain scores with pregabalin were randomized to either continue this agent or switch to placebo for 26 weeks. By the end of this study, 32% of those who continued to use pregabalin and 61% of those who switched to placebo had lost their therapeutic response.

A second agent, the serotonin and noradrenergic reuptake inhibitor duloxetine, has been shown to have similar findings to pregabalin and was approved for the treatment of fibromyalgia in 2008. Other newer antidepressants, especially those with the greatest effect on adrenergic/dopaminergic activity, also have been shown to be beneficial in this condition. NSAIDs, opioids, and corticosteroids have been shown to have limited efficacy in the treatment of this condition.

KEY POINTS

- Nonpharmacologic therapy such as regular aerobic exercise and cognitive behavioral therapy is the cornerstone of treatment of fibromyalgia and should be initiated in all affected patients.
- Low-dose amitriptyline and cyclobenzaprine are the most used therapeutic agents in patients with fibromyalgia.
- Pregabalin and duloxetine are approved by the U.S. Food and Drug Administration for the treatment of fibromyalgia.

Bibliography

Arnold LM, Lu Y, Crofford LJ, et al. A double-blind, multicenter trial comparing duloxetine with placebo in the treatment of fibromyalgia patients with or without major depressive disorder. Arthritis Rheum. 2004;50(9):2974-2984. [PMID: 15457467]

Crofford LJ, Mease PJ, Simpson SL, et al. Fibromyalgia relapse evaluation and efficacy for durability of meaningful relief (FREEDOM): a 6-month, double-blind, placebo-controlled trial with pregabalin. Pain. 2008;136(3):419-431. [PMID: 18400400]

Epstein SA, Kay G, Clauw D, et al. Psychiatric disorders in patients with fibromyalgia. A multicenter investigation. Psychosomatics. 1999; 40(1):57-63. [PMID: 9989122]

Goldenberg DL. Fibromyalgia, chronic fatigue syndrome, and myofascial pain syndrome. Curr Opin Rheumatol. 1993;5(2):199-208. [PMID: 8452771]

Pregabalin (Lyrica) for fibromyalgia. Med Lett Drugs Ther. 2007; 49 (1270):77-78. [PMID: 17878888]

The Seronegative Spondyloarthropathies

The seronegative spondyloarthropathies are a heterogeneous group of disorders that consist of ankylosing spondylitis, reactive arthritis (formerly known as Reiter syndrome), enteropathic arthritis, and psoriatic arthritis. Manifestations vary widely among these conditions, but common features include a genetic predisposition, the potential for an infectious trigger, the presence of enthesitis (inflammation at the attachment site of tendon to bone), and extra-articular involvement. The results of serologic studies, including rheumatoid factor assays, are characteristically negative in affected patients.

Undifferentiated spondyloarthropathy refers to the clinical features of a spondyloarthropathy in patients who do not meet the criteria for an individual disease process.

Pathophysiology

Various cytokines mediate the local inflammatory and destructive processes affecting the synovium, entheses, and bone. The significant efficacy of tumor necrosis factor (TNF) α inhibitors in the treatment of the spondyloarthropathies suggests that TNF is a key mediator in this inflammatory process. T-cell activation is characteristic of the pathogenesis of the spondyloarthropathies, particularly psoriatic arthritis.

Genetic Predisposition

The class I histocompatibility antigen HLA-B27 is the strongest genetic risk factor for the spondyloarthropathies. HLA-B27 is a strong risk factor for ankylosing spondylitis and reactive arthritis but is less associated with enteropathic and psoriatic arthritis. Less than 5% of HLA-B27–positive persons develop ankylosing spondylitis, whereas more than 50% of first-degree relatives of affected patients develop this condition. Compared with patients with other patterns of joint involvement, patients with psoriatic and enteropathic arthritis who have sacroiliitis and spondylitis have a higher rate of HLA-B27 positivity.

Testing for HLA-B27 positivity generally is not helpful diagnostically, because most HLA-B27–positive persons do not develop disease. In addition, not all patients with this disease have this allele.

Environmental Triggers

Infectious organisms can trigger the onset of reactive arthritis in genetically predisposed patients. Nongonococcal genitourinary tract infections (primarily *Chlamydia*) and infectious diarrhea (which may occur in large outbreaks, such as among military troops) caused by organisms including *Shigella*, *Salmonella*, *Yersinia*, and *Campylobacter* can be associated with reactive arthritis. Antibiotic treatment does not alter the course of arthritis in patients with nongonococcal disease but does in patients with gonococcal infections.

Infectious triggers have been suspected in all of the spondyloarthropathies. These triggers include the potential immunostimulatory properties of gastrointestinal flora in enteropathic arthritis and the bacteria harbored in psoriatic skin plaques.

Patients with HIV infection have an increased incidence of reactive arthritis, psoriasis, and psoriatic arthritis. These conditions may have an explosive onset and a more severe disease course in patients with HIV infection compared with HIV-negative patients. However, the causative role of HIV infection in this setting is unknown. Testing for HIV infection is indicated for patients newly diagnosed with severe psoriatic or reactive arthritis.

KEY POINTS

- *Chlamydia* infection and infectious diarrhea can be associated with reactive arthritis.
- Infectious organisms can trigger the onset of reactive arthritis in genetically predisposed patients.
- Testing for HIV infection is indicated for patients newly diagnosed with severe psoriatic or reactive arthritis.

Diagnosis and Evaluation

The cardinal feature of the spondyloarthropathies is enthesitis with subsequent reactive new bone and spur formation.

Spinal manifestations of the spondyloarthropathies include sacroiliitis and spondylitis, which most typically cause initial pain in the gluteal region that persists for more than 3 months and may progress with time to involve the rest of the spine. Unlike mechanical back pain, pain and stiffness associated with the spondyloarthropathies are characteristically worse in the morning and are alleviated with exercise.

In the spondyloarthropathies, progressive limitation in spinal mobility occurs through the years and ultimately results in spinal fusion, often in a forward-flexed position, with decreased chest expansion (**Figure 14**). Before sacroiliac joint fusion develops, these joints may be tender to palpation. Lateral compression of the pelvis with the patient in a lateral decubitus position also may elicit discomfort. The Schober test helps to monitor loss of lumbar flexion. Patients with a spondyloarthropathy also may have a loss of cervical spine mobility.

Initial radiographic irregularities along the margins of the sacroiliac joints lead to eventual ankylosis and fusion, and radiography reflects these progressive changes (**Figure 15**). Inflammation of the ligamentous attachments erodes the corners of the vertebral bodies, which produces a squared-off appearance. Over time, ossification of these ligaments leads to the development of a rigid "bamboo spine," named because the shape of the vertebrae resemble bamboo on radiography.

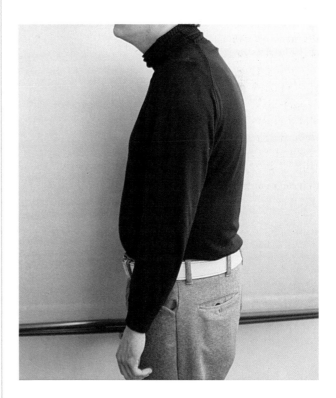

FIGURE 14.
Spinal deformity in ankylosing spondylitis.
This patient has forward flexion of the upper spine resulting in the characteristic stooped posture associated with ankylosing spondylitis.

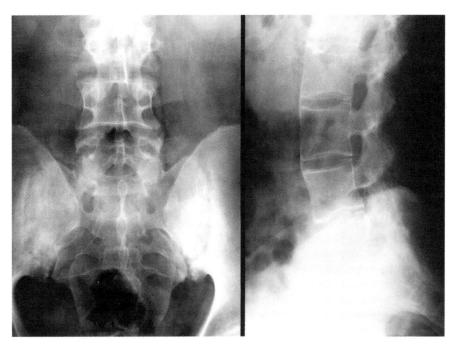

FIGURE 15.
Sacroiliitis and sacroiliac joint fusion.

MRI is the most sensitive method for detecting early inflammatory changes in the sacroiliac joints and spine.

Enthesitis and bone spurs can occur at any site of tendon attachment. Common sites include the plantar fascia and the Achilles tendon, and involvement at these sites often causes episodes of inflammation and heel pain.

The pattern and degree of peripheral joint involvement among the spondyloarthropathies vary widely (**Table 6**). The most common pattern is a large-joint asymmetrical oligoarthritis that predominantly involves the lower extremities. However, psoriatic arthritis may potentially manifest with a predominantly peripheral arthritis that involves the small joints. Histologically, the synovitis seen in patients with a spondyloarthropathy resembles that of rheumatoid arthritis.

Joint ankylosis also may occur in the seronegative spondyloarthropathies. Enthesitis is characterized by inflammation of the tendon insertion sites and contributes to dactylitis, which can cause the characteristic sausage-shaped digits associated with psoriatic and reactive arthritis (**Figure 16**).

Extra-articular manifestations of the seronegative spondyloarthropathies include inflammatory disease of the skin, eyes, lungs, gastrointestinal and genitourinary tracts, and vascular system (**Table 7**). The most overt skin manifestation is psoriasis, but other mucocutaneous involvement includes oral ulcerations, keratoderma blennorrhagicum, and circinate balanitis (plaques or ulcers involving the glans and shaft of the penis) most typical in reactive arthritis, and erythema nodosum and pyoderma gangrenosum most typical in enteropathic arthritis. Inflammatory eye disease, which can be recurrent, includes conjunctivitis, uveitis, and keratitis.

Genitourinary manifestations of the seronegative spondyloarthropathies include noninfectious urethritis, prostatitis, cervicitis, and salpingitis. Inflammatory bowel disease

TABLE 6 Pattern of Peripheral Synovitis in the Spondyloarthropathies	
Condition	**Pattern of Involvement**
Ankylosing spondylitis/reactive arthritis	Asymmetric large-joint oligoarthritis primarily involving the lower extremities
Enteropathic arthritis	Asymmetric large-joint oligoarthritis primarily involving the lower extremities Peripheral joint flares parallel the course of the bowel disease
Psoriatic arthritis	Oligoarticular disease: Asymmetric large-joint oligoarthritis primarily involving the lower extremities Polyarticular disease: Symmetric polyarthritis involving both the large and small joints resembling rheumatoid arthritis DIP joint disease: Associated with nail involvement Arthritis mutilans: Severely destructive arthritis involving the hands with shortening of the digits
DIP = distal interphalangeal.	

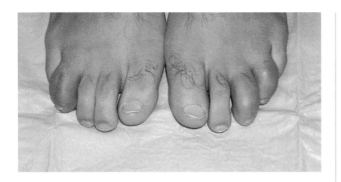

FIGURE 16.
Sausage toes.
This figure shows "sausage-shaped" digits caused by dactylitis in a patient with reactive arthritis.

Reprinted with permission from Moore G. Atlas of the Musculoskeletal Examination. Philadelphia: American College of Physicians; 2003.

is the most obvious form of gastrointestinal involvement. Pulmonary fibrosis, when present, characteristically involves the lung apices rather than the basilar regions typically affected in other systemic rheumatic diseases. Aortitis with aortic root dilatation, conduction abnormalities, and myocardial dysfunction may occur. Both pulmonary and cardiac complications are rare and more characteristic of ankylosing spondylitis than of other types of seronegative spondyloarthropathies.

> **KEY POINTS**
>
> - In patients less than 40 years of age, persistent low back pain accompanied by morning stiffness that improves with activity should raise suspicion for a spondyloarthropathy, particularly ankylosing spondylitis.
> - MRI is the most sensitive method for detecting early inflammatory changes in the sacroiliac joints and spine in patients with a seronegative spondyloarthropathy.
> - Extra-articular manifestations of the seronegative spondyloarthropathies include inflammatory disease of the skin, eyes, lungs, gastrointestinal and genitourinary tracts, and vascular system.

Classification

Ankylosing Spondylitis

Ankylosing spondylitis is the prototypical spondyloarthropathy. The prevalence of this condition in the United States is less than 1%. Ankylosing spondylitis affects men more often than women (ratio of 3:1 to 5:1), and women typically have a milder form of disease and may go undiagnosed.

The onset of ankylosing spondylitis is marked by persistent low back pain and occurs in the teenage years or 20s. The inflammatory spinal disease typically progresses cephalad and results in a characteristic stooped posture and loss of spinal mobility seen in late disease (see Figure 14). However, disease may be limited to the pelvis and sacroiliac joints (**Table 8**). Fractures, including those caused by minor trauma to the rigid spine, and spinal cord and nerve root impingement (such as the cauda equina syndrome) may complicate spinal involvement. Arthritis of the hips, which is rare in patients with rheumatoid arthritis, is common in this disease and further worsens function.

Early diagnosis of ankylosing spondylitis has become particularly important since the advent of therapeutic agents that potentially can alter the debilitating course of this disease. However, diagnosis of this condition often is delayed by many years. Persistent back pain or extra-articular manifestations (particularly eye involvement) typically prompt affected patients to seek medical attention.

Early in the disease course, plain radiographs of the pelvis and spine are normal. At this stage, patients with suspected disease should undergo MRI of the sacroiliac joints to detect early inflammatory and erosive changes.

Reactive Arthritis

Reactive arthritis is an inflammatory arthritis that presents within 2 months of an episode of bacterial gastroenteritis or nongonococcal urethritis or cervicitis in a genetically susceptible patient. Cultures for the infectious trigger in this setting are usually negative by the time arthritis develops. Serologic testing for a previous infectious exposure is rarely helpful but if positive would more strongly suggest reactive arthritis, which is generally less severe than the other spondyloarthropathies.

TABLE 7 Clinical Features in the Seronegative Spondyloarthropathies								
Condition	Spine	Joints (Arthritis)	Skin	Eyes	GI	GU	Pulmonary	Vascular
Ankylosing spondylitis	+++	++		++	+	+	+	+
Reactive arthritis	++	+++	++	+++		+++		+
Enteropathic arthritis	++	++	+	+	+++	+		+
Psoriatic arthritis	++	+++	+++	+				

GI = gastrointestinal; GU = genitourinary; + = rare; ++ = more frequent; +++ = characteristic of the disease.

TABLE 8 Musculoskeletal Examination Findings Consistent with Ankylosing Spondylitis

Loss of spinal mobility

Decreased lumbar spinal mobility in all directions

Positive modified Schober test: With the patient standing, put two marks on the skin over the lumbar area: one at the midline at the level of the sacral dimples, the other 10 cm higher. Ask the patient to bend forward as far as possible with the knees fully extended. An increase in distance between the marks ≤4 cm indicates diminished flexibility of the lumbar spine.

Decreased cervical spinal mobility in all directions

Fixed forward flexion with an increased wall-to-occiput distance

Sacroiliac joint tenderness

Decreased chest expansion

A decrease from the usual ≥5-cm chest expansion seen in normal persons on maximal inspiration after a full expiration

Enthesitis

Tenderness over the iliac crest, chest wall, Achilles and plantar insertion of the heel, spinous processes, and other bony prominences

Peripheral inflammatory joint disease

Oligoarticular inflammatory arthritis typically involving the hips, knees, and ankles with effusion, decreased range of motion, and periarticular inflammation

Modified with permission from Physician's Information and Education Resource (PIER). Philadelphia: American College of Physicians. Copyright 2009 American College of Physicians.

Diagnosis of reactive arthritis is more difficult when there is no history of a preceding infection, as occurs in asymptomatic sexually transmitted diseases.

The clinical features of reactive arthritis most likely result from bacterial antigens that trigger an immunologic reaction because of molecular mimicry between these antigens and self-proteins. Patients with rheumatoid arthritis also may have bacterial antigens, but routine synovial fluid cultures in these patients are negative.

The incidence of reactive arthritis varies according to the rate of HLA-B27 positivity in the population and the infectious organism but is approximately 1% to 2% after *Chlamydia* infection and 5% to 20% after gastroenteritis. The incidence is at least five times higher in men than women after a sexually transmitted disease but is equal in men and women after bacterial diarrhea.

Reactive arthritis has an acute onset and may present with an asymmetric oligoarthritis predominantly of the lower extremities, inflammatory back pain, or a combination of these symptoms. Symptoms of enthesitis, such as heel pain, also may be present. Extra-articular manifestations, particularly eye, genitourinary, and mucocutaneous lesions, are common and may precede the development of the arthritis. Only one third of affected patients have the classic triad of arthritis, urethritis, and conjunctivitis associated with reactive arthritis.

Acute episodes of reactive arthritis typically resolve within 4 to 6 months. In some patients, these episodes recur or evolve into a chronic destructive arthritis or progressive spinal disease. Approximately 10% to 50% of affected patients have recurrent or progressive disease.

Enteropathic Arthritis

Inflammatory arthritis can complicate Crohn disease and ulcerative colitis. Up to 20% of patients with inflammatory bowel disease develop a peripheral arthritis, which manifests as either a polyarticular arthritis resembling rheumatoid arthritis or an asymmetric oligoarthritis predominantly of the lower extremities resembling reactive arthritis. The peripheral arthritis may precede the development of gastrointestinal symptoms. The course of arthritis often fluctuates with the activity of the underlying bowel involvement. However, in a few patients, the arthritis dominates the clinical presentation and has a progressive, destructive course. Rarely, the peripheral arthritis precedes the development of gastrointestinal symptoms.

Another 10% to 20% of patients with inflammatory bowel disease have spinal involvement ranging from asymptomatic sacroiliac disease found incidentally on radiographs to a clinical presentation identical to that of ankylosing spondylitis with progressive spinal fusion. Unlike the peripheral arthritis, the progression of spinal involvement in enteropathic arthritis is independent of the course of the bowel disease.

Additional extra-articular manifestations of enteropathic arthritis include inflammatory eye disease and cutaneous lesions (particularly erythema nodosum) and occur in up to 20% of patients with this condition. The course of these extra-articular manifestations typically parallels peripheral joint and bowel inflammation.

Psoriatic Arthritis

Psoriasis affects an estimated 1% to 2% of the general population, and a total of 20% to 40% of affected patients develop arthritis. The highest incidence of psoriatic arthritis occurs in patients with extensive skin involvement. However, this condition can develop even in patients with subtle skin disease, such as that limited to the nails.

The distribution of joint involvement in psoriasis varies widely among patients. Psoriatic arthritis is classified with the spondyloarthropathies because of the potential axial involvement, the contribution of enthesitis in its pathogenesis, and its increased association with HLA-B27.

Psoriatic arthritis most commonly presents with a symmetric polyarticular arthritis that resembles rheumatoid arthritis in distribution except that psoriatic arthritis also is associated with increased involvement of the distal interphalangeal (DIP) joints (**Figure 17**). In a small subset of patients with psoriatic arthritis, the arthritis is limited almost exclusively to the DIP joints and is often associated with psoriatic fingernail changes with pitting and onycholysis (**Figure 18** and **Figure 19**). Rarely, an extensive osteolysis of the digits occurs and results in arthritis mutilans, a condition that causes severe hand deformities.

Other patients with psoriatic arthritis present with an asymmetric, predominantly oligoarthritis similar to that found in the other spondyloarthropathies. Up to 40% of patients with psoriatic arthritis have evidence of either sacroiliitis (which may be asymmetric) or spondylitis, most often accompanying a peripheral arthritis. In a small percentage of these patients, involvement is limited to the spine.

A significant overlap exists among these patterns of involvement, which may change throughout the disease course in patients with psoriatic arthritis. Typically, psoriasis predates the arthritis by years, whereas arthritis develops before skin disease in 15% of patients.

A diagnosis of psoriatic arthritis should be suspected in patients with dactylitis, marked DIP joint involvement, asymmetric joint involvement, symptoms of enthesitis, or joint ankylosis. In these patients, a thorough skin examination should be performed to evaluate for nail changes or undetected small patches of psoriasis in areas such as the scalp, periumbilical area, and intertriginous skin folds to verify the diagnosis.

KEY POINTS

- The onset of ankylosing spondylitis is marked by persistent low back pain and occurs in the teenage years or 20s.
- MRI is the most sensitive method of detecting early inflammatory and erosive changes of the sacroiliac joints in patients with ankylosing spondylitis.
- Reactive arthritis usually develops within 2 months of bacterial gastroenteritis or nongonococcal urethritis or cervicitis.
- An inflammatory peripheral arthritis or spinal disease may accompany inflammatory bowel disease.
- The presence of dactylitis, marked distal interphalangeal joint involvement, asymmetric joint involvement, symptoms of enthesitis, or joint ankylosis is suggestive of psoriatic arthritis.

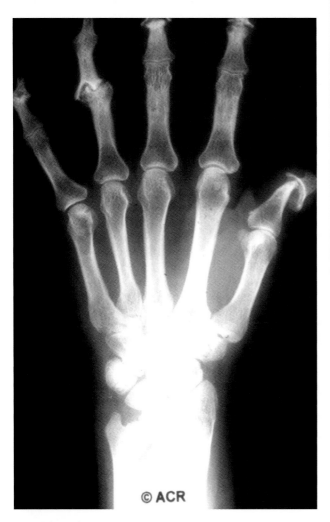

FIGURE 17.
Psoriatic arthritis involving the hand.
This radiograph shows "pencil-in-cup" deformities of the distal interphalangeal joints of the thumb and middle fingers. These deformities are caused by erosive changes associated with psoriatic arthritis.

Reprinted with permission from Clinical Slide Collection on the Rheumatic Diseases. Atlanta: American College of Rheumatology. Copyright 1972-2004 American College of Rheumatology.

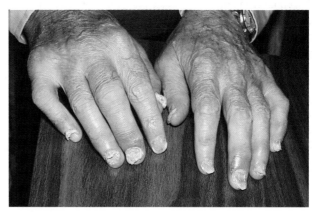

FIGURE 18.
Psoriatic arthritis of the hands with phalangeal joint and nail involvement.
This patient with psoriatic arthritis has onycholysis and onychodystrophy.

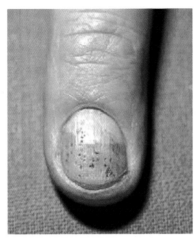

FIGURE 19.
Nail pitting in a patient with psoriasis.

Reprinted with permission from Physician's Information and Education Resource (PIER). Philadelphia: American College of Physicians. Copyright 2009 American College of Physicians.

Treatment

Many of the treatments used in rheumatoid arthritis also suppress inflammation in the joints and extra-articular structures and provide long-term prevention of joint damage and functional loss in the spondyloarthropathies. These treatments include the aggressive use of immunosuppressive, disease-modifying agents such as methotrexate or sulfasalazine. The use of tumor necrosis factor α inhibitors and disease-modifying agents should be guided by a rheumatologist.

For years, NSAIDs were the mainstay of therapy for the spondyloarthropathies, particularly before the advent of effective disease-modifying therapy for spinal involvement. These agents continue to be used as chronic therapy for joint inflammation and pain. However, NSAIDs do not alter the disease course or prevent disease progression. NSAIDs also may exacerbate inflammatory bowel disease and should be used with caution in patients with enteropathic arthritis.

Low-dose oral corticosteroids, preferably in short courses, may be used for peripheral arthritis but are not clinically useful in inflammatory spinal disease and worsen the risk for osteoporosis. In psoriatic arthritis, dramatic flares in skin disease have been reported with corticosteroid taper; therefore, corticosteroids ideally should be avoided in this patient population. Intra-articular injections may benefit patients with predominant involvement in one to two joints, but arthrocentesis through a psoriatic plaque is contraindicated secondary to the risk of joint infection.

Ankylosing Spondylitis

Tumor necrosis factor (TNF) α inhibitors are currently first-line therapy in ankylosing spondylitis (3). These agents are the first therapy to significantly suppress inflammation in the axial skeleton and therefore improve back pain and potentially halt progressive ankylosis with the subsequent loss of mobility and function (**Figure 20**). TNF-α inhibitors also have shown efficacy in peripheral arthritis and extra-articular disease. Traditional immunosuppressants, such as methotrexate or sulfasalazine, benefit patients with peripheral joint and extra-articular disease but are not effective for spinal involvement. Exercise (including physical therapy) and NSAIDs, once the primary therapeutic options in ankylosing spondylitis, are still indicated for symptomatic and functional improvement.

Reactive Arthritis

Despite the association between reactive arthritis and bacterial infection, antibiotics are indicated primarily for acute infection and generally are of dubious benefit for reactive joint disease. In some studies, a 3-month trial of minocycline or a similar agent was shown to improve the clinical course of reactive arthritis, particularly when this condition was associated with *Chlamydia* infection.

NSAIDs are first-line therapy for symptom management in reactive arthritis. Corticosteroid therapy (topical, intralesional, or intra-articular) is useful for skin lesions, eye involvement, and acute arthritis or enthesitis in this setting. Disease-modifying agents such as sulfasalazine or methotrexate can be beneficial in recurrent or chronic inflammatory disease. TNF-α inhibitors should be considered only if other interventions are ineffective or if patients have significant axial skeleton involvement or severe disease.

Enteropathic Arthritis

The immunosuppressive therapies that benefit intestinal disease in enteropathic arthritis also have efficacy in the treatment of the associated peripheral joint and extra-articular manifestations. These therapies include corticosteroids, sulfasalazine, azathioprine, methotrexate, and the TNF-α inhibitors infliximab and adalimumab. Etanercept has not shown efficacy in treating bowel symptoms in this setting.

The activity of bowel involvement typically determines therapeutic decisions. In patients with predominantly axial skeleton disease, TNF-α inhibition should be considered even if the bowel disease is quiescent.

Psoriatic Arthritis

The therapeutic options in psoriatic arthritis are similar to those in rheumatoid arthritis. Generally, immunosuppressive agents that have efficacy in psoriasis also benefit patients with joint disease. Methotrexate is beneficial for both skin and joint disease and has dominated therapy for many years. TNF-α inhibitors increasingly have been shown to be effective in psoriatic arthritis and are the preferred intervention for patients with predominant spondylitis. Leflunomide, sulfasalazine, and cyclosporine also have been used to treat psoriatic arthritis. Rarely, hydroxychloroquine has been associated with flares in skin disease.

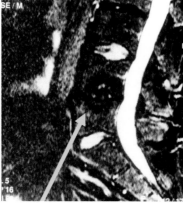

FIGURE 20.
MRI of the lumbar spine in a patient with ankylosing spondylitis pre– and post–tumor necrosis factor α inhibitor therapy.
The left panel shows edema immediately adjacent to the L4 to L5 endplates *(asterisks)* and immediately subjacent to the superior endplate of L5 *(arrow)*. The right panel shows the lumbar spine after tumor necrosis factor α inhibitor therapy was initiated and reveals resolution of active enthesitis by fatty marrow replacement *(arrow)*.

KEY POINTS

- Aggressive use of immunosuppressive, disease-modifying agents suppresses inflammation in the joints and extra-articular structures and prevents joint damage and functional loss in the spondyloarthropathies.

- NSAIDs improve symptoms in the spondyloarthropathies but do not affect the disease course.

- Tumor necrosis factor α inhibitors have proven efficacy in axial skeleton disease.

- Antibiotics are not indicated to treat joint disease in reactive arthritis.

Bibliography

Braun J, Sieper J. Ankylosing spondylitis. Lancet. 2007;369(9570): 1379-1390. [PMID: 17448825]

Mansour M, Cheema GS, Naguwa SM, et al. Ankylosing spondylitis: a contemporary perspective on diagnosis and treatment. Semin Arthritis Rheum. 2007;36(4):210-223. [PMID: 17011612]

Petersel DL, Sigal LH. Reactive arthritis. Infect Dis Clin North Am. 2005; 19:863-83. [PMID: 16297737]

Punzi L, Podswiadek M, Sfriso P, Oliviero F, Fiocco U, Todesco S. Pathogenetic and clinical rationale for the TNF-blocking therapy in psoriatic arthritis. Autoimmun Rev. 2007;6(8): 524-528. [PMID: 17854743]

Systemic Lupus Erythematosus

Pathophysiology

Systemic lupus erythematosus (SLE) is characterized pathophysiologically by the presence of autoantibodies, hypocomplementemia, and increased production of interferon-α and interferon-β that result in humoral and cellular inflammation in the skin, joints, kidneys, blood cells, nervous system, and serosal surfaces. Patients with SLE have abnormalities in immune tolerance to self-antigens and in the ability to clear cellular debris containing these antigens. Disease flares can occur when exposure to ultraviolet light causes skin cells to become apoptotic or when a viral infection causes cell necrosis.

Autoantibodies in patients with SLE can take the form of immune complexes that deposit in tissues or bond to target cells. Once deposited, these autoantibodies can cause damage by fixing complement on the surface of a cell, which causes cell lysis; binding to Fc receptors on circulating cells, which leads to their clearance in the liver or spleen; or binding to Fc receptors on macrophages, which initiates cell-mediated inflammation.

KEY POINT

- Systemic lupus erythematosus is characterized by the presence of autoantibodies, hypocomplementemia, increased production of interferon-α and interferon-β, and evidence of organ dysfunction.

Epidemiology and Risk Factors

SLE has a 9:1 female predominance and a peak age of onset between 15 and 45 years; it is more common and more severe in nonwhite patients. Estrogen may be associated with SLE. Recent studies suggest that estrogen-progestin oral contraceptives do not trigger disease flares in women with mild, stable SLE. However, these agents should be used with caution in patients with SLE and are contraindicated in patients with severe or unstable disease, antiphospholipid antibody positivity, or a history of thrombosis.

KEY POINT

- Estrogen-progestin oral contraceptives are contraindicated in patients with severe or unstable systemic lupus erythematosus, antiphospholipid antibody positivity, or a history of thrombosis.

Clinical Manifestations

Cutaneous Involvement

Approximately 80% of patients with SLE have cutaneous involvement at some point in their disease course. Immune complex deposition at the dermal-epidermal junction occurs in all patients with lupus-related rashes. Most rashes associated with SLE occur in areas exposed to the sun.

Butterfly Rash

Butterfly rash, or malar rash, occurs in approximately 25% of patients with SLE and is associated with acute disease. This rash is erythematous and sharply defined and can be flat or raised. It is localized to the cheeks and the bridge of the nose and spares the nasolabial folds; it also may involve the forehead, chin, neck, and chest (**Figure 21**). The rash resembles rosacea except that rosacea does affect the nasolabial folds and is further characterized by telangiectasias, pustules, and papules without comedones.

Subacute Cutaneous Lupus Erythematosus
Subacute cutaneous lupus erythematosus, which occurs in approximately 5% of patients with SLE, is associated with anti-Ro/SSA and anti-La/SSB antibodies. The papulosquamous form of subacute cutaneous lupus erythematosus resembles psoriasis, whereas the annular variant is characterized by scaly erythematous circular plaques with central hypopigmentation (**Figure 22**). These rashes most commonly involve the neck, trunk, and extensor surfaces of the arms. They can be chronic and recurrent but do not scar.

Discoid Lupus
Chronic discoid lupus is a form of chronic cutaneous lupus and occurs in approximately 5% of patients with SLE. This condition can exist as a primary cutaneous disease as well as a manifestation of SLE; only 10% of patients with primary discoid lupus develop SLE.

Discoid lupus manifests as erythematous indurated scaly plaques that typically develop above the neck and often involve the ear canals. Key features include peripheral expansion and central regression with plugging of the hair follicles, hyperpigmentation, and atrophic scarring. Facial scarring can be severe, and scarring on the scalp can cause irreversible patchy alopecia.

Alopecia
Alopecia occurs in up to 70% of patients with SLE, and most cases of alopecia are not associated with discoid lupus. The nonscarring form of alopecia occurs in patients with active SLE and may be associated with skin changes consistent with seborrhea, such as erythema and scaling of the scalp. In patients with SLE, alopecia is reversible once the systemic disease is controlled.

Mucosal Ulcerations
Approximately 10% of patients with SLE develop mucosal ulcerations that characteristically are localized to the tongue and hard palate but may affect the nose and entire mouth. They typically are painless but may cause pain in some patients. Aphthous ulcers and oral ulceration due to herpes simplex virus and Behçet disease are typically painful.

Raynaud Phenomenon
Raynaud phenomenon develops in 30% of patients with SLE. Arterial vasospasm causes this condition, which manifests as a triphasic color change of the fingers. The digits in affected

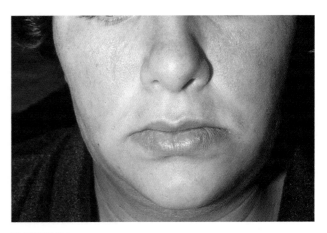

FIGURE 21.
Butterfly rash.

patients evolve from white to blue with ischemia and then become red with reperfusion.

Joint Involvement
More than 90% of patients with SLE develop joint involvement that can manifest as arthralgia or true arthritis. Joint pain is often migratory and can be oligoarticular or polyarticular, or asymmetric or symmetric. Pain typically involves the large and small joints; the wrists and metacarpophalangeal and proximal interphalangeal joints in particular are most commonly affected.

Tenderness, swelling, and warmth of the joints also can occur in patients with SLE and are often mild, and arthritis in this setting is typically nonerosive. Tendon inflammation can cause joint laxity that leads to reducible deformities that mimic rheumatoid arthritis, such as Jaccoud arthropathy. Patients with SLE also may develop fibromyalgia.

Renal Involvement
Up to 50% of patients with SLE have renal involvement. Acute forms of lupus nephritis can be asymptomatic or manifest as severe systemic illness. Renal biopsy is usually needed to diagnose lupus nephritis.

Proliferative Lupus Nephritis
Signs of proliferative lupus nephritis may include new-onset hypertension or edema. Laboratory studies in affected patients typically reveal high titers of anti–double-stranded DNA antibodies and hypocomplementemia, proteinuria, hematuria, and erythrocyte and granular casts in the urine.

Focal segmental proliferative lupus nephritis and diffuse proliferative lupus nephritis differ only in their degree of glomerular involvement. Renal biopsy specimens in patients with these conditions characteristically reveal glomerular hypercellularity, crescent formation, and immune complex deposition in the subendothelial space and may show interstitial inflammation. The presence of

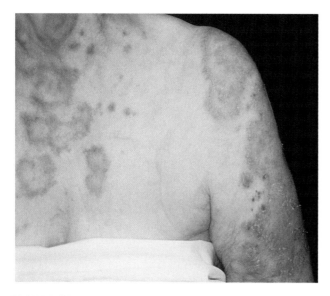

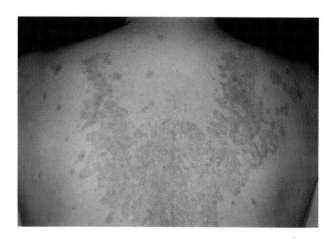

FIGURE 22.
Rash in subacute cutaneous lupus erythematosus.
The left panel shows a patient with an annular polycyclic rash characterized by scaly erythematous circular plaques with central hypopigmentation. The right panel shows a patient with a papulosquamous rash, which manifests as a silvery, erythematous scaly rash that appears in a symmetric pattern.

hypercellularity/inflammation on biopsy specimen can help to determine the degree of disease activity, and the presence of necrosis/scarring can help to determine chronicity.

Patients with early disease may not have renal insufficiency, and early treatment does not significantly affect the findings on renal biopsy. However, progression to renal failure can be rapid; therefore, patients with a strong clinical suspicion for lupus nephritis should begin high-dose corticosteroid therapy before renal biopsy is performed.

Membranous Lupus Nephritis

Patients with membranous lupus nephritis typically present with the nephrotic syndrome and usually do not have features of nephritis, such as hypertension, an active urine sediment, or renal insufficiency. High titers of anti–double-stranded DNA antibodies and hypocomplementemia also may be absent.

Membranous lupus nephritis is characterized pathologically by thickening of the basement membrane, immune complex deposition in the subepithelial area, and an absence of hypercellularity in the glomerulus. Marked proteinuria also may be present.

Membranous lupus nephritis is indolent but can lead to renal insufficiency and secondary hypertension. Treatment is recommended when this condition presents acutely, but acute disease can be refractory.

Membranoproliferative Glomerulonephritis

Some patients have both proliferative and membranous lupus nephritis; therapy is targeted towards the more aggressive proliferative disease.

Neurologic Involvement

Approximately 15% of patients with SLE have involvement of the central, peripheral, and autonomic nervous systems as a result of vasculitis of small, medium, or large vessels. Antineuronal antibodies may be present, but elevated titers of anti–double-stranded DNA antibodies and hypocomplementemia often are absent. Manifestations include peripheral neuropathy, mononeuritis multiplex, cranial neuritis, transverse myelitis, aseptic meningitis, stroke, seizure, encephalitis, and psychosis. An adverse effect of NSAIDs in patients with SLE also may be aseptic meningitis. Seizure in patients with SLE often is a manifestation of azotemia, systemic infection, meningitis, or stroke rather than of SLE itself. Subtle chronic cognitive deficits may occur in patients with SLE but can be difficult to distinguish from medication side effects and depression.

Cardiopulmonary Involvement

Up to 50% of patients with SLE have pleurisy or pericarditis. Libman-Sacks (verrucous) endocarditis, myocarditis, interstitial lung disease, pneumonitis, and pulmonary hemorrhage also may occur.

Pleurisy in patients with SLE generally is not life threatening and responds well to treatment. Pericarditis also responds to treatment, although a pericardial window to drain excess fluid rarely may be indicated to manage tamponade. The differential diagnosis of chest pain in patients with SLE includes costochondritis.

Acute lupus pneumonitis is a rare but serious condition that generally manifests as fever, cough, pleurisy, and shortness of breath accompanied by infiltrates on chest radiography.

Differentiating between acute lupus pneumonitis and infection is critical; occasionally, lung biopsy is needed for diagnosis. Alveolar hemorrhage as a manifestation of pulmonary vasculitis is suggested by alveolar infiltrates on chest radiography and an increased D_{LCO}, although some patients with dyspnea may not be able to undergo pulmonary function testing. Alveolar hemorrhage is a medical emergency and requires prompt immunosuppressive therapy.

Hematologic Involvement

Depression of the hematopoietic system commonly occurs in patients with SLE but also may develop as a side effect of the immunosuppressive therapy used to treat SLE. Leukopenia (as a result of lymphopenia, not neutropenia) is a good marker of disease activity, although the leukopenia tends to be mild and does not itself typically predispose patients to infection. SLE-related leukopenia must be distinguished from immunosuppressive drug–related leukopenia, which may develop after institution of a new agent or a change in dosage. Leukopenia also may develop when the dosage of corticosteroids, which cause leukocytosis, is tapered. Dosage adjustment is indicated for patients with medication-related leukopenia.

Approximately 5% of patients with SLE develop autoimmune (Coombs-positive) hemolytic anemia, sometimes accompanied by idiopathic thrombocytopenic purpura. Approximately 10% to 25% of patients with SLE develop mild thrombocytopenia (platelet count of 100,000/μL to 150,000/μL [100×10^9/L to 150×10^9/L]). However, a platelet count less than 20,000/μL (20×10^9/L) may develop in some patients and warrants aggressive treatment that may include splenectomy. Thrombocytopenia also may occur as a manifestation of thrombotic thrombocytopenic purpura, which is more prevalent in patients with SLE than in the general population.

The Antiphospholipid Syndrome

Approximately 40% of patients with SLE have antiphospholipid antibodies. However, not all of these patients have manifestations of the antiphospholipid syndrome, which include venous and arterial thrombosis and recurrent fetal loss. This syndrome also may be associated with thrombocytopenia, hemolytic anemia, livedo reticularis, and cardiac valvular disease.

Both SLE and the antiphospholipid syndrome can cause neurologic and renal manifestations. Therefore, determining whether the presenting condition in patients with SLE who have antiphospholipid antibodies is inflammatory or thrombotic/embolic is critical in order to initiate appropriate treatment. The presence of inflammatory markers such as an elevated erythrocyte sedimentation rate, leukopenia, elevated titers of anti–double-stranded DNA antibodies, and hypocomplementemia suggest an inflammatory process, whereas tissue infarcts in the absence of elevated inflammatory markers and thrombotic vasculopathy on tissue biopsy specimen suggest a thrombotic process. Anticoagulation is indicated in patients with thrombotic manifestations of the antiphospholipid syndrome.

KEY POINTS

- Lupus nephritis may manifest as new-onset hypertension or edema associated with high titers of anti–double-stranded DNA antibodies, hypocomplementemia, proteinuria, hematuria, and erythrocyte and granular casts in the urine.

- Patients with a strong clinical suspicion for lupus nephritis should begin high-dose corticosteroid therapy before renal biopsy is performed.

- Neurologic manifestations of systemic lupus erythematosus include peripheral neuropathy, mononeuritis multiplex, cranial neuritis, transverse myelitis, aseptic meningitis, stroke, seizure, encephalitis, and psychosis.

- Cardiopulmonary manifestations of systemic lupus erythematosus include pleurisy, pericarditis, endocarditis, myocarditis, interstitial lung disease, pneumonitis, and pulmonary hemorrhage.

- The antiphospholipid syndrome manifests as venous and arterial thrombosis and recurrent fetal loss and may be associated with thrombocytopenia, hemolytic anemia, livedo reticularis, and cardiac valvular disease.

Diagnosis and Evaluation

Characteristic clinical features and laboratory findings are used to diagnose SLE (**Table 9**). Autoantibody positivity in SLE has both diagnostic and prognostic relevance (**Table 10**). More than 99% of untreated patients with SLE have high titers of antinuclear antibodies. However, antinuclear antibodies are nonspecific and should be measured only in patients whose clinical presentation suggests at least a moderate pretest probability of SLE. Monitoring ANA titers is not warranted because these values do not reflect disease activity.

Further testing indicated in patients with symptoms suggestive of SLE include a complete blood count, erythrocyte sedimentation rate measurement, and urinalysis. Patients with a high pretest probability of SLE and antinuclear antibodies (usually a titer ≥1:160) should undergo confirmatory testing, such as measurement of C3, C4, and CH50 and more specific autoantibody testing. Antibodies to double-stranded DNA are present in approximately 50% to 70% of patients with SLE, whereas anti-Smith, antiribonucleoprotein, anti-Ro/SSA, and anti-La/SSB antibodies are present in 10% to 60% of patients with SLE. These antibodies are rarely present in patients without connective tissue disease. Patients with a new diagnosis of SLE also should also undergo screening for anticardiolipin antibodies and the lupus anticoagulant.

TABLE 9 American College of Rheumatology Classification Criteria for Systemic Lupus Erythematosus[a, b]

Malar rash

Discoid rash

Photosensitivity

Oral ulcers

Arthritis

Serositis

Renal disorder

Neurologic disorder

Hematologic disorder

Immunologic disorder (anti-dsDNA, anti-Sm, or antiphospholipid antibodies)

Antinuclear antibodies

Anti-dsDNA antibody = anti–double-stranded DNA antibody; anti-SM antibody = anti-Smith antibody.

[a]At least four of these criteria must be present.

[b]These criteria may not be useful for diagnosing mild disease.

Differential Diagnosis

Undifferentiated Connective Tissue Disease

Undifferentiated connective tissue disease (UCTD) is characterized by the presence of antinuclear antibodies accompanied by only one or two criteria for SLE. Most patients with UCTD do not have progressive disease, although some affected patients may eventually develop SLE or another connective tissue disease, such as systemic sclerosis or myositis. Treatment of UCTD involves symptomatic management.

Drug-Induced Lupus

Many medications cause an SLE-like syndrome known as drug-induced lupus (**Table 11**). Drug-induced lupus affects older patients more often than does SLE and does not have a female predominance.

Drug-induced lupus typically manifests as fever, arthralgia, and serositis accompanied by antinuclear antibodies. Affected patients also may have mild pancytopenia; renal and neurologic manifestations are uncommon, and antibodies to anti–double-stranded DNA, anti-Smith, antiribonucleoprotein, or anti-Ro/SSA or anti-La/SSB antibodies are typically absent. Up to 95% of patients have antihistone antibodies, which also are present in more than 50% of patients with SLE.

The diagnosis of drug-induced lupus is established when compatible symptoms develop after institution of a drug and resolve after its withdrawal. Symptoms typically last for 4 to 6 weeks, whereas serologic abnormalities can persist for years. Some affected patients require a short course of NSAIDS or corticosteroids.

KEY POINTS

- Patients with symptoms suggestive of systemic lupus erythematosus should undergo an antinuclear antibody assay, complete blood count, erythrocyte sedimentation rate measurement, and urinalysis.

- Patients with a high pretest probability of systemic lupus erythematosus and the presence of antinuclear antibodies should undergo measurement of C3, C4, and CH50 and assays for antibodies to anti–double-stranded DNA, anti-Smith, antiribonucleoprotein, and anti-Ro/SSA, and anti-La/SSB.

- Patients with drug-induced lupus typically have antinuclear and antihistone antibodies but do not have renal or neurologic involvement or antibodies to anti–double-stranded DNA, anti-Smith, antiribonucleoprotein, or anti-Ro/SSA or anti-La/SSB.

- In patients with drug-induced lupus, symptoms resolve 4 to 6 weeks after withdrawal of the offending drug.

TABLE 10 Autoantibodies and Their Clinical Associations in Systemic Lupus Erythematosus

Antibody	Sensitivity[a] (%)	Clinical Association
Anti-dsDNA	50-70	Glomerulonephritis, more severe SLE
Anti-Sm	20-30	Glomerulonephritis, CNS disease
Anti-RNP	30-40	Raynaud phenomenon, myositis, MCTD
Anti-Ro/SSA	20-60	SCLE, Sjögren syndrome, neonatal lupus
Anti-La/SSB	10-15	SCLE, Sjögren syndrome, neonatal lupus
Antiphospholipid	30-50	Arterial and venous thrombosis, recurrent fetal loss, thrombocytopenia
Antiribosomal P protein	15	Psychosis, depression
Antihistone	70	Present in >95% of patients with drug-induced lupus

anti-dsDNA = anti–double-stranded DNA; SLE = systemic lupus erythematosus; anti-Sm = anti-Smith; CNS = central nervous system; anti-RNP = antiribonucleoprotein; MCTD = mixed connective tissue disease; SCLE = subacute cutaneous lupus erythematosus.

[a]The specificity of antibodies to anti-dsDNA, anti-Sm, anti-RNP, anti-Ro/SSA, and anti-La/SSB is more than 95%.

TABLE 11 Medications Associated with Drug-Induced Lupus

Definite Associations with Drug-Induced Lupus[a]

Hydralazine
Procainamide
Isoniazid
Methyldopa
Chlorpromazine
Quinidine
Minocycline

Possible Associations with Drug-Induced Lupus[b]

Anticonvulsants (carbamazepine, ethosuximide, phenytoin)
Antithyroid drugs (propylthiouracil, methimazole)
Statins
β-Blockers
Thiazides
Sulfasalazine
Zafirlukast
Ticlopidine

Biologic Agents[c]

Tumor necrosis factor α inhibitors (etanercept, infliximab, adalimumab)
Interferon alfa
Interleukin-2

SLE = systemic lupus erythematosus.

[a]Well-controlled studies have demonstrated the role of these agents in inducing SLE.

[b]Associations between these agents and SLE have been shown in case reports and other less rigorous studies. When listed, drug classes indicate that all members of the class have been implicated.

[c]Biologic agents are definite causes of drug-induced lupus that most likely cause SLE via their direct effect on cytokine levels rather than indirectly via an immune response to the drug itself, as is the case in classic drug-induced lupus.

Modified from Sarzi-Puttini P, Atzeni F, Capsoni F, Lubrano E, Doria A. Drug-induced lupus erythematosus. Autoimmunity. 2005;38(7):507-518. [PMID: 16373256] Modified with permission from Taylor & Francis Ltd., www.tandf.co.uk/journals.

Treatment

Immunizations and Purified Protein Derivative Screening

Patients with SLE should receive all routinely prescribed immunizations; however, patients taking more than 20 mg/d of prednisone or who use immunosuppressive therapy should not receive live attenuated vaccines, including those for varicella, herpes zoster virus, mumps, measles, and rubella. Tuberculin skin testing using purified protein derivative also should be performed in patients with SLE in whom corticosteroid or immunosuppressive therapy will most likely be used.

NSAIDs and Hydroxychloroquine

NSAIDs can be used to relieve pain in patients with SLE who have arthralgia or serositis. Selective cyclooxygenase-2 inhibitors may increase the risk for thrombosis and therefore should be used with caution in patients with SLE who have antiphospholipid antibodies.

Hydroxychloroquine is well tolerated and has a good safety profile and significant disease-modifying properties. This agent is effective for skin and joint manifestations and helps to prevent disease flares. Hydroxychloroquine should be continued indefinitely to prevent disease reactivation, even if the disease has been quiescent for many years.

Corticosteroids

Photosensitive rashes in patients with SLE should be treated conservatively with a sunscreen that blocks UVA and UVB radiation, hydroxychloroquine, and topical corticosteroids; however, fluorinated corticosteroids should not be used on the face because of the risk of skin atrophy. Corticosteroids are the primary treatment for acute SLE. Low-dose systemic corticosteroids are beneficial in patients with mild cutaneous disease and joint involvement; moderate-dose corticosteroids may be warranted in patients with more aggressive skin disease, serositis, or mild hematologic abnormalities other than leukopenia; and high-dose corticosteroids are indicated in patients with nephritis, cerebritis, vasculitis, and life-threatening hematologic abnormalities. High-dose or intralesional corticosteroids may be indicated to treat discoid lupus until hydroxychloroquine therapy becomes effective.

Immunosuppressive Agents

Cyclophosphamide, mycophenolate mofetil, and azathioprine have a steroid-sparing effect and have been shown to improve outcomes in patients with severe SLE, particularly those with renal involvement. In patients with lupus nephritis, combination therapy with monthly intravenous cyclophosphamide and high-dose corticosteroids is superior to corticosteroids alone.

Cyclophosphamide is associated with serious toxicity; therefore, after remission of renal disease has been achieved and maintained for 3 to 6 months, switching from cyclophosphamide to mycophenolate mofetil or azathioprine should be considered. Mycophenolate mofetil is as effective as cyclophosphamide in inducing remission of lupus nephritis, but long-term outcomes of this therapy remain uncertain.

KEY POINTS

- NSAIDs can be used to relieve pain in patients with systemic lupus erythematosus who have arthralgia or serositis.

- Hydroxychloroquine is safe and effective for skin and joint manifestations of systemic lupus erythematosus.

- Hydroxychloroquine should be continued indefinitely when appropriate to help prevent flares of systemic lupus erythematosus even in patients with quiescent disease.

- In patients with lupus nephritis, combination therapy with monthly intravenous cyclophosphamide and high-dose corticosteroids is superior to corticosteroids alone.

- Once remission of renal disease associated with systemic lupus erythematosus has been achieved, switching from cyclophosphamide to mycophenolate mofetil or azathioprine should be considered to maintain remission.

Systemic Lupus Erythematosus and Pregnancy

An obstetrician with experience in high-risk pregnancy and a rheumatologist should monitor pregnant patients with SLE. Patients whose disease has been quiescent for at least 6 months before conception and who take either no medications or medications that can be continued during pregnancy typically have favorable pregnancy outcomes. Patients with recently or currently active SLE at the time of conception have an increased risk of intrauterine growth restriction, premature birth, and fetal loss. Disease activity, particularly renal manifestations, also increases the risk for preeclampsia.

The risk of disease flare during pregnancy is increased sevenfold if the disease has been active 6 months before pregnancy

or if hydroxychloroquine has been discontinued. These features are risk factors for flare in patients with SLE who are not pregnant, as well, and therefore may not be specific to pregnancy. Patients whose disease is controlled by corticosteroids, hydroxychloroquine, or azathioprine should continue therapy during pregnancy. However, cyclophosphamide, mycophenolate mofetil, methotrexate, warfarin, angiotensin-converting enzyme inhibitors, and bisphosphonates should not be used during pregnancy.

Antiphospholipid antibodies predispose patients to intrapartum and postpartum venous thromboembolism. These antibodies also are associated with second- and third-trimester pregnancy losses caused by placental thrombosis and placental insufficiency. Subcutaneous heparin should be instituted in patients with antiphospholipid antibody positivity and a history of recurrent fetal loss or thrombosis. Ideally, heparin should be initiated when patients begin trying to conceive. Low-dose aspirin is often used in conjunction with heparin.

Neonatal lupus affects 1% to 2% of children of mothers with anti-Ro/SSA or anti-La/SSB antibodies, independent of whether these women have SLE or Sjögren syndrome. Neonatal lupus can cause in utero fetal heart block and postnatal rash and hematologic and hepatic abnormalities.

Fetal cardiac disease usually develops at 16 to 24 weeks of gestation and can advance rapidly to complete heart block. Cardiac conditions associated with neonatal SLE are generally irreversible, but rash and hematologic and hepatic abnormalities resolve at 6 to 8 months of age after dissipation of maternal antibodies. Pregnant patients who have anti-Ro/SSA or anti-La/SSB antibodies should undergo regular fetal echocardiography starting at 16 weeks of gestation.

KEY POINTS

- Patients with systemic lupus erythematosus whose disease has been quiescent for at least 6 months before conception and who either take no medications or take medications that can be continued during pregnancy typically have favorable pregnancy outcomes.

- Disease activity, particularly renal manifestations, increases the risk for preeclampsia in pregnant patients with systemic lupus erythematosus.

- Antiphospholipid antibodies predispose patients with systemic lupus erythematosus to both intrapartum and postpartum venous and arterial thromboses and are associated with second-and third-trimester pregnancy losses.

- Neonatal lupus affects 1% to 2% of children of mothers with anti-Ro/SSA or anti-La/SSB antibodies, independent of whether these women have systemic lupus erythematosus or Sjögren syndrome.

- Neonatal lupus can cause in utero fetal heart block and postnatal rash and hematologic and hepatic abnormalities.

Prognosis and Follow-up

Patients with SLE should be asked about symptoms during each office visit. A complete blood count, measurement of anti–double-stranded DNA antibodies and C3, and urinalysis also are indicated to help assess disease activity.

During disease flares, anti–double-stranded DNA antibody titers increase and complement levels decrease. These fluctuations in the absence of other signs or symptoms of disease activity warrant closer follow-up.

Morbidity and mortality in patients with SLE are increasingly associated with medication side effects (such as infection, osteoporosis, or malignancy) and long-term damage from previously active disease (such as chronic kidney disease or neurologic dysfunction). Appropriate vaccinations and screening for osteoporosis are therefore indicated for these patients. Angiotensin-converting enzyme inhibitor therapy also is indicated for patients with SLE with renal involvement.

SLE is a risk factor for premature atherosclerosis and death from coronary artery disease. Atherosclerotic plaque in SLE is associated with a longer duration of disease, more end-organ damage, and less-aggressive treatment. Patients with SLE also are at increased risk for malignancy. The standardized incidence ratio for all cancers in patients with SLE (observed/expected) is 1.15; this ratio is 2.75 for hematologic malignancies and 3.64 for non-Hodgkin lymphoma.

Therefore, management of SLE also involves aggressive treatment of hypertension, hyperlipidemia, and hyperglycemia; weight control; smoking cessation; and age- and sex-appropriate malignancy screening.

Long-term survival in SLE depends on disease severity and access to care. The 5-year survival rate in patients in underserved communities is only 50%, whereas the 10-year survival rate in patients who receive optimal treatment and have strong social support is 90%.

KEY POINTS

- In patients with systemic lupus erythematosus, an increase in anti–double-stranded DNA antibody titers and a decrease in complement levels warrant closer follow-up.
- Systemic lupus erythematosus is a risk factor for premature atherosclerosis, death from coronary artery disease, and hematologic malignancy.

Bibliography

Bernatsky S, Boivin JF, Joseph L, et al. An international cohort study of cancer in systemic lupus erythematosus. Arthritis Rheum. 2005;52 (5):1481-1490. [PMID: 15880596]

Buyon JP, Petri MA, Kim MY, et al. The effect of combined estrogen and progesterone hormone replacement therapy on disease activity in systemic lupus erythematosus: a randomized trial. Ann Intern Med. 2005; 142(12 Pt 1):953-962. [PMID: 15968009]

Clowse ME. Lupus activity in pregnancy. Rheum Dis Clin North Am. 2007;33(2):237-252. [PMID: 17499705]

D'Cruz DP, Khamashta MA, Hughes GR. Systemic lupus erythematosus. Lancet. 2007;369(9561):587-596. [PMID: 17307106]

Ginzler EM, Dooley MA, Aranow C, et al. Mycophenolate mofetil or intravenous cyclophosphamide for lupus nephritis. N Engl J Med. 2005;353(21):2219-2228. [PMID: 16306519]

Tincani A, Branch W, Levy RA, et al. Treatment of pregnant patients with antiphospholipid syndrome. Lupus. 2003;12(7):524-529. [PMID: 12892392]

Systemic Sclerosis

Pathophysiology and Epidemiology

Systemic sclerosis is a disease of unknown cause. The hallmarks of this condition are microangiopathy and fibrosis of the skin and visceral organs. Common pathophysiologic findings in affected patients include endothelial cell dysfunction, abnormal fibroblast function, and autoantibody production.

Systemic sclerosis most commonly affects women and has a peak initial presentation in the third to fourth decades of life. Black individuals, particularly black women, are more likely to have more severe disease compared with other population groups.

KEY POINT

- The hallmarks of systemic sclerosis are microangiopathy and fibrosis of the skin and visceral organs.

Classification

Systemic sclerosis is classified according to the extent and pattern of skin involvement. No medical intervention has been shown to effectively treat systemic sclerosis, and treatment involves management of the disease manifestations.

Limited and Diffuse Cutaneous Systemic Sclerosis

Limited cutaneous systemic sclerosis (lcSSc) is characterized by skin disease that does not progress proximal to the elbows or knees. A subset of this condition is the CREST (calcinosis, Raynaud phenomenon, esophageal dysmotility, sclerodactyly, and telangiectasia) syndrome. Diffuse cutaneous systemic sclerosis (dcSSc) is characterized by skin thickening that involves areas proximal to the elbows and/or knees.

Both lcSSc and dcSSc can involve the face and neck. Patients with lcSSc are more likely to develop pulmonary hypertension in the absence of other pulmonary manifestations. Patients with dcSSc are more likely to develop interstitial lung disease (ILD) and/or renal disease.

Systemic Sclerosis Sine Scleroderma

Systemic sclerosis sine scleroderma is characterized by visceral disease in the absence of cutaneous involvement. Internal organ involvement in this condition parallels that in lcSSc or dcSSc, and laboratory findings and survival rates are similar to those in lcSSc.

- Treatment in patients with systemic sclerosis is limited to management of the disease manifestations.
- Systemic sclerosis sine scleroderma is characterized by visceral disease in the absence of cutaneous involvement.

Diagnosis

Diagnosis of systemic sclerosis is established in patients with sclerodermatous skin changes (tightness, thickening, and nonpitting induration) that have sclerodactyly and skin disease that extends proximal to the metacarpophalangeal joints. In the absence of these findings, diagnosis of systemic sclerosis may be established in patients with two of the following features: sclerodactyly (sclerodermatous skin changes limited to the fingers and toes), digital pitting (soft-tissue defects and scarring in the pulp space of the distal phalanges), or basilar fibrosis visible on chest radiography (**Figure 23** and **Figure 24**).

Antinuclear antibodies are present in more than 95% of patients with systemic sclerosis. A nucleolar pattern of staining is common in patients with either type of systemic sclerosis, whereas anticentromere antibody positivity is associated with lcSSc. Patients who have anticentromere antibodies appear to have a lower incidence of ILD. Anti-topoisomerase I (anti–Scl-70) antibody positivity suggests an increased risk for developing ILD and dcSSc. Serologic markers of disease activity in systemic sclerosis have not yet been identified.

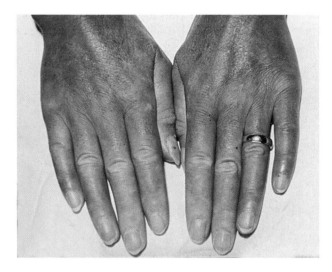

- Diagnosis of systemic sclerosis is established in patients with sclerodermatous skin changes that extend proximal to the metacarpophalangeal joints or who have two of the following features: sclerodactyly, digital pitting, or basilar fibrosis visible on chest radiography.

Clinical Manifestations and Management

Cutaneous Involvement

Initial cutaneous changes in patients with lcSSc and dcSSc usually reflect an inflammatory response in the dermis that manifests as puffiness or swelling in the hands and fingers. Hypo- or hyperpigmentation is another manifestation of this inflammatory reaction, and pruritus also may develop.

Later in the disease course, induration of the skin typically develops over the fingers and progresses proximally. Telangiectasia and subcutaneous calcinosis occur in patients with dcSSc but are more common findings in patients with lcSSc. Calcinosis usually develops over pressure points such as the fingertips, elbows, buttocks, and knees (**Figure 25**).

Skin changes generally progress during the first 2 years of the course of systemic sclerosis; during this time, lcSSc may evolve into dcSSc. After this initial period of worsening skin disease, the skin in patients with systemic sclerosis may soften; this development heralds the atrophic phase of cutaneous disease.

No agent has yet been shown to be effective in the treatment of skin thickening in systemic sclerosis. However, a study of the efficacy of cyclophosphamide in the treatment of patients with systemic sclerosis–associated lung disease showed that this agent somewhat alleviated skin thickening in this setting compared with placebo.

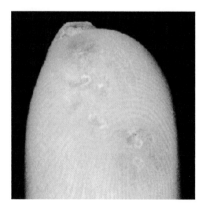

FIGURE 24.
Digital pitting.
Digital pitting (soft-tissue defects and scarring in the pulp space of the distal phalanges) in a patient with systemic sclerosis.

FIGURE 23.
Sclerodactyly.
Sclerodactyly (skin thickening over the fingers) extending proximal to the metacarpophalangeal joints in a patient with systemic sclerosis.

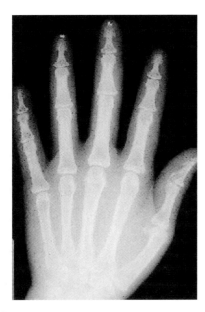

FIGURE 25.
Calcinosis.
Radiograph showing calcinosis, which commonly develops in patients with limited cutaneous systemic sclerosis but also may occur in those with diffuse cutaneous disease.

Vascular Involvement

Raynaud phenomenon due to arterial vasospasm is the initial clinical manifestation in 70% of patients with systemic sclerosis and eventually occurs in more than 95% of these patients. Episodes of Raynaud phenomenon are usually triggered by cold exposure and involve the extremities but may affect nearly any artery or arteriole. Sequelae of Raynaud phenomenon in patients with systemic sclerosis include digital pitting, ulceration, and gangrene (**Figure 26**).

Microvascular involvement in systemic sclerosis also manifests as intimal proliferation with progressive luminal obliteration. Similar abnormalities may affect the larger arteries, causing conditions such as arterial occlusions and erectile dysfunction. Therefore, patients with systemic sclerosis experience both an anatomic vascular narrowing as well as superimposed vasospasm.

Management of Raynaud phenomenon includes the use of vasodilators such as dihydropyridine calcium channel blockers, α_1-antagonists, and topical nitrates. Antiplatelet agents such as aspirin and dipyridamole also are frequently used, and sildenafil has been shown to be effective in this setting. In patients with refractory Raynaud phenomenon, surgical revascularization, sympathetic nerve blockade or sympathectomy, prostacyclin analogues, or endothelin antagonists may be warranted.

Musculoskeletal Involvement

Myalgia and arthralgia are common in patients with systemic sclerosis but usually are not associated with an underlying inflammatory arthritis or myopathy. Extensive fibrotic changes in the overlying skin may cause joint flexion contractures. Tendon friction rubs also may be present and are usually palpable over the wrists, elbows, knees, and ankles. The presence of tendon friction rubs predicts the development of aggressive diffuse skin involvement and an increased risk of internal organ involvement.

Patients with systemic sclerosis also may develop an inflammatory, typically nonerosive arthritis. This condition is similar to rheumatoid arthritis and is managed using similar interventions.

Collagen deposition in the muscle in patients with systemic sclerosis may cause a noninflammatory myopathy. This myopathy is associated with only minimal elevations in muscle enzyme levels and typically requires no intervention. An overlap syndrome with polymyositis also may occur and manifests as proximal muscle weakness accompanied by elevated muscle enzyme levels. Treatment of inflammatory myopathy associated with systemic sclerosis is similar to that of polymyositis.

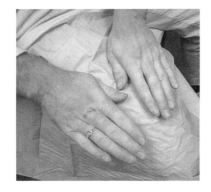
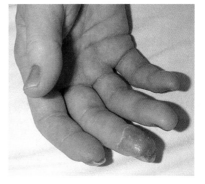

FIGURE 26.
Raynaud phenomenon.
Raynaud phenomenon associated with color change (*left panel*) and ulceration (*right panel*).

Gastrointestinal Involvement

Involvement of the gastrointestinal tract is universal in systemic sclerosis and may affect the entire alimentary canal. Gastrointestinal manifestations in systemic sclerosis often present before the diagnosis of this condition is established and are the same in both lcSSc and dcSSc.

The esophagus is the second most commonly affected organ, after the skin, in patients with systemic sclerosis. Esophageal dysfunction is the most common gastrointestinal manifestation in this setting and affects at least 80% of patients with this condition. Smooth muscle dysfunction in the distal esophagus results in dysphagia, whereas decreased lower esophageal sphincter pressure causes gastroesophageal reflux.

Potential complications of esophageal disease in patients with systemic sclerosis include esophagitis, esophageal stricture, Barrett esophagus, and aspiration pneumonitis. Management of these conditions includes the use of prokinetic agents such as metoclopramide, erythromycin, and octreotide. In addition, gastric acid suppression with proton pump inhibitors is indicated for nearly all patients with systemic sclerosis. Patients with systemic sclerosis also have an increased risk for the development of Barrett esophagus, and screening for this condition is appropriate.

Systemic sclerosis also may cause thickening of the perioral skin. This abnormality results in a narrowed oral aperture, which may compromise the ability of affected patients to eat and drink.

Mucosal telangiectasias may be present throughout the gastrointestinal tract. In the stomach, telangiectasias may result in gastric antral vascular ectasia (watermelon stomach) and may cause significant blood loss (**Figure 27**). Endoscopic laser coagulation and obliteration of these vascular ectasias may reduce the risk of gastrointestinal bleeding.

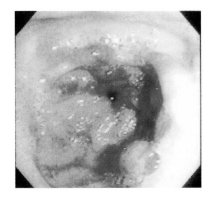

FIGURE 27.
Gastric antral vascular ectasia.
Endoscopic view of gastric antral vascular ectasia. This condition is known as watermelon stomach because the telangiectasias in the antrum resemble watermelon stripes.

Reprinted with permission from Physician's Information and Education Resource (PIER). Philadelphia: American College of Physicians. Copyright 2009 American College of Physicians.

Small- and large-bowel involvement in patients with systemic sclerosis may cause intestinal pseudo-obstruction, defined as a functional ileus that manifests as symptoms of bowel obstruction. Management of intestinal pseudo-obstruction is conservative and includes decompression and bowel rest; surgical intervention is not indicated.

Bacterial overgrowth due to dysfunctional motility may cause chronic diarrhea, alternating diarrhea and constipation, and/or malabsorption. Manifestations of bacterial overgrowth include bloating, abdominal pain, and steatorrhea. Extended courses of antibiotics are useful in patients with this condition; this therapy often involves rotating among different classes of antibiotics, with the course of each agent lasting several months.

Wide-mouthed colonic diverticula develop along the antimesenteric border of the colon but are rarely clinically significant. LcSSc also is associated with the development of biliary cirrhosis.

Pulmonary Involvement

Lung disease is the primary cause of morbidity and mortality in patients with systemic sclerosis. The principal clinical manifestations of lung disease in this setting include ILD and/or pulmonary arterial hypertension (PAH). Other manifestations of lung involvement in systemic sclerosis include recurrent aspiration, cryptogenic organizing pneumonia, recurrent aspiration, and hemorrhage due to endobronchial telangiectasia. Patients with systemic sclerosis also have an increased risk of developing carcinoma of the lung. However, the principal clinical manifestations of lung disease in this setting include ILD and PAH.

Interstitial Lung Disease

ILD occurs most often in patients with dcSSc but also may affect those with lcSSc. This condition is more likely to develop in patients with anti-topoisomerase I (anti–Scl-70) antibody positivity compared with the general population.

Patients with systemic sclerosis and ILD have a restrictive pattern with a decreased FVC and D$_{LCO}$ on pulmonary function testing. A D$_{LCO}$ less than 40% is associated with a 5-year survival rate of 9%, whereas a D$_{LCO}$ greater than 40% is associated with a 5-year survival rate of more than 75%.

ILD associated with systemic sclerosis usually manifests as dyspnea, dry cough, and decreased exercise tolerance. Fine bibasilar crackles that extend into late inspiration are heard on physical examination. High-resolution CT is more sensitive than chest radiography for ILD and reveals ground-glass and reticular linear opacities, subpleural cysts, and honeycombing in patients with advanced disease.

Oral cyclophosphamide may improve pulmonary symptoms and lung volumes in patients with ILD related to systemic sclerosis and has been shown to modestly improve lung function in this setting.

Pulmonary Arterial Hypertension

Pulmonary vascular disease may manifest as isolated PAH or as a complication of vascular obliteration in patients with ILD. Vascular intimal fibrosis, not vasculitis, causes PAH in patients with systemic sclerosis. Patients with lcSSc have the greatest risk for developing PAH not associated with interstitial lung disease, whereas patients with dcSSc most often develop secondary PAH.

Patients with PAH may present with fatigue, decreased exercise tolerance, dyspnea, or syncope. Physical examination findings include an increased P_2 and a persistently split S_2. Chest radiographs are usually normal but may reveal enlarged or prominent pulmonary arteries. A decrease in DLCO in the setting of normal or corrected lung volumes that is not associated with ILD is consistent with PAH. Echocardiography may show elevated right ventricular systolic pressures, but the gold standard for determining pulmonary artery pressure is direct measurement by right heart catheterization. Some experts recommend echocardiographic examination of all patients with systemic sclerosis at baseline and yearly intervals thereafter, with additional monitoring of pulmonary function tests and dyspnea. Clinical suspicion of PAH should prompt further assessment by right heart catheterization.

Treatment for isolated PAH includes anticoagulation with warfarin; vasodilation; and, if needed, oxygen. Vasodilating agents approved for the treatment of PAH include sildenafil; the endothelin antagonists bosentan and ambrisentan; and prostacyclin analogues such as epoprostenol, iloprost, and treprostinil, and these agents have been shown to effectively relieve symptoms of PAH associated with systemic sclerosis.

Cardiac Involvement

Up to 50% of patients with systemic sclerosis have cardiac involvement. Cardiac disease in patients with systemic sclerosis may manifest as cardiomyopathy, pericarditis, and arrhythmias or be clinically silent. Symptomatic cardiac involvement in systemic sclerosis portends a poor prognosis and is associated with a 2-year mortality rate of 60%.

Patients with systemic sclerosis may develop myocardial fibrosis and pathologic contraction band necrosis, and these conditions may cause systolic or diastolic dysfunction as well as arrhythmias. Echocardiography in patients with systemic sclerosis commonly reveals effusions but rarely shows cardiac tamponade. Autopsy results in patients with systemic sclerosis frequently reveal pericardial disease.

Renal Involvement

Scleroderma renal crisis (SRC) occurs almost exclusively in patients with early dcSSc. This condition is characterized by the acute onset of severe hypertension, renal failure, and microangiopathic hemolytic anemia. The presence of a pericardial effusion is associated with an increased risk of SRC. Use of corticosteroid therapy in the management of inflammatory disease manifestations such as myopathy is classically associated with normotensive renal failure and is also a risk factor for SRC.

SRC is a medical emergency, and patients in whom this diagnosis is established should be admitted to the hospital immediately for aggressive blood pressure control. Before the advent of angiotensin-converting enzyme (ACE) inhibitors, end-stage renal disease and associated increased mortality were the universal outcomes in patients with SRC. ACE inhibitor therapy is currently considered the cornerstone of therapy for this condition. Aggressive dosage titration of ACE inhibitors is indicated at the onset of SRC. Therapy with these agents should continue even in patients with significant renal insufficiency, because renal function has been shown to improve even after months of dialysis.

KEY POINTS

- Raynaud phenomenon due to arterial vasospasm is the initial clinical manifestation in 70% of patients with systemic sclerosis.
- Involvement of the gastrointestinal tract is universal in patients with systemic sclerosis and often presents before the diagnosis of this disease.
- Oral cyclophosphamide may improve pulmonary symptoms and lung volumes in patients with interstitial lung disease related to systemic sclerosis and has been shown to modestly improve lung function in this setting.
- Cardiac disease in patients with systemic sclerosis may manifest as cardiomyopathy, pericarditis, and arrhythmias or be clinically silent.
- Scleroderma renal crisis occurs almost exclusively in patients with early diffuse cutaneous disease and is characterized by the acute onset of severe hypertension, renal failure, and microangiopathic hemolytic anemia.

Scleroderma Spectrum Disorders

Morphea involves only the skin in the absence of other systemic manifestations of systemic sclerosis. Eosinophilic fasciitis is characterized by peripheral eosinophilia accompanied by woody induration of the skin that involves the extremities but usually spares the hands and face. Patients with eosinophilic fasciitis do not have Raynaud phenomenon or other features of systemic sclerosis (**Table 12**). Corticosteroid therapy usually is effective in patients with this condition.

KEY POINTS

- Morphea is a localized form of systemic sclerosis that involves only the skin without other systemic manifestations of systemic sclerosis.
- Eosinophilic fasciitis is characterized by peripheral eosinophilia accompanied by woody induration of the skin of the extremities without Raynaud phenomenon or other features of systemic sclerosis.

TABLE 12 Differential Diagnosis of Fibrosing Skin Disorders

Condition	Characteristic Clinical Features	Pathologic Findings	Systemic Involvement
Systemic sclerosis	Sclerodactyly and more extensive skin involvement	Dermal fibrosis	Raynaud phenomenon; pulmonary, gastrointestinal, renal, cardiac, musculoskeletal systems
Localized scleroderma	Skin plaque thickening	Dermal fibrosis (identical to features of systemic sclerosis)	None
Eosinophilic fasciitis	Woody induration of arms/legs; spares hands and face	Inflammation and fibrosis of fascia (plasma cells and lymphocytes)	None
Buschke scleredema	Affects shoulder girdle, neck, upper arms	Excess large collagen fibers; ground substance	Diabetes mellitus; association with monoclonal gammopathy
Scleromyxedema	Affects face, upper trunk, arms; papular and nodular lesions	Mucin deposition; stellate fibroblasts	Association with monoclonal gammopathy/ paraproteinemia; neurologic, gastrointestinal, cardiac systems
Nephrogenic systemic fibrosis[a]	Brawny hyperpigmentation, papular lesions; spares fingers	Disorganized collagen bundles, increased clefts, increased spindle cells	Renal insufficiency/failure

[a]This condition has been associated with use of gadolinium-containing contrast agents.

Pregnancy and Systemic Sclerosis

Systemic sclerosis does not affect fertility and most likely does not increase the rate of miscarriage. In addition, no good evidence exists to suggest that pregnancy exacerbates systemic sclerosis. However, pregnancy in patients with systemic sclerosis is considered high risk and is associated with an increased risk of small full-term infants and premature births.

SRC poses the greatest risk in pregnant patients with systemic sclerosis. The therapy indicated for this condition, ACE inhibitors, is associated with an increased risk to the fetus. However, the mortality rate of untreated SRC is high enough to warrant the use of these agents in pregnant patients despite the risk to the fetus.

KEY POINT

- Pregnancy in patients with systemic sclerosis is considered high risk and is associated with an increased risk of small full-term infants and premature births.

Bibliography

Mayes MD. Scleroderma epidemiology. Rheum Dis Clin North Am. 2003;29(2):239-254. [PMID: 12841293]

Poormoghim H, Lucas M, Fertig N, Medsger TA Jr. Systemic sclerosis sine scleroderma: demographic, clinical, and serologic features and survival in forty-eight patients. Arthritis Rheum. 2000;43(2):444-451. [PMID: 10693887]

Rose S, Young MA, Reynolds JC. Gastrointestinal manifestations of scleroderma. Gastroenterol Clin North Am. 1998; 27(3):563-594. [PMID: 9891698]

Steen VD. Pregnancy in scleroderma. Rheum Dis Clin North Am. 2007; 33(2):345-358. [PMID: 17499711]

White B, Moore WC, Wigley FM, Xiao HQ, Wise RA. Cyclophosphamide is associated with pulmonary function and survival benefit in patients with scleroderma and alveolitis. Ann Intern Med. 2000; 132(12):947-954. [PMID: 10858177]

Sjögren Syndrome

Pathology and Epidemiology

Sjögren syndrome is a slowly progressive autoimmune inflammatory disorder associated with lymphoproliferation and mononuclear cell infiltration of the exocrine glands. This condition has a 9:1 female predominance and usually affects patients in midlife.

Sjögren syndrome may occur as a primary disorder but commonly presents secondary to another autoimmune disease. This condition most often develops in association with rheumatoid arthritis and systemic lupus erythematosus but also occurs in patients with systemic sclerosis and inflammatory myopathy.

Clinical Manifestations

Sjögren syndrome is characterized by keratoconjunctivitis sicca, which causes xerophthalmia (dry eyes), and xerostomia (dry mouth). In affected patients, the absence of oral mucosal moisture often causes difficulty with mastication and swallowing and increases the risk for dental caries and periodontal disease; patients with xerophthalmia are at increased risk for corneal lesions. Vaginal dryness and parotid gland enlargement are frequently present, and fatigue and arthralgia are common. Some patients with Sjögren syndrome also may develop an inflammatory polyarthritis.

Additional systemic features of Sjögren syndrome include cutaneous vasculitis, peripheral neuropathy, vasculitis that may be associated with mononeuritis multiplex, and interstitial nephritis with associated distal renal tubular acidosis. Pulmonary involvement may develop in patients with Sjögren syndrome and most commonly manifests with interstitial lung disease; however, bronchial and bronchiolar disease also may occur.

Because Sjögren syndrome is associated with B-cell clonal expansion, affected patients have an increased risk for developing lymphoma. Lymphoma is particularly likely to develop in patients with primary Sjögren syndrome, who reportedly have up to a 44-fold increased incidence of this condition.

Diagnosis

A full physical examination is required to document oral, ocular, and extraglandular manifestations of Sjögren syndrome. Autoantibody formation occurs in primary Sjögren syndrome. Approximately 50% of patients with this syndrome are antinuclear antibody positive. Extractable nuclear antigens are frequently present; 60% to 75% of patients with primary Sjögren syndrome are anti-Ro/SSA antibody positive, and approximately 40% of these patients are anti-La/SSB antibody positive. A total of 60% to 80% of patients with this condition are rheumatoid factor positive.

Abnormal findings on the Schirmer test, which measures moisture under the lower eyelids, are consistent with Sjögren syndrome. Referral to an ophthalmologist for rose bengal staining also may be warranted. In this study, visualization of small conjunctival and corneal punctate lesions caused by microtrauma associated with ocular dryness suggests a diagnosis of Sjögren syndrome.

The presence of xerophthalmia and xerostomia accompanied by anti-Ro/SSA and anti-La/SSB antibody positivity and abnormal findings on the Schirmer test or rose bengal staining have 94% sensitivity and specificity for primary Sjögren syndrome.

Pathologic diagnosis of this condition can be confirmed if biopsy specimens of a labial salivary gland reveal focal lymphocytic infiltration.

In addition to Sjögren syndrome, the differential diagnosis of parotid gland enlargement includes bacterial, mycobacterial, fungal, or viral infection; lymphoma; sarcoidosis; amyloidosis; alcohol abuse; bulimia; and HIV infection.

Treatment

Treatment of Sjögren syndrome is largely symptomatic. NSAIDs or hydroxychloroquine is helpful for arthralgia;

hydroxychloroquine also helps fatigue. Oral pilocarpine and cevimeline can be useful for xerophthalmia and are even more effective in xerostomia. Frequent use of artificial tear eye drops also can relieve symptoms of xerophthalmia, whereas cyclosporine eye drops may benefit patients with continued ocular symptoms. Systemic corticosteroid therapy or other immunosuppressants may be warranted in patients with severe extraglandular manifestations of Sjögren syndrome. Diligent attention to dental care is important to prevent dental caries and the need for dental extractions.

KEY POINTS

- Sjögren syndrome commonly presents secondary to rheumatoid arthritis, systemic lupus erythematosus, systemic sclerosis, and inflammatory myopathy.
- Sjögren syndrome is characterized by xerophthalmia and xerostomia.
- Patients with Sjögren syndrome have an increased risk for developing lymphoma.
- The presence of xerophthalmia and xerostomia accompanied by anti-Ro/SSA and anti-La/SSB antibody positivity and abnormal findings on the Schirmer test or rose bengal staining have 94% sensitivity and specificity for primary Sjögren syndrome.
- Diligent attention to dental care is important in patients with Sjögren syndrome to prevent dental caries and the need for dental extractions.

Bibliography
Ramos-Casals M, Tzioufas AG, Font J. Primary Sjögren's syndrome: new clinical and therapeutic concepts. Ann Rheum Dis. 2005;64 (3):347-354. [PMID: 15498797]

Vitali C, Bombardieri S, Moutsopoulos HM, et al. Preliminary criteria for the classification of Sjögren's syndrome: results of a prospective concerted action supported by the European Community. Arthritis Rhem. 1993:36(3):340-347. [PMID: 8452579]

Mixed Connective Tissue Disease

Mixed connective tissue disease (MCTD) is characterized by features of systemic sclerosis, myositis, rheumatoid arthritis, and systemic lupus erythematosus and is by definition associated with high titers of antiribonucleoprotein antibodies. The condition has a 9:1 female predominance.

Clinical Manifestations and Diagnosis

A total of 95% of patients with MCTD have arthralgia or arthritis, and arthritis in this setting can be erosive. Raynaud phenomenon is present in 85% of affected patients. Serositis and an inflammatory muscle disease that typically has a milder presentation than polymyositis are present in 60% of patients with MCTD, and 50% of patients with this condition have mild Sjögren syndrome.

Some patients with MCTD have sclerodactyly or edema of the hands. MCTD also may be associated with pulmonary hypertension, pulmonary fibrosis, trigeminal neuralgia, or esophageal dysmotility. Scleroderma renal crisis is uncommon but may develop in this setting, and proliferative glomerulonephritis and serious central nervous system disease are rarely present.

Diagnosis of MCTD is established in patients with a compatible clinical presentation who have high titers of antiribonucleoprotein antibodies. Various diagnostic criteria exist for this condition, but diagnosis generally requires high titers of antiribonucleoprotein antibodies accompanied by three of the following features: Raynaud phenomenon, synovitis, swollen hands, and myositis. Whether antiribonucleoprotein antibodies are pathogenic remains uncertain. Diagnosis of MCTD is established in patients with features of connective tissue diseases who do not meet criteria for a specific disease.

Treatment and Prognosis

Treatment in patients with MCTD involves managing the individual disease manifestations. Corticosteroids and other immunosuppressive agents are used in patients with myositis, whereas NSAIDs, antimalarial agents, or more potent agents such as azathioprine, methotrexate, or mycophenolate mofetil are indicated for those with arthritis. Vasodilatory agents are beneficial in patients with pulmonary arterial hypertension, and angiotensin-converting enzyme inhibitors help to treat renovascular disease.

Prognosis in MCTD is generally good except in the presence of pulmonary arterial hypertension.

KEY POINTS

- Mixed connective tissue disease is characterized by features of systemic sclerosis, myositis, and systemic lupus erythematosus accompanied by antiribonucleoprotein antibody positivity.

- Mixed connective tissue disease typically manifests with arthralgia or arthritis, Raynaud phenomenon, serositis, and an inflammatory muscle disease.

- Treatment of patients with mixed connective tissue disease involves managing the individual disease manifestations.

Bibliography

Venables PJ. Mixed connective tissue disease. Lupus. 2006;15(3):132-137. [PMID 16634365]

Crystal-Induced Arthropathies

Gout

Gout (monosodium urate deposition disease) refers to the group of clinical disorders associated with hyperuricemia (**Table 13**).

Pathophysiology and Epidemiology

Uric acid is the end product of purine metabolism and is present in the serum and tissues in the form of monosodium urate. In patients with serum uric acid levels higher than 6.7 mg/dL (0.40 mmol/L), monosodium urate supersaturates the serum and precipitates into tissues. With prolonged tissue deposition, gouty arthropathy and tophi develop.

Most patients with elevated levels of uric acid do not experience clinical disease. An acute gouty attack occurs when monosodium urate crystals are released or form *de novo* in the joint space. Trauma, surgery, or the initiation of medications such as allopurinol or uricosuric or diuretic agents can abruptly alter uric acid levels and incite an attack of gout.

Transplant recipients who take cyclosporine have a significantly increased incidence of both hyperuricemia and gout. Patients with gout who are younger than 25 years and have normal renal function typically are genetically predisposed to gout because of an enzymatic defect in uric acid metabolism.

Screening and Prevention

Screening measurement of uric acid levels or treatment of asymptomatic hyperuricemia is not indicated in patients without clinical evidence of gout; few patients with hyperuricemia develop gout, and potential reactions to medications may outweigh benefits in asymptomatic individuals. Prophylactic use of uric acid–lowering agents is only indicated when a patient's renal function is compromised.

Clinical Manifestations

Gout manifests as acute intermittent attacks of joint and tenosynovial inflammation characterized by redness, swelling, and intense pain with accompanying fever and chills. Attacks often begin during the night and peak within the first 12 hours from disease onset.

Early attacks of gout are typically monoarticular and involve joints in the lower extremities. Half of initial episodes manifest as gouty involvement of the first metatarsophalangeal joint (**Figure 28**).

Acute attacks of gout, which vary in intensity and duration, typically last 5 to 7 days, but a severe attack may last up to 2 weeks. Gouty attacks are self-limited and eventually resolve spontaneously. Early attacks are followed by asymptomatic periods that can last for years. Over time, these attacks

TABLE 13 Disorders Associated with Hyperuricemia		
Condition	**Clinical Presentation**	**Cause**
Gouty arthritis	Inflammatory erosive arthritis	Inflammatory response to monosodium urate crystals deposited into synovial tissues, bursae, and tendon sheaths due to chronic supersaturation of sera. These deposits produce joint and tissue destruction over time.
Tophi	Painless, persistent, generally noninflammatory nodules that develop in tissues and tendons that are palpable on physical examination but also may occur as nodular lesions within joints or tissues	Chronic deposition of monosodium urate crystals into synovial tissues, bursae, and tendon sheaths due to chronic supersaturation of sera. Tophi develop concomitantly with progressive gouty arthritis. Although typically noninflammatory, acute inflammation reactions and local damage can occur at these sites analogous to the acute gouty flares in the joints.
Nephrolithiasis	Formation of uric acid and calcium oxalate renal stones	Increase in uric acid concentrations in the urinary collecting system serves as a nidus for both uric acid and calcium oxalate stone formation
Nephropathy	Loss of renal function secondary to severe, typically acute increases in serum uric acid levels, such as occur in patients with tumor lysis syndrome	Deposition of monosodium urate crystals in the renal interstitium

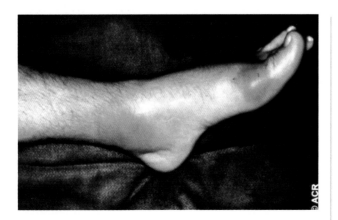

FIGURE 28.
Podagra.
This patient has podagra, or acute pain in the great toe caused by an attack of gout. As the attack subsides, the superficial skin of the involved toe may peel.

Reprinted with permission from Clinical Slide Collection on the Rheumatic Diseases. Atlanta: American College of Rheumatology. Copyright 1972-2004 American College of Rheumatology.

become more frequent and increasingly polyarticular and begin to involve joints in the upper extremities (**Figure 29**).

Chronic tophaceous gout is characterized by the deposition of urate crystals into the connective tissue either as soft-tissue nodules that are clinically apparent or as masses or erosive deposits detectable on radiography. Tophi may be asymptomatic or become acutely or chronically inflamed. They commonly develop at the pressure areas of the forearms and at joints and bursae, particularly the olecranon.

Chronic tophaceous gout may manifest as a chronic polyarticular deforming arthritis that particularly involves the hands, especially in affected women (**Figure 30**). This condition may be difficult to differentiate in clinical appearance from rheumatoid arthritis.

Diagnosis and Evaluation

Distinguishing an acute attack of gout from septic arthritis or cellulitis can be difficult. Definitive diagnosis of gout requires the identification of monosodium urate crystals on arthrocentesis or aspiration of a tophus, although a presumptive diagnosis can be made based on a patient's clinical course and presentation (**Table 14**). An elevated serum uric acid level is not diagnostic of gout, and a normal or low serum uric acid level does not exclude gout.

During an attack of gout, needle-shaped monosodium urate crystals that typically appear engulfed by the neutrophils are visible on compensated polarized light microscopy (**Figure 31**). The synovial fluid leukocyte count can increase to $15,000/\mu L$ or higher with a predominance of neutrophils. Leukocyte counts higher than $50,000/\mu L$ should raise suspicion for a concurrent bacterial joint infection even when monosodium urate crystals have been identified. Until culture results exclude infection, empiric antibiotic therapy is indicated in this setting. Monosodium urate crystals also may be visible on joint aspiration when an acute flare is not occurring.

Determining whether a patient with hyperuricemia is an underexcretor or overproducer of uric acid is usually not necessary and rarely affects treatment. Patients who both under- and overexcrete urine uric acid respond to allopurinol. However, when uricosuric therapy is being considered, for example, in patients who are intolerant of allopurinol, verification that the patient does not have a history of nephrolithiasis and is a urine uric acid underexcretor is necessary.

Radiographs of patients with chronic advanced gout typically reveal asymmetric erosions with overhanging edges.

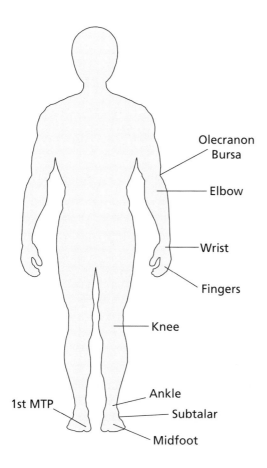

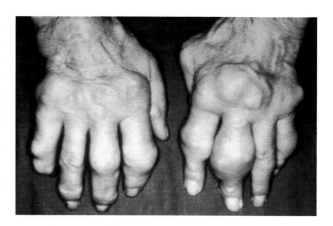

FIGURE 30.
Polyarticular chronic tophaceous gout.
Joint and nodular changes of the hands in a patient with long-standing tophaceous gout.

Treatment

Gouty Arthritis

NSAIDs, corticosteroids, and colchicine are options in the treatment of an acute attack of gout. NSAIDs (including selective cyclooxygenase-2 inhibitors) are highly effective when administered during an acute attack, but they should be used with caution in patients at risk for renal impairment, bleeding, or ulcer disorders, especially in the elderly.

Oral, intra-articular, or intravenous corticosteroid therapy is also effective in acute gouty attacks. However, oral therapy generally requires doses in the range of 40 mg/d or greater, which may be problematic in patients with diabetes mellitus. The dose can be tapered when the attack has

FIGURE 29.
Common sites of gout involvement in patients with advanced disease.

MTP = metatarsophalangeal.

TABLE 14 American College of Rheumatology Criteria for the Classification of Acute Arthritis of Primary Gout
The presence of characteristic urate crystals in the joint fluid, OR
A tophus proved to contain urate crystals by chemical means or polarized light microscopy, OR

The presence of 6 of the following clinical, laboratory, and radiographic findings, even in the absence of crystal identification:
    More than one attack of acute arthritis
    Maximum inflammation developed within 1 day
    Monoarthritis attack
    Redness observed over joints
    First metatarsophalangeal joint painful or swollen
    Unilateral first metatarsophalangeal joint attack
    Unilateral tarsal joint attack
    Tophus (suspected)
    Hyperuricemia
    Asymmetric swelling within a joint visible on physical examination or radiography
    Subcortical cysts without erosions visible on radiography
    Monosodium urate monohydrate microcrystals in joint fluid during attack
    Joint fluid culture negative for organisms during attack

Modified from Wallace SL, Robinson H, Masi AT, Decker JL, McCarty DJ, Yü TF. Preliminary criteria for the classification of the acute arthritis of primary gout. Arthritis Rheum. 1977;20(3):895-900. [PMID: 856219] Copyright 1977 American College of Rheumatology. Modified with permission from John Wiley & Sons, Inc.

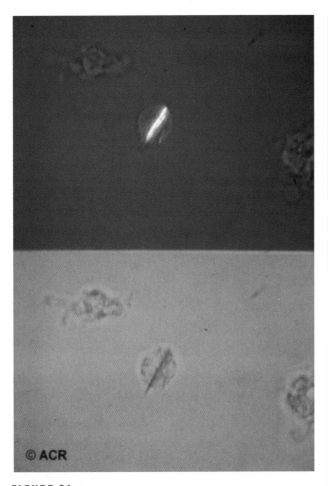

FIGURE 31.
Monosodium urate crystals.
Compensated polarized light microscopy of monosodium urate monohydrate crystals phagocytosed by a polymorphonuclear leukocyte in the synovial fluid during an acute attack of gout.

improved. Once infection has been excluded, intra-articular injections of corticosteroids also can be beneficial.

Colchicine is most effective in patients with monoarticular involvement and when used within the first 24 hours of symptoms and can abort a severe attack. At the first sign of an attack in patients with normal renal function, this agent is usually administered twice or three times daily until the patient experiences symptomatic relief, develops gastrointestinal toxicity, or reaches a maximum dose of 6 mg per attack. Colchicine also should be used at a reduced dosage in patients with renal impairment. Intravenous colchicine is associated with potential bone marrow and neuromuscular toxicity and should therefore generally be avoided.

Hyperuricemia
Dietary purine restriction, weight loss, and discontinuation of alcohol may help to decrease uric acid levels in patients with

mild hyperuricemia and symptomatic gout. Medications that raise serum uric acid levels, such as thiazide diuretics and low-dose salicylates, should be discontinued if alternative therapy is appropriate. However, most patients with recurrent gouty attacks, particularly those with tophaceous deposits, require pharmacologic therapy to lower serum levels of uric acid.

Criteria for initiating treatment of hyperuricemia in patients with symptomatic gout include the presence of tophi or renal stones or a history of a decreasing period between attacks. Uric acid–lowering therapy typically is not initiated until a patient experiences two documented acute attacks.

Rapid control of serum uric acid levels generally is not necessary during an acute attack, and acute increases and decreases in the uric acid level alter the steady state and may prolong the current attack or precipitate new attacks. Discontinuing chronic therapy also alters serum uric acid levels and may precipitate attacks. Therefore, discontinuation of chronic therapy during an acute attack is not necessary and may actually worsen symptoms.

The goal in uric acid–lowering therapy is to achieve a serum uric acid level less than 6.0 mg/dL (0.35 mmol/L), not just levels within the normal range. When the uric acid levels are below 6.0 mg/dL (0.35 mmol/L), monosodium urate crystals from within the joint and from soft-tissue tophaceous deposits are reabsorbed. Suppression therefore eventually leads to alleviation of the arthritis.

Allopurinol is the agent of choice for patients with over-production of uric acid, renal insufficiency, nephrolithiasis, tophi, or intolerance to uricosuric therapy. Because allopurinol is primarily cleared by the kidney, initial doses must be adjusted downward for patients with renal impairment. Patients with renal insufficiency, especially those with concomitant use of hydrochlorothiazide, who are treated with allopurinol have an increased risk for a rare but potentially fatal hypersensitivity syndrome characterized by severe dermatitis, fever, eosinophilia, hepatic necrosis, and acute nephritis; in addition to discontinuation of allopurinol, therapy is primarily supportive.

Expert consultation is indicated before initiating allopurinol therapy in patients who use azathioprine, such as transplant recipients, because serious potential drug interactions may occur. To permit treatment with allopurinol in this setting, a switch from azathioprine to mycophenolate mofetil may be warranted.

The uricosuric agents probenecid and sulfinpyrazone are relatively contraindicated in patients with impaired renal function or those at risk for renal stones. Newer uric acid–lowering agents such as pegylated uricase are under investigation and show promise for the treatment of refractory gout.

Prophylactic colchicine, low-dose corticosteroids (10 mg/d or less), or NSAIDs initiated at least 1 week before beginning or adjusting the dose of uric acid–lowering therapy help to prevent disease flares associated with changes in uric acid levels and may need to be continued until therapeutic serum uric acid levels have been achieved. Prolonged use of these agents may be indicated in patients with chronic tophaceous gout until the disease is controlled.

KEY POINTS

- Maximal-dose NSAID therapy is highly effective during an acute attack of gout.
- Colchicine is most effective in patients with monoarticular involvement and when used within the first 24 hours of symptoms of gout and can abort the development of a severe attack.
- Criteria for initiating treatment of hyperuricemia in patients with symptomatic gout include the presence of tophi and renal stones and a history of at least two documented gouty attacks.
- The goal of uric acid–lowering therapy in gout is to achieve a serum uric acid level less than 6.0 mg/dL (0.35 mmol/L).
- Allopurinol is the agent of choice for patients with overproduction of uric acid, renal insufficiency, nephrolithiasis, tophi, or intolerance to uricosuric therapy.

Calcium Pyrophosphate Dihydrate Deposition Disease

Pathophysiology and Epidemiology

Alterations of inorganic pyrophosphate metabolism within the cartilage matrix and abnormalities in calcium metabolism predominantly favor the formation of calcium pyrophosphate dihydrate (CPPD) crystals. These crystals develop within the cartilage and may provoke an acute inflammatory response. The presence of CPPD crystals also stimulates mediators of cartilage degradation.

The prevalence of CPPD deposition disease increases with age, as does chondrocalcinosis (calcification within the joint cartilage secondary to CPPD deposition). Neither of these conditions, however, is considered a normal consequence of the aging process. Hypophosphatasia, hypomagnesemia, hypothyroidism, hemochromatosis, and hyperparathyroidism may be associated with CPPD deposition disease.

Clinical Manifestations

Many patients with CPPD deposition disease are asymptomatic. Symptom presentation is highly variable, including pseudogout, pseudo-osteoarthritis, pseudorheumatoid arthritis, and pseudoneuropathic joint disease. CPPD deposition disease is commonly known as pseudogout because acute mono- or pauciarticular inflammatory joint attacks of this condition mimic acute attacks of gout. Pseudogout attacks may be precipitated by surgery or illness. Pseudo-osteoarthritis, which is a more common presentation than pseudogout,

mimics osteoarthritis but involves the wrists, metacarpophalangeal joints, shoulders, ankles, hips, and knees. Pseudorheumatoid arthritis is a rare presentation of CPPD deposition disease that manifests as a symmetric polyarticular disease accompanied by the morning stiffness, fatigue, and swelling. Pseudoneuropathic joint disease, named for its resemblance to neuropathic arthropathy, is also rare and manifests as severely destructive monoarticular arthritis that develops in neurologically intact patients.

Diagnosis

CPPD deposition disease is diagnosed by the identification of weakly positive birefringent CPPD crystals on synovial fluid analysis. Inflammatory synovial fluid occurs in patients with pseudogout attacks and those who have pseudorheumatoid arthritis, whereas noninflammatory fluid is associated with pseudo-osteoarthritis. The presence of chondrocalcinosis on radiography also suggests a diagnosis of CPPD deposition disease (**Figure 32**).

In asymptomatic patients, CPPD deposition disease is diagnosed by the incidental identification of crystals on joint fluid analysis or chondrocalcinosis on radiography. Screening for underlying conditions includes measurement of serum calcium, phosphorus, magnesium, alkaline phosphatase, ferritin, and iron levels, as well as the total iron binding capacity.

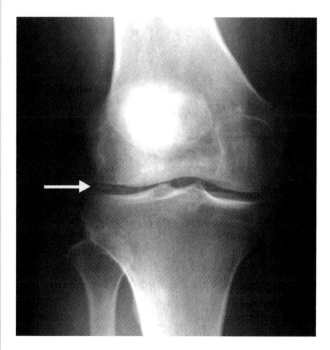

FIGURE 32.
Chondrocalcinosis.
This radiograph shows chondrocalcinosis in a patient with calcium pyrophosphate dihydrate deposition disease.

Reprinted with permission from Yee AMF and Paget SA, eds. Expert Guide to Rheumatology. Philadelphia: American College of Physicians; 2004.

Treatment

The treatment of acute attacks of CPPD deposition disease is the same as for acute attacks of gout. NSAIDs are the primary therapy for chronic disease, but maintenance therapy with colchicine is effective in some patients.

KEY POINTS

- Calcium pyrophosphate dihydrate deposition disease is usually asymptomatic but may manifest as pseudogout; pseudo-osteoarthritis; or, rarely, pseudorheumatoid arthritis or pseudoneuropathic joint disease.
- Calcium pyrophosphate dihydrate deposition disease is diagnosed by the identification of weakly positive birefringent calcium pyrophosphate dihydrate crystals on synovial fluid analysis.
- NSAIDs are the primary therapy for chronic calcium pyrophosphate dihydrate deposition disease, but maintenance therapy with colchicine is effective in some patients.

Basic Calcium Phosphate Deposition Disease

Basic calcium phosphate (BCP) crystals are composed of carbonate-substituted hydroxyapatite, octacalcium phosphate, and tricalcium phosphate. They are too small to be identified on polarized light microscopy and are poorly understood and under-recognized. BCP crystals can be identified in approximately 50% of osteoarthritic joints, which raises speculation as to their role in osteoarthritis.

BCP crystals are most commonly associated with a large-joint destructive process such as Milwaukee shoulder, which typically affects elderly women and manifests as chronic shoulder pain and a large noninflammatory effusion that may be bloody. Active motion is markedly limited because of the destruction of articular cartilage and associated tendon structures that develop in this setting, whereas passive motion is preserved. BCP crystals also may develop in other joints and have been associated with acute calcific periarthritis, asymptomatic periarticular calcification, diffuse idiopathic skeletal hyperostosis, and calcification of spinal ligaments and disks. Therapy includes NSAIDs, joint aspiration and injection, physical therapy, and occasionally surgical intervention.

KEY POINT

- Basic calcium phosphate crystals are most commonly associated with Milwaukee shoulder, which manifests as chronic shoulder pain and a large noninflammatory effusion.

Bibliography
Choi HK, Mount DB, Reginato AM; American College of Physicians; American Physiological Society. Pathogenesis of gout. Ann Intern Med. 2005;143(7):499-516. [PMID: 16204163]

Keith MP, Gilliland WR. Updates in the management of gout. Am J Med. 2007;120(3):221-224. [PMID: 17349440]

Roddy E, Zhang W, Doherty M. The changing epidemiology of gout. Nat Clin Pract Rheumatol. 2007;3(8):443-449. [PMID: 17664951]

Stamp LK, O'Donnell JL, Chapman PT. Emerging therapies in the long-term management of hyperuricaemia and gout. 2007;37(4):258-266. [PMID: 17388867]

Infectious Arthritis

Septic arthritis is a medical emergency. Hematogenous spread is the most common mechanism of joint infection because the synovium has no basement membrane and is therefore particularly vulnerable to infection. Inoculation of the joint from a bite, thorn, invasive procedure, or other trauma also may cause infection. Risk factors for septic arthritis include systemic and local factors.

Diagnosis

Septic arthritis should be considered in any patient who presents with the sudden onset of monoarthritis or the acute worsening of chronic joint disease. In patients with underlying rheumatologic disorders, a sudden joint flare that is not accompanied by other features of the pre-existing disorder and is unresponsive to usual therapy particularly suggests a diagnosis of infectious arthritis.

Clinical Manifestations

A history of joint pain, joint swelling, and fever are the only findings associated with septic arthritis that occur in more than 50% of affected patients. Approximately 85% to 90% of patients have involvement of only one joint. Common sites of infection include the knee, wrists, ankles, and hips.

Physical Examination

The pattern of joint involvement and associated tendinitis or enthesitis should be assessed in patients with suspected septic arthritis. The hallmark of a septic joint is pain on passive range of motion in the absence of trauma, and an infected joint typically appears swollen and warm with overlying erythema. The presence of tenosynovitis is suggestive of gonococcal arthritis.

A complete dermatologic examination should be performed to evaluate for pustular lesions, ecchymoses, petechiae, bullae, and necrotic lesions located over the mucosal surfaces, trunk, hands, and upper and lower extremities. These lesions suggest bacteremia, particularly disseminated gonococcal infection. Evaluation of other organ systems and sites of possible infection, such as the urinary tract and intra-abdominal area, also is warranted.

Laboratory Studies

Synovial fluid analysis, including cell count, Gram stain, culture, and crystal identification, is indicated in all patients with monoarthritis.

The synovial fluid in patients with septic arthritis is cloudy and less viscous than that in patients with other forms of arthritis. Infected fluid is usually purulent, with a leukocyte count higher than 50,000/µL and a predominance of polymorphonuclear cells. A synovial fluid leukocyte count near 100,000/µL with 90% neutrophils is specific for acute bacterial infection. However, patients who are immunosuppressed, have infection caused by *Mycobacterium* or *Neisseria* species, or have a prosthetic joint infection may have a lower synovial fluid leukocyte count. A count between 10,000/µL and 30,000/µL with 50% neutrophils suggests mycobacterial or fungal arthritis. Gram staining of synovial fluid may help to guide initial antibiotic coverage until culture results are available.

Septic arthritis can develop in patients with gout or pseudogout, and the presence of crystals in synovial fluid does not exclude a concomitant infection. Therefore, empiric antibiotic treatment is indicated in patients whose condition is suspicious for septic arthritis and have crystal formation visible on synovial fluid analysis. Blood cultures are indicated in all patients with suspected septic arthritis, particularly those who have features suggestive of or risk factors for endocarditis, such as an intravascular catheter.

Plain radiographs of the infected joint are indicated to identify joint damage and the remote possibility of concomitant osteomyelitis. CT scanning or MRI may be more sensitive than radiography for diagnosing osteomyelitis in early disease and are particularly useful in the evaluation of the hip, sternoclavicular, or sacroiliac joints. CT scanning helps to guide aspiration of the hip; MRI helps to reveal adjacent soft-tissue edema and periarticular abscesses and to facilitate adequate débridement and drainage.

Biopsy of the synovium occasionally is indicated for patients with an indolent infection who have persistently negative cultures and a poor response to empiric therapy.

KEY POINTS

- Septic arthritis should be considered in patients with sudden-onset monoarthritis or the acute worsening of chronic joint disease in a single joint.
- The hallmark of a septic joint is pain on passive range of motion in the absence of known trauma.
- Synovial fluid analysis should be performed in all patients with monoarthritis and should include cell count, Gram stain, cultures, and crystal analysis.
- Septic arthritis can develop in patients with gout or pseudogout, and the presence of crystals in synovial fluid does not exclude a concomitant infection.
- Empiric antibiotic treatment is indicated in patients whose condition is suspicious for septic arthritis and who have crystal formation visible on microscopic synovial fluid analysis.

Common Causes

Infection with Gram-Positive Organisms

Staphylococcus aureus is the most common gram-positive organism affecting native and prosthetic joints, and infection with the methicillin-resistant strain is becoming increasingly common (**Table 15**). Coagulase-negative staphylococci often cause septic arthritis in patients with prosthetic joints, hardware, or the presence of foreign bodies in the joint; these pathogens also are resistant to certain antibiotics, including methicillin.

Non–group A β-hemolytic streptococcal septic arthritis is caused by bacteremia associated with either an intravascular focus or increased permeability due to inflammation or perforation of the mucosa of the gastrointestinal or genitourinary tract. Patients infected with non–group A β-hemolytic streptococci usually present with monoarthritis, although more than one third of patients with *Streptococcus pneumoniae* infection have polyarticular involvement.

TABLE 15 Common Causes of Septic Arthritis

Gram-Positive Organisms
Staphylococcus aureus
Coagulase-negative staphylococcal species
Non–group A β-hemolytic streptococcal species
Streptococcus pyogenes
Streptococcus agalactiae
Streptococcus pneumoniae
Gram-Negative Organisms
Escherichia coli
Pseudomonas aeruginosa
Haemophilus influenzae
Gonococcal Infection
Neisseria gonorrhoeae
Mycobacterial Organisms
Mycobacterium tuberculosis
Mycobacterium marinum
Fungal Organisms
Sporothrix schenckii
Histoplasma species
Cryptococcus species
Blastomyces species
Viral Organisms
Parvovirus B19
Hepatitis B
Hepatitis C
Rubella

Infection with Gram-Negative Organisms

Gram-negative infections are more common in elderly, immunosuppressed, and postoperative patients and those with intravenous catheters. The most common gram-negative pathogens that cause septic arthritis are rod-shaped enteric organisms, such as *Escherichia coli* and hospital-acquired *Pseudomonas aeruginosa*. Infection with these organisms is associated with a high rate of complications from the underlying condition and the severity of the arthritis. *Haemophilus influenzae* only occasionally causes septic arthritis, and infection with this organism is easier to manage compared with other gram-negative rod-shaped pathogens.

Disseminated Gonococcal Infection

Gonococcal arthritis is the most common form of bacterial arthritis in young sexually active persons in the United States. This condition manifests as either a purulent arthritis or a syndrome of disseminated gonococcemia. The arthritis usually involves one or two joints, most commonly the knees, wrists, ankles, or elbows. Disseminated gonococcemia is characterized by a prodrome of tenosynovitis, polyarthralgia, and cutaneous lesions that progress from papules or macules to pustules and usually are sterile on culture (**Figure 33**). Fever and rigors are common.

Most patients with purulent gonococcal arthritis do not have systemic features or cutaneous involvement. Gonococcal arthritis should be considered in sexually active patients who present with migratory tenosynovitis and arthralgia. Blood cultures for *N. gonorrhoeae* are positive in 50% of infected patients, particularly in those with disseminated gonococcal disease who have the characteristic pustular rash and tenosynovitis. Obtaining culture specimens from the pharynx, genitals, and rectum in addition to synovial fluid cultures increases the diagnostic yield for *N. gonorrhoeae*. All patients with gonorrhea also should be evaluated for HIV infection, syphilis, and *Chlamydia* infection. Treatment for presumed coinfection with *Chlamydia* is indicated.

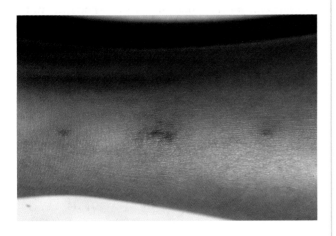

FIGURE 33.
Cutaneous lesions associated with disseminated gonococcal infection.

Infection with Mycobacterial Organisms

Mycobacterium tuberculosis

Tuberculous disease of the bones or joints is believed to be a reactivation of a focus of bacilli that becomes lodged in the bone after a remote primary infection. Therapy with tumor necrosis factor α inhibitors is a risk factor for reactivation tuberculosis.

Tuberculous infection of the joints manifests as osteomyelitis more often than arthritis. The most common sites of infection are the lower thoracic and lumbar spine. The most commonly involved peripheral joints are the large, weight-bearing joints, such as the hip and knee.

Tuberculous arthritis usually is indolent, typically does not cause systemic features, and is not typically associated with a delayed-type hypersensitivity response to purified protein derivative testing. Therefore, it is often diagnosed late in the disease course after patients have not responded to therapy for joint pain or empiric antibiotic therapy.

Synovial fluid cultures for *M. tuberculosis* are the gold standard for diagnosis of tuberculous arthritis. Synovial fluid in patients with tuberculous arthritis usually is inflammatory with a predominance of polymorphonuclear cells. Gram staining for this pathogen usually is negative.

When synovial fluid culture results are negative despite a high index of suspicion for *M. tuberculosis* infection, synovial biopsy may be warranted. Molecular testing for *M. tuberculosis* also may be helpful.

Mycobacterium marinum

M. marinum is an atypical mycobacterium associated with exposure to freshwater or saltwater, swimming pools, and fish tanks. Infection is acquired by local inoculation through swimming, handling fish, boating, or other marine activities.

The hand is the most common site of infection with *M. marinum*. Infection often initially manifests as mild, slowly progressive tenosynovitis, although dysfunction of the flexor tendons can be functionally limiting. Nodular cutaneous papules that progress to shallow ulcerated lesions also may develop.

Positive culture results for *M. marinum* are highly desirable to establish a diagnosis, but empiric treatment based on the clinical presentation may be indicated.

Infection with Fungal Organisms

Fungal arthritis is rare, occurring most frequently in immunosuppressed patients. The most common infecting organisms are *Candida*, *Aspergillus*, and *Cryptococcus* species. Fungal arthritis also may affect patients who live in endemic areas for *Sporothrix schenckii* and *Blastomyces*, *Coccidioides*, or *Histoplasma* species.

Fungal arthritis typically manifests as subacute monoarthritis in patients with a systemic fungal infection. Fungal arthritis due to hematogenous spread of *Candida* in native or prosthetic joints has been increasing in frequency because of the rising incidence of *Candida* infections in hospitalized and chronically ill patients. Cryptococcal arthritis is rare and usually is caused by local spread of disease from adjacent osteomyelitis in immunosuppressed patients.

S. schenckii arthritis can occur through local inoculation into the joint or by hematogenous spread. This pathogen is associated with plant litter and other organic materials, but rose thorns are the most well-known vectors.

S. schenckii arthritis usually manifests as progressive joint pain, swelling, and loss of range of motion. Osteomyelitis also can occur because of spread from an adjacent joint, and draining sinuses often develop in the overlying skin.

Coccidioidomycosis, blastomycosis, and histoplasmosis usually manifest as primary pulmonary infections that disseminate to involve the joints and bones. Erythema nodosum also may be associated with fungal arthritis.

Infection with Viral Organisms

Viral arthritis usually is a mild to moderate polyarticular self-limited condition. It also may be associated with rash.

Viral arthritis usually resolves within a few weeks to months with supportive therapy. Patients with chronic hepatitis B and C virus infection often have chronic polyarthralgia, but a true inflammatory arthritis is less common.

Parvovirus B19

Parvovirus B19 is transmitted through hand-to-hand contact or respiratory secretions. Infection occurs most commonly during the winter and spring. Mothers of young children and day care workers are at higher risk for acquiring the virus from infected children than is the general population.

The presentation of parvovirus B19 infection may be indistinguishable from early rheumatoid arthritis or systemic lupus erythematosus. Manifestations include a symmetric nonerosive arthritis that usually involves the small joints of the hands and feet and the knees. Erythema infectiosum, or "slapped cheek" rash, often develops in infected children but is uncommon in adults.

Many adults with parvovirus B19 infection develop autoantibodies, particularly rheumatoid factor and antinuclear antibodies, which may persist for years. Diagnosis is confirmed by the presence of specific IgM antibodies.

Rubella

Acute rubella is characterized by rash, fever, and lymphadenopathy. A self-limited symmetric arthritis also may occur with primary infection or after rubella vaccination.

Joint symptoms in patients with acute rubella usually manifest at the time of onset of the acute infection, whereas arthritis associated with rubella vaccination usually manifests 2 weeks after inoculation. Arthritis usually resolves within weeks; joint pain may persist, but destructive joint disease does not develop.

Prosthetic Joint Infections

Complicated joint replacement procedures, such as revision arthroplasty, are associated with a higher rate of infection than simpler procedures. Overlying skin infection in a patient who has recently undergone arthroplasty strongly suggests a prosthetic joint infection.

Prosthetic joint infections that occur within the first post-operative year likely result from contamination of the operative wound and commonly manifest as fever, swelling, pain, and poor wound healing.

Infections that occur after the first postoperative year are related to the hematogenous spread of organisms to the prosthetic joint or a delayed response to low-intensity pathogens, such as coagulase-negative staphylococci. Pain may be the only manifestation in these later-onset infections, which might be confused with loosening of the implanted prosthesis.

The gold standard for the diagnosis of prosthetic joint infections is tissue sampling via arthrocentesis or open débridement. Measurement of erythrocyte sedimentation rate or C-reactive protein may help in the diagnosis. Imaging modalities such as radionuclide bone scanning also are not specific. Plain films may show prosthesis loosening, which can be present in both infected and uninfected prosthetic joints.

Surgery may be warranted in patients with a prosthetic joint infection and involves removing the infected prosthesis, placing an antibiotic-impregnated articulating spacer, and initiating antibiotic therapy for at least 4 to 6 weeks. Once the joint is sterile, a new prosthesis is implanted. This two-stage procedure is associated with significant morbidity and prolonged immobilization.

Débridement and prolonged antibiotic therapy without removal of the prosthesis may be appropriate for some patients, including frail patients who should not undergo two-stage replacement arthroplasty. Such treatment is most effective in patients with early-onset postoperative infection or early-onset hematogenous infection caused by penicillin-susceptible streptococci who do not have infection with *Staphylococcus aureus*. Additional factors associated with a positive outcome include a history of arthroscopic drainage within 7 days of symptom onset and an absence of radiologic signs of prosthesis loosening or osteitis. This method has a high failure rate, is associated with significant drug toxicity, and commonly causes superinfection.

Infections in Previously Damaged Joints

Joints that have been previously damaged are more likely to become infected than structurally normal joints. Septic arthritis also is more likely to be associated with a poor outcome in patients who have a pre-existing arthritis.

Patients with rheumatoid arthritis usually have used intra-articular corticosteroids and/or immunosuppressive agents at some point in their disease course and are therefore particularly susceptible to infection. Septic arthritis also is more likely to have a polyarticular presentation in patients with pre-existing rheumatoid arthritis than in other patients.

- *Staphylococcus aureus* is the most common organism that affects both native and prosthetic joints.
- Gram-negative joint infections are more common in elderly, immunosuppressed, and postoperative patients and those with intravenous catheters in place.
- Disseminated gonococcemia is characterized by a prodrome of tenosynovitis, polyarthralgia, migratory arthritis, and cutaneous lesions and should be considered in sexually active young persons.
- Overlying skin infection in a patient who has recently undergone arthroplasty strongly suggests a prosthetic joint infection.
- The gold standard for the diagnosis of prosthetic joint infections is tissue sampling via arthrocentesis or open débridement.

Management

Pharmacologic Therapy

In patients with suspected septic arthritis, empiric systemic antibiotic therapy is indicated until culture results are available (**Table 16**). Vancomycin or another broad-spectrum agent active against gram-positive bacteria is the empiric therapy of choice unless the patient's presentation or Gram stain results suggest infection with a methicillin-susceptible pathogen.

In patients with *N. gonorrhoeae* septic arthritis, antibiotic therapy for 2 weeks or less is usually sufficient; initially, parenteral therapy is given but oral therapy can usually be started 24 to 48 hours after clinical improvement is demonstrated. However, in nongonococcal septic arthritis, the duration of parenteral therapy is determined by the infecting pathogen, the site of infection, and the presence of comorbidities. Some patients infected with particularly virulent pathogens may require 6 weeks or more of parenteral therapy.

Topical or intra-articular antibiotic therapy is not indicated in septic arthritis. Patients infected with unusual organisms or who have a poor response to therapy should be referred to a rheumatologist or infectious disease specialist.

Nonpharmacologic Therapy

Arthrocentesis is critical to control acute infection but may not be needed in patients who demonstrate an early clinical response to pharmacologic therapy. Arthrocentesis can be performed at least once daily and should be continued until the synovial fluid leukocyte count decreases and the fluid becomes sterile.

Patients who do not respond well to arthrocentesis or have infection in a previously damaged or difficult to access joint may require surgical drainage via arthroscopy or arthrotomy. Surgical drainage also may be indicated if sufficient staff qualified to perform repeated arthrocentesis are not available.

In patients who undergo surgical drainage, the involved joint should be immobilized for a few days. To prevent joint contractures and help restore baseline function, patients should be instructed to begin a progressive approach to moving the joint, ranging from gentle range-of-motion exercises to more intensive types of physical therapy until maximal improvement has been achieved.

TABLE 16 Empiric and Definitive Antibiotic Treatment for Septic Native Joint Arthritis

Gram Stain Results	Likely or Identified Pathogen	First-Line Therapy	Second-Line Therapy
Gram-positive cocci	*Staphylococcus aureus*, other staphylococcal species	Oxacillin/nafcillin or cefazolin	Cefazolin or nafcillin
	If MRSA is a concern (risk factors or known MRSA carrier)	Vancomycin or linezolid	Teicoplanin
Gram-negative cocci	*Neisseria gonorrhoeae*	Ceftriaxone	Fluoroquinolones
Gram-negative bacilli	Enteric gram-negative bacilli	Ceftriaxone or cefotaxime	Fluoroquinolones
	Pseudomonas aeruginosa	Ceftazidime (plus gentamicin if proven)	Carbapenems, cefepime, piperacillin-tazobactam, fluoroquinolones
Gram stain unavailable	At risk for *N. gonorrhoeae* infection	Ceftriaxone or cefotaxime	
	No risk for *N. gonorrhoeae*; *S. aureus* or gram-negative bacilli are likely	Nafcillin plus ceftazidime	Nafcillin plus quinolone

MRSA = methicillin-resistant *Staphylococcus aureus*.

- Vancomycin or another broad-spectrum agent active against gram-positive bacteria is the empiric therapy of choice for septic arthritis unless the patient's presentation or Gram stain results suggest infection with a methicillin-susceptible pathogen.

- Repeated arthrocentesis is critical in controlling acute septic joint infection.

- Surgical drainage may be warranted if patients do not respond well to percutaneous drainage or have an infection in a previously damaged or difficult-to-access joint.

Bibliography

Coakley G, Mathews C, Field M, et al; British Society for Rheumatology Standards, Guidelines and Audit Working Group. BSR & BHPR, BOA, RCGP, BSAC guidelines for management of the hot swollen joint in adults. Rheumatology (Oxford). 2006;45(8):1039-1041. [PMID: 16829534]

Gardam M, Lim S. Mycobacterial osteomyelitis and arthritis. Infect Dis Clin North Am. 2005;19(4):819-830. [PMID: 16297734]

Gracia-De La Torre I. Advances in the management of septic arthritis. Infect Dis Clin North Am. 2006;20(4):773-788. [PMID: 17118290]

Margaretten ME, Kohlwes J, Moore D, Bent S. Does this adult patient have septic arthritis? JAMA. 2007;297(13):1478-1488. [PMID: 17405973]

Rice PA. Gonococcal arthritis (disseminated gonococcal infection). Infect Dis Clin North Am. 2005;19(4):853-861. [PMID: 16297736]

Sia IG, Berbari, EF, Karchmer AW. Prosthetic joint infections. Infect Dis Clin North Am. 2005;19(4):885-914. [PMID: 16297738]

Titov AG, Vyshnevskaya EB, Mazurenko SI, Santavirta S, Konttinen YT. Use of polymerase chain reaction to diagnose tuberculous arthritis from joint tissues and synovial fluid. Arch Pathol Lab Med. 2004;128(2):205-209. [PMID: 14736282]

Idiopathic Inflammatory Myopathies

The idiopathic inflammatory myopathies are a heterogeneous group of immune-mediated disorders (**Table 17**). These disorders are characterized by the insidious onset of symmetric proximal muscle weakness that typically progresses within 3 to 6 months, the presence of a mononuclear infiltrate in multiple muscles, and autoantibody formation.

Pathophysiology and Epidemiology

The inflammatory myopathies are believed to be caused by an immune response triggered by environmental factors, especially viral infections, in genetically predisposed persons. Polymyositis and inclusion body myositis (IBM) are diseases of cellular immunity with evidence of T-cell–mediated cytotoxicity, whereas dermatomyositis is a disorder of humoral immunity.

Polymyositis may develop in patients with HIV infection early in the course of infection and may be the presenting clinical manifestation of HIV infection in these patients. However, the role of HIV infection in the development of polymyositis is not known. The inflammatory myopathies also can occur as part of other systemic autoimmune disorders, including systemic lupus erythematosus, systemic sclerosis, mixed connective tissue disease, and Sjögren syndrome or as a paraneoplastic syndrome.

The peak incidence of the idiopathic inflammatory myopathies is between 45 and 65 years of age. Patients with an inflammatory myopathy who have an underlying systemic connective tissue disease are generally younger, whereas those with IBM and a malignancy-associated myopathy are more frequently older than 60 years.

Classification and Clinical Manifestations

Muscle Involvement

Dermatomyositis and polymyositis manifest as symmetric muscle weakness that usually affects the proximal muscles. IBM is a distinct clinical disorder separate from dermatomyositis and polymyositis. Muscle weakness in patients with IBM typically is symmetric and involves both proximal and distal muscle groups. Asymmetric atrophy and neuropathic changes, such as loss of deep tendon reflexes, also may occur. IBM has a more indolent disease course than dermatomyositis and polymyositis and typically progresses over several years.

Affected patients may have difficulty with activities that involve raising their hands above their head and have difficulty rising from a chair and climbing stairs. Neck flexor muscles may be affected, and involvement of the pharyngeal muscles predisposes patients to aspiration. Muscle pain in patients with an inflammatory myopathy is atypical and, if present, is generally mild. Significant myalgia suggests an alternative diagnosis, such as arthritis, polymyalgia rheumatica, or fibromyalgia.

With disease progression, more distal muscle and respiratory muscle groups are affected, progressive loss of all mobility develops, and respiratory failure ultimately occurs. Neurologic defects such as abnormalities in sensation, coordination, and cranial nerve or autonomic function do not occur in patients with an inflammatory myopathy and when present should raise suspicion for an intracerebral, spinal cord, or neurologic disorder.

Cutaneous Involvement

Cutaneous manifestations of dermatomyositis may precede muscle disease. Gottron papules are pathognomonic for dermatomyositis, and a periorbital heliotrope rash, shawl and V signs, and mechanic's hands are characteristic (**Table 18**) (**Figure 34** and **Figure 35**). Patients with dermatomyositis

TABLE 17 The Inflammatory Myopathies

Condition	Notes
Polymyositis	An inflammatory muscle disease associated with symmetric muscle weakness. This condition initially involves the proximal muscles and progresses over months.
Dermatomyositis	An inflammatory muscle disease clinically similar to polymyositis but associated with characteristic cutaneous manifestations that may precede the onset of muscle disease.
Myositis associated with collagen vascular disease (SLE, systemic sclerosis, Sjögren syndrome, mixed connective tissue disease)	Poly- or dermatomyositis that manifests in a patient with another pre-existing or co-existing disorder such as a systemic autoimmune disorder, or as a component of mixed connective tissue disease.
Inclusion body myositis	A combination of proximal and distal weakness that may be asymmetric. More common in older people than polymyositis and has a more indolent course than this condition. This condition is characterized by the presence of inclusion bodies.
Juvenile dermatomyositis	Dermatomyositis in children.
Myositis associated with malignancy	Myositis that occurs in association with a malignancy. The muscle disease may precede the diagnosis of malignancy.

SLE = systemic lupus erythematosus.

also may have nailfold capillary abnormalities, such as periungual erythema and telangiectasias, as well as cuticle hypertrophy.

Calcinosis can develop over extensor surfaces, such as the elbows, and at sites of trauma; patients with this condition may have a sheet-like appearance within the muscle on radiography. Calcinosis occurs most commonly in patients with juvenile dermatomyositis and is a source of long-term morbidity.

Amyopathic dermatomyositis is a rare subset of dermatomyositis. Patients with this condition develop the cutaneous manifestations characteristic of dermatomyositis in the absence of muscle involvement.

Cardiopulmonary Involvement

Interstitial lung disease (ILD) with progressive pulmonary fibrosis and secondary pulmonary arterial hypertension is one of the leading causes of death in patients with polymyositis and dermatomyositis. ILD may be prominent at the onset of myopathy or develop over the course of the disease. The presence of anti–Jo-1 antibodies is associated with an increased risk for ILD.

Patients with ILD have progressive dyspnea, basilar crackles, bibasilar infiltrates on chest radiographs, and restrictive changes on pulmonary function studies. Differentiating between pulmonary manifestations due to pulmonary fibrosis and those due to aspiration pneumonia and respiratory muscle weakness is critical. Pulmonary symptoms in patients with aspiration pneumonia typically have a more acute or intermittent course and a more asymmetric infiltrative pattern on chest radiographs. Swallowing studies may be necessary to document the aspiration. Respiratory muscle failure may develop in patients with profound end-stage loss of muscle function; however, this feature can be detected earlier on pulmonary function testing.

Cardiac involvement in patients with an inflammatory myopathy is rare and includes arrhythmias and cardiomyopathy.

Additional Systemic Manifestations

Additional systemic manifestations of the inflammatory myopathies include constitutional symptoms, such as fever, weight loss, and malaise. Arthralgia or inflammatory arthritis and Raynaud phenomenon with possible digital ischemia also may occur. Gastrointestinal involvement includes motility disorders accompanied by regurgitation and reflux. Vasculitis may be present but is more common in patients with juvenile dermatomyositis.

KEY POINTS

- Dermatomyositis and polymyositis manifest as symmetric muscle weakness that usually affects the proximal muscles.

- Muscle weakness in patients with inclusion body myositis typically is symmetric and involves both proximal and distal muscle groups.

- Muscle pain in patients with an inflammatory myopathy is atypical and, if present, is generally mild.

- Gottron papules are pathognomonic for dermatomyositis, and a periorbital heliotrope rash, shawl and V signs, and mechanic's hands are characteristic of this condition.

- Interstitial lung disease is one of the leading causes of death in patients with polymyositis and dermatomyositis.

Diagnosis

A diagnosis of an inflammatory myopathy is established in patients with a compatible clinical presentation accompanied

TABLE 18 Rashes Associated with Dermatomyositis

Condition	Findings
Gottron papules	Violaceous to pink plaques with scaling overlying the extensor surface of the hand joints, knees, and elbows
Heliotrope rash	Violaceous discoloration of the eyelids accompanied by periorbital edema
Macular erythema	Photosensitive rash involving the face and neck
	Shawl sign: rash involves the posterior neck, upper back, and shoulders
	V sign: rash involves the anterior neck and chest
Mechanic's hands	Rough, scaly lesions with fissuring of the skin over the lateral margins and pads of the fingers

by elevated muscle enzyme levels and characteristic pathologic findings on muscle biopsy. Characteristic muscle changes on electromyography and/or MRI may help support the diagnosis, exclude alternative conditions such as neurologic disorders, and help identify an appropriate biopsy site. The presence of a myositis-specific autoantibody or a rash that is characteristic of dermatomyositis may help to establish a diagnosis.

Laboratory Studies

Patients with an inflammatory myopathy may have an elevated erythrocyte sedimentation rate or C-reactive protein levels. However, these findings are not helpful diagnostically or in monitoring disease activity.

Muscle Enzymes

Creatine kinase measurement is the most sensitive and specific laboratory study for muscle damage and is therefore useful in diagnosing and monitoring disease activity in patients with an inflammatory myopathy. At presentation, more than 95% of patients with an inflammatory myopathy have creatine kinase levels more than twice the normal range.

However, the magnitude of the creatine kinase level may not correlate with disease severity. Despite the presence of muscle weakness and evidence of active disease, creatine

kinase levels may be normal or only slightly elevated in patients who have an indolent disease course, low levels of muscle inflammation, low muscle mass, or extensive muscle atrophy. IBM is associated with only modestly elevated creatine kinase levels.

Once the creatine kinase levels in patients with an inflammatory myopathy decrease, several weeks may pass before muscle strength improves. Elevated levels also are not specific for the inflammatory myopathies. Other causes for elevations in these levels include trauma, statin use, thyroid disease, electrolyte abnormalities, and other neuromuscular disorders.

Active muscle disease is associated with an increase in aspartate aminotransferase, alanine aminotransferase, lactate dehydrogenase, and aldolase levels. However, none of these enzymes are specific for muscle disease and do not help to establish the diagnosis.

Autoantibodies

Autoantibody assays may be useful in distinguishing an inflammatory myopathy from other causes of muscle weakness. Up to 80% of patients with an inflammatory myopathy have antinuclear autoantibodies, and most of these patients have a speckled pattern. However, the predictive value of a positive antinuclear antibody assay is low because this study has a low specificity.

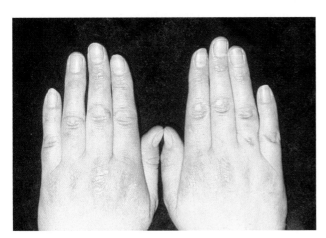

FIGURE 34.
Gottron papules.
Gottron papules affecting the hand joints in a patient with dermatomyositis.

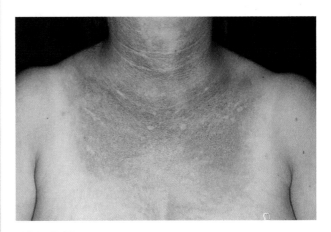

FIGURE 35.
V sign.
This V-shaped photosensitive erythematous rash is characteristic of dermatomyositis.

Certain autoantibodies are so specific for the inflammatory myopathies that they are diagnostic in patients with a compatible clinical presentation. In this setting, further invasive studies such as muscle biopsy are not needed. Anti–Jo-1 antibodies occur in up to 20% of affected patients. Assays for this antibody also are the most commercially available autoantibody assays for the inflammatory myopathies. Anti–Jo-1 antibodies are part of a family of autoantibodies directed against various transfer RNA synthetases and are specific for histidyl-transfer RNA synthetase. Patients with anti–Jo-1 antibodies are more likely to have ILD, inflammatory arthritis, fever, and Raynaud phenomenon than other patients with inflammatory myopathy, as well as a higher mortality rate.

Patients with an inflammatory myopathy who have antiribonucleoprotein antibodies, which are associated with mixed connective tissue disease, often have features of systemic sclerosis and systemic lupus erythematosus.

Imaging Studies

MRI of the proximal muscles, particularly the thighs, is increasingly being used in assessing the degree of muscle inflammation and damage and can help to localize a biopsy site. Fat-suppressed T2-weighted MRI can reveal active muscle inflammation with edema, whereas T1-weighted MRI can demonstrate atrophy and fatty infiltration. However, these changes are not specific for myositis. Furthermore, the usefulness of MRI as an ancillary diagnostic test is unknown, as studies supporting the use of MRI are few and include only small numbers of patients.

Electromyography

Electromyography and nerve-conduction velocity studies can suggest a myopathic process and help to exclude other disorders, such as neuropathic conditions.

Changes on electromyography that are characteristic but not diagnostic of an active myopathy include increased insertional activity, fibrillations, high-frequency discharges, and polyphasic motor unit potentials of low amplitude and short duration. Results of electromyography in patients with IBM frequently reveal mixed myopathic and neuropathic patterns.

Muscle Biopsy

Muscle biopsy is the gold standard for diagnosing an inflammatory myopathy, and an open biopsy is preferred to a needle biopsy. Biopsy can confirm the inflammatory changes associated with the inflammatory myopathies and exclude other causes of an elevated creatine kinase level, such as mitochondrial myopathy and enzyme deficiencies. However, muscle involvement in the myopathies may be patchy, and the false-negative rate for muscle biopsy can be as high as 25%.

The diagnostic yield of muscle biopsy is highest when a clinically involved muscle is biopsied and may be maximized if MRI is used to identify a biopsy site. Biopsy of a muscle on which electromyography has recently been performed should be avoided because the local inflammation caused by the electromyography needle can be mistaken for an inflammatory myopathy. In patients who have undergone electromyography, biopsy specimens should be obtained from the contralateral side of that studied by electromyography.

Polymyositis and Dermatomyositis

Polymyositis and dermatomyositis can often be distinguished on biopsy by the localization and composition of the inflammatory infiltrate. Biopsy specimens in patients with polymyositis reveal a lymphocytic infiltrate predominantly composed of CD8 cells localized within the muscle fascicles. In patients with dermatomyositis, B cells and CD4 cells predominate in the inflammatory infiltrate. In addition, inflammation in patients with dermatomyositis is localized to the perivascular regions and the areas surrounding the muscle fascicles. Biopsy specimens in patients with polymyositis or dermatomyositis can show varying stages of necrosis and regeneration.

Inclusion Body Myositis

Biopsy specimens in patients with IBM reveal an endomysial inflammatory infiltrate similar to that in patients with polymyositis, as well as characteristic rimmed vacuoles. Electron microscopy of these specimens in patients with IBM reveals intracellular tubular or filamentous inclusions.

KEY POINTS

- More than 95% of patients with an inflammatory myopathy have elevated creatine kinase levels.
- Anti–Jo-1 antibodies are highly specific for the inflammatory myopathies and are associated with an increased risk for interstitial lung disease and death.
- In patients with muscle weakness or elevated creatine kinase levels, electromyography and nerve-conduction velocity studies can suggest a myopathic process and help to exclude neuropathic conditions.
- Muscle biopsy is the gold standard for diagnosing an inflammatory myopathy.
- In patients who have undergone electromyography, biopsy specimens should be obtained from the contralateral side of that studied by electromyography.

Treatment

Physical and occupational therapy are crucial adjuncts to pharmacologic therapy in patients with an inflammatory myopathy. Exercise improves aerobic capacity and strength and provides cardiopulmonary benefits. Exercise also is not typically associated with increases in muscle enzyme levels, which are indicative of muscle dysfunction.

High-dose oral corticosteroid therapy is first-line treatment for polymyositis and dermatomyositis. However, patients with profound muscle disease or life-threatening manifestations may require intravenous pulse corticosteroid administration.

Patients with an inflammatory myopathy who are using corticosteroids should undergo regular muscle strength monitoring and measurement of creatine kinase. Most patients respond at least partially to corticosteroid therapy, and a clinical response typically occurs over weeks to months of therapy. Initially, the creatine kinase levels decrease, then muscle strength improves. In patients with polymyositis or dermatomyositis treated with corticosteroids, progressive weakness accompanied by significant improvement in muscle enzyme levels should raise suspicion for a corticosteroid-induced myopathy. In addition, the corticosteroid dosage must be tapered gradually over the first several months to avoid flares of muscle inflammation.

Baseline bone mineral density testing is indicated in patients who undergo long-term high-dose corticosteroid therapy. These patients also should begin prophylactic therapy for osteoporosis with calcium and vitamin D supplementation and bisphosphonates.

Additional or alternative immunosuppressive therapy is indicated for patients with polymyositis or dermatomyositis who have refractory disease, an inadequate treatment response, or intolerable side effects. Additional immunosuppressive therapy also is used as steroid-sparing agents to facilitate corticosteroid tapering in patients with persistent disease that warrants long-term corticosteroid use.

Methotrexate and azathioprine are the most commonly used adjunctive immunosuppressive agents, but monthly administration of intravenous immune globulin is increasingly used in patients with refractory disease. Other immunosuppressive agents used include cyclophosphamide, 6-mercaptopurine, chlorambucil, and cyclosporine. Hydroxychloroquine may help to treat cutaneous manifestations of dermatomyositis but not muscle involvement. Patients with IBM respond poorly to immunosuppressive therapy, and whether aggressive therapy is appropriate in this setting remains uncertain.

KEY POINTS

- High-dose oral corticosteroid therapy is first-line treatment for polymyositis and dermatomyositis.
- In patients with polymyositis or dermatomyositis treated with corticosteroids, progressive weakness accompanied by significant improvement in muscle enzyme levels should raise suspicion for a corticosteroid-induced myopathy.
- Additional or alternative immunosuppressive therapy is indicated for patients with polymyositis or dermatomyositis treated with corticosteroids who have refractory disease, an inadequate treatment response, or intolerable side effects to this therapy.
- Patients with inclusion body myositis respond poorly to immunosuppressive therapy.

Malignancy and the Idiopathic Inflammatory Myopathies

Screening for an occult malignancy is indicated in patients newly diagnosed with an inflammatory myopathy and should be considered in patients whose disease is refractory to aggressive immunosuppressive treatment. The history and physical examination findings should guide this screening, which should include recommended age-appropriate and sex-specific screening tests.

Typically, malignancy occurs in older patients and more often develops in those with dermatomyositis. Malignancy may predate or present within the first few years after the development of an inflammatory myopathy. The types of malignancies are similar to those in an age-matched population without myopathy except that women with this condition have a higher rate of ovarian cancer. It is reasonable to consider endoscopic and imaging studies to exclude nasopharyngeal, gastrointestinal, pulmonary, intra-abdominal, and pelvic (particularly ovarian) malignancies; Asian patients in particular are likely to develop nasopharyngeal malignancies.

KEY POINTS

- Screening for an occult malignancy is indicated in adult patients newly diagnosed with an inflammatory myopathy.
- Malignancy associated with the inflammatory myopathies typically occurs in older patients and more often develops in those with dermatomyositis.

Prognosis

Improved diagnostic capabilities and increased use of immunosuppressive therapy have markedly increased long-term survival in patients with inflammatory myopathies. The 5-year survival rate exceeds 80%. However, less than one third of affected patients achieve long-term remission.

Some patients with an inflammatory myopathy have a relapsing-remitting disease course, whereas others require long-term immunosuppressive therapy. The following features are associated with a poorer prognosis: profound muscle weakness; older age at diagnosis; associated malignancy; delayed initiation of corticosteroid therapy or a refractory response to therapy; and the presence of pulmonary disease, including aspiration pneumonia and interstitial fibrosis.

KEY POINTS

- Some patients with an inflammatory myopathy have a relapsing-remitting disease course, whereas others require long-term immunosuppressive therapy.
- In patients with an inflammatory myopathy, poor prognosis is associated with profound muscle weakness; older age at diagnosis; associated malignancy; delayed initiation of corticosteroid therapy or a refractory response to this therapy; and the presence of pulmonary disease.

Bibliography

Fathi M, Lundberg IE, Tornling G. Pulmonary complications of the polymyositis and dermatomyositis. Semin Respir Crit Care Med. 2007;28(4):451-458. [PMID: 17764062]

Hengstman GJ. Advances in the immunopathophysiology of the idiopathic inflammatory myopathies: not as simple as suspected. Curr Rheumatol Rep. 2007;9(4):280-285. [PMID: 17688836]

Needham M, Mastaglia FL. Inclusion body myositis: current pathogenetic concepts and diagnostic and therapeutic approaches. Lancet Neurol. 2007;6(7):620-631. [PMID: 17582362]

Targoff IN. Myositis specific autoantibodies. Curr Rheumatol Rep. 2006;8(3):196-203. [PMID: 16901077]

Tomasová Studynková J, Charvát F, Jarosová K, Vencovsky J. The role of MRI in the assessment of polymyositis and dermatomyositis. Rheumatology (Oxford). 2007;46(7):1174-1179. [PMID: 17500079]

Ytterverg SR. Treatment of refractory polymyositis and dermatomyositis. Curr Rheumatol Rep. 2006;8(3):167-173. [PMID: 16901073]

Systemic Vasculitis

Vasculitis refers to an inflammation in the blood vessel walls that causes vessel narrowing, blockage, aneurysm, or rupture. This condition is classified according to the size of the vessels affected (**Table 19**).

Vasculitis can be a primary disease, occur secondary to another condition, or develop in response to a medication or infection. Patients with vasculitis may present with purpura, constitutional symptoms that reflect the systemic nature of this condition, or manifestations of ischemia in affected organs (**Table 20**).

Large-Vessel Vasculitis

Giant Cell Arteritis

Pathophysiology and Epidemiology

Giant cell arteritis (GCA) is a granulomatous vasculitis that most commonly affects the large and medium-sized arteries of the head and neck, including the temporal, ophthalmic, and posterior ciliary arteries. Subclinical involvement of the proximal and distal aorta also is common. In addition, GCA may involve the internal and external carotid arteries but typically spares the intracranial vessels. It occurs in patients older than 50 years and has a 2:1 female predominance.

Clinical Manifestations and Diagnosis

Most patients with GCA present with headache that typically involves the temporal area. Approximately 33% of affected patients have symptoms of polymyalgia rheumatica or visual

TABLE 19 Primary Vasculitic Diseases	
Condition	**Characteristics**
Large-Vessel Vasculitis	
Giant cell arteritis	Headache, visual abnormalities, jaw claudication, constitutional symptoms, polymyalgia rheumatica
Polymyalgia rheumatica	Aching in the shoulders, neck, and hip girdle region; fatigue, malaise
Takayasu arteritis	An inflammatory phase characterized by fever, arthralgias, myalgias, malaise, weight loss; a pulseless phase characterized by arm or leg claudication, hypertension, headache
Medium-Sized Vessel Vasculitis	
Polyarteritis nodosa	Mononeuritis multiplex, hypertension, testicular pain, abdominal pain, arthralgias, fever, weight loss; cutaneous, renal, mesenteric, or nerve involvement
Kawasaki disease	Fever, conjunctivitis, erythema of the oral mucous membranes, erythema or edema of the extremities, cervical lymphadenopathy, coronary aneurysms; occurs in children
Small-Vessel Vasculitis	
Wegener granulomatosis	Upper-airway disease (sinusitis, epistaxis), mononeuritis multiplex, c-ANCA positivity; pulmonary, ocular, or renal disease
Microscopic polyangiitis	Renal or pulmonary involvement, fever, arthralgias, purpura, mononeuritis multiplex, c-ANCA positivity
Churg-Strauss syndrome	Asthma, rhinitis, sinusitis, migratory pulmonary infiltrates, mononeuritis multiplex, purpura, fever, arthralgias, myalgias; cardiac, renal, or gastrointestinal involvement; 50% of affected patients have positive titers of p-ANCA
Henoch-Schönlein purpura	Purpura, abdominal pain, renal disease, arthritis; occurs more frequently in children
Essential cryoglobulinemic vasculitis	Purpura, arthralgias, lymphadenopathy, hepatosplenomegaly, renal disease, mononeuritis multiplex, hypocomplementemia; associated with hepatitis C virus infection
Cutaneous leukocytoclastic vasculitis	Palpable purpura; occurs in patients with connective tissue diseases and as a reaction to drugs or viruses

TABLE 20 Differential Diagnosis of Vasculitis	
Disease	**Characteristics**
Infection (sepsis, endocarditis, hepatitis)	Heart murmur, rash, and/or musculoskeletal symptoms can occur in bacterial endocarditis or viral hepatitis. Obtain blood cultures, hepatitis B and C serologic studies, and an echocardiogram.
Drug toxicity/poisoning	Cocaine, amphetamines, ephedra alkaloids, and phenylpropanolamine may produce vasospasm, resulting in symptoms of ischemia. Perform toxicology screen.
Coagulopathy	Occlusive diseases (disseminated intravascular coagulation, antiphospholipid syndrome, thrombotic thrombocytopenic purpura) can produce ischemic symptoms. Perform coagulation panel and test for hypercoagulability.
Malignancy	Paraneoplastic vasculitis is rare. Any organ system may be affected, but the skin and nervous system are the most common. Vasculitic symptoms may precede, occur simultaneously with, or follow diagnosis of cancer. Lymphoma occasionally may involve the blood vessels and mimic vasculitis. Consider malignancy in patients with incomplete or no response to therapy for idiopathic vasculitis.
Atrial myxoma	Classic triad of symptoms: embolism, intracardiac obstruction leading to pulmonary congestion or congestive heart failure, and constitutional symptoms (fatigue, weight loss, fever). Skin lesions can be identical to those seen in leukocytoclastic vasculitis. Atrial myxomas are rare, but they are the most common primary intracardiac tumor. Myxomas also can occur in other cardiac chambers.
Multiple cholesterol emboli	Typically seen in patients with severe atherosclerosis. Embolization may occur after abdominal trauma, aortic surgery, or angiography. May also occur after heparin, warfarin, or thrombolytic therapy. Patients may have livedo reticularis, petechiae and purpuric lesions, and localized skin necrosis.

abnormalities. Some of these patients may develop visual loss, which is a medical emergency that requires immediate parenteral corticosteroid therapy.

Patients with GCA can have jaw claudication and constitutional symptoms, such as fever, weight loss, or fatigue. A small subset of affected patients present with arm or leg claudication. Predictive physical examination findings include temporal artery beading (positive likelihood ratio, 4.6); prominence (positive likelihood ratio, 4.3); and tenderness (positive likelihood ratio, 2.6).

GCA is associated with a markedly elevated erythrocyte sedimentation rate (ESR) and C-reactive protein levels, and in some patients with anemia and thrombocytosis. However, a temporal artery biopsy specimen showing destruction of the internal elastic lamina, intimal thickening, and inflammatory infiltrates is diagnostic of this condition. Giant cells are present in the inflammatory infiltrate in only 50% of affected patients.

Duplex ultrasonography of the temporal artery can reveal a characteristic halo sign in patients with GCA, and positron emission tomography scanning often shows thoracic aorta uptake.

Treatment

In patients with a strong suspicion for GCA, high-dose corticosteroid therapy is indicated before biopsy to decrease the risk for visual loss; if biopsy is performed within 4 weeks of initiating this therapy, biopsy results will not be affected. Once the symptoms of GCA have resolved and the ESR has normalized, the corticosteroid dosage can be tapered by 10% every 1 to 2 weeks. In addition, aspirin may lower the risk for cerebral ischemia.

GCA recurs in more than 50% of affected patients during the first year. When symptoms recur, the corticosteroid dosage should be increased to 10 mg above the dosage that previously controlled the disease. Neither methotrexate nor infliximab is an effective steroid-sparing agent for this condition.

Polymyalgia Rheumatica

Clinical Manifestations and Diagnosis

Polymyalgia rheumatica is twice as common as GCA, but the two entities appear to be different manifestations of the same disease. Polymyalgia rheumatica is characterized by aching in the shoulders, neck, and hip girdle region; fatigue; and malaise that develop over weeks to months. ESR and C-reactive protein levels are elevated. Affected patients respond rapidly and dramatically to low-dose prednisone (10 to 20 mg/d). Once symptoms have subsided, the prednisone dosage can be tapered by 2.5 mg weekly or monthly to 10 mg/d, then by 2.5 mg monthly.

Treatment

Polymyalgia rheumatica commonly recurs, and slower corticosteroid tapering often is warranted. Methotrexate is an effective steroid-sparing agent in this condition, but infliximab is not.

Takayasu Arteritis

Pathophysiology and Epidemiology

Takayasu arteritis is an inflammatory disease that affects the aorta and its branches as well as the pulmonary arteries.

Vascular pathologic changes are similar to those in GCA. Takayasu arteritis most commonly affects young women and children and has an 8:1 female predominance.

Clinical Manifestations and Diagnosis

Takayasu arteritis has an initial inflammatory phase followed by a pulseless phase. The initial phase is characterized by fever, arthralgia, myalgia, malaise, and weight loss that can last weeks to months. ESR and C-reactive protein are elevated. The pulseless phase is characterized by symptoms of vascular insufficiency, such as arm or leg claudication, or hypertension that is usually caused by renal artery stenosis. Many patients with Takayasu arteritis do not seek medical attention until they enter this disease phase.

A diagnosis of Takayasu arteritis is established in patients with a compatible clinical presentation accompanied by great-vessel narrowing visible on imaging studies (**Table 21**). Angiography, ultrasonography, CT angiography, MRI, and magnetic resonance angiography are useful imaging modalities for diagnosis (**Figure 36**). Vessel narrowing is most marked at branch points in the aorta. Positron emission tomography scanning can occasionally identify sites of vessel inflammation that are not clinically apparent.

Treatment

High-dose corticosteroid therapy is indicated in the inflammatory phase. Elevated inflammatory markers, constitutional symptoms, or evidence of progressive arterial narrowing indicate the need for treatment. Uncontrolled trials suggest that methotrexate and tumor necrosis factor α inhibitors are effective steroid-sparing agents. In addition, cyclophosphamide is used in patients with severe refractory Takayasu arteritis.

After the inflammatory phase of Takayasu arteritis has been controlled, affected patients may still have symptoms of vascular insufficiency due to fixed arterial narrowing. Aspirin may be used in this setting, but some patients require vascular intervention with revascularization. The outcome of coronary artery bypass graft surgery, angioplasty, and stenting is not optimal in these patients, and revascularization is not indicated until inflammation has been controlled.

KEY POINTS

- Visual loss in patients with giant cell arteritis is a medical emergency that requires immediate parenteral corticosteroid therapy.

- In patients with a strong suspicion for giant cell arteritis, high-dose corticosteroid therapy is indicated before temporal artery biopsy.

- A rapid and dramatic clinical response to low-dose prednisone is characteristic of polymyalgia rheumatica.

- A diagnosis of Takayasu arteritis is established in patients with a compatible clinical presentation accompanied by great-vessel narrowing visible on angiography, ultrasonography, CT angiography, MRI, or magnetic resonance angiography.

- Aspirin may be used to manage symptoms of vascular insufficiency in patients with Takayasu arteritis once the inflammatory phase has been controlled with high-dose corticosteroids, but some patients require revascularization.

Medium-Sized Vessel Vasculitis

Polyarteritis Nodosa

Pathophysiology and Epidemiology

Polyarteritis nodosa is a necrotizing vasculitis of the medium-sized arteries. The affected vessels are characterized by necrosis and inflammation in a patchy distribution.

Polyarteritis nodosa has a peak age of onset between 40 and 60 years. Approximately 50% of cases of polyarteritis nodosa are associated with hepatitis B virus infection, usually of recent acquisition. The disorders also occur, but less frequently, in patients with hepatitis C virus infection.

Clinical Manifestations and Diagnosis

Patients with polyarteritis nodosa typically present with fever, abdominal pain, arthralgia, and weight loss that develop over days to months. Two thirds of these patients have mononeuritis multiplex, and one third have hypertension, testicular

---

TABLE 21 Diagnostic Criteria for Takayasu Arteritis[a]
Age at disease onset ≤40 years
Claudication of the extremities
Decreased pulsation of one or both brachial arteries
Difference of at least 10 mm Hg in systolic blood pressure between the arms
Bruit over one or both subclavian arteries or the abdominal aorta
Arteriographic studies showing narrowing or occlusion of the entire aorta, its primary branches, or large arteries in the proximal upper or lower extremities that is not related to arteriosclerosis, fibromuscular dysplasia, or other causes
[a]A diagnosis of Takayasu arteritis is established in patients who meet three or more of these criteria.

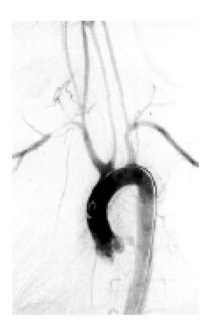

FIGURE 36.
Takayasu arteritis.
This angiogram of the aorta demonstrates high-grade stenosis of the proximal right subclavian artery as well as the left subclavian artery just below the origin of the left vertebral artery. Incidentally noted is anatomic variation with a common origin of the right brachiocephalic artery and the left common carotid artery.

pain, and cutaneous involvement including nodules, ulcers, purpura, and livedo reticularis.

The kidneys, peripheral nerves, and heart also are commonly affected. Aneurysm formation is common, especially in the mesenteric vessels. Ischemia, not glomerulonephritis, causes renal disease in patients with this condition.

Patients with polyarteritis nodosa usually have anemia, leukocytosis, and an elevated ESR. ANCA assays are almost always negative, particularly in patients with concomitant hepatitis B virus infection. In patients with a compatible clinical presentation, biopsy is generally taken from the skin or a sural nerve. Radiographic imaging of the mesenteric or renal arteries can also be used to establish a definitive diagnosis of polyarteritis nodosa. Characteristic findings of this condition include aneurysms and stenoses of the medium-sized vessels.

Treatment and Prognosis
High-dose corticosteroid therapy is indicated initially to treat polyarteritis nodosa. After the inflammatory process has been controlled, the dosage can be tapered.

Predictors of a poor prognosis include renal, gastrointestinal, central nervous system, or cardiac involvement. The 5-year survival rate in patients without such involvement is 90%; the 5-year survival rate in patients with any one of these features is 65%.

Patients with a poor prognosis or with disease that is not controlled by corticosteroids should receive cyclophosphamide

in addition to corticosteroid therapy. Short-term high-dose corticosteroid therapy accompanied by an antiviral agent such as lamivudine is indicated in patients with concomitant hepatitis B virus infection. A large retrospective study demonstrated that 50% of patients with hepatitis B e antigen (HBeAg)–positive polyarteritis nodosa treated with combination therapy seroconverted to anti–hepatitis Be antibody positivity and their vasculitis remitted.

KEY POINTS

- Approximately 50% of cases of polyarteritis nodosa are associated with hepatitis B virus infection.

- Biopsy of the skin or sural nerve or radiographic imaging of the mesenteric or renal arteries is used to establish a diagnosis of polyarteritis nodosa.

- Patients with polyarteritis nodosa who have a poor predicted prognosis or disease that is not controlled by corticosteroids should receive cyclophosphamide in addition to corticosteroid therapy.

- Short-term high-dose corticosteroid therapy accompanied by an antiviral agent such as lamivudine is indicated in patients with polyarteritis nodosa with concomitant hepatitis B virus infection.

Small-Vessel Vasculitis
Antineutrophil Cytoplasmic Antibodies and Vasculitis
The ANCA-associated vasculitides include Wegener granulomatosis, microscopic polyangiitis, and Churg-Strauss syndrome (CSS). These conditions are characterized by vasculitis of the small to medium-sized vessels, pauci-immune necrotizing glomerulonephritis, and pulmonary and renal involvement.

The presence of ANCAs may be pathogenic and not just a marker of disease; ANCA titers correlate with disease activity but should not be used to guide treatment.

Immunofluorescence testing is used to detect ANCAs. The c-ANCA pattern of staining generally reflects reactivity to neutral serine proteinase-3 and is highly sensitive and specific for Wegener granulomatosis. The p-ANCA pattern reflects reactivity to myeloperoxidase and typically is associated with microscopic polyangiitis and CSS.

Antibodies to other proteins also can produce a p-ANCA pattern. These atypical ANCAs are present in patients with conditions such as rheumatoid arthritis and inflammatory bowel disease and are not associated with vasculitis. An enzyme-linked immunosorbent assay is indicated to directly measure reactivity to proteinase-3 and myeloperoxidase in ANCA-positive patients, because only antibodies to these antigens are specific for vasculitis.

Wegener Granulomatosis

Clinical Manifestations and Diagnosis

Wegener granulomatosis is a necrotizing vasculitis that typically affects the respiratory tract and the kidneys. More than 70% of affected patients present with upper-airway symptoms, particularly sinusitis. Nasal, inner ear, or laryngotracheal involvement can also occur. Cartilage and tissue destruction can result in nasal septal perforation or a saddle nose deformity.

Up to 90% of patients have pulmonary manifestations that can include cough, hemoptysis, or pleurisy. Radiographs in these patients show infiltrates or nodules that are often cavitary, as well as pulmonary hemorrhage (**Figure 37**).

Renal involvement occurs in 80% of patients. Renal manifestations usually are preceded by pulmonary disease and can be rapidly progressive. Other commonly affected organs include the eyes (scleritis, keratitis, uveitis, and an inflammatory soft-tissue mass in the orbital fossa known as retro-orbital pseudotumor), skin (purpura, nodules, and ulcers), and nerves (mononeuritis multiplex). Patients with Wegener granulomatosis also have an increased risk for venous thromboembolism.

In most patients with Wegener granulomatosis, lung tissue demonstrates vasculitis, necrosis, or granulomatous inflammation; however, all three features are rarely present in the same biopsy specimen. Biopsy of the sinuses or

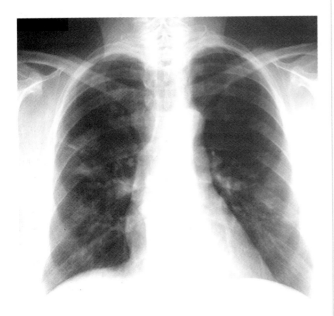

FIGURE 37.
Pulmonary disease in Wegener granulomatosis.
Radiograph of a patient with Wegener granulomatosis showing pulmonary nodules.

Reprinted with permission from Yee AMF and Paget SA, eds. Expert Guide to Rheumatology. Philadelphia: American College of Physicians; 2004.

transbronchial lung biopsy rarely is used to confirm a diagnosis of Wegener granulomatosis.

Renal biopsy specimens reveal a necrotizing focal segmental glomerulonephritis. Granulomas and vasculitis are rarely found in the kidneys, and immune complex deposition is absent. In patients with a classic presentation (a systemic illness accompanied by pulmonary infiltrates, upper-airway findings, and hematuria) who have antiproteinase-3 antibodies, the diagnosis can be established without tissue biopsy. Patients with isolated upper- or lower-airway disease or isolated renal disease generally should undergo tissue biopsy to establish a diagnosis, even if antiproteinase-3 antibodies are present.

Treatment and Prognosis

High-dose corticosteroid therapy accompanied by a 3- to 6-month course of oral cyclophosphamide is used to treat Wegener granulomatosis. After remission has been achieved, cyclophosphamide can be switched to azathioprine or methotrexate. Treatment should be continued for at least 18 months.

In patients without severe renal involvement, methotrexate can be used instead of cyclophosphamide. However, methotrexate therapy is associated with a higher rate of relapse and usually is reserved for patients with mild disease, such as that localized to the upper airways. Etanercept is not effective in Wegener granulomatosis, but rituximab has shown therapeutic promise in one open-label trial.

Up to 90% of patients with Wegener granulomatosis achieve remission. Relapse occurs in 30% of patients still on treatment and in another 30% of patients after discontinuation of treatment.

Microscopic Polyangiitis

Clinical Manifestations and Diagnosis

Microscopic polyangiitis is a necrotizing vasculitis that typically involves the kidneys and lungs. It can affect patients of any age but has a peak age of onset between 30 and 50 years of age. Affected patients frequently present with glomerulonephritis that is often rapidly progressive and commonly results in renal failure; 50% of patients have pulmonary involvement that usually manifests as pulmonary hemorrhage. Fever, arthralgia, purpura, and mononeuritis multiplex can also occur.

Antimyeloperoxidase antibodies are present in 60% to 85% of patients with microscopic polyangiitis; only 10% of affected patients have antiproteinase-3 antibodies.

Renal biopsy specimens reveal a pauci-immune necrotizing glomerulonephritis that is indistinguishable from that found in patients with Wegener granulomatosis. Lung biopsy specimens reveal a characteristic pulmonary capillaritis and may reveal inflammatory infiltrates.

Treatment

Treatment for microscopic polyangiitis consists of corticosteroids and cyclophosphamide to induce remission, followed by maintenance therapy using azathioprine or methotrexate.

Churg-Strauss Syndrome

Clinical Manifestations and Diagnosis

Virtually all patients with CSS have asthma; up to 80% of affected patients have a history of rhinitis or sinusitis. Migratory pulmonary infiltrates, mononeuritis multiplex, and purpura are each present in 50% of patients; cardiac and gastrointestinal involvement in 33%; and glomerulonephritis in 20%. Fever, arthralgia, and myalgia may also occur.

Tissue inflammation in patients with CSS is manifested as eosinophilic tissue infiltration or a necrotizing small-vessel vasculitis. The vasculitis can be granulomatous or nongranulomatous and involves both small arteries and veins.

More than 95% of patients with CSS have eosinophilia, and 40% have ANCAs that are virtually always antimyeloperoxidase antibodies. Patients who have ANCAs are more likely to have glomerulonephritis, alveolar hemorrhage, mononeuritis multiplex, and purpura. Conversely, patients without ANCAs are more likely to have pulmonary infiltrates and cardiomyopathy, which are the result of eosinophilic tissue infiltration.

Treatment and Prognosis

High-dose corticosteroids are indicated to treat CSS and should be accompanied by cyclophosphamide in patients with renal, gastrointestinal, central nervous system, or cardiac involvement.

Up to 80% of patients achieve remission, but relapse occurs in 40% of such patients. The 10-year survival rate is 80%, and 75% of deaths are caused by the disease itself, usually from cardiac involvement.

Henoch-Schönlein Purpura

Clinical Manifestations and Diagnosis

Henoch-Schönlein purpura (HSP) most commonly develops in children but occasionally affects adults, in whom this disease is much more severe. This condition is characterized by purpura, arthritis, abdominal pain, and renal disease. HSP usually resolves in days to weeks, but a subset of patients has persistent, progressive renal disease.

Skin biopsy specimens demonstrate leukocytoclastic vasculitis and IgA deposition. Renal biopsy specimens reveal a glomerulonephritis with IgA deposition that is indistinguishable from that in patients with IgA nephropathy.

Treatment and Prognosis

In children, corticosteroid therapy may control nonrenal symptoms but does not prevent renal disease. There are no effective treatments for adults with HSP-associated renal disease. However, high-dose corticosteroids are sometimes considered for patients with severe glomerulonephritis.

After 5 years of follow-up, 40% of affected adults develop hematuria and 10% develop renal insufficiency.

Cryoglobulinemic Vasculitis

Pathophysiology

Cryoglobulins are immunoglobulins that precipitate in the cold and have rheumatoid factor activity. Type I cryoglobulins are monoclonal rheumatoid factors that can be associated with hyperviscosity and can produce ischemic ulcerations in acral areas exposed to the cold, such as the ears, nose, and finger tips. Type I cryoglobulins are present in patients with multiple myeloma and Waldenström macroglobulinemia.

Type II cryoglobulins are monoclonal rheumatoid factors that can be associated with small-vessel vasculitis. Type III cryoglobulins, which are not typically associated with vasculitis, are polyclonal rheumatoid factors that are present in patients with such chronic inflammatory diseases as hepatitis B and C virus infection, endocarditis, systemic lupus erythematosus (SLE), and rheumatoid arthritis.

Clinical Manifestations and Diagnosis

Type II cryoglobulinemic vasculitis manifests as palpable purpura, mononeuritis multiplex, hepatosplenomegaly, hypocomplementemia, and glomerulonephritis. Approximately 80% to 95% of patients with type II cryoglobulinemic vasculitis have hepatitis C virus infection, although only 5% of patients with hepatitis C virus infection and cryoglobulins develop vasculitis. A diagnosis of cryoglobulinemic vasculitis is established by the presence of cryoglobulins in the serum.

Treatment

Interferon alfa and ribavirin are effective in 75% of patients with mild to moderate cryoglobulinemic vasculitis and hepatitis C virus infection. However, disease may recur if antiviral therapy is discontinued and hepatitis C virus has not been eradicated.

In patients with severe disease, a short course of corticosteroids occasionally accompanied by cyclophosphamide is indicated but should be discontinued once the acute phase of the condition has subsided.

Cutaneous Leukocytoclastic Vasculitis

Cutaneous leukocytoclastic vasculitis can develop in patients with various localized and systemic disorders: 40% of cases are idiopathic; 20% are associated with medications; 22% are related to a recent infection; and 12% are a result of connective tissue diseases, primarily SLE and rheumatoid arthritis. The remaining cases occur in the context of a systemic vasculitis (**Table 22**).

Clinical Manifestations and Diagnosis

Cutaneous leukocytoclastic vasculitis can manifest as palpable purpura, skin nodules, ulcerations, livedo reticularis, or urticaria (**Figure 38**). The vasculitis typically occurs on the lower extremities, particularly below the knees, or where tightly fitting clothing is worn. Involvement of the upper extremities, trunk, head, or neck should raise suspicion for more severe disease or an associated illness. Symptoms of

TABLE 22 Causes of Secondary Vasculitis
Medications
Antimicrobial agents
Vaccines
Antithyroid agents
Anticonvulsant agents
Antiarrhythmic agents
Diuretics
Other cardiovascular drugs
Anticoagulants
Antineoplastic agents
Hematopoietic growth factors
NSAIDs
Leukotriene inhibitors
Psychotropic drugs
Sympathomimetic agents
Allopurinol
TNF modulatory agents
Interferon alfa
Infections
Hepatitis A, B, and C virus
HIV
Bacterial endocarditis
Parvovirus B19
Neoplasms
Hairy cell leukemia (associated with polyarteritis nodosa)
Other hematologic and solid malignancies
Autoimmune Diseases
Systemic lupus erythematosus
Rheumatoid arthritis
Sjögren syndrome
Inflammatory myopathies
Systemic sclerosis
Relapsing polychondritis
Inflammatory bowel disease
Primary biliary cirrhosis

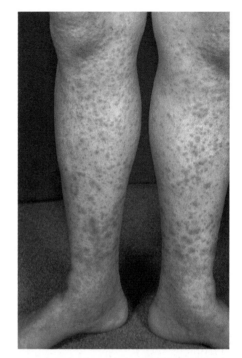

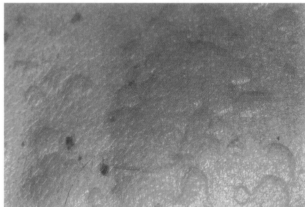

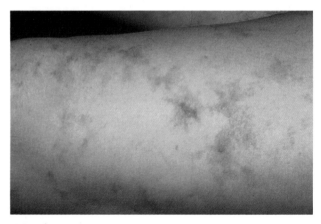

FIGURE 38.
Dermatologic manifestations of cutaneous leukocytoclastic vasculitis.
The top panel shows palpable purpura, the center panel shows urticaria, and the bottom panel shows livedo reticularis.

Reprinted with permission from Alguire PA. Internal Medicine Essentials for Clerkship Students 2. Philadelphia: American College of Physicians; 2009.

medication-induced cutaneous vasculitis typically manifest 7 to 21 days after initial exposure to the triggering agent.

Treatment

NSAIDs, antihistamines, colchicine, or dapsone is used to manage symptomatic and persistent cutaneous leukocytoclastic vasculitis. Low-dose corticosteroid therapy is indicated if these agents are not effective, and use of a steroid-sparing agent such as methotrexate or azathioprine may be warranted in this setting. Treatment of medication-induced cutaneous leukocytoclastic vasculitis consists of discontinuing the triggering agent.

KEY POINTS

- Microscopic polyangiitis is characterized by renal and pulmonary disease as well as the presence of antimyeloperoxidase antibodies.

- High-dose corticosteroid therapy accompanied by a 3- to 6-month course of oral cyclophosphamide is used to initially treat Wegener granulomatosis and microscopic polyangiitis.

- Patients with Churg-Strauss syndrome typically have asthma, a history of rhinitis or sinusitis, and eosinophilia.

- Henoch-Schönlein purpura is characterized by purpura, arthritis, abdominal pain, and renal disease.

- Most cases of type II cryoglobulinemic vasculitis are associated with hepatitis C virus infection.

Secondary Vasculitis

Vasculitis can occur as a manifestation of an underlying condition as well as a primary disease (see Table 22). Secondary vasculitis is usually cutaneous but can be systemic, particularly when associated with connective tissue diseases, such as SLE or Sjögren syndrome.

Certain medications, particularly hydralazine and propylthiouracil, have been associated with p-ANCA–related systemic vasculitis. Viral disease also has been associated with vasculitis.

Malignancies, particularly lymphomas and leukemias, also have been associated with vasculitis. In rare circumstances, vasculitis occurs in patients with lung, colon, or gastrointestinal carcinomas.

Management of secondary vasculitis involves treating the underlying disease or discontinuing the triggering agent.

KEY POINT

- Management of secondary vasculitis involves treating the underlying disease or discontinuing the triggering agent.

Bibliography

De Groot K, Rasmussen N, Bacon PA, et al. Randomized trial of cyclophosphamide versus methotrexate for induction of remission in early systemic antineutrophil cytoplasmic antibody-associated vasculitis. Arthritis Rheum. 2005;52(8):2461-2469. [PMID: 16052573]

Guillevin L, Mahr A, Callard P, et al; French Vasculitis Study Group. Hepatits B virus-associated polyarteritis nodosa: clinical characteristics, outcome, and impact of treatment in 115 patients. Medicine (Baltimore). 2005;84(5):313-322. [PMID: 16148731]

Hoffman GS, Cid MC, Rendt-Zagar KE, et al; Infliximab-GCA Study Group. Infliximab for maintenance of glucocorticosteroid-induced remission of giant cell arteritis: a randomized trial. Ann Intern Med. 2007;146(9):621-630. [PMID: 17470830]

Karassa FB, Matsagas MI, Schmidt WA, Ioannidis JP. Meta-analysis: test performance of ultrasonography for giant-cell arteritis. Ann Intern Med. 2005;142(5):359-369. [PMID: 15738455]

Merkel PA, Lo GH, Holbrook JT, et al; Wegener's Granulomatosis Etanercept Trial Research Group. Brief communication: high incidence of venous thrombotic events among patients with Wegener granulomatosis: the Wegener's Clinical Occurrence of Thrombosis (WeCLOT) Study. Ann Intern Med. 2005;142(8):620-626. [PMID: 15838068]

Salvarani C, Macchioni P, Manzini C, et al. Infliximab plus prednisone or placebo plus prednisone for the initial treatment of polymyalgia rheumatica: a randomized trial. Ann Intern Med. 2007;146(9):631-639. [PMID: 17470831]

Sinico RA, Di Toma L, Maggiore U, et al. Prevalence and clinical significance of antineutrophil cytoplasmic antibodies in Churg-Strauss syndrome. Arthritis Rheum. 2005;52(9):2926-2935. [PMID: 16142760]

Smetana GW, Shmerling RH. Does this patient have temporal arteritis? JAMA. 2002;287(1):92-101. [PMID: 11754714]

The Wegener's Granulomatosis Etanercept Trial (WGET) Research Group. Etanercept plus standard therapy for Wegener's granulomatosis. N Engl J Med. 2005;352(4):351-361. [PMID: 15673801]

Vanoli M, Daina E, Salvarani C, et al; Itaka Study Group. Takayasu's arteritis: A study of 104 Italian patients. Arthritis Rheum. 2005;53(1):100-107. [PMID: 15696576]

Other Systemic Autoinflammatory Diseases

Behçet Disease

Behçet disease is a rare systemic disorder characterized by vasculitis and potential involvement of multiple visceral organs. The most important diagnostic clues for Behçet disease are intermittent mucous membrane, cutaneous, and ocular involvement. Gastrointestinal, pulmonary, musculoskeletal, and neurologic manifestations also may be present.

Death occurs early in the disease course in patients with vascular and/or neurologic involvement. Vascular events, especially aneurysm rupture, are the chief cause of death in patients with Behçet disease; pulmonary artery aneurysms in particular have a high risk of rupture and subsequent death.

Clinical Manifestations

Nearly all patients with Behçet disease have oral ulcerations at some point in their disease course. These ulcerations, which are similar to those in inflammatory bowel disease, are typically painful, may have a pseudomembrane, and are nonscarring (**Figure 39**).

Painful genital ulcerations, which are similar in appearance to the oral ulcerations and typically develop on the vulva or the scrotum, cause scarring in 75% of patients (**Figure 40**). Additional cutaneous manifestations include erythema nodosum, cutaneous pustular vasculitis, inflammatory plaques, and lesions similar in appearance to pyoderma gangrenosum.

Inflammatory eye disease typically develops early in the disease course and is associated with an approximately 20% incidence of blindness. Specific manifestations may include anterior uveitis, which may manifest as pain, redness of the eye, and hypopyon; posterior uveitis, which manifests as

floaters in the visual field; and retinal vasculitis, which classically manifests as a painless decrease in vision that may be accompanied by visual field defects and floaters.

Vascular involvement in patients with Behçet disease includes arterial occlusions and aneurysms and venous thrombosis. Venous involvement is more common and manifests as deep venous thrombosis but also may involve the superior and inferior vena cava, dural sinuses, and portal vein. Abdominal aortic aneurysms also can develop and may rupture.

Gastrointestinal involvement is caused by mucosal inflammation and ulcerations; ileocecal involvement commonly occurs. Gastrointestinal manifestations include abdominal pain, nausea, and diarrhea.

Pulmonary involvement is less common but can be associated with high mortality rates. Pulmonary manifestations include pleuritis, cough, fever, and/or hemoptysis. Pulmonary artery aneurysms, which have a high risk of rupture, may occur.

The most common musculoskeletal manifestation is arthralgia. Up to 50% of patients with Behçet disease develop a nonerosive oligoarthritis that primarily involves the large joints of the lower extremities.

Neurologic manifestations typically present later in the disease course and include aseptic meningitis; vascular thrombotic events such as dural sinus thrombosis; inflammation of the brain stem; and organic brain syndrome, which is characterized by confusion, seizures, and memory loss.

Diagnosis

The International Study Group criteria for Behçet disease are highly sensitive and specific for the disease and consist of the presence of oral ulcerations that recur at least three times in 1 year and at least two of the following manifestations: recurrent genital ulcerations, inflammatory eye disease, cutaneous lesions, and positive results on a pathergy test. This test is performed by inserting a 20- to 25-gauge needle 0.5 cm intradermally, usually into the forearm. Results are considered positive if an erythematous papule or pustule more than 2 mm in diameter develops at the site of the needlestick 48 hours later. The pathergy test has a specificity of 95% to 100% for Behçet disease, but results are typically negative in American and European patients.

Treatment

Oral corticosteroids, often in high doses, are used to treat patients with Behçet disease who have severe mucocutaneous involvement. Colchicine, dapsone, and thalidomide are effective in treating mucosal ulcerations.

Azathioprine and cyclosporine have been shown to be effective in the treatment of inflammatory eye disease associated with Behçet disease. Cyclophosphamide or chlorambucil may be used to treat pulmonary vascular disease and neurologic manifestations. Recent case reports have suggested that

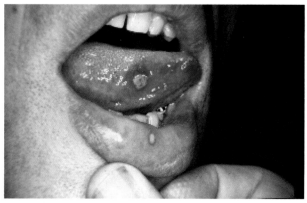

FIGURE 39.
Aphthous oral ulcerations in a patient with Behçet disease.

Reprinted with permission from Physician's Information and Education Resource (PIER). Philadelphia: American College of Physicians. Copyright 2009 American College of Physicians.

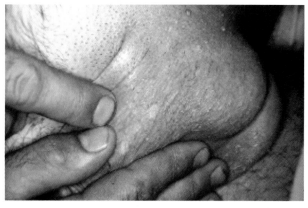

FIGURE 40.
Genital ulcerations in a patient with Behçet disease.

Reprinted with permission from Physician's Information and Education Resource (PIER). Philadelphia: American College of Physicians. Copyright 2009 American College of Physicians.

infliximab may be effective in patients with Behçet disease. Because thrombotic disorders related to Behçet disease are caused by inflammation and not a hypercoagulable state, anticoagulation typically is not indicated in this setting.

Relapsing Polychondritis

Relapsing polychondritis is a systemic disorder characterized by inflammation of cartilage with involvement of the ears, nose, larynx, trachea, and joints. This condition can occur in conjunction with other autoimmune diseases such as vasculitis, rheumatoid arthritis, and systemic lupus erythematosus. This condition also may be associated with myelodysplastic syndromes.

The disease course may be relapsing-remitting, but some patients have a rapidly fatal course characterized by airway inflammation and respiratory failure. The most common causes of death in affected patients are infectious complications caused by immunosuppression and pneumonia due to upper-airway obstruction. Death also may result from airway collapse or inflammation of vessels with aneurysm rupture.

Clinical Manifestations

Auricular inflammation is present in 85% of affected patients and consists of redness, swelling, and tenderness of the auricle (**Figure 41**). Additional manifestations of the disorder include low-grade fever, fatigue, arthralgia, and arthritis.

Serous otitis media and cartilaginous inflammation of the eustachian tube may develop and can cause hearing loss. Vestibular hearing loss due to arteritis of the branches of the internal auditory artery also may occur. Inflammatory lesions can destroy nasal cartilage, which may result in a saddle-nose deformity.

Patients with inflammation of the tracheal cartilage may develop upper-airway obstruction with stridor; bronchial chondritis, which can rapidly progress to airway collapse and respiratory failure, also may occur.

Cardiovascular involvement includes valvulitis with aortic and/or mitral valve insufficiency. Vascular involvement also may include aneurysm formation, particularly of the ascending aorta.

Up to 50% of patients develop inflammatory eye disease, including episcleritis, scleritis, or uveitis. Ocular pseudotumors

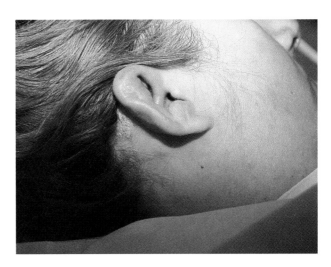

FIGURE 41.
Auricular inflammation in a patient with relapsing polychondritis.

(orbital mucosa-associated lymphoid tissue [MALT]–type cell lymphoma) also may occur.

Cartilaginous inflammation of the joints results in arthritis. Nervous system involvement includes peripheral neuropathy; mononeuritis multiplex; cranial neuropathies; and, less commonly, aseptic meningitis or cerebral vasculitis.

Diagnosis

Relapsing polychondritis is associated with inflammation of the auricular, nasal, and/or laryngeal cartilage, and the diagnosis is established by inflammation in two of these areas. If only one area is involved, two of the following features must be present: ocular inflammation, audiovestibular manifestations, and/or inflammatory arthritis, which need not occur simultaneously. Affected patients may develop a normocytic, normochromic anemia and an elevated erythrocyte sedimentation rate and C-reactive protein level. A macrocytic anemia is suggestive of a myelodysplastic syndrome.

The differential diagnosis includes other systemic vasculitides, such as Wegener granulomatosis, Takayasu arteritis, sarcoidosis, and amyloidosis.

Treatment

High-dose corticosteroids are the mainstay of treatment in patients with relapsing polychondritis. The inflammatory eye disease is treated with corticosteroid eye drops. Systemic corticosteroids or steroid-sparing agents such as azathioprine or methotrexate can be used as second-line treatment. Management of inflammatory airway disease may include methotrexate, azathioprine, or cyclosporine.

Tracheostomy may be warranted in patients with upper-airway obstruction and stridor. Patients with postinflammatory fibrotic airway disease may require airway stenting.

Adult-Onset Still Disease

Adult-onset Still disease (AOSD) is a systemic inflammatory disorder with multisystem involvement that is associated with fever, evanescent rash, and arthritis; the disorder has a 2:1 female predominance.

Some affected patients have self-limited disease that lasts less than 1 year, whereas others have a chronic relapsing-remitting course. The disorder also can manifest as a chronic articular disease that usually is associated with a destructive arthropathy and a worse prognosis.

Clinical Manifestations

The clinical features of AOSD include a quotidian fever in which the temperature usually spikes once daily and then returns to subnormal (**Table 23**). Patients typically have constitutional symptoms, including fatigue, malaise, arthralgia, and myalgia, that worsen during febrile episodes. Proteinuria and serositis also may be present during these episodes. Rash occurs in the juvenile form of this disease but is much less common in affected adults. Joint manifestations include an intense but typically nonerosive inflammatory arthritis; some patients also have profound joint stiffness without obvious signs of inflammation.

Diagnosis

AOSD is typically a diagnosis of exclusion, and the differential diagnosis is broad.

Ferritin levels are elevated in AOSD, and serum levels higher than 2500 ng/mL (2500 mg/L) are highly specific for this condition and reflect disease activity. Levels of proinflammatory cytokines, including tumor necrosis factor α, interleukin-1, and interleukin-6, may be elevated.

Treatment

NSAIDs are generally used as first-line agents in the treatment of AOSD, but corticosteroids may be helpful in patients whose disease is refractory to NSAIDs. In patients with disease refractory to NSAIDs and prednisone, therapy with methotrexate, a tumor necrosis factor α inhibitor, or the interleukin-1 receptor antagonist anakinra may be helpful.

Bibliography

Efthimiou P, Paik PK, Bielory L. Diagnosis and management of adult onset Still's disease. Ann Rheum Dis. 2006;65(5):564-572. [PMID: 16219707]

Kent PD, Michet CJ Jr, Luthra HS. Relapsing polychondritis. Curr Opin in Rheumatol. 2004;16(1):56-61. [PMID: 14673390]

Lin P. Liang G. Behcet disease: recommendation for clinical management of mucocutaneous lesions. J Clin Rheumatol. 2006;12(6):282-286. [PMID: 17149058]

Mat MC, Goksugur N, Engin B, Yurdakul S, Yazici H. The frequency of scarring after genital ulcers in Behcet syndrome: a prospective study. Int J Dermatol. 2006;45(5):554-556. [PMID: 16700790]

McAdam LP, O'Hanlan MA, Bluestone R, Pearson CM. Relapsing polychondritis: prospective study of 23 patients and a review of literature. Medicine (Baltimore). 1976;55(3):193-215. [PMID: 775252]

TABLE 23 Yamaguchi Criteria for the Diagnosis of Adult-Onset Still Disease[a]
Major Criteria
Fever of at least 39.0 °C (102.2 °F) lasting at least 1 week
Arthralgias or arthritis lasting at least 2 weeks
A salmon-colored nonpruritic macular or maculopapular rash usually found over the trunk or extremities during febrile episodes
Leukocytosis (leukocyte count ≥10,000/µL [10 × 10^9/L]) with at least 80% granulocytes
Minor Criteria
Sore throat
Lymphadenopathy
Hepatomegaly or splenomegaly
Abnormal liver chemistry studies, particularly elevations in aspartate and alanine aminotransferase and lactate dehydrogenase levels
Negative results on rheumatoid factor and antinuclear antibody assays

[a]Adult-onset Still disease can be diagnosed in patients with at least five of these features, including at least two major criteria.

Self-Assessment Test

This self-assessment test contains one-best-answer multiple-choice questions. Please read these directions carefully before answering the questions. Answers, critiques, and bibliographies immediately follow these multiple-choice questions. The American College of Physicians is accredited by the Accreditation Council for Continuing Medical Education (ACCME) to provide continuing medical education for physicians.

The American College of Physicians designates MKSAP 15 Rheumatology for a maximum of 11 *AMA PRA Category 1 Credits*™. Physicians should only claim credit commensurate with the extent of their participation in the activity. Separate answer sheets are provided for each book of the MKSAP program. Please use one of these answer sheets to complete the Rheumatology self-assessment test. Indicate in Section H on the answer sheet the actual number of credits you earned, up to the maximum of 11, in ¼-credit increments. (One credit equals one hour of time spent on this educational activity.)

Use the self-addressed envelope provided with your program to mail your completed answer sheet(s) to the MKSAP Processing Center for scoring. Remember to provide your MKSAP 15 order and ACP ID numbers in the appropriate spaces on the answer sheet. The order and ACP ID numbers are printed on your mailing label. If you have *not* received these numbers with your MKSAP 15 purchase, you will need to acquire them to earn CME credits. E-mail ACP's customer service center at custserv@acponline.org. In the subject line, write "MKSAP 15 order/ACP ID numbers." In the body of the e-mail, make sure you include your e-mail address as well as your full name, address, city, state, ZIP code, country, and telephone number. Also identify where you have made your MKSAP 15 purchase. You will receive your MKSAP 15 order and ACP ID numbers by e-mail within 72 business hours.

CME credit is available from the publication date of July 31, 2009, until July 31, 2012. You may submit your answer sheets at any time during this period.

Self-Scoring Instructions: Rheumatology

Compute your percent correct score as follows:

Step 1: Give yourself 1 point for each correct response to a question.

Step 2: Divide your total points by the total number of questions: 79.

The result, expressed as a percentage, is your percent correct score.

	Example	Your Calculations
Step 1	67	
Step 2	67 ÷ 79	÷ 79
% Correct	85%	

Item 1

A 56-year-old woman is evaluated for a 6-week history of arthralgia, prolonged morning stiffness involving the hands and feet, and severe fatigue. She has a history of hypothyroidism well controlled with levothyroxine. She takes ibuprofen, which has not helped to relieve her joint pain. Her mother has osteoarthritis of the knees.

On physical examination, temperature is 36.8 °C (98.2 °F), blood pressure is 135/78 mm Hg, pulse rate is 90/min, and respiration rate is 16/min. BMI is 32. Cardiopulmonary examination is normal. There is no rash. Musculoskeletal examination reveals tenderness and swelling of the second and third metacarpophalangeal joints bilaterally. The elbows are stiff but have a full range of motion and are without synovitis. There is squeeze tenderness of the metatarsophalangeal joints bilaterally.

Laboratory studies:

Complete blood count	Normal
Rheumatoid factor	Negative
Thyroid-stimulating hormone	1.8 µU/mL (1.8 mU/L)
Anti–cyclic citrullinated peptide antibodies	Positive
IgG antibodies against parvovirus B19	Positive
IgM antibodies against parvovirus B19	Negative

Which of the following is the most likely diagnosis?

(A) Hypothyroidism
(B) Parvovirus B19 infection
(C) Polymyalgia rheumatica
(D) Rheumatoid arthritis
(E) Systemic lupus erythematosus

Item 2

A 35-year-old woman with a 3-year history of systemic lupus erythematosus is admitted to the hospital with a blood pressure of 180/90 mm Hg and evidence of acute kidney injury. Her last lupus flare was 1 year ago, and she is currently asymptomatic. Five years ago, she developed deep venous thrombosis and pulmonary embolism after an automobile accident. She has had three first-trimester miscarriages. Her only medication is hydroxychloroquine.

On physical examination, temperature is normal, blood pressure is 200/96 mm Hg, pulse rate is 102/min, and respiration rate is 20/min. Cardiopulmonary examination is normal except for an S_4 gallop. Abdominal examination is unremarkable. There is no rash, lymphadenopathy, or oral ulcers.

Laboratory studies:

Hemoglobin	12.3 g/dL (123 g/L)
Leukocyte count	5300/µL (5.3 × 10⁹/L)
Platelet count	122,000/µL (122 × 10⁹/L)
Reticulocyte count	1.9% of erythrocytes
Serum creatinine	3.2 mg/dL (244.2 µmol/L)

Serum complement (C3 and C4)	Normal
Antinuclear antibodies	1:1280 (speckled pattern)
Anti–double-stranded DNA antibodies	Negative
IgM-specific anticardiolipin antibodies	>100 U/mL
IgG-specific anticardiolipin antibodies	>100 U/mL
Lupus anticoagulant	Positive
Urinalysis	2+ protein; 1+ blood; 2-3 leukocytes, 3-5 erythrocytes/hpf
Urine protein-creatinine ratio	1.2 mg/mg

A direct antiglobulin test (Coombs test) is negative. Peripheral blood smear reveals rare schistocytes. Renal ultrasonography reveals normal-sized kidneys with no obstruction or renal vein thrombosis. Renal biopsy shows capillary congestion and intracapillary fibrin thrombi consistent with thrombotic microangiopathy. Immunofluorescence testing reveals deposition of fibrin but not IgG, IgM, or C3.

Which of the following is the most appropriate next step in this patient's treatment?

(A) Heparin
(B) Prednisone
(C) Prednisone plus cyclophosphamide
(D) Plasmapheresis plus fresh frozen plasma
(E) Rituximab

Item 3

A 52-year-old man is evaluated in the emergency department for a 2-day history of acute pain and swelling in the left knee. He lives in Memphis, works in an office, and does not participate in outdoor recreational activities. There is no history of skin rash or trauma. He has type 2 diabetes mellitus. Medications are insulin glargine and insulin lispro.

On physical examination, temperature is 38.0 °C (100.4 °F), blood pressure is 144/88 mm Hg, pulse rate is 88/min, and respiration rate is 18/min. The left knee is swollen and warm, has overlying erythema, and is tender to palpation. Range of motion of the left knee elicits pain and is limited. The remainder of the musculoskeletal examination is normal.

Laboratory studies:

Hemoglobin	10 g/dL (100 g/L) (normal indices)
Leukocyte count	11,300/µL (11.3 × 10⁹/L) (76% neutrophils)
Erythrocyte sedimentation rate	78 mm/h
Uric acid	8.2 mg/dL (0.48 mmol/L)
Serum creatinine	2.0 mg/dL (152.6 µmol/L)

Which of the following is the most appropriate next step in this patient's management?

(A) Arthrocentesis

(B) Prednisone and allopurinol

(C) Radiography of the left knee

(D) Serologic testing for Lyme disease

Item 4

A 37-year-old man is evaluated for a 4-month history of progressively worsening red, scaly lesions involving the scalp, trunk, and extremities. During the past month, he also has had pain in the hands and feet and has lost 4.5 kg (10.0 lb). Aspirin and acetaminophen have helped to relieve his joint symptoms. He does not drink alcoholic beverages, has no other medical problems, and takes no additional medications. He denies allergies. He has sex with men and women and uses condoms inconsistently.

On physical examination, vital signs are normal. The appearance of lesions found on the arms, hands, upper torso, back, inside the umbilicus, and legs is shown.

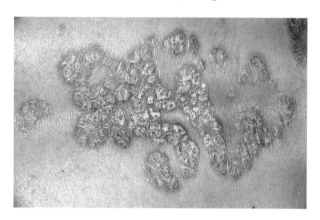

There is swelling of the first and fourth digits on the left hand and of the feet. The left first metatarsophalangeal joint and left ankle are swollen and tender to palpation.

Which of the following diagnostic studies should be performed next in this patient?

(A) Anti–cyclic citrullinated peptide antibody assay

(B) Antinuclear antibody assay

(C) Hepatitis C virus antibody assay

(D) HLA-B27 testing

(E) Serologic testing for HIV antibodies

Item 5

A 78-year-old man with a 15-year history of osteoarthritis is evaluated for severe pain and swelling of the left knee of 4 days' duration. He also has hypertension, type 2 diabetes mellitus, and chronic kidney disease. Medications are glyburide, lisinopril, and low-dose aspirin.

On physical examination, vital signs are normal. He is unable to bear weight on the left leg because of pain. The left knee is swollen and warm, and range of motion of this joint is limited and elicits pain. There are no tophi.

Laboratory studies:

Leukocyte count	15,600/µL (15.6 × 10⁹/L) (90% polymorphonuclear cells, 10% lymphocytes)
Glucose (random)	210 mg/dL (11.7 mmol/L)
Serum creatinine	2.2 mg/dL (167.9 µmol/L)
Serum uric acid	10.7 mg/dL (0.63 mmol/L)
Urinalysis	Normal

Arthrocentesis of the left knee is performed. Synovial fluid leukocyte count is 24,000/µL (90% polymorphonuclear cells, 10% lymphocytes). Polarized light microscopy reveals intra- and extracellular monosodium urate crystals. Gram stain is negative.

Which of the following is the most appropriate treatment for this patient?

(A) Allopurinol

(B) Colchicine

(C) Ibuprofen

(D) Intra-articular methylprednisolone

(E) Prednisone

Item 6

A 25-year-old woman is evaluated for a 2-week history of bilateral lower-extremity pain and skin lesions that she describes as "red knots." Ibuprofen has not alleviated her discomfort, and she has continued to develop new skin lesions. Six months ago, she developed vulvar ulcers that were negative for herpes simplex virus on a polymerase chain reaction assay; these lesions healed within 3 weeks. Two years ago, she developed uveitis that was treated with prednisolone drops. She also has a 7-year history of Raynaud phenomenon and a long-standing history of recurrent oral ulcers. She has had no recent infections and currently has no vulvar ulcers.

On physical examination, vital signs and cardiopulmonary and abdominal examinations are normal. There is no conjunctival injection. There are two ulcers on her tongue. Cutaneous examination reveals several subcutaneous reddish-colored nodules that are tender to palpation located on the lower extremities bilaterally. There is no synovitis, and range of motion of all joints is full.

Laboratory studies:

Complete blood count	Normal
Erythrocyte sedimentation rate	95 mm/h
Metabolic panel	Normal
Rheumatoid factor	Negative
Antinuclear antibodies	Negative
ANCA	Negative
Urinalysis	Normal

A chest radiograph is normal.

Which of the following is the most appropriate treatment for this patient?

(A) Leflunomide
(B) Penicillin
(C) Prednisone
(D) Sulfasalazine

Item 7

An 82-year-old woman with a 2-year history of osteoarthritis of the knees is evaluated for persistent swelling and pain in the right knee of 3 months' duration. She now uses a cane for ambulation and is unable to go grocery shopping. Medications are naproxen and hydrocodone-acetaminophen as needed.

On physical examination, vital signs are normal. The right knee has a large effusion and a valgus deformity. There is decreased flexion of the right knee secondary to pain and stiffness, and she is unable to fully extend this joint. Range of motion of both knees elicits coarse crepitus.

Laboratory studies reveal a serum creatinine level of 1.1 mg/dL (83.9 µmol/L) and a serum uric acid level of 8.2 mg/dL (0.48 mmol/L).

Radiograph of the right knee reveals a large effusion and changes consistent with end-stage osteoarthritis. Aspiration of the right knee is performed. Synovial fluid leukocyte count is 3200/µL. Polarized light microscopy of the fluid demonstrates rhomboid-shaped weakly positively birefringent crystals. Results of Gram stain and cultures are pending.

Which of the following is the most likely diagnosis?

(A) Calcium pyrophosphate dihydrate deposition disease
(B) Chronic apatite deposition disease
(C) Gout
(D) Septic arthritis

Item 8

A 76-year-old man comes for a preoperative evaluation before total joint arthroplasty of the right knee. He has a 24-year history of rheumatoid arthritis. His disease has been stable, but he has had progressive pain and loss of range of motion of the right knee. He has no other medical problems and has never been admitted to the hospital. Medications are methotrexate, a folic acid supplement, hydroxychloroquine, and prednisone.

On physical examination, temperature is 37.2 °C (99.0 °F), blood pressure is 136/80 mm Hg, pulse rate is 90/min, and respiration rate 18/min. BMI is 23. Cardiopulmonary examination is normal. There is mild puffiness of the metacarpophalangeal joints bilaterally. He also has bilateral ulnar deviation and swan neck deformities involving the third digit of the right hand and the fourth digit of the left hand. Extension of the cervical spine is painful and decreased. There is a bony deformity of the right knee. Extension of the right knee is decreased by 10

degrees and flexion is limited to 110 degrees. Neurologic examination is unremarkable.

Laboratory studies are normal, including the complete blood count and serum creatinine level. Chest radiograph and electrocardiogram are normal.

Which of the following preoperative diagnostic studies should be performed in this patient?

(A) B-type natriuretic peptide hormone
(B) Cervical spine radiograph
(C) Spirometry
(D) Urinalysis

Item 9

A 48-year-old woman is evaluated for a rash on her legs, arthralgia and myalgia, low-grade fever, and fatigue of 4 weeks' duration. Over the past week, she has had numbness and burning pain in her left foot; she also feels that this foot is slightly "dragging," and she has tripped and fallen several times. Fifteen years ago, she used illicit injection drugs for a 3-year period.

On physical examination, temperature is 37.7 °C (99.8 °F), blood pressure is 150/100 mm Hg, pulse rate is 88/min, and respiration rate is 18/min. Cardiopulmonary examination is normal. Skin examination findings are shown.

Abdominal examination reveals hepatomegaly. She has a left foot drop, and there is no synovitis.

Laboratory studies:

Hemoglobin	9.9 g/dL (99 g/L)
Leukocyte count	10,400/μL (10.4 × 10^9/L)
Platelet count	323,000/μL (323 × 10^9/L)
Total protein	7.9 g/dL (79 g/L)
Albumin	2.9 g/dL (29 g/L)
Serum creatinine	1.6 mg/dL (122.1 μmol/L)
Total bilirubin	0.9 mg/dL (15.4 μmol/L)
Alkaline phosphatase	84 U/L
Alanine aminotransferase	95 U/L
Aspartate aminotransferase	108 U/L
Rheumatoid factor	232 U/mL (232 kU/L)
C3	32 mg/dL (320 mg/L)
C4	8 mg/dL (80 mg/L) (normal range, 13-38 mg/dL [130-380 mg/L])
Antinuclear antibodies	Negative
Urinalysis	3+ protein; 2+ blood; 15-20 erythrocytes, 5-10 leukocytes/hpf

A chest radiograph is normal.

Which of the following diagnostic studies should be performed next?

(A) ANCA

(B) Anti–cyclic citrullinated peptide antibodies

(C) Anti–double-stranded DNA antibodies

(D) Serum cryoglobulin

Item 10

A 69-year-old woman is evaluated for a 5-day history of pain and swelling in the right knee that developed after a prolonged period of gardening in her backyard. Her pain worsens when she walks and is relieved with rest. She has no morning stiffness.

On physical examination, temperature is normal, blood pressure is 128/72 mm Hg, pulse rate is 88/min, and respiration rate is 17/min. BMI is 32. The right knee has a moderate effusion but is not warm or erythematous. Range of motion of the right knee elicits pain. The remainder of the musculoskeletal examination is normal.

Plain radiographs of the right knee show osteophytes and medial joint-space narrowing. Arthrocentesis is performed, and synovial fluid analysis reveals 250 leukocytes/μL (88% lymphocytes, 12% macrophages).

Which of the following is the most likely diagnosis?

(A) Bacterial arthritis

(B) Crystal-induced arthritis

(C) Fungal arthritis

(D) Osteoarthritis

Item 11

A 45-year-old woman is hospitalized for shortness of breath of 2 days' duration. For the past 2 weeks, she has had ankle edema and a low-grade fever and cough productive of white sputum for which she began taking azithromycin 1 week ago. She has a 15-year history of allergic rhinitis and asthma treated with albuterol and fluticasone-salmeterol inhalers. Two months ago, her asthma worsened despite an increased fluticasone-salmeterol dosage and the addition of montelukast to her regimen. She also takes mometasone furoate aqueous nasal spray.

On physical examination, temperature is 37.7 °C (99.9 °F), blood pressure is 120/65 mm Hg, pulse rate is 112/min, and respiration rate is 32/min. Cardiopulmonary examination reveals tachycardia, an S$_3$ gallop, diffuse crackles, and wheezes. There is no rash, lymphadenopathy, splenomegaly, or synovitis, but there is 2+ edema of the ankles.

Laboratory studies:

Hemoglobin	10.3 g/dL (103 g/L)
Leukocyte count	16,000/μL (16 × 10^9/L) (21% eosinophils; no immature forms)
Platelet count	605,000/μL (605 × 10^9/L)
Serum creatinine	1.4 mg/dL (106.8 μmol/L)
Liver enzyme studies	Normal
Antinuclear antibodies	Negative
p-ANCA	Positive
Antimyeloperoxidase antibodies	Positive
Urinalysis	2+ protein; 3+ blood; 20-30 leukocytes, 15-20 erythrocytes/hpf; rare erythrocyte casts
Urine protein-creatinine ratio	1.3 mg/mg

Chest radiograph reveals cardiomegaly; small bilateral effusions; and pulmonary infiltrates in the right lower lobe, right middle lobe, and left lower lobe. Echocardiography shows an ejection fraction of 35%, diffuse hypokinesis, and no valvular or wall motion abnormalities. Bone marrow biopsy reveals 8% eosinophils and no abnormal cells.

In addition to methylprednisolone, which of the following is the most appropriate treatment for this patient?

(A) Cyclophosphamide

(B) Hydroxyurea

(C) Imatinib

(D) No additional therapy

Item 12

A 41-year-old woman is evaluated for intermittent pain and cyanosis of the fingers that is usually associated with exposure to cold temperatures or stress. She does not smoke, and her efforts to keep room temperatures warm and to wear gloves and layers of clothing to maintain her core temperature have not been successful in managing her symptoms.

She was diagnosed with limited cutaneous systemic sclerosis 1 year ago. She also has gastroesophageal reflux disease. Her only medication is omeprazole.

On physical examination, temperature is 37.0 °C (98.6 °F), blood pressure is 128/72 mm Hg, and pulse rate is 88/min. Cutaneous examination of the hands shows sclerodactyly. Radial and ulnar pulses are 2+ and equal bilaterally.

Which of the following is the most appropriate additional treatment for this patient?

(A) Amlodipine
(B) Isosorbide dinitrate
(C) Prednisone
(D) Propranolol

Item 13

A 75-year-old woman is evaluated for a sudden loss of vision in the left eye that began 30 minutes ago. She has a 2-week history of fatigue; malaise; and pain in the shoulders, neck, hips, and lower back. She also has a 5-day history of mild bitemporal headache.

On physical examination, temperature is 37.3 °C (99.1 °F), blood pressure is 140/85 mm Hg, pulse rate is 72/min, and respiration rate is 16/min. BMI is 31. The left temporal artery is tender. Funduscopic examination reveals a pale, swollen optic disc. Range of motion of the shoulders and hips elicits moderate pain.

Laboratory studies:

Hemoglobin	9.9 g/dL (99 g/L)
Leukocyte count	7300/µL (7.3 × 10⁹/L)
Platelet count	456,000/µL (456 × 10⁹/L)
Erythrocyte sedimentation rate	116 mm/h

Which of the following is the most appropriate next step in this patient's management?

(A) Brain MRI
(B) High-dose intravenous methylprednisolone
(C) Low-dose oral prednisone
(D) Temporal artery biopsy

Item 14

A 32-year-old woman is evaluated in the emergency department for a 4-day history of pain and swelling of the right wrist and low-grade fever. She has a 7-year history of severe rheumatoid arthritis. She does not recall any specific trauma involving the wrist but has recently been very physically active. Medications are methotrexate, a folic acid supplement, etanercept, prednisone, and ibuprofen.

On physical examination, temperature is 37.8 °C (100.0 °F), blood pressure is 118/68 mm Hg, pulse rate is 90/min, and respiration rate is 18/min. BMI is 22. Cardiopulmonary examination is normal. There is no rash. The right wrist is swollen and tender and has a decreased range of motion. There are a subcutaneous nodule and small flexion deformity on the left elbow but no active synovitis. Mild synovitis is present on the second metacarpophalangeal joints bilaterally. The hips, knees, and feet are not tender or swollen and have full range of motion.

Which of the following diagnostic studies of the wrist will be most helpful in establishing this patient's diagnosis?

(A) Arthrocentesis
(B) Arthroscopy
(C) Bone scan
(D) MRI
(E) Radiography

Item 15

A 68-year-old woman is admitted to the hospital for an 8-month history of progressive proximal muscle weakness. Muscle biopsy of the right quadriceps performed when symptoms first began was consistent with dermatomyositis. At the time of diagnosis, chest radiograph, breast examination, mammography, pelvic examination, Pap smear, and colonoscopy were normal. High-dose prednisone accompanied by alendronate and calcium and vitamin D supplements was begun 6 months ago but has not helped to alleviate her symptoms. She is now unable to bathe or dress herself, requires assistance rising from a chair, and uses a wheelchair because of frequent falls. She also occasionally chokes when eating. Since diagnosis of her condition, the serum creatine kinase level has been between 1000 and 2000 U/L. She has no additional symptoms.

On physical examination, she appears frail with facial fullness. Vital signs are normal. BMI is 21. Cardiopulmonary examination is unremarkable. Cutaneous examination reveals a V-shaped erythematous macular eruption on the anterior chest. On musculoskeletal examination, she is unable to raise the upper arms or thighs against gravity, and the distal muscles are weak against resistance.

Laboratory studies:

Hemoglobin	10.8 g/dL (108 g/L)
Erythrocyte sedimentation rate	120 mm/h
Creatine kinase	3845 U/L

Which of the following should be done next?

(A) CT of the chest, abdomen, and pelvis
(B) Discontinue prednisone
(C) MRI of the thigh muscles
(D) Repeat muscle biopsy

Item 16

A 33-year-old woman is evaluated during a follow-up visit. She was diagnosed with rheumatoid arthritis 3 months ago; at that time, she began methotrexate therapy and a folic acid supplement. She also takes ibuprofen and acetaminophen. Despite this treatment, she still has 2 to 3 hours of morning stiffness daily and wakes frequently during the night with pain and stiffness. She also has persistent pain in the hands and feet.

On physical examination, vital signs are normal. The neck and shoulders are stiff but have full range of motion. Small nodules are present on the elbows. The right elbow has a small effusion and has 15 degrees of flexion contracture. The wrists and metacarpophalangeal joints are tender bilaterally, and there is synovitis of the wrists. The left knee has a small effusion. The metatarsophalangeal joints also are tender bilaterally.

Laboratory studies:

Hemoglobin	12.2 g/dL (122 g/L)
Platelet count	460,000/μL (460 × 10⁹/L)
Erythrocyte sedimentation rate	45 mm/h

Radiographs of the hands show periarticular osteopenia and erosions of the right ulnar styloid and the base of the left fifth metacarpal bone.

Which of the following is the most appropriate next step in this patient's treatment?

(A) Add etanercept
(B) Add hydroxychloroquine
(C) Add cyclophosphamide
(D) Discontinue methotrexate; begin sulfasalazine

Item 17

A 57-year-old man is evaluated in the emergency department for the acute onset of rapidly worsening dyspnea. For the past 10 weeks, he has had pain and swelling in the small joints of the hands and in the knees; he was diagnosed with seronegative symmetric inflammatory polyarthritis 2 weeks ago and was started on low-dose methotrexate, a folic acid supplement, low-dose prednisone, and naproxen at that time. He also has a history of refractory otitis media and underwent bilateral tympanostomy tube placement 6 months ago.

He is in respiratory failure and is intubated, mechanically ventilated, and admitted to the hospital. Blood is noted when he is intubated. On physical examination on admission, temperature is 38.5 °C (101.3 °F), blood pressure is 135/95 mm Hg, pulse rate is 125/min, and respiration rate is 24/min. There is no bleeding from the gums. Pulmonary examination reveals diffuse crackles throughout all lung fields. The metacarpophalangeal and proximal interphalangeal joints are swollen, and both knees have medium-sized effusions. Palpable purpura is present on the calves.

Laboratory studies:

Hemoglobin	10 g/dL (100 g/L)
Leukocyte count	12,500/μL (12.5 × 10⁹/L) (80% neutrophils)
Serum creatinine	2.6 mg/dL (198.4 μmol/L)
Rheumatoid factor	Negative
Antinuclear antibodies	Negative
c-ANCA	Positive
Anti–cyclic citrullinated peptide antibodies	Negative
Antiproteinase-3 antibodies	Positive
Serologic test for HIV antibodies	Negative
Urinalysis	2+ protein; 1+ blood; 15 erythrocytes/hpf

A chest radiograph shows normal heart size and diffuse alveolar infiltrates in both lung fields.

Ceftriaxone, azithromycin, and hydrocortisone are started. His previous medications are discontinued.

Which of the following is the most likely diagnosis?

(A) Interstitial pneumonitis
(B) Methotrexate-induced pneumonitis
(C) *Pneumocystis* pneumonia
(D) Wegener granulomatosis

Item 18

A 55-year-old woman is evaluated for progressive polyarthralgia, photosensitive rash, and lower-extremity purpura of 7 weeks' duration. She also has daily low-grade fever and intermittent pleuritic chest pain. She has an 11-year history of rheumatoid arthritis treated with oral methotrexate and intravenous infliximab. Her disease has been mostly stable except for occasional flares treated with prednisone.

On physical examination, vital signs are normal except for a temperature of 38.0 °C (100.4 °F). Malar rash is present. Cardiopulmonary examination reveals normal breath sounds, and no rubs are heard. She is unable to take a deep breath because of pain. Several small 1-cm maculopapular eruptions are visible on the lower extremities bilaterally. Musculoskeletal examination reveals synovitis of the metacarpophalangeal and proximal interphalangeal joints and the wrists bilaterally. The left elbow has a nodule. Range of motion of the right wrist is decreased.

Laboratory studies:

Rheumatoid factor	Positive
Antinuclear antibodies	Titer of 1:640
Anti–double-stranded DNA antibodies	Positive

Chest radiograph reveals small bilateral pleural effusions.

Which of the following is the most appropriate next step in this patient's treatment?

(A) Add sulfasalazine
(B) Discontinue infliximab; begin prednisone
(C) Discontinue methotrexate; begin hydroxychloroquine
(D) Discontinue methotrexate; begin sulfasalazine

Item 19

A 21-year-old man is evaluated for a 5-day history of pain and swelling in the right ankle. Seven days ago, he developed a nodule on the left leg. He has no history of trauma to either of these sites. He is otherwise asymptomatic.

On physical examination, vital signs are normal. The right ankle is warm and swollen, and range of motion elicits pain. He also has a warm, firm 2-cm erythematous nodule over the anterior left lower extremity that is tender to palpation and has been present for 7 days. The remainder of the physical examination is normal.

Chest radiograph is shown.

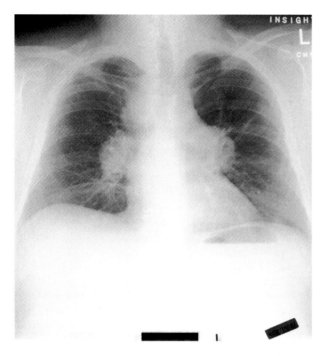

A plain radiograph of the right ankle is normal. Arthrocentesis of the right ankle is performed, and synovial fluid analysis reveals a leukocyte count of 3000/µL (80% lymphocytes, 12% macrophages). There are no crystals.

Which of the following is the most likely diagnosis?

(A) Bacterial arthritis
(B) Crystal-induced arthritis
(C) Osteoarthritis
(D) Sarcoidosis

Item 20

A 24-year-old woman is evaluated for a 1-year history of scaly plaques on her face and scalp. Results of a skin biopsy 1 week ago are consistent with chronic cutaneous lupus. She has ongoing mild fatigue, a 10-day history of lower back pain, and occasional migraine headaches for which she takes sumatriptan as needed. She also has a history of partial-onset seizures that began at age 13 years for which she currently takes phenytoin.

On physical examination, temperature is 37.0 °C (98.6 °F), blood pressure is 125/73 mm Hg, pulse rate is 72/min, and respiration rate is 16/min. Cutaneous examination reveals scattered circular plaques on the cheeks, nose, scalp, and ear canals. Within the plaques, there is follicular plugging and atrophic scarring. She also has patches of alopecia where the rash is present on the scalp. Cardiopulmonary examination is normal. There is no lymphadenopathy or oral ulcers. Abdominal examination is unremarkable. Musculoskeletal examination reveals no synovitis, and neurologic examination is normal.

Laboratory studies:

Hemoglobin	14 g/dL (140 g/L)
Leukocyte count	6300/µL (6.3 × 10⁹/L)
Erythrocyte sedimentation rate	16 mm/h
Serum creatinine	0.8 mg/dL (61.0 µmol/L)
Serum complement (C3 and C4)	Normal
Antinuclear antibodies	Titer of 1:160
Anti–double-stranded DNA antibodies	Negative
Anti-Ro/SSA antibodies	Negative
Anti-La/SSB antibodies	Negative
Anti-Smith antibodies	Negative
Antiribonucleoprotein antibodies	Negative
Antihistone antibodies	Negative
Urinalysis	Normal

Which of the following is the most likely diagnosis?

(A) Discoid lupus
(B) Drug-induced lupus
(C) Mixed connective tissue disease
(D) Systemic lupus erythematosus

Item 21

A 56-year-old woman is evaluated during a follow-up visit for persistent rheumatoid arthritis. She was diagnosed with this condition 1 year ago and began treatment with methotrexate, 20 mg weekly, and hydroxychloroquine, 400 mg/d; etanercept was added 6 months ago. For the past 2 months, she has had persistent pain and swelling in the hands and knees as well as increased morning stiffness that lasts up to 3 hours daily. These symptoms interfere with her daily activities. Prednisone, 5 mg/d, was added 4 weeks ago and has provided only modest benefits.

Medical history is significant for osteopenia. She also takes alendronate and calcium, vitamin D, and folic acid supplements.

On physical examination, vital signs are normal. Range of motion of the shoulders is decreased. There are nodules on the elbows bilaterally and bilateral synovitis of the wrists. Grip strength is decreased. There are small effusions on the knees and squeeze tenderness of the metatarsophalangeal joints bilaterally.

Laboratory studies:

Hemoglobin	11 g/dL (110 g/L)
Leukocyte count	8000/µL (8 × 10⁹/L)
Erythrocyte sedimentation rate	56 mm/h
Rheumatoid factor	Positive
Anti–cyclic citrullinated peptide antibodies	Positive

Radiograph of the hands shows erosions of the right second metacarpophalangeal joint and at the base of the left fifth metacarpal bone. Diffuse periarticular osteopenia also is visible.

Which of the following is the most appropriate next step in this patient's management?

(A) Add infliximab

(B) Discontinue etanercept; switch to infliximab

(C) Discontinue methotrexate; switch to sulfasalazine

(D) Increase prednisone

Item 22

A 58-year-old man is evaluated for a 3-year history of recurrent episodes of pain and swelling of the joints of the lower extremities. These episodes have an acute onset, are monoarticular, reach maximum intensity within 1 day, and last between 2 and 7 days. The right great toe is most often affected, but the knee also is involved. During the past 6 months, he has had three episodes.

On physical examination, vital signs are normal. Musculoskeletal examination is normal except for bony enlargement of the right first metatarsophalangeal joint with valgus deformity. There are no tophi.

Which of the following diagnostic studies will be most helpful in establishing this patient's diagnosis?

(A) 24-Hour urine uric acid

(B) Radiography of the right foot

(C) Serum uric acid

(D) Synovial fluid leukocyte count

Item 23

A 28-year-old woman is evaluated for a 3-week history of pain and swelling of the right knee and ankle. For the past 6 weeks, she has had diffuse, crampy abdominal pain. For the past week, the pain has been accompanied by four to six daily episodes of bloody diarrhea and fecal urgency. She has lost approximately 1.5 kg (3.3 lb) since the onset of her symptoms. She has not noticed a rash or other joint or soft-tissue involvement. She has not traveled outside of her hometown and has a monogamous sexual relationship with her husband. She has no other medical problems and does not take any medications.

On physical examination, temperature is 37.7 °C (99.9 °F), blood pressure is 128/72 mm Hg, pulse rate is 98/min, and respiration rate is 18/min. The abdomen is soft and diffusely tender to palpation. Bowel sounds are normal, and there is no organomegaly. Rectal examination reveals tenderness of the rectal canal and stool associated with bright red blood. The right ankle and knee are swollen and slightly warm to the touch, and range of motion of these joints elicits pain. The remainder of the physical examination is normal.

Plain radiographs of the ankle and knee are normal. Arthrocentesis is performed. Synovial fluid analysis reveals a leukocyte count of 14,000/µL (92% polymorphonuclear cells, 8% macrophages).

Which of the following is the most likely cause of this patient's joint symptoms?

(A) Crystal-induced arthritis

(B) Enteropathic arthritis

(C) Gonococcal arthritis

(D) Whipple disease

Item 24

A 42-year-old woman with systemic lupus erythematosus is admitted to the hospital for a 1-week history of worsening headache and a 2-day history of confusion, personality change, and emotional lability. She was diagnosed with lupus 1 year ago, and her condition has been well controlled with prednisone, hydroxychloroquine, and ibuprofen. Four months ago, prednisone was discontinued.

Two months ago, she developed fatigue, intermittent low-grade fevers, and occasional headache. Two weeks ago, she was evaluated in the office for a 1-month history of purpuric lesions on her legs, palms, and soles. Biopsy specimen of a lesion showed leukocytoclastic vasculitis. At that time, prednisone, 40 mg/d, was initiated, and the purpuric lesions began to fade.

On physical examination today, temperature is 37.9 °C (100.2 °F), blood pressure is 150/80 mm Hg, pulse rate is 102/min, and respiration rate is 20/min. She is confused and combative. She is oriented to name only, intermittently laughs and cries, and has paranoid ideation. Cardiopulmonary examination is normal. She does not have photophobia or nuchal rigidity. Abdominal examination is unremarkable. She has livedo reticularis involving the arms and legs, and there are purpuric lesions on the palms, fingertips, legs, soles, and toes. There is no synovitis. Neurologic examination is nonfocal.

Laboratory studies:

Hemoglobin	11.1 g/dL (111 g/L)
Leukocyte count	3500/µL (3.5 × 10⁹/L)
Platelet count	200,000/µL (200 × 10⁹/L)
Erythrocyte sedimentation rate	83 mm/h
Serum complement (C3 and C4)	Decreased
Antinuclear antibodies	Titer of 1:2560

Cerebrospinal fluid findings:	
Leukocyte count	55/µL (100% lymphocytes)
Erythrocyte count	1/µL
Protein	72 mg/dL (720 mg/L)
Gram stain	Negative
VDRL	Negative

Culture results are pending. T2-weighted MRI of the brain reveals scattered punctate areas of increased signal in the periventricular and subcortical white matter.

Which of the following is the most appropriate next step in this patient's treatment?

(A) Begin ampicillin and gentamicin

(B) Begin methylprednisolone and cyclophosphamide

(C) Discontinue ibuprofen

(D) Schedule plasmapheresis

Item 25

A 34-year-old woman is evaluated for a 4-month history of heartburn and regurgitation that occurs several times daily. She has a 2-month history of swelling and aching in the hands. Six months ago, she also began to develop episodes of pain and cyanosis involving the fingers upon exposure to cold temperatures. She has no other medical problems and takes no medications.

On physical examination, temperature is 37.0 °C (98.6 °F), blood pressure is 100/60 mm Hg, pulse rate is 78/min, and respiration rate is 18/min. There is skin thickening over the fingers. There is no evidence of joint swelling, synovitis, or tendinitis. The remainder of the physical examination is normal. Laboratory studies, including complete blood count, basic metabolic profile, and urinalysis, are normal except for an antinuclear antibody titer of 1:640 (speckled pattern).

The patient received counseling about avoiding the cold and other environmental protection.

Which of the following is the most appropriate additional treatment for this patient?

(A) Cyclophosphamide
(B) Enalapril
(C) Methotrexate
(D) Omeprazole
(E) Prednisone

Item 26

A 70-year-old male dairy farmer is evaluated for a 1-year history of pain in the left knee that worsens with activity and is relieved with rest. On physical examination, vital signs are normal. A small effusion is present on the left knee, but there is no erythema or warmth. Range of motion of the left knee elicits pain and is slightly limited. Extension of this joint is limited to approximately 10 degrees, but flexion is nearly full. The remainder of the musculoskeletal examination is normal.

The erythrocyte sedimentation rate is 15 mm/h. A standing radiograph of the left knee is shown.

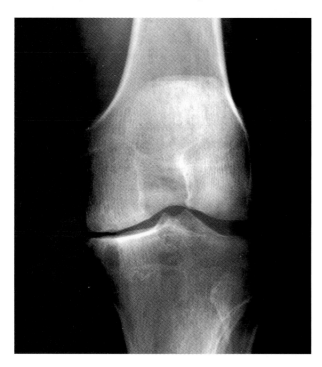

Which of the following is the most likely diagnosis?

(A) Avascular necrosis
(B) Osteoarthritis
(C) Rheumatoid arthritis
(D) Torn medial meniscus

Item 27

A 31-year-old man with systemic lupus erythematosus is evaluated for new-onset hypertension, peripheral edema, hematuria, and proteinuria. He also has hypocomplementemia, elevated anti–double-stranded DNA antibodies, and a serum creatinine level of 1.8 mg/dL (137.3 µmol/L). He was diagnosed with lupus 1 year ago, and his disease had been well controlled with prednisone and hydroxychloroquine. Additional medications are calcium and vitamin D supplements. Renal biopsy reveals World Health Organization class IV proliferative glomerulonephritis. His prednisone dosage is increased from 5 mg/d to 60 mg/d, and he begins intravenous cyclophosphamide, 1 g monthly, and lisinopril. Hydroxychloroquine therapy is continued.

At a follow-up evaluation 6 months later, he is asymptomatic. His prednisone has been tapered to 5 mg/d, and his most recent dose of cyclophosphamide was administered 3 weeks ago. On physical examination, temperature is 36.4 °C (97.6 °F), blood pressure is 130/80 mm Hg, pulse rate is 64/min, and respiration rate is 16/min. Physical examination is unremarkable.

Laboratory studies:

Hemoglobin	12.3 g/dL (123 g/L)
Leukocyte count	4200/µL (4.2 × 10⁹/L)
Platelet count	155,000/µL (155 × 10⁹/L)
Serum creatinine	1.2 mg/dL (91.6 µmol/L)
Serum complement (C3 and C4)	Normal
Anti–double-stranded DNA antibodies	Positive (low titers)
Urinalysis	1+ protein; 3-5 leukocytes, 3-5 erythrocytes/hpf
Urine protein-creatinine ratio	0.5 mg/mg

Which of the following is the most appropriate treatment for this patient?

(A) Continue monthly cyclophosphamide
(B) Discontinue cyclophosphamide
(C) Discontinue cyclophosphamide; start methotrexate
(D) Discontinue cyclophosphamide; start mycophenolate mofetil

Item 28

A 26-year-old woman is evaluated for a 2-month history of pain and swelling in the hands and daily morning stiffness that lasts for 3 to 4 hours. She is 4 months postpartum, and her pregnancy was without complications. She has no history of rash and is otherwise well. Her only medication is ibuprofen, which has not sufficiently relieved her symptoms.

On physical examination, temperature is normal, blood pressure is 110/68 mm Hg, pulse rate is 82/min, and respiration rate is 16/min. The second and third proximal interphalangeal and metacarpophalangeal joints and the wrists are tender and swollen bilaterally.

Laboratory studies show an erythrocyte sedimentation rate of 67 mm/h, and titers of IgM antibodies against parvovirus B19 are negative.

Which of the following is the most likely diagnosis?

(A) Gout
(B) Osteoarthritis
(C) Parvovirus B19 infection
(D) Rheumatoid arthritis

Item 29

A 45-year-old man is evaluated for an 8-week history of bilateral knee and ankle pain. There is no history of trauma. He also has daily morning stiffness that lasts up to 2 hours and fatigue that has caused him to limit his activities. He consumes approximately 12 beers on weekends and is unwilling to limit his alcohol consumption. He has been taking ibuprofen, but this has not relieved his joint symptoms.

On physical examination, temperature is 37.6 °C (99.7 °F), blood pressure is 140/80 mm Hg, and pulse rate is 88/min. BMI is 30. There is no rash. The wrists and knees are swollen bilaterally. He is unable to fully extend the right knee.

Laboratory studies:

Hemoglobin	14 g/dL (140 g/L)
Leukocyte count	10,500/µL (10.5 × 10⁹/L)
Erythrocyte sedimentation rate	28 mm/h
Rheumatoid factor	Positive
Alanine aminotransferase	35 U/L
Aspartate aminotransferase	35 U/L
Anti–cyclic citrullinated peptide antibodies	Negative

Arthrocentesis of the right knee is performed. Synovial fluid analysis reveals a leukocyte count of 13,500/µL. Polarized light microscopy of the fluid is negative for crystals, and synovial fluid culture is negative.

Radiographs of the hands are normal. Radiographs of the knees show moderate joint effusions.

Which of the following is the most appropriate treatment for this patient?

(A) Leflunomide
(B) Methotrexate
(C) Prednisone
(D) Sulfasalazine

Item 30

A 25-year-old woman is evaluated during a follow-up visit for a 6-month history of diffuse muscle and joint pain above and below the waist, fatigue, and difficulty sleeping. She has a 2-year history of hypothyroidism treated with levothyroxine. Her only other medication is hydrocodone-acetaminophen, which has not relieved her pain.

On physical examination, temperature is 37.0 °C (98.6 °F), blood pressure is 125/78 mm Hg, pulse rate is 85/min, and respiration rate is 12/min. Cardiopulmonary examination is normal. Musculoskeletal examination reveals diffuse periarticular tenderness, including bilateral tenderness in the biceps brachii, thighs, and calves. Muscle strength testing cannot be completed because of pain. The joints are not swollen, and she does not have lower-extremity edema.

Laboratory studies:

Complete blood count	Normal
Complete metabolic panel	Normal
Erythrocyte sedimentation rate	10 mm/h
Creatine kinase	100 U/L
Antinuclear antibodies	Titer of 1:640
Thyroid-stimulating hormone	1.5 µU/mL (1.5 mU/L)
Urinalysis	Normal

Which of following is the most likely diagnosis?

(A) Fibromyalgia
(B) Polymyositis
(C) Sjögren syndrome
(D) Systemic lupus erythematosus

Item 31

A 65-year-old man is evaluated for a 2-year history of increasing weakness of the hands and legs. Medical history is insignificant, and he takes no medications or vitamin supplements.

On physical examination, vital signs are normal. Cardiopulmonary examination is unremarkable. There are red, flaking patches predominantly involving the scalp, eyebrows, nasolabial folds, ears, and chest.

Strength in the left wrist flexor, left hip flexor, and right quadriceps muscles is decreased. The remainder of the physical examination is normal.

Laboratory studies reveal a serum creatine kinase level of 320 U/L.

Electromyography demonstrates a mixed pattern of myopathic and neurogenic changes. Muscle biopsy specimen shows endomysial inflammation and basophilic vacuoles. On electron microscopy, the vacuoles contain particles resembling myxovirus or paramyxovirus.

Which of the following is the most likely diagnosis?

(A) Dermatomyositis
(B) Fibromyalgia
(C) Inclusion body myositis
(D) Mixed connective tissue disease
(E) Polymyositis

Item 32

A 62-year-old man is evaluated for a 2-year history of enlargement and discomfort of the metacarpophalangeal joints of both hands. He works as a bank manager and leads a sedentary lifestyle. He does not have morning stiffness. He was diagnosed with type 2 diabetes mellitus 3 months ago for which he takes metformin.

On physical examination, vital signs are normal. Examination of the skin reveals generalized hyperpigmentation. There is bony enlargement of the metacarpophalangeal joints bilaterally but no evidence of synovial proliferation. Range of motion of the hands is full, and he can make a strong fist. Examination of the proximal and distal interphalangeal joints, knees, and hips is normal.

Laboratory studies:

Hemoglobin A_{1c}	7.3%
Erythrocyte sedimentation rate	13 mm/h
Glucose (fasting)	100 mg/dL (5.6 mmol/L)
Rheumatoid factor	Negative
Anti–cyclic citrullinated peptide antibodies	Negative

Hand radiographs show joint-space narrowing and hook-shaped osteophyte formation in the metacarpophalangeal joints. Radiographs of the hips and knees are normal. These imaging studies reveal no evidence of chondrocalcinosis.

Which of the following is the most likely diagnosis?

(A) Calcium pyrophosphate deposition disease
(B) Diabetic cheiroarthropathy (stiff hand syndrome)
(C) Hemochromatosis
(D) Primary osteoarthritis
(E) Rheumatoid arthritis

Item 33

A 64-year-old man is evaluated during a 3-month follow-up visit for rheumatoid arthritis. He was diagnosed with this condition 15 years ago. He has approximately 20 minutes of morning stiffness daily. He has chronic pain in the right knee; however, this pain has not worsened since his last visit. His last disease flare was 1 year ago, and he does not have fatigue, difficulty sleeping, or fever. His weight and functional level have been stable. Medications are methotrexate, hydroxychloroquine, naproxen, and a folic acid supplement.

On physical examination, vital signs are normal. BMI is 33. There is bony enlargement of the second and third metacarpophalangeal joints bilaterally but no tenderness. There are swan-neck deformities of the third and fourth digits on the right hand. Range of motion of the knees elicits crepitus bilaterally, and extension of the right knee is restricted by 5 degrees. There is subluxation of the right second and left third metatarsophalangeal joints.

Laboratory studies reveal a hemoglobin level of 12.5 g/dL (125 g/L) and an erythrocyte sedimentation rate of 44 mm/h.

Radiographs of the hands and feet show marginal joint erosions that are unchanged from those obtained 2 years ago. Radiograph of the right knee reveals significant uniform joint-space narrowing and prominent osteophytes.

Which of the following is the most appropriate medical treatment for this patient?

(A) Etanercept
(B) Prednisone
(C) Sulfasalazine
(D) No additional therapy

Item 34

A 24-year-old woman with systemic lupus erythematosus is evaluated during a follow-up visit for a lupus flare. She was diagnosed with lupus 5 years ago. For the past year, her disease had been controlled with hydroxychloroquine and prednisone, 10 mg/d. Three months ago, she developed malar rash; oral ulcers; fatigue; pleuritis; and arthralgia involving the hands, wrists, and elbows. After her prednisone dosage was increased to 30 mg/d, her symptoms began to resolve, and the prednisone dosage was again tapered to 10 mg/d over a 6-week period. Three weeks ago, her symptoms recurred and her prednisone dosage was again increased to 30 mg/d. During an evaluation 2 weeks ago, she was asymptomatic. At that time, her prednisone dosage was decreased to 20 mg/d and azathioprine was added. She also takes calcium and vitamin D supplements.

On physical examination, temperature is 36.4 °C (97.6 °F), blood pressure is 130/76 mm Hg, pulse rate is 76/min, and respiration rate is 16/min. She has cushingoid features. Cardiopulmonary examination is normal. She does not have oral ulcers, lymphadenopathy, or rash. Abdominal examination is unremarkable. Musculoskeletal examination reveals no synovitis.

Laboratory studies:

Hemoglobin	
3 months ago	12.6 g/dL (126 g/L)
2 weeks ago	13.5 g/dL (135 g/L)
Today	9.5 g/dL (95 g/L)

Leukocyte count	
3 months ago	3200/µL (3.2×10^9/L)
2 weeks ago	6300/µL (6.3×10^9/L)
Today	1600/µL (1.6×10^9/L)

Platelet count	
3 months ago	176,000/µL (176×10^9/L)
2 weeks ago	245,000/µL (245×10^9/L)
Today	135,000/µL (135×10^9/L)

Complement (C3 and C4)	
3 months ago	Decreased
2 weeks ago	Normal
Today	Normal

Anti–double-stranded DNA antibodies	
3 months ago	Positive
2 weeks ago	Negative
Today	Negative

Which of the following is the most appropriate treatment for this patient?

(A) Discontinue azathioprine
(B) Discontinue hydroxychloroquine
(C) Increase prednisone
(D) Start intravenous immune globulin

Item 35

A 28-year-old woman is hospitalized with a 7-week history of daily fever spikes to 38.0 °C and 39.0 °C (101.4 °F and 102.2 °F) followed by return to normal. She also has chest pain and pain in the hips, shoulders, proximal interphalangeal joints, wrists, and knees. She does not have dyspnea, nausea, vomiting, diarrhea, or rash. Her only current medication is ibuprofen, which has somewhat alleviated her joint pain.

On physical examination, temperature is 37.1 °C (98.8 °F), blood pressure is 122/76 mm Hg, pulse rate is 78/min, and respiration rate is 14/min. Cardiac examination reveals a normal S_1 and S_2, and a three-component friction rub. The lungs are clear to auscultation. Shotty anterior cervical lymphadenopathy is present. There are no oral ulcers, and the oropharynx is clear. The wrists and proximal interphalangeal joints are swollen and tender bilaterally. Range of motion of the shoulders, hips, and knees elicits pain, but palpation of these joints reveals no appreciable swelling. The spleen tip is palpable, and there is no hepatomegaly.

Laboratory studies:

Hemoglobin	9.2 g/dL (92 g/L)
Leukocyte count	14,500/μL (14.5 × 10⁹/L)
Platelet count	525,000/μL (525 × 10⁹/L)
Alanine aminotransferase	138 U/L
Aspartate aminotransferase	105 U/L
Ferritin	12,000 ng/mL (12,000 mg/L)
Rheumatoid factor	Negative
Serum complement (C3 and C4)	Normal
Antinuclear antibodies	Negative
ANCA	Negative
Anti–double-stranded DNA antibodies	Negative
Urinalysis	Normal

A chest radiograph reveals an enlarged cardiac silhouette, no pulmonary infiltrates, and clear costophrenic angles. Blood cultures are negative.

Which of the following is the most likely diagnosis?

(A) Adult-onset Still disease
(B) Relapsing polychondritis
(C) Systemic lupus erythematosus
(D) Wegener granulomatosis

Item 36

A 24-year-old woman is evaluated in the emergency department for nausea, vomiting, and fatigue of 4 days' duration. She has an 18-month history of diffuse cutaneous systemic sclerosis complicated by gastroesophageal reflux disease and Raynaud phenomenon. She also has a 12-year history of asthma. Two weeks ago, she was evaluated in the emergency department for an asthma flare; at that time, her blood pressure was 100/70 mm Hg and her complete blood count, renal function studies, and urinalysis were normal. She began a course of prednisone, 40 mg/d, for 10 days. Additional medications are inhaled fluticasone-salmeterol, amlodipine, omeprazole, and inhaled albuterol as needed.

On physical examination, temperature is 37.0 °C (98.6 °F), blood pressure is 130/75 mm Hg, pulse rate is 78/min, and respiration rate is 16/min. Cardiopulmonary examination is normal except for several diffuse expiratory wheezes. There is skin thickening over the face, chest, arms, hands, and legs. There is 1+ edema of the lower extremities bilaterally.

Laboratory studies:

Hemoglobin	9.8 g/dL (98 g/L)
Platelet count	100,000/μL (100 × 10⁹/L)
Blood urea nitrogen	92 mg/dL (32.8 mmol/L)
Serum creatinine	5.7 mg/dL (434.9 μmol/L)
Urinalysis	2+ protein; 3-5 erythrocytes/hpf; no casts

A peripheral blood smear shows schistocytes.

The addition of which of the following is the most appropriate management option for this patient?

(A) Captopril
(B) Cyclosporine
(C) Plasma exchange
(D) Prednisone

Item 37

A 52-year-old woman is evaluated for a 4-day history of swelling and pain of the left ankle. She has a 6-year history of Crohn disease associated with joint involvement of the knees and ankles. Her last disease flare was 2 years ago; at that time, she was treated with a 3-month course of tapering prednisone and infliximab. She has continued taking infliximab. She also has been on azathioprine for 3 years.

On physical examination, temperature is 38.0 °C (100.5 °F), pulse rate is 88/min, and respiration rate is 18/min. The left ankle is warm and swollen, and passive range of motion of this joint elicits pain. The knees are mildly tender to palpation bilaterally but do not have effusions, warmth, or erythema. Range of motion of the knees elicits crepitus bilaterally. The remainder of the musculoskeletal examination is normal.

Arthrocentesis of the left ankle is performed and yields 3 mL of cloudy yellow fluid. The synovial fluid leukocyte count is 75,000/μL (92% neutrophils). Polarized light microscopy of the fluid shows no crystals, and Gram stain is negative. Culture results are pending.

Which of the following is the most likely diagnosis?

(A) Avascular necrosis of the ankle
(B) Crohn disease arthropathy
(C) Crystal-induced arthritis
(D) Septic arthritis

Item 38

A 72-year-old woman is evaluated for a 1-year history of progressive pain in the right knee. The pain is most acute along the medial aspect of the joint, worsens with activity, and is relieved with rest. She has no stiffness in the morning and has had no swelling. She also has not experienced locking or giving away of this joint.

On physical examination, vital signs are normal. There is bony enlargement of the proximal and distal interphalangeal joints. There is no evidence of a right knee effusion. Passive flexion and extension of the right knee are painful.

Laboratory studies, including complete blood count, erythrocyte sedimentation rate, and C-reactive protein, are normal. Radiograph of the right knee also is normal.

In addition to acetaminophen as needed, which of the following is the most appropriate next step in this patient's management?

(A) Arthroscopy
(B) Aspiration of the knee
(C) MRI of the knee
(D) Physical therapy

Item 39

A 44-year-old man is evaluated for a 2-year history of joint pain in the wrists, hands, knees, ankles, and feet. He also has a 12-year history of plaque psoriasis. His current medications include acetaminophen for joint pain, topical hydrocortisone and calcipotriene ointments, and a tar-based shampoo. He does not drink alcoholic beverages and has no history of liver disease.

On physical examination, vital signs are normal. There are large erythematous plaques with an overlying silvery scale on the elbows, knees, sacrum, and scalp. The wrists are swollen and warm bilaterally, and there is bilateral synovitis of the metacarpophalangeal joints. There are effusions on both knees. The appearance of the toes is shown.

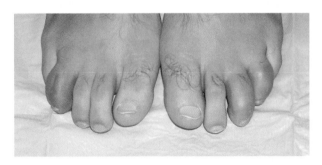

Screening laboratory tests, including metabolic profile, renal function, and liver chemistry tests, are normal.

After discussing medication options, the patient refuses to begin therapy with tumor necrosis factor α inhibitors because of concern about possible side effects.

Which of the following is the most appropriate treatment for this patient?

(A) Hydroxychloroquine

(B) Ibuprofen
(C) Methotrexate
(D) Prednisone
(E) Sulfasalazine

Item 40

A 45-year-old woman is evaluated for a 2-week history of pleuritic chest pain. She has a 6-month history of arthralgia and a 2-month history of myalgia and mild proximal muscle weakness. She has difficulty climbing stairs, rising from a chair, and removing dishes from a high cabinet. She also has a 10-year history of Raynaud phenomenon.

On physical examination, temperature is 36.4 °C (97.6 °F), blood pressure is 125/78 mm Hg, pulse rate is 90/min, and respiration rate is 18/min. Cardiopulmonary examination is normal. Abdominal examination is unremarkable. There are healed ulcerations on the second and third fingers of the right hand. There is no synovitis. Proximal upper- and lower-extremity muscle strength is 4/5 and is associated with mild muscle tenderness.

Laboratory studies:

Hemoglobin	12 g/dL (120 g/L)
Erythrocyte sedimentation rate	63 mm/h
Serum creatinine	0.9 mg/dL (68.7 µmol/L)
Creatine kinase	896 U/L
Alanine aminotransferase	98 U/L
Aspartate aminotransferase	67 U/L
Alkaline phosphatase	80 U/L
Antinuclear antibodies	Titer of 1:2560
Urinalysis	Normal

A chest radiograph shows blunting of the costophrenic angles.

Which of the following antibody assays will confirm the most likely diagnosis?

(A) Antimitochondrial
(B) Antiribonucleoprotein
(C) Anti-Ro/SSA
(D) Anti-Smith
(E) Antitopoisomerase I (anti–Scl-70)

Item 41

An 83-year-old woman is evaluated for persistent pain related to osteoarthritis of the left knee, which was diagnosed 3 years ago. She continues to ambulate with a cane as instructed by a physical therapist but is unable to walk more than 4 blocks without sitting down because of pain. She currently takes acetaminophen, but her pain remains severe. Previous treatment with acetaminophen with codeine was discontinued because of severe constipation, and tramadol was discontinued because of dizziness. Medical history is significant for hypertension, heart failure, and chronic kidney disease. She also takes lisinopril, metoprolol, and furosemide. She currently prefers medical therapy to surgical intervention, if possible.

On physical examination, the left knee has slight valgus angulation and a medium-sized effusion without warmth or erythema. There is no tenderness along the joint line. On laboratory studies, erythrocyte sedimentation rate is 10 mm/h, C-reactive protein is normal.

A radiograph of the left knee shows moderate lateral joint-space narrowing and osteophyte formation.

Which of the following is the most appropriate next step in this patient's management?

(A) Celecoxib
(B) Hyaluronan injections
(C) Hydrocodone with acetaminophen
(D) Referral for total knee arthroplasty

Item 42

A 53-year-old man is evaluated for a 6-week history of fatigue, fever, numbness and tingling in the hands and feet, mild abdominal pain, and a nodular rash on the hands, arms, and legs. He also has lost 4.1 kg (9.0 lb).

On physical examination, temperature is 37.9 °C (100.3 °F), blood pressure is 150/82 mm Hg, pulse rate is 96/min, and respiration rate is 14/min. Cardiopulmonary examination is normal. Examination of the hands reveals numerous subcutaneous nodules. There is shotty cervical, axillary, and inguinal lymphadenopathy. Abdominal examination reveals hepatomegaly and mild diffuse abdominal tenderness without rebound. The testes are tender. There is no synovitis on musculoskeletal examination.

Laboratory studies:

Hemoglobin	8.6 g/dL (86 g/L)
Leukocyte count	15,200/μL (15.2 × 10⁹/L)
Platelet count	523,000/μL (523 × 10⁹/L)
Erythrocyte sedimentation rate	113 mm/h
Alanine aminotransferase	73 U/L
Aspartate aminotransferase	85 U/L
Antinuclear antibodies	Negative
ANCA	Negative
Hepatitis B surface antigen (HBsAg)	Positive
Antibody to hepatitis B surface antigen (anti-HBs)	Negative
Hepatitis B e antigen (HBeAg)	Positive
Antibody to hepatitis C virus (anti-HCV)	Negative
Serologic test for HIV antibodies	Negative

Skin biopsy specimen is consistent with necrotizing vasculitis.

Which of the following is the most appropriate treatment for this patient?

(A) Cyclophosphamide
(B) Prednisone
(C) Prednisone plus cyclophosphamide
(D) Prednisone plus lamivudine

Item 43

A 25-year-old female preschool teacher is evaluated for a 2-week history of symmetric pain and stiffness in the small joints of the hands and feet. Three weeks ago, she developed a macular, nonpruritic, erythematous rash on the upper extremities that resolved within 3 days. At that time, she also developed low-grade fever, myalgia, and malaise that also resolved within a few days. She states that many children at her workplace have had fever and rash. She does not have a history of Raynaud phenomenon, photosensitivity, serositis, kidney disease, or anemia.

On physical examination, vital signs are normal. Cardiopulmonary examination is unremarkable. Cutaneous examination reveals no rash or scarring, and there are no oral ulcerations. There is mild diffuse soft-tissue swelling of the hands and feet bilaterally. The metacarpophalangeal and metatarsophalangeal joints are tender to palpation.

Laboratory studies:

Complete blood count	Normal
Rheumatoid factor	Negative
Antinuclear antibodies	Titer of 1:40
Urinalysis	Normal

Which of the following antibody assays will be most helpful in establishing this patient's diagnosis?

(A) Anti–cyclic citrullinated peptide antibodies
(B) Anti–double-stranded DNA antibodies
(C) Anti-topoisomerase I (anti–Scl-70) antibodies
(D) IgM antibodies against parvovirus B19

Item 44

A 43-year-old man comes for evaluation of joint pain. For the past 8 months, he has had morning stiffness that lasts approximately 30 minutes daily and polyarthralgia involving the wrists and fingers. His symptoms have not interfered with his daily activities. He has hepatitis C virus infection for which he is not currently receiving therapy. Ibuprofen has been ineffective in relieving his joint pain. His mother and younger sister have severe rheumatoid arthritis.

On physical examination, temperature is 37.0 °C (98.6 °F), blood pressure is 128/62 mm Hg, pulse rate is 68/min, and respiration rate is 12/min. Musculoskeletal examination reveals tenderness of the metacarpophalangeal and proximal interphalangeal joints bilaterally without swelling. Range of motion of all joints is full.

Laboratory studies:

Alanine aminotransferase	55 U/L
Aspartate aminotransferase	46 U/L
Alkaline phosphatase	100 U/L
Rheumatoid factor	Positive
Hepatitis C virus antibodies	Positive

Radiographs of the hands show periarticular osteopenia but no erosions.

Which of the following is the most appropriate management for this patient?

(A) Begin methotrexate
(B) Begin prednisone

(C) Obtain radiographs of the feet

(D) Perform anti–cyclic citrullinated peptide antibody assay

Item 45

A 60-year-old woman is evaluated for a 4-month history of progressive fatigue and dyspnea on exertion. She does not smoke cigarettes and denies chest pain, palpitations, dizziness, or syncope. She has a 12-year history of limited cutaneous systemic sclerosis. A screening cardiopulmonary evaluation 3 years ago was normal. She also has gastroesophageal reflux disease and Raynaud phenomenon and intermittently develops ulcers on the fingertips. Current medications are amlodipine, omeprazole, and nitroglycerin ointment.

On physical examination, temperature is 37.0 °F (98.6 °F), blood pressure is 120/80 mm Hg, pulse rate is 84/min, and respiration rate is 16/min. Cardiac examination reveals a loud pulmonic component of S_2 with fixed splitting and a 2/6 early systolic murmur at the lower left sternal border that increases with inspiration. The lungs are clear to auscultation. The abdominal examination is unremarkable. Sclerodactyly is present, and pitting scars are visible over several fingertips. There is no peripheral edema.

Complete blood count and erythrocyte sedimentation rate are normal. Electrocardiogram shows evidence of right ventricular hypertrophy. Chest radiograph shows no infiltrates.

Pulmonary function studies:

FVC	84% of predicted
FEV_1/FVC	0.8
DLCO	44% of predicted

Which of the following is the most likely diagnosis?

(A) Atrial septal defect

(B) Interstitial lung disease

(C) Left ventricular failure

(D) Pulmonary arterial hypertension

Item 46

A 62-year-old man is evaluated in the emergency department for a 1-month history of nonproductive cough, progressive dyspnea on exertion, fever, arthritis, and weakness. He has had increasing difficulty rising from a chair, climbing stairs, and holding his arms up to comb his hair. For the past week, he has noticed pain and color changes of his digits when exposed to the cold. His medical history is otherwise unremarkable, and he takes no medications.

On physical examination, temperature is 38.7 °C (101.6 °F), blood pressure is 148/88 mm Hg, pulse rate is 100/min, and respiration rate is 34/min. Pulse oximetry shows 92% oxygen saturation with the patient breathing 2 L/min of supplemental oxygen. There is no jugular venous distension. Cardiac examination reveals normal heart sounds without extra sounds, murmurs, or rubs. On pulmonary examination, late bilateral fine crackles are noted over the lower half of the lung fields. The sides of the fingers appear rough and cracked. He has tenderness

and synovial thickening involving the wrists and the second and third metacarpophalangeal joints. Grip strength is intact, but he has evidence of weakness in the muscles of the upper arms and legs and neck flexors.

Laboratory studies:

Hemoglobin	13.8 g/dL (138 g/L)
Leukocyte count	10,600/µL (10.6 × 10⁹/L)
Creatine kinase	5400 U/L
Antinuclear antibodies	Titer of 1:640
Anti–double-stranded DNA antibodies	Negative
Anti-Smith antibodies	Negative
Anti-Scl-70 antibodies	Negative
Anti-Jo-1 antibodies	Positive

Chest radiograph is shown.

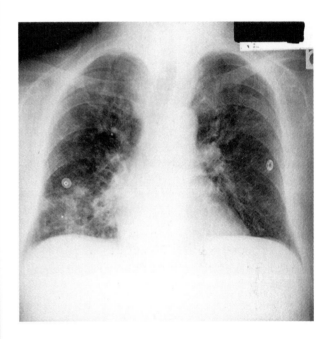

Which of the following is the most likely diagnosis?

(A) Antisynthetase syndrome

(B) Idiopathic pulmonary fibrosis

(C) Systemic lupus erythematosus

(D) Systemic sclerosis

Item 47

A 75-year-old woman is evaluated during a follow-up examination for severe pain associated with osteoarthritis of the knee. For the past 10 years, she has had gradually progressive right knee pain. Originally, her pain increased with activity and was relieved with rest; however, she now also has discomfort at rest, which disturbs her sleep. Acetaminophen, ibuprofen, naproxen, and celecoxib have been ineffective in controlling her pain; tramadol provided only modest pain relief. Three months ago, she received an intraarticular corticosteroid injection, which alleviated her pain for 1 week. Medical history is significant for hypertension and compensated heart failure. She also takes metoprolol, lisinopril, low-dose aspirin, and furosemide. Currently, the knee pain is the single condition that is impairing the quality of her life.

On physical examination, there is a 15-degree varus angulation of the right knee in the standing position. There is no effusion or other signs of inflammation. Standing radiographs of the right knee show severe medial joint-space narrowing and mild lateral joint-space narrowing.

Which of the following is the most appropriate next step in the management of this patient's knee pain?

(A) Add diclofenac
(B) Add hydrocodone-acetaminophen
(C) Refer for total knee arthroplasty
(D) Repeat intra-articular corticosteroid injection

Item 48

A 50-year-old woman is evaluated for an 8-week history of diarrhea and abdominal pain. Stools are semiformed and greasy, and bowel movements seem to be stimulated by eating. She has not had nocturnal diarrhea. She also has lost 2.0 kg (4.4 lb) over the past month. She has an 8-year history of limited cutaneous systemic sclerosis associated with gastroesophageal reflux disease and Raynaud phenomenon. She has not traveled recently, used antibiotics, ingested raw or undercooked foods, or been exposed to anyone with a diarrheal illness. Current medications are amlodipine and omeprazole.

On physical examination, temperature is 37.0 °C (98.6 °F), blood pressure is 120/80 mm Hg, pulse rate is 84/min, and respiration rate is 16/min. BMI is 22. Cardiopulmonary examination is normal. The abdomen is slightly distended and has mild diffuse tenderness to palpation; there is no organomegaly.

Laboratory studies:

Erythrocyte sedimentation rate	21 mm/h
Complete blood count	Normal
Albumin	2.8 g/dL (28 g/L)
Serum thyroid-stimulating hormone	4.1 µU/mL (4.1 mU/L)

An abdominal radiographic series shows no free air under the diaphragm and a nonspecific bowel gas pattern.

Which of the following is the most likely diagnosis?

(A) Bacterial overgrowth
(B) *Clostridium difficile*–associated colitis
(C) Irritable bowel syndrome
(D) Microscopic colitis

Item 49

An 82-year-old woman is evaluated for a flare of polymyalgia rheumatica manifested by aching in the shoulders and hips that began 2 weeks ago. She also has fatigue and malaise. She was diagnosed with polymyalgia rheumatica 8 months ago. At that time, she was prescribed prednisone,

20 mg/d; her symptoms promptly resolved; and her prednisone dosage was gradually tapered. Four months ago, her prednisone dosage was decreased from 7.5 mg/d to 5 mg/d, and her symptoms returned. Her prednisone dosage was then increased to 10 mg/d followed by a slow taper of this agent. Her prednisone dosage was most recently decreased from 7 mg/d to 6 mg/d, which is her current dosage. She also takes calcium and vitamin D supplements and a bisphosphonate.

On physical examination, vital signs are normal. Range of motion of the shoulders, neck, and hips elicits mild pain. There is no temporal artery tenderness.

Which of the following is the most appropriate treatment for this patient?

(A) Increase prednisone to 20 mg/d
(B) Increase prednisone to 7.5 mg/d; add methotrexate
(C) Increase prednisone to 20 mg/d; add methotrexate
(D) Increase prednisone to 7.5 mg/d; add infliximab

Item 50

A 52-year-old woman is evaluated during a follow-up office visit. She has hypercholesterolemia that was treated with atorvastatin for 5 years. Six months ago, she developed achy thigh muscles. At that time, laboratory studies revealed a serum creatine kinase level of 430 U/L, and she was switched to cholestyramine. Since then, her creatine kinase levels have remained elevated. Her last evaluation 2 months ago revealed a creatine kinase level of 448 U/L. She has remained minimally symptomatic with myalgia during this time. She does not drink alcoholic beverages, and her only large muscle exercise includes walking approximately 1 mile daily. There is no family history of muscle disorders.

On physical examination, vital signs are normal. BMI is 31. There is no rash. On musculoskeletal examination, proximal and distal muscle strength is intact. Neurologic examination is normal.

Laboratory studies reveal a serum creatine kinase level of 550 U/L and a normal serum thyroid-stimulating hormone level.

Which of the following diagnostic studies would be warranted for this patient?

(A) Aldolase
(B) Antinuclear antibody
(C) Erythrocyte sedimentation rate
(D) MRI of the thigh muscles

Item 51

A 67-year-old man comes for evaluation of knee pain. Two months ago, he developed pain in the right knee that worsened when he played tennis and was relieved with rest. He now has pain with most activities and occasionally at rest that is often associated with swelling. He has no morning stiffness. Maximum doses of acetaminophen provide only mild to moderate relief of pain. One year ago, he was diagnosed with coronary artery disease with a myocardial infarction and underwent intracoronary stent placement. He also has hypertension and hyperlipidemia. Current medications are atorvastatin, atenolol, isosorbide mononitrate, and low-dose aspirin.

On physical examination, blood pressure is 130/80 mm Hg. Cardiac examination shows an S_4, normal S_1 and S_2, and no murmurs or rubs. Range of motion of the right knee is painful and limited. The remainder of the musculoskeletal examination is normal.

Radiograph of the right knee shows medial joint-space narrowing, subchondral sclerosis, and osteophytes.

Which of the following is the most appropriate next therapeutic step for this patient's knee pain?

(A) Arthroscopic lavage and débridement
(B) Celecoxib
(C) Ibuprofen
(D) Total knee arthroplasty
(E) Tramadol

Item 52

A 28-year-old woman is evaluated in the emergency department for a 1-day history of nausea, vomiting, and blood per rectum. For the past several months, she has had fatigue and malaise. Two weeks ago, she developed arthralgia involving the hands and feet, intermittent pleuritic chest pain, and abdominal pain. She also has a 1-week history of low-grade fever and worsening of her abdominal pain.

On physical examination, she appears ill. Temperature is 38.3 °C (100.9 °F), blood pressure is 145/85 mm Hg, pulse rate is 112/min, and respiration rate is 16/min. There is an erythematous rash over the cheeks and forehead. Cardiopulmonary examination reveals a friction rub. Abdominal examination reveals mild distention, rare bowel sounds, and diffuse abdominal tenderness. The wrists are tender and mildly swollen. Bilateral 1+ peripheral edema is present. A stool specimen is positive for occult blood.

Laboratory studies:

Hemoglobin	8.9 g/dL (89 g/L)
Leukocyte count	2800/µL (2.8 × 10⁹/L)
Platelet count	48,000/µL (48 × 10⁹/L)
Erythrocyte sedimentation rate	116 mm/h
Reticulocyte count	2.6% of erythrocytes
Haptoglobin	5 mg/dL (50 mg/L)
Serum creatinine	1.8 mg/dL (137.3 µmol/L)
Lactate dehydrogenase	580 U/L
Serum complement (C3 and C4)	Decreased
ANCA	Negative
Antinuclear antibodies	Titer of 1:1280
Anti–double-stranded DNA antibodies	Positive
Hepatitis B surface antigen (HBsAg)	Negative
Urinalysis	2+ protein; 2+ blood; 15 leukocytes, 15-20 erythrocytes/hpf; occasional erythrocyte casts
Direct antiglobulin (Coombs) test	Positive

A peripheral blood smear is normal. Chest radiograph shows a small pleural effusion, and radiograph of the abdomen shows dilatation of the bowel loops without obstruction or free air. CT of the abdomen reveals symmetric thickening of the bowel wall, dilatation of bowel segments, and an increased number of vessels in a comb-like pattern consistent with bowel ischemia. Colonoscopy reveals scattered ulcerations suggestive of ischemia.

Which of the following is the most likely diagnosis?

(A) Crohn disease
(B) Hemolytic uremic syndrome
(C) Henoch-Schönlein purpura
(D) Polyarteritis nodosa
(E) Systemic lupus erythematosus

Item 53

A 19-year-old woman is evaluated for a 6-month history of pain and swelling of the hands. Her hands develop blue and white color changes when exposed to cold temperatures, and she has small, painful, slowly healing lesions on the tips of her fingers. She also has progressive fatigue and weakness. She takes no medications.

On physical examination, she rocks back and forth and reaches forward and uses her arms to push herself up when rising from her chair. She also has difficulty getting onto the examination table. Vital signs are normal. The appearance of a finger is shown.

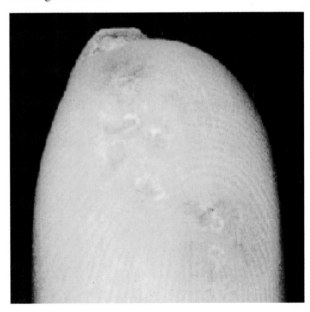

Proximal muscle strength is 3/5 in the upper and lower extremities. There are effusions of the metacarpophalangeal, wrist, and knee joints bilaterally. The remainder of the physical examination is normal.

Laboratory studies:

Hemoglobin	10.2 g/dL (102 g/L)
Leukocyte count	1900/µL (1.9 × 10⁹/L) (15% lymphocytes)
Platelet count	85,000/µL (85 × 10⁹/L)

Erythrocyte sedimentation rate	85 mm/h
Creatine kinase	5500 U/L
Alanine aminotransferase	320 U/L
Aspartate aminotransferase	270 U/L
Total bilirubin	0.8 mg/dL (13.7 μmol/L)
Antinuclear antibodies	Titer of 1:2560
Antiribonucleoprotein antibodies	Positive

Which of the following is the most appropriate next step in this patient's management?

(A) Bone marrow biopsy

(B) CT of the chest, abdomen, and pelvis

(C) Liver biopsy

(D) Prednisone

Item 54

A 27-year-old woman in the twelfth week of pregnancy is admitted to the hospital for hypertension and proteinuria. She has a 2-year history of diffuse cutaneous systemic sclerosis associated with gastroesophageal reflux disease and Raynaud phenomenon. She had been taking omeprazole but discontinued this agent when she became pregnant. Her only current medications are over-the-counter calcium carbonate and prenatal vitamins.

On physical examination, temperature is 37.0 °C (98.6 °F), blood pressure is 194/104 mm Hg, pulse rate is 84/min, and respiration rate is 17/min. Cardiopulmonary examination is normal except for an S_4 gallop. There is skin thickening over the face, chest, abdomen, arms, hands, and feet. Funduscopic examination is normal. Abdominal examination reveals a normal for pregnancy gravid uterus. Tendon friction rubs are present over the anterior lower extremities.

Laboratory studies:

Hemoglobin	7.4 g/dL (74 g/L)
Leukocyte count	8000/μL (8 × 10⁹/L)
Platelet count	66,000/μL (66 × 10⁹/L)
Serum creatinine	2.4 mg/dL (183.1 μmol/L)
Urinalysis	3+ protein; no leukocytes or erythrocytes/hpf
Alanine aminotransferase	35 U/L
Aspartate aminotransferase	32 U/L
Lactate dehydrogenase	300 U/L

A peripheral blood smear shows schistocytes.

Which of the following is the most appropriate management for this patient?

(A) Captopril

(B) Immediate delivery of the fetus

(C) Methyldopa

(D) Plasma exchange

Item 55

A 46-year-old woman is evaluated during a follow-up visit. Six months ago, she was diagnosed with dermatomyositis that manifested as proximal muscle weakness, Gottron

papules, and a serum creatine kinase level of 2300 U/L. Her disease responded well to prednisone, 60 mg/d, and this dosage was gradually tapered. One month ago, her creatine kinase level was 340 U/L, and her prednisone dosage was tapered to 20 mg/d. Her symptoms have been well controlled on this decreased dosage. Additional medications are risedronate and calcium and vitamin D supplements.

On physical examination, vital signs are normal. Proximal and distal muscle strength testing is 5/5.

Laboratory studies:

Glucose (fasting)	183 mg/dL (10.2 mmol/L)
Creatine kinase	1250 U/L
Alanine aminotransferase	87 U/L
Aspartate aminotransferase	68 U/L

Which of the following is the most appropriate management for this patient?

(A) Add cyclosporine

(B) Add methotrexate

(C) Add rituximab

(D) Increase prednisone dosage

Item 56

A 75-year-old man is evaluated for a 2-year history of pain in the left groin that radiates down the medial thigh. His pain worsens with walking and is relieved with rest. Acetaminophen provides only minimal relief for his pain. He was diagnosed with hypertension 10 years ago and also has type 2 diabetes mellitus and chronic kidney disease due to hypertensive nephropathy. Medications are glyburide, pioglitazone, and lisinopril.

On physical examination, his blood pressure is 130/80 mm Hg. The FABERE (Flexion, ABduction, External Rotation, Extension) maneuver performed on the left hip reproduces pain on external rotation. The femoral pulses are intact, and there is no femoral lymphadenopathy.

Laboratory studies:

Serum creatinine	1.9 mg/dL (145.0 μmol/L)
Blood urea nitrogen	24 mg/dL (8.6 mmol/L)
Urinalysis	Normal

Radiograph of the left hip shows superior joint-space narrowing, subchondral sclerosis, and osteophytes.

Which of the following is the most appropriate treatment of this patient's groin pain?

(A) Celecoxib

(B) Ibuprofen

(C) Sulindac

(D) Tramadol

Item 57

A 42-year-old woman is evaluated during a follow-up visit for a 3-year history of polyarthralgia involving the metacarpophalangeal and proximal interphalangeal joints of the hands, wrists, elbows, shoulders, knees, and ankles accompanied by occasional swelling of the wrists and hands. Over the past 3 months, her joint symptoms have worsened, and she has had intermittent mouth ulcers, redness of the cheeks, and pain on inspiration. She was started on naproxen 1 week ago, and she states today that her joint and chest pain has decreased by approximately 80%. She takes no other medications.

On physical examination, temperature is 37.1 °C (98.7 °F), blood pressure is 134/82 mm Hg, pulse rate is 84/min, and respiration rate is 16/min. Cardiopulmonary examination is normal. There is mild malar erythema, and there is one ulcer on the palate. Shotty cervical and axillary lymphadenopathy is present. Abdominal examination is unremarkable. Examination of her hands reveals ulnar deviation and metacarpal subluxation. The deformities in her hands are reducible, and she has full range of motion of all joints. The wrists and ankles are mildly tender.

Laboratory studies:

Hemoglobin	12.9 g/dL (129 g/L)
Leukocyte count	3900/μL (3.9 × 10⁹/L)
Erythrocyte sedimentation rate	42 mm/h
Rheumatoid factor	50 U/mL (50 kU/L)
C3	40 mg/dL (400 mg/L)
C4	10 mg/dL (100 mg/L) (normal range 13-38 mg/dL [130-380 mg/L])
Antinuclear antibodies	Titer of 1:640
Anti-Ro/SSA antibodies	Positive

Radiograph of the hands shows no erosions.

Which of the following is the most appropriate treatment for this patient?

(A) Etanercept
(B) Hydroxychloroquine
(C) Methotrexate
(D) No additional treatment

Item 58

A 73-year-old man is evaluated during a follow-up visit for dermatomyositis. His condition was diagnosed 6 months ago. His serum creatine kinase level at that time was 3000 U/L. His disease responded well to prednisone, 60 mg/d, which was gradually tapered to 20 mg/d. He also takes azathioprine, 150 mg/d; alendronate; and calcium and vitamin D supplements. He mentions that his muscle weakness has increased over the past month but denies myalgia, tenderness, or side effects related to azathioprine.

On physical examination, there are cushingoid facial changes. There is no rash. Muscle strength in the hip flexors and upper arms is 4/5. The muscles of the neck, back, upper arms, and legs are not tender to palpation.

Laboratory studies reveal a leukocyte count of 9800/μL (9.8 × 10⁹/L) and a serum creatine kinase level of 170 U/L.

Which of the following is the most appropriate next step in this patient's management?

(A) Decrease prednisone dosage
(B) Increase azathioprine dosage
(C) Substitute cyclosporine for azathioprine
(D) Substitute methotrexate for azathioprine

Item 59

A 54-year-old woman with rheumatoid arthritis is evaluated for a 3-month history of increased morning stiffness. She has not had joint swelling. She was diagnosed with rheumatoid arthritis 4 years ago and began treatment with methotrexate at that time; etanercept was added 1 year ago, and she began prednisone, 5 mg/d, 6 months ago. She also takes a folic acid supplement. Three weeks ago, she was diagnosed with superficial spreading melanoma on the leg. A wide excision was performed, and the surgical margins were clear.

On physical examination, vital signs are normal. There is a small nodule on the left elbow. The right wrist has mild synovitis and a slightly decreased range of motion. Grip strength is normal, and the metacarpophalangeal and proximal interphalangeal joints are not swollen or tender to palpation. There is a surgical wound on the patient's right leg that is healing well. The remainder of the examination is normal.

Which of the following is the most appropriate next step in this patient's treatment?

(A) Begin leflunomide
(B) Discontinue etanercept
(C) Increase the prednisone dosage
(D) No change in treatment

Item 60

A 23-year-old man is evaluated in the emergency department for a 5-day history of headache, blurred vision, and right eye pain. His eye pain increases when he attempts to read or when exposed to light. He also has a 3-year history of back stiffness that is worse in the morning and tends to improve as he becomes more active. He does not have arthralgia, arthritis, or rash. He takes no medications and is monogamous.

On physical examination, temperature is 36.8 °C (98.2 °F), blood pressure is 130/76 mm Hg, pulse rate is 85/min, and respiration rate is 14/min. There are no skin lesions. The appearance of the right eye is shown.

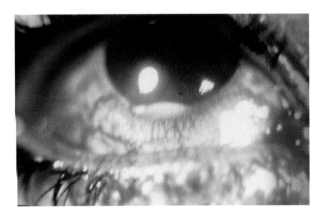

Photophobia is present during the penlight examination of the pupil. Both pupils react to light. An emergency referral is made to an ophthalmologist.

Following resolution of the eye problem, this patient should be evaluated for which of the following systemic diseases?

(A) Ankylosing spondylitis

(B) Sarcoidosis

(C) Sjögren syndrome

(D) Systemic lupus erythematosus

Item 61

A 25-year-old woman is evaluated during a routine follow-up visit. Four months ago, she was diagnosed with systemic lupus erythematosus that manifested as fatigue, malar rash, oral ulcers, pleuritis, and arthralgia. At that time, she began treatment with hydroxychloroquine and a 1-month course of low-dose prednisone.

On physical examination today, she states that her symptoms have resolved somewhat but that she still has slight fatigue and mild arthralgia in her hands, feet, and knees. Temperature is 36.4 °C (97.6 °F), blood pressure is 130/92 mm Hg, pulse rate is 84/min, and respiration rate is 18/min. She has a mild malar flush, a painless ulcer on the hard palate, and trace bilateral ankle edema. The remainder of the examination is normal.

Laboratory studies:

Hemoglobin	10 g/dL (100 g/L)
Leukocyte count	2300/μL (2.3 × 10⁹/L)
Platelet count	132,000/μL (132 × 10⁹/L)
Erythrocyte sedimentation rate	45 mm/h
Serum creatinine	1.0 mg/dL (76.3 μmol/L)
Albumin	3.1 g/dL (31 g/L)
Serum complement (C3 and C4)	Decreased
Urinalysis	2+ protein; 3+ blood; 5-10 leukocytes, 15-20 erythrocytes, and 1 erythrocyte cast/hpf

Which of the following is the next best step in this patient's treatment?

(A) Amlodipine

(B) High-dose prednisone

(C) Ibuprofen

(D) Low-dose prednisone

Item 62

A 31-year-old woman is evaluated during a follow-up visit. Five years ago, she was diagnosed with systemic lupus erythematosus that manifested as malar rash, arthralgia, mild hemolytic anemia, and thrombocytopenia; until now, her condition had been well controlled with hydroxychloroquine and low-dose prednisone. She became pregnant 7 months ago but 1 month ago developed new-onset hypertension and proteinuria and experienced a late second-trimester fetal loss. At that time, laboratory studies showed a serum creatinine level of 1.5 mg/dL (114.5 μmol/L), hypocomplementemia, anti–double-stranded DNA antibodies, and hematuria; renal biopsy revealed World Health Organization class IV lupus nephritis. Treatment with high-dose prednisone and lisinopril was begun, and she received her first dose of monthly intravenous cyclophosphamide. She also experienced a first-trimester fetal loss 1 year ago. Additional medications are calcium and vitamin D supplements.

On physical examination today, temperature is 36.4 °C (97.6 °F), blood pressure is 140/85 mm Hg, pulse rate is 88/min, and respiration rate is 16/min. Cardiopulmonary examination is normal. There is no rash or lymphadenopathy. Abdominal examination is unremarkable. There is no synovitis. There is bilateral 1+ peripheral edema.

Laboratory studies:

Serum creatinine	1.2 mg/dL (91.6 μmol/L)
Serum complement (C3 and C4)	Decreased
Antinuclear antibodies	Titer of 1:2560
Anti–double-stranded DNA antibodies	Positive
IgG-specific anticardiolipin antibodies	Elevated
Urinalysis	2+ protein; 2+ blood; 5-10 leukocytes, 10-15 erythrocytes/hpf

She would like to attempt pregnancy again after successful management of the lupus nephritis and seeks advice on how to maintain her fertility until that time.

Which of the following is the most appropriate next step in the management of this patient's reproductive health?

(A) Oral dehydroepiandrosterone

(B) Leuprolide acetate injections

(C) Oral contraceptives

(D) Placement of an intrauterine device

Item 63

A 26-year-old female electrical engineer is evaluated for a 2-year history of persistent pain and stiffness involving the low back. These symptoms are worse in the morning and are alleviated with exercise and hot showers. There are no radicular symptoms. Her only medication is ibuprofen, which has helped to relieve her symptoms. She is married and is sexually monogamous with her husband. She has no other medical problems and takes no additional medications. Family history is negative for arthritis.

On physical examination, vital signs are normal. Cutaneous examination is normal. Palpation of the pelvis and low back elicits pain. There is loss of normal lumbar lordosis, and forward flexion of the lumbar spine is decreased. Reflexes and strength are intact.

Radiographs of the lumbar spine and pelvis are normal.

Which of the following studies is most likely to establish the diagnosis in this patient?

(A) Anti–cyclic citrullinated peptide antibodies

(B) Bone scan

(C) Erythrocyte sedimentation rate

(D) HLA-B27

(E) MRI of the sacroiliac joints

Item 64

A 55-year-old woman is evaluated for a 3-month history of fatigue, morning stiffness lasting for 1 hour, and decreased grip strength. She drinks two glasses of wine daily and is unwilling to stop. Her only medication is over-the-counter ibuprofen, 400 mg three times daily, which has helped to relieve her joint stiffness.

On physical examination, vital signs are normal. Musculoskeletal examination reveals swelling of the metacarpophalangeal and proximal interphalangeal joints of the hands and decreased grip strength. There are effusions on both knees. The remainder of the physical examination is normal.

Laboratory studies:

Erythrocyte sedimentation rate	35 mm/h
C-reactive protein	Normal
Rheumatoid factor	Positive
Antinuclear antibodies	Positive
Anti–cyclic citrullinated peptide antibodies	Positive
Alanine aminotransferase	25 U/L
Aspartate aminotransferase	28 U/L

Radiographs of the hands show soft-tissue swelling but no erosions or joint-space narrowing. Radiographs of the feet are normal.

Which of the following is the most appropriate treatment for this patient?

(A) Add hydroxychloroquine
(B) Add methotrexate
(C) Add subcutaneous etanercept
(D) Increase ibuprofen dosage

Item 65

A 34-year-old man is evaluated in the emergency department for progressively worsening shortness of breath that began this morning; he is accompanied by his wife.

He is unable to provide a history due to respiratory distress. His wife states that he developed redness of the eyes approximately 6 months ago that resolved with the use of prescription eye drops but has otherwise been healthy. He currently takes no medications.

On physical examination, he is in marked respiratory distress and is using accessory muscles to breathe. Temperature is 37.1 °C (98.8 °F), blood pressure is 165/98 mm Hg, pulse rate is 135/min, and respiration rate is 50/min. Cardiac examination is normal. Tracheal stridor is heard, and tenderness is noted over the thyroid cartilage and anterior trachea. The lungs are clear to auscultation. There is no skin rash, conjunctival injection, or jaundice. The oropharynx is clear. The abdomen is soft and nontender, and there is no organomegaly. Musculoskeletal examination reveals large knee effusions bilaterally.

Laboratory studies:

Hemoglobin	14.8 g/dL (148 g/L)
Leukocyte count	17,000/µL (17 × 10⁹/L)
Erythrocyte sedimentation rate	100 mm/h
Urinalysis	Normal

Chest radiograph is normal, with no cardiomegaly and no pulmonary infiltrates. Anesthesia staff are standing by for intubation, if needed.

Which of the following is the most likely diagnosis?

(A) Goodpasture syndrome
(B) Polymyositis
(C) Relapsing polychondritis
(D) Rheumatoid arthritis
(E) Systemic sclerosis

Item 66

A 29-year-old woman with systemic lupus erythematosus (SLE) is evaluated in the office after obtaining positive results on a home pregnancy test. She has a 1-month history of nausea but is otherwise asymptomatic. Her last menstrual period was 2 months ago. This is her first pregnancy. Her SLE is well controlled with hydroxychloroquine, and her last flare was 10 months ago.

On physical examination, temperature is 36.2 °C (97.2 °F), blood pressure is 110/72 mm Hg, pulse rate is 76/min, and respiration rate is 16/min. Physical examination is normal. A repeat pregnancy test is positive.

Laboratory studies:

Hemoglobin	12.1 g/dL (121 g/L)
Leukocyte count	5400/µL (5.4 × 10⁹/L)
Platelet count	342,000/µL (342 × 10⁹/L)
Serum creatinine	0.7 mg/dL (53.4 µmol/L)
Serum complement (C3 and C4)	Normal
Antinuclear antibodies	Titer of 1:2560
Anti-Ro/SSA antibodies	Positive
Anti–double-stranded DNA antibodies	Negative
Anti-Smith antibodies	Positive
Urinalysis	Normal

She seeks advice on how to manage her SLE during her pregnancy.

Which of the following is the most appropriate management of this patient?

(A) Discontinue hydroxychloroquine
(B) Recommend termination of pregnancy
(C) Start prednisone
(D) No change in management

Item 67

A 19-year-old female college student is evaluated in the emergency department for a 10-day history of fever and a 9-day history of migratory arthralgia and swelling of the joints. She initially developed pain and swelling in the right third and fourth proximal interphalangeal joints and the left second and third metacarpophalangeal joints, which resolved within 3 days. These symptoms then manifested in the right knee and also resolved within 3 days. She now has pain and swelling of the right wrist of 3 days' duration. Her last menstrual period was 12 days ago. Her only medication is an oral contraceptive pill.

On physical examination, temperature is 38.0 °C (100.4 °F), blood pressure is 124/88 mm Hg, and pulse rate is 90/min. The oropharynx is clear. There is tenderness and puffiness of the dorsum of the right hand that extends to the distal forearm. The appearance of the right forearm is shown.

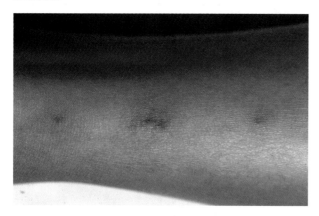

The right wrist is tender, swollen, and has a decreased range of motion. The remainder of the physical examination is normal.

Arthrocentesis is performed. The synovial fluid leukocyte count is 40,000/µL (90% polymorphonuclear cells). Polarized light microscopy of the fluid is negative for crystals, and Gram stain is negative. Culture results are pending.

Which of the following is the most likely diagnosis?

(A) Disseminated gonococcal infection
(B) Nongonococcal septic arthritis
(C) Parvovirus B19 infection
(D) Rheumatic fever

Item 68

A 20-year-old woman is evaluated for a 5-month history of malaise, fatigue, myalgia, occasional headaches, and an unintentional 4.5-kg (10.0-lb) weight loss. Five weeks ago, she began to develop pain in her arms and legs when exercising at the gym; this pain resolves with rest.

On physical examination, temperature is 37.3 °C (99.2 °F), blood pressure is 180/95 mm Hg in the right arm and 110/70 mm Hg in the left arm, pulse rate is 84/min, and respiration rate is 16/min. A bruit is heard over the left subclavian artery and left flank. The radial pulse is absent on the left side, and the dorsalis pedis pulses are absent bilaterally.

Laboratory studies:

Hemoglobin	9.2 g/dL (92 g/L)
Leukocyte count	14,000/µL (14 × 10⁹/L)
Platelet count	575,000/µL (575 × 10⁹/L)
Erythrocyte sedimentation rate	125 mm/h
Serum creatinine	1.1 mg/dL (83.9 µmol/L)
Urinalysis	Normal

Chest radiograph is normal.

Which of the following is the most likely cause of this patient's hypertension?

(A) Glomerulonephritis
(B) Pheochromocytoma
(C) Polyarteritis nodosa
(D) Renal artery stenosis

Item 69

A 35-year-old woman is evaluated in the office before the initiation of infliximab for rheumatoid arthritis. She was diagnosed with rheumatoid arthritis 5 years ago, and her disease is inadequately controlled on methotrexate and naproxen. She has no other complaints or medical problems and has no risk factors for tuberculosis. She has never been screened for tuberculosis.

Her physical examination is unremarkable except for changes compatible with active rheumatoid arthritis involving her hands and feet. A chest radiograph is normal. Forty-eight hours after administering the PPD skin test, there is 5 mm of induration at the injection site.

Which of the following is the most appropriate next step in this patient's management?

(A) Infliximab
(B) Isoniazid
(C) Isoniazid and infliximab
(D) Isoniazid, rifampin, pyrazinamide, and ethambutol

Item 70

A 67-year-old man is evaluated in the emergency department for a 2-week history of pain involving the left hip. He has had no fever. Four years ago, he underwent total arthroplasty of the left hip joint to treat osteoarthritis. One month ago, he underwent tooth extraction for an abscessed tooth.

On physical examination, temperature is 36.6 °C (98.0 °F), blood pressure is normal, and pulse rate is 90/min. Cardiopulmonary examination is normal. A well-healed surgical scar is present over the left hip, and there is no warmth or tenderness. External rotation of the left hip joint is markedly painful.

Laboratory studies reveal an erythrocyte sedimentation rate of 88 mm/h.

Radiograph of the left hip shows a normally seated left hip prosthesis. Fluoroscopic-guided arthrocentesis is performed. The synovial fluid leukocyte count is 38,000/µL (90% neutrophils). Polarized light microscopy of the fluid shows no crystals, and Gram stain is negative. Culture results are pending.

Which of the following is the most likely diagnosis?

(A) Aseptic loosening
(B) Gout
(C) Pigmented villonodular synovitis
(D) Prosthetic joint infection

Item 71

A 32-year-old man is evaluated for a 10-year history of low back pain and stiffness that are alleviated with exercise and hot showers. He does not have a history of skin, eye, or bowel disease. He has not had previous infections of the gastrointestinal or genitourinary systems.

On physical examination, vital signs are normal. The sacroiliac joints and lumbar spine are tender to palpation. There is complete loss of forward flexion in the lower spine. When standing upright against a wall, he is unable to touch the occiput to the wall.

Radiographs of the spine reveal complete fusion of the sacroiliac joints bilaterally and squaring of the vertebral bodies throughout the lumbar and thoracic spine.

In addition to starting an NSAID and physical therapy, which of the following is the most appropriate treatment for this patient?

(A) Etanercept
(B) Low-dose prednisone
(C) Methotrexate
(D) Sulfasalazine

Item 72

A 22-year-old woman is evaluated for pain and swelling of the left knee of 3 months' duration. She has pain with weight bearing, at rest, and during the night but no morning stiffness, warmth, or erythema. Four years ago, she was diagnosed with systemic lupus erythematosus. She also has a 2-year history of glomerulonephritis. She recently completed an extended course of mycophenolate mofetil and a tapering course of high-dose prednisone. Current medications are low-dose prednisone and hydroxychloroquine.

On physical examination, temperature is normal, blood pressure is 128/72 mm Hg, pulse rate is 88/min, and respiration rate is 20/min. There is a large effusion on the left knee but no warmth or erythema. Range of motion of the left knee elicits pain.

Synovial fluid leukocyte count is 800/µL (78% lymphocytes, 22% macrophages). Plain radiograph of the left knee shows no bony abnormalities.

Which of the following is the most likely diagnosis?

(A) Avascular necrosis
(B) Bacterial septic arthritis
(C) Crystal-induced arthritis
(D) Fungal arthritis

Item 73

A 48-year-old woman is evaluated for a 4-month history of pain in the shoulders, neck, and lower back. She also has fatigue and difficulty sleeping. She does not have rash, chest pain, joint pain, anorexia, weight loss, fever, or depressed mood.

On physical examination, vital signs are normal. Thyroid examination is normal. Musculoskeletal examination reveals widespread soft-tissue pain. The joints are not swollen. Muscle strength testing is limited because of pain. Deep-tendon reflexes and sensation are intact.

Laboratory studies:
Complete blood count — Normal
Erythrocyte sedimentation rate — 18 mm/h
Serum creatine kinase — 164 U/L
Serum thyroid-stimulating hormone — 3.0 µU/mL (3.0 mU/L)

Which of the following is the most appropriate next step in this patient's management?

(A) Aerobic exercise program
(B) Antinuclear antibody assay
(C) Electromyography
(D) Ibuprofen
(E) Prednisone

Item 74

A 53-year-old man is evaluated in the emergency department for a 2-day history of acute swelling and pain in the right knee. He also has had fever up to 38.3 °C (101.0 °F). Three weeks ago, he was evaluated in the emergency department for cellulitis. Medical history is significant for chronic tophaceous gout and hypertension. Medications are allopurinol, atenolol, and enalapril. He has a monogamous sexual relationship with his wife of 30 years.

On physical examination, temperature is 38.1 °C (100.5 °F), blood pressure is 124/50 mm Hg, and pulse rate is 88/min. Cardiopulmonary examination is normal. Tophi are present on both elbows. The right fourth proximal interphalangeal joint and left third metacarpophalangeal joint have soft-tissue swelling but no warmth or erythema. The right knee is markedly swollen and has overlying warmth and erythema. Palpation of this joint elicits pain.

Laboratory studies reveal a leukocyte count of 15,000/µL (15 × 10⁹/L).

Arthrocentesis is performed. The synovial fluid leukocyte count is 110,000/µL (95% neutrophils). Polarized light microscopy of the fluid reveals negatively birefringent monosodium urate crystals. Gram stain of the aspirated fluid is negative. Culture results are pending.

Which of the following is the most appropriate treatment for this patient?

(A) Ciprofloxacin
(B) Intra-articular corticosteroids
(C) Prednisone
(D) Vancomycin

Item 75

A 24-year-old woman is evaluated for a 2-week history of persistent pain and swelling in the right foot and knee and the left heel. One month ago, she developed an episode of conjunctivitis that resolved spontaneously. She also had an episode of severe diarrhea 2 months ago while traveling to Central America that was successfully treated with a 3-day course of ciprofloxacin and loperamide. She has not had other infections of the gastrointestinal or genitourinary tract, rash, or oral ulcerations. Her weight has been stable, and she has not had abdominal pain, blood in the stool, or changes in her bowel habits. She has had only one sexual partner 6 years ago. She otherwise feels well, has no other medical problems, and takes no medications other than acetaminophen for joint pain.

On physical examination, vital signs, including temperature, are normal. Cutaneous examination, including the nails and oral mucosa, is normal. There is no evidence of conjunctivitis or iritis. Musculoskeletal examination reveals swelling, warmth, and tenderness of the right knee and ankle. There is tenderness to palpation at the insertion site of the left Achilles tendon.

Which of the following is the most likely diagnosis?

(A) Enteropathic arthritis

(B) Psoriatic arthritis

(C) Reactive arthritis

(D) Rheumatoid arthritis

Item 76

A 19-year-old woman is evaluated for a 5-day history of pain and swelling of the cartilage of the left ear. There is no discharge from the ear, and she has not had fever. Three months ago, she developed redness and pain 1 week after getting the cartilage of the right ear pierced; at that time, she was prescribed a 10-day course of amoxicillin-clavulanate, and her symptoms resolved. She pierced her left nosrtil and umbilicus 9 months ago but did not develop any unusual symptoms.

On physical examination, temperature is 37.7 °C (99.8 °F), blood pressure is 110/72 mm Hg, pulse rate is 88/min, and respiration rate is 18/min. The left pinna is swollen, red, tender, and warm; the lobe of the left ear is spared. The conjunctivae and tympanic membranes are not injected, and the sclerae and oropharynx are clear. Cardiovascular examination reveals a normal S_1 and S_2 and no murmurs. The lungs are clear. Abdominal and musculoskeletal examinations are normal. There is no peripheral edema.

Which of the following is the most likely diagnosis?

(A) Churg-Strauss syndrome

(B) Cogan syndrome

(C) Relapsing polychondritis

(D) Wegener granulomatosis

Item 77

A 44-year-old woman is evaluated for a 6-week history of progressive fatigue. She was diagnosed with limited cutaneous systemic sclerosis 6 years ago. She also has gastroesophageal reflux disease well controlled with omeprazole and Raynaud phenomenon for which she takes amlodipine. She has no other medical problems and does not drink alcoholic beverages or take NSAIDs.

On physical examination, temperature is 37.0 °C (98.6 °F), blood pressure is 98/68 mm Hg, pulse rate is 96/min, and respiration rate is 18/min. Physical examination is normal except for sclerodactyly and widespread telangiectasias. Abdominal examination is unremarkable with no evidence of hepatosplenomegaly.

Laboratory studies:

Hemoglobin	8.4 g/dL (84 g/L)
Mean corpuscular volume	78 fL
Ferritin	10 ng/mL (10 mg/L)

Upper endoscopy is performed and reveals longitudinal rows of flat, reddish stripes radiating from the pylorus into the antrum consisting of ectatic and sacculated mucosal blood vessels.

Which of the following is the most likely diagnosis?

(A) Erosive gastropathy

(B) Gastric antral vascular ectasia (GAVE)

(C) Gastric lymphoma

(D) Portal hypertensive gastropathy

Item 78

A 25-year-old man is evaluated in the emergency department for acute abdominal pain that began earlier today. For the past week, he has had progressive diffuse, crampy abdominal pain that is worse in the umbilical area and is exacerbated by food. Three weeks ago, he developed persistent low-grade fever, fatigue, malaise, nasal congestion, cough, and sore throat. For the past 2 weeks, he has had a rash on his legs. He also has a 1-week history of arthralgia.

On physical examination, temperature is 37.8 °C (100.1 °F), blood pressure is 130/80 mm Hg, pulse rate is 96/min, and respiration rate is 18/min. Cardiopulmonary examination is normal. Palpable purpura is present on the legs. There is diffuse abdominal tenderness without rebound. No synovitis is present. A stool specimen is positive for occult blood.

Laboratory studies:

Hemoglobin	10.5 g/dL (105 g/L)
Leukocyte count	12,400/µL (12.4 × 10⁹/L)
Platelet count	472,000/µL (472 × 10⁹/L)
Erythrocyte sedimentation rate	54 mm/h
Serum creatinine	1.1 mg/dL (83.9 µmol/L)
Blood urea nitrogen	25 mg/dL (8.9 mmol/L)
Urinalysis	2+ protein; 3+ blood; 2-3 leukocytes, 5-10 erythrocytes/hpf; no casts

Radiographs of the chest and abdomen are normal. Skin biopsy reveals a leukocytoclastic vasculitis. Immunofluorescence testing shows perivascular IgA deposition.

Which of the following is the most appropriate initial treatment for this patient?

(A) Prednisone

(B) Prednisone plus cyclophosphamide

(C) Prednisone plus cyclophosphamide and plasmapheresis

(D) Prednisone plus infliximab

(E) Prednisone plus rituximab

Item 79

A 63-year-old woman is evaluated during a follow-up visit for a 4-week history of fatigue; pain in the proximal interphalangeal joints, knees, and hips; and low-grade fever. She has not had joint swelling, chest pain, or shortness of breath. Over the past 4 years, she has had progressive dryness of the eyes and mouth. She has a 5-month history of Raynaud phenomenon, which has been less symptomatic since beginning nifedipine 4 months ago.

On physical examination, temperature is 38.2 °C (100.8 °F), blood pressure is 125/72 mm Hg, pulse rate is 74/min, and respiration rate is 18/min. Cardiac examination is normal, and the lungs are clear. She has bilateral parotid gland enlargement, a firm 4-cm left axillary lymph node, and a shotty 0.3-cm left anterior cervical lymph node. Musculoskeletal examination reveals bilateral crepitus of the knees. There is no joint swelling.

Laboratory studies:

Hemoglobin	11.6 g/dL (116 g/L)
Leukocyte count	3400/µL (3.4 × 10⁹/L)
Platelet count	120,000/µL (120 × 10⁹/L)
Rheumatoid factor	76 U/mL (76 kU/L)
Antinuclear antibodies	Positive
Anti-Ro/SSA antibodies	Positive
Anti-La/SSB antibodies	Positive
Urinalysis	Normal
Blood cultures	No growth

A chest radiograph and mammogram are normal.

Which of the following is the next best step in this patient's management?

(A) Excisional axillary lymph node biopsy

(B) Minor salivary gland biopsy

(C) Prednisone

(D) Transthoracic echocardiography

Answers and Critiques

Item 1   Answer: D

Educational Objective: Diagnose early rheumatoid arthritis.

This patient most likely has early rheumatoid arthritis. This condition has a peak age of onset in the mid 50s. Rheumatoid arthritis most often manifests as symmetric polyarthritis involving the small joints of the hands and feet, and patients with early disease may have fever and fatigue. Rheumatoid factor assays detect the presence of IgM reactive against IgG, and rheumatoid factor is present in approximately 50% of patients with early rheumatoid arthritis. However, rheumatoid factor is not specific for rheumatoid arthritis and is present in patients with systemic lupus erythematosus, Sjögren syndrome, sarcoidosis, and other autoimmune diseases, as well as chronic infections. Anti–cyclic citrullinated peptide (CCP) antibodies are a more specific marker for rheumatoid arthritis and may be present in patients with early disease who do not have rheumatoid factor. Anti-CCP antibody assays also help to predict more severe disease, radiologic progression, and poorer functional outcomes.

Hypothyroidism may cause fatigue and is occasionally associated with polyarthralgia. However, this patient's normal thyroid-stimulating hormone level excludes a diagnosis of hypothyroidism.

Parvovirus B19 infection may manifest as fatigue, fever, rheumatoid factor positivity, and joint manifestations that resemble rheumatoid arthritis. This condition is usually self limited and resolves after several months. Affected adults commonly have nonspecific rashes but only rarely develop the characteristic rash of erythema infectiosum that defines infection in children, which is known as the "slapped cheek" rash. The presence of anti-CCP antibodies and the absence of IgM antibodies against parvovirus B19 in this patient argue against active parvovirus B19 infection. This patient's IgG antibodies against parvovirus B19 may be related to a previous infection with this virus that has since resolved.

Polymyalgia rheumatica is characterized by fatigue, aching, and morning stiffness that involve the shoulder and hip girdles and is sometimes associated with giant cell arteritis. Fever, frank joint swelling, and symmetric involvement of the small joints of the hands and feet occur in a minority of patients with polymyalgia rheumatica. Patients with this condition usually have a markedly elevated erythrocyte sedimentation rate and anemia. This patient's lack of shoulder and hip girdle symptoms argues against this diagnosis.

Systemic lupus erythematosus develops more frequently in women of reproductive age compared with the general population. This condition may be associated with polyarthritis and constitutional symptoms but is unlikely in the absence of systemic manifestations, such as rash, pleuritis, and cytopenias.

> **KEY POINT**
> - Anti–cyclic citrullinated peptide antibodies are a more specific marker for rheumatoid arthritis than rheumatoid factor and may be present in patients with early disease who do not have rheumatoid factor.

Bibliography

Majithia V, Geraci SA. Rheumatoid arthritis: diagnosis and management. Am J Med. 2007;120(11):936-939. [PMID: 17976416]

Item 2   Answer: A

Educational Objective: Treat thrombotic microangiopathy associated with the antiphospholipid antibody syndrome in a patient with systemic lupus erythematosus.

This patient has a 3-year history of systemic lupus erythematosus (SLE). Her history of deep venous thrombosis, pulmonary embolism, and three first-trimester miscarriages also is strongly suggestive of the antiphospholipid antibody syndrome (APS). This diagnosis is confirmed by the presence of anticardiolipin antibodies and a lupus anticoagulant. APS is characterized by the presence of at least one type of autoantibody known as an antiphospholipid antibody and at least one recognized clinical feature of this condition, which may include venous or arterial thromboses, recurrent fetal loss, or thrombocytopenia.

This patient now presents with new-onset hypertension, proteinuria, renal failure, and a thrombotic microangiopathy seen on renal biopsy. These findings are most likely caused by her APS, and the most appropriate treatment is heparin. Although corticosteroids, plasmapheresis, and rituximab have been used in patients with catastrophic APS, anticoagulation is considered first-line treatment for APS-related microangiopathy.

Determining whether acute kidney injury in patients with SLE who have antiphospholipid antibodies is associated with inflammation, which would be suggestive of SLE, or thrombosis, which would be suggestive of APS, is critical in order to initiate appropriate treatment. The presence of a thrombotic microangiopathy on renal biopsy in a patient with anticardiolipin antibodies and a lupus anticoagulant suggests that this patient's renal failure is a manifestation of APS and therefore thrombotic in origin. The therapy for APS is the same regardless of whether the disorder is primary or secondary to SLE. Anticoagulation therapy with heparin, followed by warfarin, is indicated in patients with thrombotic-associated manifestations of this condition.

Prednisone and cyclophosphamide are used in the treatment of lupus nephritis. However, this patient currently has no symptoms of active SLE. In addition, her renal biopsy reveals no evidence of inflammation consistent with lupus nephritis, anti–double-stranded DNA antibody assay is negative, and her complement levels are normal.

Plasmapheresis plus fresh frozen plasma is indicated to treat thrombotic thrombocytopenic purpura-hemolytic uremic syndrome (TTP-HUS), which may be associated with SLE. Rituximab also has been used to treat this condition. The presentation of TTP-HUS is similar to that of APS-associated thrombotic microangiopathy, and renal biopsy results in patients with TTP-HUS and APS-associated thrombotic microangiopathy can be indistinguishable. However, TTP-HUS would not explain the presence of antiphospholipid antibodies. In addition, patients with TTP-HUS often have fever, mental status changes, and severe thrombocytopenia. The microangiopathic hemolytic anemia associated with TTP-HUS is characterized by numerous schistocytes on peripheral blood smear and usually is associated with a high reticulocyte count, both of which are absent in this patient.

KEY POINT

- **Anticoagulation therapy with heparin followed by warfarin is indicated in patients who have thrombotic microangiopathy associated with the antiphospholipid antibody syndrome.**

Bibliography
Fischer MJ, Rauch J, Levine JS. The antiphospholipid syndrome. Semin Nephrol. 2007; 27(1):35-46. [PMID: 17336687]

Item 3   Answer: A

Educational Objective: Manage acute monoarticular arthritis.

Acute monoarticular arthritis should be presumed to be infectious until proven otherwise by synovial fluid analysis and culture via arthrocentesis; the presence of a synovial fluid leukocyte count higher than 50,000/μL would strongly suggest an infectious process. The most appropriate next step in this patient's management is therefore arthrocentesis of the left knee. Because infectious arthritis is associated with significant morbidity and mortality, patients whose clinical presentation is suspicious for this condition should be treated immediately with empiric antibiotic therapy until culture results are available.

This patient's diabetes mellitus places him at increased risk for infectious arthritis, and the presence of fever as well as erythema and swelling of the involved joint further raises suspicion for this condition.

The differential diagnosis of acute monoarticular arthritis includes gouty arthritis, fracture, and Lyme disease. Allopurinol therapy would not be indicated for a first attack of gout or during an acute flare of gout. Also,

crystal-induced arthritis and infectious arthritis may coexist, and infection must be excluded via synovial fluid analysis before beginning therapy for gout.

In patients with long-standing gout, joint radiographs may reveal accumulated effects of inflammation, such as joint-space narrowing and destruction of the joint surface. Although highly suggestive of gout, radiographic abnormalities are not diagnostic of this condition and are usually absent in a first attack of acute gouty arthritis. Patients with acute calcium pyrophosphate deposition disease may have no radiographic abnormalities, and, conversely, chondrocalcinosis may be present in asymptomatic patients. In infectious arthritis, changes seen on joint radiographs may include bone damage but are relatively late findings. Early in the course of septic arthritis, soft-tissue fullness and joint effusions are often the only initial radiographic findings.

Serologic testing for Lyme disease would not be the most appropriate next step in the management of a patient who does not have definite risk of exposure for this condition, such as living in an endemic area. Furthermore, arthritis typically is a late manifestation of Lyme disease and manifests subacutely. In patients with Lyme arthritis, swelling is usually more prominent than pain and significant erythema is rare.

KEY POINT

- **Acute monoarticular arthritis should be presumed to be infectious until proven otherwise by synovial fluid analysis and culture via arthrocentesis.**

Bibliography
Pascual E, Jovaní V. Synovial fluid analysis. Best Pract Res Clin Rheumatol. 2005;19(3):371-386. [PMID: 15939364]

Item 4   Answer: E

Educational Objective: Diagnose HIV-related psoriatic arthritis.

This patient should be tested for HIV infection. He has extensive new-onset psoriasis accompanied by asymmetric peripheral arthritis that predominantly involves the small joints and dactylitis. This constellation of symptoms is consistent with psoriatic arthritis. Psoriasis, psoriatic arthritis, or reactive arthritis may be presenting signs of HIV infection or may appear after the diagnosis of HIV infection is established. Compared with psoriasis that develops in the general population, HIV-associated psoriasis is more likely to have an explosive onset and more severe disease course that may include nail changes, palmar and plantar involvement, and erythroderma. Underlying HIV infection should therefore be excluded in all patients with new-onset psoriasis or psoriatic arthritis, as well as in those with mild forms of these conditions who experience an explosion of their disease. Diagnosis of HIV infection is important for the purposes of identifying and managing a comorbidity but also because a patient's immune status may affect the selection of treatment for psoriasis; for example, immunosuppressive therapy would not be indicated in a patient with HIV infection.

The presence of anti–cyclic citrullinated peptide antibodies is relatively specific for rheumatoid arthritis. However, rheumatoid arthritis is unlikely in a patient with an asymmetric pattern of joint disease and would not explain the temporal association between this patient's arthritis and new-onset psoriasis.

Patients with systemic lupus erythematosus (SLE) and hepatitis C virus infection may have musculoskeletal and cutaneous manifestations. However, joint involvement in SLE, which is associated with antinuclear antibodies, typically manifests as symmetric arthritis that involves the small and large joints. In addition, patients with SLE may present with many types of cutaneous lesions, including photosensitivity, malar rash, subacute cutaneous lupus, and discoid lupus. However, none of these conditions resembles the erythematous plaque with a thick silvery scale that is characteristic of chronic plaque psoriasis.

Joint involvement in patients with hepatitis C virus infection also is more likely to be symmetric and more commonly manifests as arthralgia instead of frank arthritis. Furthermore, skin disease in these patients usually consists of ulcerations and purpuric rash that is often limited to the lower extremities.

The spondyloarthropathies are associated with an increased incidence of HLA-B27 compared with the general population. However, patients with psoriatic arthritis that predominantly manifests as peripheral joint involvement are only slightly more likely to have HLA-B27 than the general population. Furthermore, most HLA-B27–positive patients do not develop a spondyloarthropathy. This study therefore would not help to diagnose this patient's condition because it lacks both sensitivity and specificity.

KEY POINT

- **Underlying HIV infection should be excluded in all patients with new-onset psoriasis or psoriatic arthritis, as well as in those with mild forms of these conditions who experience an explosion of their disease.**

Bibliography
Mamkin I, Mamkin A, Ramanan SV. HIV-associated psoriasis. Lancet Infect Dis. 2007;7(7):496. [PMID: 17597572]

Item 5   Answer: D

Educational Objective: Treat an acute attack of gout.

This patient has gout, which manifests as acute, intermittent attacks of severe pain, redness, and swelling of a joint accompanied by intracellular urate crystals seen on polarized light microscopy of the synovial fluid. The most appropriate treatment for this patient is an intra-articular corticosteroid injection. Early attacks of gout are typically monoarticular and usually involve a joint in the lower extremities, particularly the first metatarsophalangeal joint. Affected joints may be exquisitely tender to the touch and have a painful range of motion. Gout also is associated with an inflammatory synovial fluid leukocyte count during an acute attack and an elevated serum uric acid level, although many patients with hyperuricemia do not develop gout.

Intra-articular corticosteroid injection has been shown to rapidly treat acute gout. This therapy is particularly useful in patients in whom NSAIDs or oral or parenteral corticosteroids are contraindicated. Furthermore, local injection therapy with a corticosteroid only minimally affects glycemic control. However, infectious arthritis must be excluded before this treatment is administered.

Allopurinol would help to decrease this patient's uric acid level. However, use of uric acid–lowering agents during an acute attack does not ameliorate the attack of gout and may prolong an attack or cause a more frequent attack rate. Furthermore, allopurinol may cause a rare but serious hypersensitivity syndrome in patients who have renal insufficiency. Therefore, this agent should be used with caution starting at a low dose in this population group.

Effective treatment of acute attacks of gout involves high-dose therapy with NSAIDs, corticosteroids, or colchicine. Immediately initiating NSAID treatment at anti-inflammatory doses is most likely more important than the specific agent used. However, NSAIDs are contraindicated in this patient because of his chronic kidney disease.

Colchicine is most effective for the treatment of acute gout when used within the first 24 hours of symptom onset but would be less efficacious in this patient, whose symptoms began 4 days ago. This agent is associated with potential bone marrow toxicity, particularly in patients with renal insufficiency.

Corticosteroids may be given orally, intramuscularly, or by intra-articular injection. These agents have similar efficacy to NSAIDs, but a high-dose oral or parenteral corticosteroid may exacerbate this patient's diabetes mellitus and is therefore relatively contraindicated.

KEY POINT

- **Intra-articular injections of corticosteroids have been shown to be effective in the treatment of acute gout attacks and are useful in patients who cannot take NSAIDs or oral and parenteral corticosteroids.**

Bibliography
Keith MP, Gilliland WR. Updates in the management of gout. Am J Med. 2007;120(3):221-224. [PMID: 17349440]

Item 6   Answer: C

Educational Objective: Treat Behçet disease.

This patient's lower-extremity lesions are consistent with erythema nodosum. She also has oral ulcers, an elevated erythrocyte sedimentation rate, and a history of genital mucosal ulcers and uveitis. This clinical presentation strongly suggests a diagnosis of Behçet disease, and the most appropriate management for this patient is prednisone.

Diagnostic criteria for Behçet disease consist of the presence of oral ulcerations that recur at least three times in 1 year and at least two of the following manifestations: recurrent genital ulcerations, inflammatory eye disease, cutaneous lesions, and positive results on a pathergy test (characterized by a papule developing 48 hours after insertion of a 20-gauge needle intradermally). Patients with Behçet disease also may have central nervous system vasculitis; a nonerosive arthritis that involves the medium and large joints; and elevated markers of inflammation, such as the erythrocyte sedimentation rate. Other manifestations include arterial and venous thromboses, and patients with Behçet disease have a high mortality rate associated with arterial aneurysm rupture.

Treatment of Behçet disease is directed toward the involved organ system. Although erythema nodosum can be treated with NSAIDs, use of these agents has not alleviated this patient's symptoms. Treatment with a corticosteroid such as prednisone is therefore reasonable.

Leflunomide and sulfasalazine are indicated to treat rheumatoid arthritis but are not useful in patients with erythema nodosum or Behçet disease. Rheumatoid arthritis may present with Raynaud phenomenon and subcutaneous nodules. However, rheumatoid nodules typically develop on pressure points and are not tender or erythematous. Rheumatoid arthritis also is characterized by swelling and tenderness in and around the joints and may manifest as joint stiffness, synovial hypertrophy, synovitis, joint effusion, and loss of normal range of motion. These findings are absent in this patient.

Sulfasalazine also is used to treat inflammatory bowel disease, which may be associated with erythema nodosum. However, this patient has no gastrointestinal manifestations.

KEY POINT

- **Treatment in patients with Behçet disease is directed toward the involved organ system.**

Bibliography

Yurdakul S. Evidence-based treatment of Behçet's syndrome [erratum in Clin Exp Rheumatol. 2007;25(3):507-508]. Clin Exp Rheumatol. 2006;24(5 Suppl 42):S53-S55. [PMID: 17067428]

Item 7   Answer: A

Educational Objective: Diagnose calcium pyrophosphate dihydrate deposition disease.

This patient has calcium pyrophosphate dihydrate (CPPD) deposition disease presenting as pseudogout. Pseudogout manifests as acute or subacute attacks of warmth and swelling in one to two joints that resemble acute gouty arthropathy. Pseudogout is associated with inflammatory synovial fluid and the presence of CPPD crystals that are weakly positively birefringent and rhomboid in shape seen on polarized light microscopy. Treatment of an acute pseudogout attack primarily involves NSAIDs, but a corticosteroid or colchicine would be appropriate alternative choices.

This patient's radiographic and physical examination findings also are suggestive of osteoarthritis. Osteoarthritis that manifests in patients with CPPD deposition or the presence of chondrocalcinosis on radiography is known as pseudo-osteoarthritis. This degenerative condition mimics osteoarthritis except that it may affect joints not typically involved in osteoarthritis, such as the wrists, metacarpophalangeal joints, shoulders, and ankles. The synovial fluid in patients with pseudo-osteoarthritis is noninflammatory. Both pseudo-osteoarthritis and pseudogout may be present in the same patient. The treatment of pseudo-osteoarthritis is no different than the treatment of osteoarthritis and includes adequate analgesia, physical and occupational therapy, and arthroplasty for symptomatic disease unresponsive to more conservative therapy.

Characteristic features of chronic apatite deposition disease include large, minimally inflammatory effusions that usually develop in the shoulder or knee, destruction of associated tendon structures, and chronic pain. Calcium apatite crystals may only appear as amorphous nonbirefringent crystalline clumps on synovial fluid analysis and therefore are not identified on routine examination. Identification of these crystals requires special staining or crystal analysis that is not routinely available. The absence of these crystals in this patient excludes this condition.

Gout is caused by the deposition of monosodium urate crystals in the tissues of and around the joints. Early attacks of gout are monoarticular and most commonly involve the first metatarsophalangeal joint, whereas chronic gout may manifest as symmetric involvement of the small joints of the hands and feet accompanied by tophi and subcortical erosions on radiography. Definitive diagnosis of gout is established by the presence of strongly negatively birefringent needle-shaped crystals on polarized light microscopy of synovial fluid or fluid from a tophus, which is not consistent with this patient's findings.

The diagnosis of septic arthritis should be considered in all patients with acute monoarthritis and a sudden increase in pain in a chronically damaged joint. This patient's joint fluid is inflammatory, but the leukocyte count is not sufficiently elevated to suggest septic arthritis.

- Pseudogout is associated with acute or sub-acute attacks of warmth and swelling in one to two joints that resemble acute gouty arthropathy and weakly positive birefringent crystals that are rhomboid in shape seen on polarized light microscopy of synovial fluid.

Bibliography

Rosenthal AK. Update in calcium deposition diseases. Curr Opin Rheumatol. 2007;19(2):158-162. [PMID: 17278931]

Item 8   Answer: B

Educational Objective: Diagnose cervical spine instability in a patient with rheumatoid arthritis.

Patients with long-standing rheumatoid arthritis have a significant risk of cervical instability at the atlantoaxial articulation, and this patient's painful, decreased extension of the cervical spine raises suspicion for this condition. Additional manifestations of cervical instability at this site include occipital headaches, loss of coordination, paresthesias of the hands and feet, and urinary retention or incontinence, although this condition may be relatively asymptomatic until late in the disease course.

Cervical spine radiographs with flexion and extension views are indicated for any patient with aggressive or long-standing rheumatoid arthritis to evaluate for cervical instability at this site. Evaluation for this condition is particularly important in the perioperative setting, when extension of the neck for intubation may lead to spinal cord compromise and resultant paraplegia.

Patients with compensated, asymptomatic heart failure can generally undergo surgery if other risk factors are acceptable. Because this patient has no history of heart failure and a normal physical examination and electrocardiogram, cardiac risk is low and further preoperative evaluation is unnecessary. The role of B-type natriuretic peptide hormone in preoperative risk assessment is currently undefined and is not recommended for asymptomatic individuals.

Rheumatoid arthritis may be associated with pulmonary involvement, but routine spirometry is not indicated for patients without pulmonary disease before surgery. Preoperative spirometry does not improve risk assessment over that of clinical evaluation alone.

In the presence of a normal serum creatinine level, routine urinalysis is unlikely to detect the presence of significant kidney disease. Moreover, current evidence does not support a relationship between asymptomatic urinary tract infection and surgical infection. Therefore, routine preoperative urinalysis is not recommended for most surgical procedures.

- Cervical spine radiographs with flexion and extension views are indicated for any patient with aggressive or long-standing rheumatoid arthritis to evaluate for cervical instability at the atlantoaxial articulation and are particularly important in patients who may undergo intubation.

Bibliography

Neva MH, Häkkinen A, Mäkinen H, Hannonen P, Kauppi M, Sokka T. High prevalence of asymptomatic cervical spine subluxation in patients with rheumatoid arthritis waiting for orthopaedic surgery. Ann Rheum Dis. 2006;65(7):884-888. [PMID: 16269427]

Item 9   Answer: D

Educational Objective: Evaluate cryoglobulinemic vasculitis.

This patient has constitutional symptoms, palpable purpura, and a foot drop consistent with mononeuritis multiplex. In addition, her elevated blood pressure, elevated serum creatinine level, proteinuria, and hematuria are suggestive of glomerulonephritis. This clinical presentation is compatible with many forms of vasculitis, but cryoglobulinemic vasculitis is the most likely diagnosis in a patient with hepatomegaly, abnormal liver chemistry studies, hypergammaglobulinemia (suggested by the elevated total protein and low albumin level), profound hypocomplementemia, and the presence of rheumatoid factor. A serum cryoglobulin assay is the most appropriate next diagnostic step in this patient.

Cryoglobulins are immunoglobulins that precipitate in the cold and have rheumatoid factor activity (that is, they bind to the Fc portion of immunoglobulins). Type II cryoglobulinemia is most commonly associated with vasculitis, and cryoglobulins in this setting are monoclonal and are bound to polyclonal IgG. Approximately 85% to 95% of cases of type II cryoglobulinemia are associated with hepatitis C virus infection, which this patient most likely has based on her constitutional symptoms, history of injection drug use, and liver chemistry study abnormalities.

The ANCA-associated vasculitides (Wegener granulomatosis, microscopic polyangiitis, and Churg-Strauss syndrome) may be associated with purpura, mononeuritis multiplex, and glomerulonephritis. However, none of these conditions would explain this patient's hypocomplementemia, hypergammaglobulinemia, or high titers of rheumatoid factor.

An anti–cyclic citrullinated peptide antibody assay would be warranted in a patient in whom rheumatoid arthritis is suspected. This patient is rheumatoid factor positive, but her clinical presentation is more consistent with vasculitis than rheumatoid arthritis. Palpable purpura is rarely associated with rheumatoid arthritis and usually develops only in patients with long-standing erosive rheumatoid arthritis, which is not compatible with this patient's history. Rheumatoid arthritis occasionally is associated with the presence of cryoglobulins, but cryoglobulins in patients with rheumatoid arthritis are typically polyclonal (type III) and are not associated with vasculitis.

Anti–double-stranded DNA antibodies are highly specific for systemic lupus erythematosus (SLE). SLE may manifest as mononeuritis multiplex, purpura, glomerulonephritis, and hypocomplementemia but is not usually associated with abnormal results on liver chemistry studies. In addition, more than 99% of patients with SLE have antinuclear antibodies, which are absent in this patient.

Because patients with hepatitis C virus infection commonly have coinfection with HIV and share the same risk factors for hepatitis B, screening for infection with hepatitis B and C virus as well as HIV also would be indicated in this patient.

KEY POINT

- **Cryoglobulinemic vasculitis secondary to hepatitis C virus infection may be associated with hepatomegaly, abnormal findings on liver chemistry studies, hypergammaglobulinemia, hypocomplementemia, and the presence of rheumatoid factor.**

Bibliography

Ferri C, Mascia MT. Cryoglobulinemic vasculitis. Curr Opin Rheumatol. 2006;18(1):54-63. [PMID: 16344620]

Item 10   Answer: D

Educational Objective: Diagnose acute osteoarthritis.

This patient most likely has osteoarthritis of the knee. Osteoarthritis may manifest as acute monoarticular arthritis and is usually noninflammatory. This condition is characterized by pain on activity that is relieved with rest and most commonly involves the proximal and distal interphalangeal and first carpometacarpal joints of the hands as well as the weight-bearing joints such as the knees and hips. Range of motion of the involved joint in patients with osteoarthritis is usually painful and may be limited. This patient's radiographic findings of joint-space narrowing and osteophytes are consistent with osteoarthritis. The synovial fluid leukocyte count in patients with osteoarthritis is typically between 200 and 2000/µL and may be associated with a predominance of lymphocytes.

Bacterial, crystal-induced, and fungal arthritis also may manifest as monoarticular arthritis. However, these conditions typically are associated with inflammation and would typically cause morning stiffness, warmth, and erythema of the involved joint. Bacterial and fungal arthritis would most likely be associated with a synovial fluid leukocyte count of at least 10,000/µL with a predominance of neutrophils,

and the synovial fluid leukocyte count in patients with bacterial arthritis often exceeds 100,000/µL. Finally, bacterial and crystal-induced arthritis often have an acute presentation, whereas fungal arthritis is usually chronic in nature at the time of presentation.

KEY POINT

- **The acute presentation of a noninflammatory monoarthritis involving a weight-bearing joint is suggestive of osteoarthritis.**

Bibliography

Hunter DJ. In the clinic. Osteoarthritis. Ann Intern Med. 2007; 147(3):ITC8-1-ITC8-16. [PMID: 17679702]

Item 11   Answer: A

Educational Objective: Treat Churg-Strauss syndrome.

This patient has a long history of allergic rhinitis and asthma that has worsened over the past 2 months. She now presents with a multisystem illness characterized by fever, eosinophilia, pulmonary infiltrates, cardiomyopathy, and positive antimyeloperoxidase antibody titers. In addition, the presence of erythrocyte casts on urinalysis and her hypertension, hematuria, proteinuria, and elevated serum creatinine level are consistent with glomerulonephritis. This clinical presentation is strongly suggestive of Churg-Strauss syndrome, and the most appropriate management for this patient is methylprednisolone plus cyclophosphamide.

The Churg-Strauss syndrome is a multisystem disorder characterized by the presence of allergic rhinitis, asthma, and eosinophilia. This condition has a mean age of diagnosis of 48 years, and the most commonly involved organ in affected patients is the lung followed by the skin. However, involvement of any organ may occur in patients with this condition, including the cardiovascular, gastrointestinal, renal, and central nervous systems. High-dose corticosteroids are indicated to treat this condition; affected patients with cardiac, gastrointestinal, renal, or central nervous system involvement also should receive cyclophosphamide.

Hydroxyurea, imatinib, and bone marrow transplantation are used to manage hypereosinophilic syndromes, and imatinib is particularly effective in patients with platelet-derived growth factor receptor-β rearrangements. Hypereosinophilic syndromes can present with eosinophilia and multisystem disease but would not cause positive ANCA titers. The absence of immature cells on peripheral blood smear or splenomegaly and her relatively low levels of bone marrow hypereosinophilia also argue against a clonal hypereosinophilic syndrome.

KEY POINT

- **Patients with Churg-Strauss syndrome who have cardiac, gastrointestinal, renal, or central nervous system involvement should be treated with cyclophosphamide in addition to high-dose corticosteroids.**

Bibliography
Bosch X, Guilabert A, Espinosa G, Mirapeix E. Treatment of antineu-trophil cytoplasmic antibody-associated vasculitis: a systematic review. JAMA. 2007;298(6):655-669. [PMID: 17684188]

Item 12   Answer: A

Educational Objective: Treat Raynaud phenomenon associated with systemic sclerosis.

This patient has Raynaud phenomenon, which is present in more than 95% of patients with systemic sclerosis and is particularly likely to develop in patients with limited cutaneous disease. The most appropriate treatment for this patient is amlodipine.

Systemic sclerosis is classified according to the degree of skin involvement. Systemic sclerosis with limited cutaneous involvement, or CREST syndrome (calcinosis, Raynaud phenomenon, esophageal dysmotility, sclerodactyly, and telangiectasia), manifests as skin thickening distal to the elbows and knees. Conversely, systemic sclerosis with diffuse cutaneous involvement is associated with skin thickening proximal to the elbows and knees. Diffuse and limited cutaneous systemic sclerosis may affect the face.

Episodes of Raynaud phenomenon are often precipitated by cold exposure or stress and usually involve the extremities. In patients with Raynaud phenomenon, cigarette smoking is contraindicated and avoidance of cold is recommended; pharmacologic therapy is warranted for patients in whom these interventions do not provide sufficient relief. Dihydropyridine calcium channel blockers such as amlodipine have been shown to reduce the frequency and severity of attacks in patients with both primary and secondary Raynaud phenomenon, and these agents are frequently used as first-line treatment in this condition. Other agents used to manage Raynaud phenomenon include peripherally acting α-1 blockers, phosphodiesterase inhibitors, and endothelin receptor antagonists.

Topical nitrates applied to the finger webs are often used in the treatment of Raynaud phenomenon but are usually used as second-line therapy. Oral therapy with nitroglycerin is less effective and less well tolerated than amlodipine and is not indicated as a first-line drug for this condition.

Raynaud phenomenon is caused by microvascular involvement in patients with systemic sclerosis and is characterized by intimal proliferation and progressive luminal obliteration, as well as digital spasm. This process does not respond to anti-inflammatory agents; therefore, prednisone is not indicated in the treatment of Raynaud phenomenon.

β-Blockers such as propranolol are not indicated in the treatment of Raynaud phenomenon and may actually worsen symptoms by preventing β-adrenergic–mediated vasodilation.

KEY POINT
- Use of a dihydropyridine calcium channel blocker is warranted in patients with Raynaud phenomenon in whom cold avoidance does not provide sufficient relief.

Bibliography
Henness S, Wigley FM. Current drug therapy for scleroderma and secondary Raynaud's phenomenon: evidence-based review. Curr Opin Rheumatol. 2007;19(6):611-618. [PMID: 17917543]

Item 13   Answer: B

Educational Objective: Manage giant cell arteritis.

This patient's headache, temporal artery tenderness, acute visual loss, fever, and mild anemia are strongly suggestive of giant cell arteritis (GCA). Immediate high-dose intravenous methylprednisolone is indicated for this patient. Pain in the shoulder and hip girdle accompanied by a significant elevation in the erythrocyte sedimentation rate is consistent with polymyalgia rheumatica, which is present in approximately 33% of patients with GCA. Anterior ischemic optic neuropathy usually causes acute and complete visual loss in patients with GCA, and funduscopic examination of these patients typically reveals a pale, swollen optic nerve.

Rarely, patients with GCA regain vision if treated immediately with high doses of an intravenous corticosteroid such as methylprednisolone (1 g/d or 100 mg every 8 hours for 3 days) followed by oral prednisone (1 to 2 mg/kg/d). More importantly, this aggressive regimen helps to prevent blindness in the contralateral eye. Therefore, although temporal artery biopsy is the gold standard for diagnosing GCA, diagnostic testing should not precede treatment in patients whose clinical presentation is suspicious for this condition.

Even in the absence of visual loss, GCA is a medical emergency. In a patient whose condition is suspicious for GCA but who does not have visual loss, immediate initiation of high-dose oral prednisone before diagnostic testing is performed also is indicated. Whether intravenous corticosteroid therapy is more effective than oral administration of prednisone for patients with GCA and visual loss remains uncertain. Nevertheless, intravenous therapy seems reasonable in this circumstance and is recommended by many experts, even though rigorous studies have not validated this approach. However, it is clear that low-dose oral prednisone, which is an adequate treatment for isolated polymyalgia rheumatica, does not sufficiently treat GCA.

A process in the brain is unlikely to cause monocular visual loss, and patients with GCA typically have normal findings on brain MRI. Therefore, this study would most likely be unhelpful in this patient.

In patients whose condition raises a strong suspicion of GCA, temporal artery biopsy should be performed after corticosteroid therapy is begun. Corticosteroid therapy will not affect the results of temporal artery biopsy as long as biopsy is performed within 2 weeks of initiating this therapy; positive biopsy results have been seen as late as 6 weeks after institution of high-dose corticosteroid therapy, but the yield of biopsy is higher when this study is performed sooner.

KEY POINT

- **In patients whose clinical presentation is suspicious for giant cell arteritis, corticosteroid therapy should be instituted immediately, before diagnostic testing is performed.**

Bibliography

Fraser JA, Weyand CM, Newman NJ, Biousse V. The treatment of giant cell arteritis. Rev Neurol Dis. 2008;5(3):140-152. [PMID: 18838954]

Item 14   Answer: A

Educational Objective: Diagnose septic arthritis in a patient with rheumatoid arthritis.

This patient most likely has septic arthritis, which usually manifests as acute monoarthritis and is characterized by pain on passive range of motion in the absence of known trauma. Arthrocentesis of the wrist will most likely help to establish a diagnosis in this patient.

Septic arthritis should particularly be suspected in patients with underlying rheumatologic disorders such as rheumatoid arthritis who present with a sudden single joint flare that is not accompanied by other features of the pre-existing disorder. However, all patients who present with acute monoarthritis should be presumed to have septic arthritis until synovial fluid analysis via arthrocentesis excludes this condition. Synovial fluid analysis is the only definitive way to diagnose septic arthritis and is critical to guide antibiotic treatment. Patients with suspicion for this condition should begin empiric systemic antibiotic therapy until culture results are available.

Surgical drainage or débridement via arthroscopy may be warranted in patients with septic arthritis who do not respond to repeated percutaneous drainage and appropriate antibiotic therapy but would not be an appropriate initial intervention.

Joint and bone damage due to infection are relatively late radiographic findings. In acute septic arthritis, nonspecific soft-tissue fullness and joint effusions are often the only initial radiographic findings and do not establish the diagnosis of infection. Bone scans are more sensitive in detecting inflammatory lesions in bones and joints but also are not specific for infection.

MRI of the affected joint is especially useful in detecting avascular necrosis, soft-tissue masses, and collections of fluid not visualized by other imaging modalities but would not establish the diagnosis of infection.

KEY POINT

- **All patients who present with acute monoarthritis should be presumed to have septic arthritis until synovial fluid analysis via arthrocentesis excludes this condition.**

Bibliography

Kherani RB, Shojania K. Septic arthritis in patients with pre-existing inflammatory arthritis. CMAJ. 2007;176(11):1605-1608. [PMID: 17515588]

Item 15   Answer: A

Educational Objective: Manage refractory dermatomyositis.

Despite high-dose corticosteroid therapy, this patient has active dermatomyositis manifested by progressive weakness, a persistently elevated creatine kinase level, and a characteristic V sign on the anterior chest on cutaneous examination. CT of the chest, abdomen, and pelvis is indicated for this patient. Evaluation for an occult malignancy is warranted in patients with dermatomyositis who are refractory to treatment, particularly those who are older than 60 years of age. The types of malignancies associated with the inflammatory myopathies have been shown to be similar to those in an age-matched population except that women with these conditions have a higher rate of ovarian cancer. Malignancy may predate or develop after myositis, but these conditions most often occur concomitantly. In some patients, symptoms of myositis are decreased or remit when the malignancy is resolved.

This patient received the minimally appropriate evaluation for malignancy at the time of diagnosis, which consisted of a chest radiograph and sex- and age-appropriate screening. Although many experts recommend more extensive screening at the time of diagnosis, there are no data from controlled studies to support this practice. Therefore, decisions regarding screening must be guided by the patient's risk factors and symptoms and should be determined on an individual basis.

MRI of the thigh muscles would most likely reveal ongoing active muscle inflammation consistent with this patient's persistently elevated creatine kinase level but would not further explain her refractory disease or help in the management.

Repeat muscle biopsy to diagnose inclusion body myositis is not indicated for this patient. Inclusion body myositis is known to respond poorly to corticosteroid therapy, but this condition characteristically manifests as slowly progressive asymmetric proximal and distal muscle weakness that develops over many years and is not associated with the classic V-neck rash seen in this patient. Furthermore, serum creatine kinase levels in patients with inclusion body myositis are typically less than 1000 U/L.

Worsening proximal muscle weakness despite corticosteroid therapy also may be caused by corticosteroid-induced myopathy. However, patients with this condition experience a decrease in the creatine kinase level; this patient's persistently elevated creatine kinase level excludes this diagnosis, and stopping the corticosteroid therapy is therefore not indicated.

> **KEY POINT**
>
> - The risk for malignant disease is increased in patients with dermatomyositis, and minimum evaluation for these patients should include age- and sex-appropriate screening tests.

Bibliography

Buchbinder R, Hill CL. Malignancy in patients with inflammatory myopathy. Curr Rheumatol Rep. 2002;4(5):415-426. [PMID: 12217247]

Item 16   Answer: A

Educational Objective: Treat persistent, aggressive rheumatoid arthritis.

This patient has early, aggressive rheumatoid arthritis, and the addition of etanercept is indicated. Methotrexate is the most commonly used and safest among the more effective disease-modifying antirheumatic drugs (DMARDs), has the greatest potential for modifying disease compared with hydroxychloroquine and sulfasalazine, and is central to most treatments for rheumatoid arthritis. Despite treatment with methotrexate, this patient has persistent morning stiffness, numerous tender and swollen joints, and elevated erythrocyte sedimentation rate. When adequate disease control is not achieved with one or more oral DMARDs, biologic therapy is indicated. The preferred initial biologic agent in this setting is a tumor necrosis factor α inhibitor such as etanercept, which is usually added to baseline methotrexate therapy. Use of a tumor necrosis factor α inhibitor in addition to methotrexate is significantly more effective in controlling joint damage and improving function compared with single-agent therapy with either medication. Screening for tuberculosis is indicated before beginning therapy with any biologic agent, and patients who test positive for latent tuberculosis should be treated with isoniazid before beginning this therapy.

Hydroxychloroquine is an effective agent in the treatment of early, mild, and nonerosive rheumatoid arthritis but most likely would not be beneficial in a patient with aggressive disease, functional limitations, and radiographic evidence of joint erosion. Even the addition of hydroxychloroquine to methotrexate is unlikely to be as helpful for erosive rheumatoid arthritis as is the combination of methotrexate and a tumor necrosis factor α inhibitor.

Cyclophosphamide is not indicated for the treatment of active rheumatoid arthritis except in patients with rheumatoid vasculitis in whom major organ function is compromised. However, this patient does not have manifestations consistent with rheumatoid vasculitis, such as cutaneous ulcers and mononeuritis multiplex.

Sulfasalazine is often administered in combination with methotrexate and/or hydroxychloroquine in the treatment of early rheumatoid arthritis. Single-agent therapy with sulfasalazine also may be used when there are contraindications to the use of methotrexate. However, sulfasalazine is less effective than methotrexate in the treatment of rheumatoid arthritis and is not likely to benefit this patient if substituted for methotrexate.

> **KEY POINT**
>
> - When adequate control of rheumatoid arthritis is not achieved with one or more oral disease-modifying antirheumatic drugs, the addition of biologic therapy with a tumor necrosis factor α inhibitor is usually indicated.

Bibliography

Keystone EC. Strategies to control disease in rheumatoid arthritis with tumor necrosis factor antagonists-an opportunity to improve outcomes. Nat Clinc Pract Rheumatol. 2006;2(11):594-601. [PMID: 17075598]

Item 17   Answer: D

Educational Objective: Diagnose Wegener granulomatosis.

This patient most likely has Wegener granulomatosis, a necrotizing vasculitis that typically affects the upper- and lower-respiratory tract and the kidneys. This patient's purpura is consistent with vasculitis. His diffuse pulmonary infiltrates (generally associated with alveolar hemorrhage), history of refractory otitis media, renal failure, and urinalysis findings that suggest glomerulonephritis particularly raise suspicion for Wegener granulomatosis.

Wegener granulomatosis may be associated with inflammatory arthritis involving the small and large joints and joint effusions. The presence of c-ANCA and antiproteinase-3 antibodies is approximately 90% specific for this condition. The presentation of Wegener granulomatosis is highly nonspecific and evolves slowly over a period of months; therefore, diagnosis of this condition is often delayed by several months.

Patients with severe, long-standing rheumatoid arthritis may develop interstitial pneumonitis, and this condition is particularly likely to develop in men. Radiographs of patients with this condition usually show bibasilar interstitial markings. Interstitial lung disease associated with rheumatoid arthritis most characteristically has an insidious onset and is associated with seropositive, erosive joint disease. In most patients, the lung disease appears 5 years or more after the diagnosis of rheumatoid arthritis.

Methotrexate-induced pneumonitis can occur at any time in the course of therapy with this agent, regardless of the dosage or duration of treatment. However, this condition would not explain this patient's entire clinical picture, including c-ANCA positivity, vasculitis, renal failure, and his urinalysis findings.

Pneumocystis pneumonia may manifest as fever, dyspnea, tachypnea, and crackles heard on pulmonary examination. However, dyspnea is typically progressive and not acute and would not result in rapid pulmonary failure. Chest radiography in patients with this condition may show diffuse infiltrates. *Pneumocystis* pneumonia also usually develops in patients who are significantly immunosuppressed, whereas this patient has received only a short course of low-dose methotrexate. Furthermore, *pneumocystis* pneumonia would not explain this patient's additional findings.

KEY POINT

- **Wegener granulomatosis should be considered in patients with upper- and lower-airway manifestations, renal involvement, and inflammatory arthritis.**

Bibliography

Bosch X, Guilabert A, Font J. Antineutrophil cytoplasmic antibodies. Lancet. 2006;368(9533):404-418. [PMID: 16876669]

Item 18   Answer: B

Educational Objective: Treat drug-induced lupus.

This patient most likely has drug-induced lupus caused by the tumor necrosis factor α inhibitor infliximab. The most appropriate next step in this patient's management is to discontinue infliximab and begin prednisone.

Many patients who use tumor necrosis factor α inhibitors develop autoantibodies, including antinuclear, anti–double-stranded DNA, and anti-Smith antibodies; rarely, these patients develop drug-induced lupus. Patients with this condition may present with typical manifestations of systemic lupus erythematosus but are particularly likely to have cutaneous and pleuropericardial involvement. Renal and neurologic manifestations are extremely rare.

The most appropriate management of a patient with drug-induced lupus caused by a tumor necrosis factor α inhibitor is discontinuation of the offending agent, which usually resolves this condition. Prednisone also should be added to this patient's medication regimen to control pleuritis and synovitis associated with drug-induced lupus.

Although this patient's worsening joint symptoms may be related to her underlying rheumatoid arthritis, her rheumatoid arthritis had been well controlled on her current medication regimen. If her flare were related to active rheumatoid arthritis, her symptoms would most likely be alleviated by initiation of sulfasalazine or an increase in her infliximab dosage. However, her musculoskeletal features, fever, malar rash, photosensitivity, purpura, symptoms of pleuritis, antinuclear and anti–double-stranded DNA antibody positivity, and findings on chest radiography also raise strong suspicion for drug-induced lupus. Therefore, progressive rheumatoid arthritis is a less likely explanation for this patient's current symptoms than is drug-induced lupus,

and initiation of sulfasalazine or an increase in her infliximab dosage would not be indicated.

Hydroxychloroquine may be useful for the treatment of systemic lupus erythematosus and drug-induced lupus and could be added to this patient's existing medication regimen, but discontinuing methotrexate would not be appropriate.

KEY POINT

- **The most appropriate management of a patient with drug-induced lupus caused by a tumor necrosis factor α inhibitor is discontinuation of the offending agent.**

Bibliography

Ramos-Casals M, Brito-Zerón P, Muñoz S, et al. Autoimmune diseases induced by TNF-targeted therapies: analysis of 233 cases. Medicine (Baltimore). 2007;86(4):242-251. [PMID: 17632266]

Item 19   Answer: D

Educational Objective: Diagnose sarcoidosis.

This patient most likely has Löfgren syndrome, a variant of sarcoidosis characterized by acute monoarticular arthritis typically involving the ankles, erythema nodosum, and hilar lymphadenopathy that usually has a good prognosis. This patient has acute monoarticular arthritis involving a lower extremity, and the presence of tenderness, warmth, and swelling of the involved joint suggests that his condition is inflammatory; a synovial fluid leukocyte count higher than 2000/µL confirms the inflammatory nature of his condition. In addition, the tender, erythematous, indurated subcutaneous lesion over the right lower extremity is consistent with erythema nodosum, and a chest radiograph reveals hilar lymphadenopathy.

Bacterial and crystal-induced arthritis may manifest as acute monoarticular arthritis and are often accompanied by signs and symptoms of inflammation, including the presence of inflammatory synovial fluid. However, the synovial fluid leukocyte count in patients with bacterial arthritis would be significantly higher than 3000/µL and often exceeds 50,000/µL and would be associated with a predominance of neutrophils. In addition, crystal-induced arthritis is unlikely in the absence of crystals on polarized light microscopy of the synovial fluid.

Osteoarthritis usually manifests as pain that occurs with activity and is relieved with rest. This condition also typically is chronic in nature at the time of presentation and would be unusual in a young patient in the absence of trauma. Furthermore, osteoarthritis is not commonly associated with signs and symptoms of inflammation and does not typically involve the ankle.

Finally, bacterial or crystal-induced arthritis or osteoarthritis would not explain this patient's erythema nodosum or hilar lymphadenopathy.

- Löfgren syndrome is a variant of sarcoidosis that manifests as acute inflammatory arthritis and typically involves the ankles, erythema nodosum, and hilar lymphadenopathy.

Bibliography

Ahmed I, Harshad SR. Subcutaneous sarcoidosis: is it a specific subset of cutaneous sarcoidosis frequently associated with systemic disease? J Am Acad Dermatol. 2006;54(1):55-60. [PMID: 16384755]

Item 20   Answer: A

Educational Objective: Diagnose discoid lupus.

This patient has discoid lupus, which is a form of chronic cutaneous lupus. Rash in this condition is characterized by sharply marginated, red-to-pink indurated papules and plaques. These lesions are round, oval, or polycyclic and have an adherent scale involving the face, scalp, and ear canals accompanied by follicular plugging. These papules and plaques expand peripherally with central clearing; with time, central atrophic scarring and hypopigmentation develop. Scarring on the scalp may cause patchy alopecia, which is irreversible. These lesions can last for years and may be slightly pruritic but are generally asymptomatic. Discoid lupus can exist as a primary condition in the absence of associated systemic disease; approximately 5% of patients with systemic lupus erythematosus (SLE) have discoid lupus, but only 10% of patients with discoid lupus develop SLE.

Certain agents, including phenytoin, can cause drug-induced lupus. This condition usually manifests as fever, arthralgia, and serositis; antihistone antibodies also are universally present. This patient does not have any of these features. In addition, rash in patients with drug-induced lupus typically manifests as nonscarring scaly circular erythematous plaques that affect the neck, trunk, and extensor surfaces of the arms, which is not consistent with this patient's cutaneous findings.

Mixed connective tissue disease is an overlap syndrome in which patients present with features of systemic sclerosis, myositis, and SLE. Diagnosis of this condition is established in patients with at least three of the following features: antiribonucleoprotein antibodies, Raynaud phenomenon, myositis, swelling of the hands, synovitis, and acrosclerosis. All of these features are absent in this patient.

The presence of antinuclear antibodies is consistent with SLE, but patients with this condition typically have high titers of these antibodies. This patient also does not have anti–double-stranded DNA, anti-La/SSB, anti-Ro/SSA, anti-Smith, and antiribonucleoprotein antibodies, which are more specific for SLE than antinuclear antibodies. Fatigue, headache, and musculoskeletal involvement may occur in patients with SLE. However, fatigue is a nonspecific condition, migraine headaches are common in the general population, and lower back pain is not a musculoskeletal manifestation of SLE. Furthermore, this patient has no other features suggestive of SLE, such as oral ulcers, arthritis, serositis, renal disease, or hematologic abnormalities. Seizures may be associated with SLE but are more often caused by metabolic abnormalities, stroke, or infection. Furthermore, seizures due to SLE usually occur only in patients with acute, severely active disease, whereas this patient has a long history of seizures in the absence of serious systemic illness.

- Discoid lupus is characterized by the presence of red-to-pink round, oval, or polycyclic papules and plaques involving the face, scalp, and ear canals accompanied by follicular plugging and eventual development of atrophic scarring and hypopigmentation.

Bibliography

Rothfield N, Sontheimer RD, Bernstein M. Lupus erythematosus: systemic and cutaneous manifestations. Clin Dermatol. 2006;24(5): 348-362. [PMID: 16966017]

Item 21   Answer: B

Educational Objective: Treat aggressive rheumatoid arthritis.

This patient has aggressive rheumatoid arthritis and should discontinue etanercept and switch to an alternative tumor necrosis factor α inhibitor. The goal of treatment in patients with rheumatoid arthritis is to maintain no evidence of disease. Frequent monitoring is therefore indicated to ensure a continued response to therapy, and medications often must be adjusted to achieve adequate disease control. Serial measurement of factors such as the number of swollen and tender joints and acute phase reactants can help to evaluate disease progression and guide treatment decisions. Periodic radiography also helps to confirm that erosive disease has not progressed despite therapy.

Despite treatment with appropriate dosages of methotrexate and a tumor necrosis factor α inhibitor, this patient has numerous tender and swollen joints, positive rheumatoid factor, positive anti–cyclic citrullinated peptide antibodies, anemia, and an elevated erythrocyte sedimentation rate. She also has evidence of erosive disease on radiography. A change in therapy is therefore warranted. The three currently available tumor necrosis factor α inhibitors, etanercept, infliximab, and adalimumab, all have similar efficacy. However, many patients who do not respond to one of these agents have a positive response to a different agent in this class.

In patients with rheumatoid arthritis, concomitant therapy with two or more biologic agents does not enhance their efficacy and poses a risk for toxicity due to infection. Therefore, the addition of infliximab to this patient's current therapeutic regimen would not be recommended.

Sulfasalazine is often administered as combination therapy with methotrexate and/or hydroxychloroquine. This agent can be used as a single agent in patients with mild rheumatoid arthritis and often is added to methotrexate in the treatment of moderate to severe disease. However, sulfasalazine is unlikely to be effective as a single agent in a patient with progressive erosive disease.

Increasing this patient's prednisone dosage would most likely help to relieve her signs and symptoms of active disease but would not prevent further disease progression. Furthermore, long-term corticosteroid therapy, particularly at an increased dosage, places this patient at higher risk for corticosteroid toxicity.

KEY POINT

- **Many patients with rheumatoid arthritis who do not respond to therapy with a tumor necrosis factor α inhibitor have a positive response to a different agent in this class.**

Bibliography

Hyrich KL, Lunt M, Dixon WG, Watson KD, Symmons DP; BSR Biologics Register. Effects of switching between anti-TNF therapies on HAQ response in patients who do not respond to their first anti-TNF drug. Rheumatology (Oxford). 2008;47(7):1000-1005. [PMID: 18420660]

Item 22   Answer: B

Educational Objective: Evaluate gouty arthropathy.

Gout typically manifests as acute intermittent attacks of joint and tenosynovial inflammation associated with redness, swelling, and intense pain. Early attacks of gout are typically monoarticular and involve joints in the lower extremities, particularly the first metatarsophalangeal joint. These episodes usually last between several days and 2 weeks. As the disease progresses, these attacks become more frequent and increasingly polyarticular and involve the upper extremities. Because this patient's presentation is classic for gout, a presumptive diagnosis can be established based solely on his history and a supportive radiograph.

In patients with gout, radiographs often reveal bony asymmetric erosions with overhanging edges that usually involve the feet. These changes are supportive of the diagnosis but are not diagnostic.

Gout is often associated with hyperuricemia, but an elevated serum uric acid level is not diagnostic of this condition. More than 20% of patients with gout have normal or low uric acid levels during an acute attack; similarly, approximately 5% of the adult general population has elevated uric acid levels, but most of these patients remain asymptomatic. A 24-hour urine measurement of uric acid excretion would help to determine whether this patient is an underexcretor or overproducer of uric acid. Results of this study would therefore help to guide treatment but would not confirm the diagnosis.

Synovial fluid analysis during an acute attack of gout may not reveal monosodium urate crystals in up to 25% of affected patients. Therefore, aspiration of an affected joint during a subsequent attack may be appropriate if crystals are not initially seen on synovial fluid analysis in suspected gout. However, a synovial fluid analysis documenting a synovial fluid leukocyte count higher than 15,000/μL is compatible with gout but does not help to establish the diagnosis.

KEY POINT

- **A presumptive diagnosis of gout can be established based solely on a patient's history and a supportive radiograph.**

Bibliography

Schlesinger N. Diagnosis of gout. Minerva Med. 2007;98(6):759-767. [PMID: 18299687]

Item 23   Answer: B

Educational Objective: Diagnose enteropathic arthritis.

This patient's joint symptoms are most likely caused by enteropathic arthritis. She has a 6-week history of crampy abdominal pain and the recent onset of bloody diarrhea and rectal urgency. She also has had weight loss. This clinical presentation raises suspicion for inflammatory bowel disease.

For the past 3 weeks, this patient also has had acute arthritis of the right knee and ankle accompanied by inflammatory features such as tenderness and swelling; her synovial fluid findings confirm the presence of an inflammatory process. The presence of acute oligoarticular arthritis involving the lower extremities in a patient with an inflammatory diarrheal illness is suggestive of enteropathic arthritis; enteropathic arthritis also may manifest as axial arthritis, such as a spondyloarthropathy.

Crystal-induced arthritis typically manifests as acute monoarticular arthritis and would be unlikely in a premenopausal woman.

Gonococcal arthritis may be associated with oligoarticular arthritis, and joint manifestations in this condition may be migratory. However, patients with gonococcal arthritis commonly have tenosynovitis and cutaneous involvement, which are not present in this patient. Furthermore, neither gonococcal nor crystal-induced arthritis would explain this patient's diarrhea and abdominal pain.

Whipple disease is an extremely rare infectious syndrome caused by *Tropheryma whippelii*. The most common presenting symptom in affected patients is arthritis; other symptoms include diarrhea, malabsorption, and central nervous system and constitutional symptoms. Joint involvement is usually migratory and follows a chronic course.

KEY POINT

- **The presence of acute oligoarticular arthritis involving the lower extremities in a patient with inflammatory bowel disease is suggestive of enteropathic arthritis.**

Bibliography

Holden W, Orchard T, Wordsworth P. Enteropathic arthritis. Rheum Dis Clin North Am. 2003;29(3):513-530, viii. [PMID: 12951865]

Item 24   Answer: B

Educational Objective: Treat central nervous system lupus.

This patient has a history of systemic lupus erythematosus (SLE) and presents with headache, psychosis, and lymphocytic pleocytosis. In addition, this patient has cutaneous vasculitis, an elevated erythrocyte sedimentation rate, and hypocomplementemia. This clinical presentation strongly suggests a diagnosis of central nervous system (CNS) lupus. The most appropriate next step in her management is the addition of methylprednisolone and cyclophosphamide.

CNS lupus can be caused by vasculitis of the small vessels of the brain but also has been associated with the presence of antineuronal antibodies. MRI of the brain in affected patients may be normal or may reveal small areas of ischemia in the periventricular and subcortical white matter. Seizure also may develop in patients with this condition.

CNS lupus is a severe manifestation of SLE that is generally treated aggressively. Although few controlled trials on the treatment of CNS lupus have been performed to date, one small study demonstrated better outcomes in those treated with monthly pulse cyclophosphamide compared with monthly pulse methylprednisolone, with both of these agents used in conjunction with prednisone, 1 mg/kg/d.

Treatment with ampicillin and gentamicin would be warranted in a patient with *Listeria monocytogenes* meningitis, which is rare but occurs more frequently in patients with immunosuppression and collagen vascular disorders. However, *L. monocytogenes* meningitis usually is associated with nuchal rigidity and would not explain this patient's psychotic symptoms. Furthermore, lymphocytic pleocytosis on cerebrospinal fluid analysis and a negative Gram stain argue strongly against this condition.

Ibuprofen is an unlikely cause of this patient's clinical presentation. NSAIDs may be associated with aseptic meningitis, particularly in patients with SLE, but generally do not cause mental status changes or cutaneous vasculitis.

Plasmapheresis is an extracorporeal technique that results in the removal of large-molecular-weight substances from the plasma, such as autoantibodies, immune complexes, cryoglobulins, and myeloma light chains. This intervention is used to treat thrombotic thrombocytopenic purpura but has not been shown to be beneficial in CNS lupus and may be associated with an increased risk of infection, including catheter-related infection.

KEY POINT

- **Aggressive treatment with corticosteroids accompanied by monthly pulse cyclophosphamide is indicated to treat patients with central nervous system lupus.**

Bibliography

Barile-Fabris L, Ariza-Andraca R, Olguín-Ortega L, et al. Controlled clinical trail of IV cyclophosphamide versus IV methylprednisolone in severe neurological manifestations in systemic lupus erythematosus. Ann Rheum Dis. 2005;64(4):620-625. [PMID: 15769918]

Item 25   Answer: D

Educational Objective: Treat gastrointestinal manifestations of systemic sclerosis.

This patient's recent onset of skin thickening, Raynaud phenomenon, and symptoms consistent with gastroesophageal reflux disease is suggestive of systemic sclerosis. The most appropriate treatment for this patient is omeprazole.

Systemic sclerosis most commonly affects women in their 30s and 40s and is strongly associated with the presence of antinuclear antibodies. This condition may involve the skin and visceral organs. Treatment of systemic sclerosis consists of symptomatic management of the disease manifestations. Therefore, treatment with a proton pump inhibitor such as omeprazole would be appropriate to treat this patient's gastroesophageal reflux disease. Avoidance of cold also would benefit her symptoms of Raynaud phenomenon; if this intervention is not effective, a dihydropyridine calcium channel blocker may be warranted.

In patients with systemic sclerosis, cyclophosphamide has been shown to improve pulmonary symptoms and lung volumes and has been shown to modestly improve lung function, thickening of the skin, and quality of life. However, this agent has not been evaluated in randomized clinical trials for the treatment of skin disease in the absence of pulmonary involvement.

Angiotensin-converting enzyme inhibitors such as enalapril are the treatment of choice for scleroderma renal crisis but have no role in prophylactic treatment of this condition.

Randomized placebo-controlled clinical trials of methotrexate for the treatment of scleroderma skin disease have been promising, but the group differences were small and not statistically significant. These findings suggest that methotrexate is not effective in the treatment of early systemic sclerosis.

Prednisone has not been shown to alter the disease course in early systemic sclerosis. Moreover, use of this agent is a risk factor for the development of scleroderma renal crisis in patients with systemic sclerosis.

KEY POINT

- **Treatment of systemic sclerosis consists of symptomatic management of the disease manifestations.**

Bibliography

Tashkin DP, Elashoff R, Clements PJ, et al; Scleroderma Lung Study Research Group. Cyclophosphamide versus placebo in scleroderma lung disease. N Engl J Med. 2006;354(25):2655-2666. [PMID: 16790698]

Item 26   Answer: B

Educational Objective: Diagnose osteoarthritis of the knee.

This patient most likely has osteoarthritis of the knee. He has two risk factors for this condition, advanced age and an occupation involving repetitive bending and physical labor. Osteoarthritis commonly affects weight-bearing joints such as the knees and is characterized by pain on activity that is relieved with rest. Swelling in patients with this condition is usually minimal, and range of motion may be limited. According to the American College of Rheumatology, osteoarthritis of the knee can be diagnosed if knee pain is accompanied by at least three of the following features: age greater than 50 years, morning stiffness lasting less than 30 minutes, crepitus, bony tenderness, bony enlargement, and an absence of palpable warmth. This patient's radiographic findings of osteophytes, joint-space narrowing, sclerosis, and cyst formation are typical of this condition. Arthrocentesis is not necessary to establish a diagnosis of osteoarthritis.

Patients with avascular necrosis of the knee typically experience pain on weight bearing and may have a painful, limited range of motion. However, this condition also is associated with pain on rest and most commonly occurs in patients who use corticosteroids, have systemic lupus erythematosus, or consume excessive amounts of alcoholic beverages. Radiographs in patients with avascular necrosis usually reveal density changes; subchondral radiolucency; cysts; sclerosis; and, eventually, joint-space narrowing.

Rheumatoid arthritis may be associated with a limited range of motion and joint-space narrowing visible on radiography. Patients with rheumatoid arthritis usually have symmetric arthritis that affects at least three joints as well as an elevated erythrocyte sedimentation rate and is associated with morning stiffness that persists for more than 30 minutes. In addition, rheumatoid arthritis also would not explain the presence of subchondral sclerosis and osteophytes on radiography.

A torn medial meniscus would cause pain in the knee and can occur in the elderly in association with osteoarthritis. Patients with acute meniscal damage often describe a twisting injury with the foot in a weight-bearing position in which a popping or tearing sensation is felt, followed by severe pain; in addition, this condition is characterized by the sensation that the knee "locks" or "gives out."

KEY POINT

- **Physical examination findings consistent with osteoarthritis of the knee include crepitus, bony tenderness, bony enlargement, and an absence of palpable warmth.**

Bibliography

Felson DT. Clinical practice. Osteoarthritis of the knee [erratum in N Engl J Med. 2006;354(23):2520]. N Engl J Med. 2006;354(8): 841-848. [PMID: 16495396]

Item 27   Answer: D

Educational Objective: Treat proliferative lupus nephritis.

This patient has proliferative lupus nephritis; treatment of this condition involves two phases, remission induction and remission maintenance. The most appropriate treatment for this patient is to discontinue cyclophosphamide and start mycophenolate mofetil.

This patient has been treated with corticosteroids and cyclophosphamide for the past 6 months. He is currently asymptomatic and has normal complement levels and only low titers of anti–double-stranded DNA antibodies. He has proteinuria, but this finding alone is not indicative of active lupus nephritis; mild proteinuria commonly persists even after effective resolution of lupus nephritis and is most likely caused by damage to the basement membrane. However, immunosuppression should not be stopped at this early stage. Nearly 50% of patients with proliferative lupus nephritis relapse after reduction or cessation of cyclophosphamide or other immunosuppressant therapy. Therefore, once remission is achieved, immunosuppression should be continued to maintain remission and prevent end-stage renal disease.

Because of the risk for toxicity, prolonged monthly cyclophosphamide use is not recommended to maintain remission in patients with lupus nephritis. Once remission has been induced with 3 to 6 months of cyclophosphamide therapy, patients with this condition can safely be switched to mycophenolate mofetil or azathioprine. Methotrexate has not been studied for this indication. Alternatively, after six monthly cyclophosphamide infusions have been administered, the frequency of cyclophosphamide infusions can be reduced to every 3 months for an additional 18 months.

KEY POINT

- **Once remission is achieved with cyclophosphamide therapy, patients with lupus nephritis can safely be switched to mycophenolate mofetil or azathioprine to avoid cyclophosphamide toxicity.**

Bibliography

Buhaescu I, Covic A, Deray G. Treatment of proliferative lupus nephritis—a critical approach. Semin Arthiritis Rheum. 2007;36(4): 224-237 [PMID: 17067659]

Item 28   Answer: D

Educational Objective: Diagnose rheumatoid arthritis.

This patient most likely has rheumatoid arthritis, which is the most common cause of chronic, inflammatory polyarthritis in premenopausal women. Rheumatoid arthritis commonly affects the metacarpophalangeal, proximal interphalangeal, and wrist joints. This patient's swelling, prolonged morning stiffness, and elevated erythrocyte sedimentation rate are consistent with this diagnosis. Furthermore, women are three times more likely to develop rheumatoid arthritis than men and have a slightly increased risk of developing this condition during the first 3 months postpartum.

Gout may involve the hand and wrist and is associated with inflammatory features. However, gout usually has an asymmetric presentation and is unlikely to develop in a premenopausal woman.

Osteoarthritis may manifest as chronic arthritis involving the proximal interphalangeal joints but would not affect the metacarpophalangeal joints or the wrists. Secondary osteoarthritis related to trauma or a metabolic condition such as hemochromatosis may explain this patient's pattern of joint involvement, but this condition would be unlikely in a 26-year-old woman. Osteoarthritis also would not have an inflammatory presentation.

Viral arthritis usually is self limited except when associated with hepatitis B and C virus infection. Parvovirus B19 infection in adults may induce an acute rheumatoid factor–positive oligo- or polyarthritis. Most adult patients with parvovirus B19 infection also develop rash, but only rarely in adults does rash manifest as the classic rash seen in childhood erythema infectiosum, the "slapped cheek" rash. Diagnosis of acute parvovirus B19 infection may be established by detecting circulating IgM antibodies against parvovirus B19.

Viral arthritis usually resolves within 3 weeks, although a minority of patients may develop persistent arthritis. The arthritis associated with acute parvovirus B19 infection does not cause joint destruction, and supportive analgesic therapy with NSAIDs is appropriate as tolerated. Parvovirus B19 infection is unlikely in this patient considering the duration of her symptoms, absence of rash, and negative titers of IgM antibodies against parvovirus B19.

KEY POINT

- **Rheumatoid arthritis is the most common cause of chronic, inflammatory polyarthritis in premenopausal women.**

Bibliography

Majithia V, Geraci SA. Rheumatoid arthritis: diagnosis and management. Am J Med. 2007;120(11):936-939. [PMID: 17976416]

Item 29   Answer: D

Educational Objective: Treat early rheumatoid arthritis.

This patient has early nonerosive rheumatoid arthritis, which usually manifests as fatigue, low-grade fever, and symmetric arthritis. The most appropriate treatment for this patient is sulfasalazine.

Rheumatoid arthritis most often involves the small joints of the hands and feet and usually has a symmetric pattern of involvement; the larger joints, such as the knees, also

may be affected. Additional manifestations of rheumatoid arthritis may include morning stiffness that lasts for more than 1 hour, synovitis, joint effusions, and loss of normal range of motion.

Rheumatoid factor is present in more than 75% of patients with established rheumatoid arthritis, but the prevalence of rheumatoid factor in early disease is lower. An antibody against filaggrin, anti–cyclic citrullinated peptide, is less sensitive than rheumatoid factor but highly specific (96%) for rheumatoid arthritis. Plain radiographs in patients with early rheumatoid arthritis are often normal but may reveal soft-tissue swelling, uniform joint-space narrowing, and juxta-articular demineralization. This patient's synovial fluid analysis also is compatible with an inflammatory process, which further supports the diagnosis of rheumatoid arthritis.

In most patients, rheumatoid arthritis is associated with progressive, irreversible joint destruction that causes increasing functional limitation. Disease-modifying antirheumatic drug (DMARD) therapy should be instituted within 3 months of the diagnosis of rheumatoid arthritis to prevent irreversible joint damage. Hydroxychloroquine and sulfasalazine are DMARDs that may be useful in patients with mild disease, which is often defined as a presentation of 5 to 10 inflamed joints with mild functional limitation, a minimally elevated erythrocyte sedimentation rate and C-reactive protein levels, and no erosions or anemia. Either sulfasalazine or hydroxychloroquine would be appropriate as initial therapy to treat this patient who has early, mild, nonerosive disease.

Methotrexate is a DMARD that is often used in patients with active rheumatoid arthritis but would be contraindicated in a patient with abnormal liver chemistry study results or underlying liver disease, or in those who regularly consume alcoholic beverages. Leflunomide is similarly associated with hepatotoxicity and should be avoided in patients who consume significant amounts of alcohol.

Prednisone would most likely help relieve this patient's joint symptoms and is often used as part of combination therapy in patients with rheumatoid arthritis. However, this agent has no disease-modifying properties and as a single agent would not help to prevent disease progression.

KEY POINT

- **Disease-modifying antirheumatic drug therapy should be instituted within 3 months of the diagnosis of rheumatoid arthritis.**

Bibliography

Majithia V, Geraci SA. Rheumatoid arthritis: diagnosis and management. Am J Med. 2007;120(11):936-939. [PMID: 17976416]

Item 30   Answer: A

Educational Objective: Diagnose fibromyalgia.

This patient most likely has fibromyalgia. This condition is characterized by diffuse pain on both sides of the body and above and below the waist as well as axial skeletal pain, or, according to the original American College of Rheumatology criteria, the presence of pain in at least 11 of 18 specified potential tender points. However, expert opinion now states that these tender points are arbitrary and not essential in the diagnosis of fibromyalgia.

Most patients with this condition have fatigue and sleep disturbance. Fibromyalgia also may be associated with dry eyes and mouth. Studies that have assessed the comorbidity of fibromyalgia with other symptom-defined syndromes have found high rates of chronic fatigue syndrome, migraine, irritable bowel syndrome, pelvic pain, and temporomandibular joint pain in patients with fibromyalgia.

Polymyositis may manifest as muscle pain and fatigue but is unlikely in the absence of significant proximal muscle weakness or an elevated creatine kinase level.

Up to 25% of patients with systemic inflammatory conditions, such as systemic lupus erythematosus (SLE) and rheumatoid arthritis, have symptoms consistent with fibromyalgia in the initial stages of their illness. This patient's fatigue, polyarthralgia, dry eyes and mouth, and strongly positive titers of antinuclear antibodies are consistent with SLE and Sjögren syndrome. However, patients with SLE usually have anemia, leukopenia, or lymphopenia. Similarly, joint involvement in Sjögren syndrome typically manifests as inflammatory arthritis. Furthermore, patients with SLE and Sjögren syndrome may have systemic manifestations, including cutaneous, neurologic, and renal involvement, which are absent in this patient.

The presence of antinuclear antibodies is not diagnostic of SLE or Sjögren syndrome. These antibodies are often present in the general population and particularly in patients with autoimmune thyroid disease or in first-degree relatives of patients with SLE. In addition, high titers of antinuclear antibodies do not necessarily indicate the presence of autoimmune disease.

KEY POINT

- **Fibromyalgia is characterized by diffuse pain on both sides of the body and above and below the waist as well as axial skeletal pain.**

Bibliography

Chakrabarty S, Zoorob R. Fibromyalgia. Am Fam Physician. 2007;76(2):247-254. [PMID: 17695569]

Item 31   Answer: C

Educational Objective: Diagnose inclusion body myositis.

This patient most likely has inclusion body myositis (IBM), which is the most common form of myositis in patients older than 60 years. This condition typically manifests as muscle weakness that affects the proximal and distal muscles and often has an asymmetric pattern of involvement. The quadriceps, wrist, and finger flexor muscles are commonly involved. IBM characteristically has an insidious onset and is associated with only moderately elevated serum creatine kinase levels that are typically less than 1000 U/L. The presence of mixed myopathic and neurogenic findings on electromyography is characteristic of this condition. IBM responds poorly to immunosuppressive therapy that is usually effective in inflammatory myositis.

Dermatomyositis and polymyositis also have an insidious onset and manifest as muscle weakness often in the absence of pain that typically causes progressive difficulty with routine activities, such as rising from a chair, climbing stairs, or hair combing. These conditions are characterized by symmetric proximal muscle weakness, whereas this patient has an asymmetric pattern of involvement that also prominently affects the distal muscles.

Furthermore, although dermatomyositis and polymyositis may be associated with serum creatine kinase levels that range from normal to several thousand U/L, a creatine kinase level of 320 U/L would be more typical of IBM. This patient's cutaneous findings are most consistent with seborrheic dermatitis, which is not associated with dermatomyositis.

Mixed connective tissue disease is characterized by features of systemic lupus erythematosus, inflammatory myopathy, and systemic sclerosis. This patient's absence of sclerodactyly, Raynaud phenomenon, digital pitting, serositis, and joint pain makes this an unlikely diagnosis.

The central features of fibromyalgia are widespread musculoskeletal pain with localized tenderness unexplained by any other diagnosis as well as sleep disturbance and fatigue. IBM is not associated with fibromyalgia. Furthermore, fibromyalgia would not explain this patient's muscle weakness and elevated serum creatine kinase level.

Finally, polymyositis, dermatomyositis, mixed connective tissue disease, or fibromyalgia would not explain this patient's electromyographic or biopsy findings.

KEY POINT

- **Inclusion body myositis typically manifests as the insidious onset of asymmetric proximal and distal muscle weakness associated with only moderately elevated creatine kinase levels.**

Bibliography

Askanas V, Engel WK. Inclusion-body myositis, a multifactorial muscle disease associated with aging: current concepts of pathogenesis. Curr Opin Rheumatol. 2007;19(6):550-559. [PMID: 17917534]

Item 32   Answer: C

Educational Objective: Diagnose secondary osteoarthritis.

This patient most likely has secondary osteoarthritis associated with hemochromatosis. Approximately 40% to 60% of patients with hemochromatosis develop an arthropathy with a presentation similar to that of osteoarthritis. The presence of symmetric pain and bony enlargement of the joints accompanied by radiographic findings of joint-space narrowing and osteophytes is consistent with osteoarthritis. However, primary osteoarthritis does not typically involve the metacarpophalangeal joints; if this occurs, suspicion should be raised for secondary osteoarthritis. Similarly, radiographs of the metacarpophalangeal joints may reveal hook-shaped osteophytes that are significantly different from radiographs of patients with primary osteoarthritis. Hemochromatosis arthropathy also may involve the proximal interphalangeal joints and, less frequently, the shoulders, hips, knees, and ankles. Finally, primary osteoarthritis usually affects patients with advanced age or who have occupations involving repetitive bending or manual labor.

Secondary osteoarthritis usually involves joints not affected by primary osteoarthritis. Secondary arthritis develops because of another condition, such as trauma, previous inflammatory arthritis, or metabolic disorders such as hemochromatosis or chondrocalcinosis. In this patient, the presence of skin hyperpigmentation and diabetes mellitus raises strong suspicion for hemochromatosis, which is particularly associated with involvement of the metacarpophalangeal joints in patients without primary osteoarthritis.

Symptoms of osteoarthritis that involve the second and third metacarpophalangeal joints also may be caused by calcium pyrophosphate deposition disease. However, radiographs of patients with this condition would typically reveal chondrocalcinosis, which occurs most frequently in the knees, symphysis pubis, and triangular fibrocartilage of the wrist.

Diabetic cheiroarthropathy (stiff hand syndrome) more commonly occurs in patients with long-standing diabetes. This condition manifests as joint stiffness, limited range of motion in the absence of pain, and skin thickening of the fingers, which is not compatible with this patient's presentation or radiographic findings.

Rheumatoid arthritis may involve the metacarpophalangeal joints in a symmetric pattern and may be present in patients without rheumatoid factor. This condition also may manifest as rheumatoid nodules (subcutaneous nodules that develop over bony prominences at sites such as the extensor surfaces of the hand) that may resemble the bony enlargement associated with osteoarthritis. However, rheumatoid arthritis is unlikely in the absence of morning stiffness and joint swelling.

KEY POINT

- Secondary osteoarthritis usually involves joints not affected by primary osteoarthritis and develops because of another condition, such as trauma, previous inflammatory arthritis, or metabolic disorders such as hemochromatosis or chondrocalcinosis.

Bibliography
Pietrangelo A. Hereditary hemochromatosis—a new look at an old disease. N Engl J Med. 2004;350(23):2383-2397. [PMID: 15175440]

Item 33　　Answer:　D
Educational Objective: Treat rheumatoid arthritis.

This patient has long-standing seropositive erosive rheumatoid arthritis associated with swan-neck deformities, subluxations of the metatarsophalangeal joints, and post-inflammatory osteoarthritis in the right knee that manifests as uniform joint-space narrowing and prominent osteophyte formation. However, he does not have evidence of active inflammatory disease, which usually manifests as morning stiffness that lasts longer than 1 hour, fatigue, progressive loss of function, weight loss, or tenderness and swelling of numerous joints. Furthermore, his symptoms have not worsened since his last visit 3 months ago, and radiography reveals no further signs of erosive joint damage.

In addition, although this patient's erythrocyte sedimentation rate is elevated, treatment decisions in patients with rheumatoid arthritis should be guided by signs and symptoms of their condition, and this patient has no evidence of active inflammatory disease. Therefore, a change in this patient's medication regimen is not warranted.

Evidence shows that rapidly escalating therapy with a multidrug regimen is the most effective means of controlling rheumatoid arthritis. The addition of prednisone or sulfasalazine would be warranted in a patient whose disease is not controlled. Similarly, etanercept would be helpful in the setting of an inadequate response to therapy with an oral disease-modifying antirheumatic drug. However, the addition of any of these agents would not be appropriate for this patient, whose disease is currently well controlled.

KEY POINT

- Active inflammatory disease in patients with rheumatoid arthritis manifests as morning stiffness lasting longer than 1 hour, fatigue, anorexia, weight loss, loss of function, tenderness and swelling of numerous joints, elevated acute phase reactant levels, and progressive joint damage visible on radiography.

Bibliography
Smolen JS, Aletaha D. Activity assessments in rheumatoid arthritis. Curr Opin Rheumatol. 2008;20(3):306-313. [PMID: 18388523]

Item 34　　Answer:　A
Educational Objective: Treat pancytopenia in a patient with systemic lupus erythematosus.

This patient has new-onset pancytopenia. This condition is a common manifestation of systemic lupus erythematosus (SLE) but also can be induced by a viral infection or the use of certain drugs. This patient developed pancytopenia 2 weeks after starting azathioprine, which suggests that azathioprine toxicity is the inciting agent. The most appropriate treatment for this patient is discontinuation of azathioprine.

Azathioprine is a purine analog that acts as a cell cycle–specific antimetabolite. This agent is metabolized by the enzymes xanthine oxidase and thiopurine methyltransferase; low thiopurine methyltransferase activity or inhibition of xanthine oxidase by drugs such as allopurinol can cause an increase in serum levels of azathioprine and can result in azathioprine toxicity. This toxicity may manifest as myelosuppression.

Most, but not all, patients with severe azathioprine-induced myelosuppression have low or absent thiopurine methyltransferase activity. Some experts recommend thiopurine methyltransferase activity measurement before beginning azathioprine therapy.

Discontinuation of hydroxychloroquine is not indicated for this patient. This agent is not associated with cytopenias, and she has been using it for 5 years. Furthermore, discontinuing this agent would most likely worsen her disease activity.

Although this patient has recently experienced a flare of her SLE, she is now asymptomatic, has normal complement levels, and does not have anti–double-stranded DNA antibodies. These features demonstrate that this patient's SLE is well controlled and that her condition has improved since her flare 3 months ago. Therefore, her pancytopenia is unlikely to be caused by her SLE, and an increase in her prednisone dosage or the addition of a new agent to help manage her SLE, such as intravenous immune globulin, would not be warranted.

KEY POINT

- Cytopenia is a manifestation of systemic lupus erythematosus but also can be induced by a viral infection or the use of certain drugs, such as azathioprine.

Bibliography

Jun JB, Cho DY, Kang C, Bae SC. Thiopurine S-methyltransferase polymorphisms and the relationship between the mutant alleles and the adverse effects in systemic lupus erythematosus patients taking azathioprine. Clin Exp Rheumatol. 2005;23(6):873-876. [PMID: 16396707]

Item 35   Answer: A

Educational Objective: Diagnose adult-onset Still disease.

This patient most likely has adult-onset Still disease (AOSD). AOSD is a clinical diagnosis established in patients who have five features cited in the diagnostic criteria for this condition, including at least two major criteria. The major criteria present in this patient are fever that spikes once or twice daily, polyarthritis, and leukocytosis. She also has lymphadenopathy, splenomegaly, and abnormal liver chemistry studies, which are among the minor criteria. Additional manifestations of AOSD may include cough, serositis manifested as pleuritic chest pain, and pericarditis. Patients with AOSD also may have normocytic,

normochromic anemia; elevated inflammatory markers; a markedly elevated serum ferritin level that may exceed 2500 ng/mL (2500 mg/L); and an absence of antinuclear antibodies or rheumatoid factor. Affected children also often develop a salmon-colored rash during febrile episodes, whereas rash occurs less frequently in adults with this condition. AOSD is typically a diagnosis of exclusion; when establishing a diagnosis of this condition, excluding infection and a malignant etiology is therefore critical.

Relapsing polychondritis is associated with inflammation of cartilaginous areas, including the trachea, airways, ears, and joints. This condition may manifest as polyarthritis; cough; fever; nasal congestion and rhinorrhea; and, in rare cases, pericarditis. Relapsing polychondritis is unlikely in the absence of auricular inflammation or inflammatory eye disease.

This patient's fever, polyarthritis, pericarditis, lymphadenopathy, and splenomegaly are consistent with systemic lupus erythematosus (SLE). However, this patient does not have antinuclear antibodies, which are present in more than 99% of patients with SLE. Typical laboratory findings in patients with SLE also may include positive titers of anti–doubled-stranded DNA antibodies and hypocomplementemia, which are absent in this patient.

Patients with Wegener granulomatosis may have polyarthritis; serositis; fever; and rhinorrhea and sinus pain. However, these findings typically would not be present in the absence of pulmonary and renal involvement. Wegener granulomatosis also is associated with positive ANCA titers, which this patient does not have. Wegener granulomatosis and relapsing polychondritis also would not explain this patient's lymphadenopathy and splenomegaly.

KEY POINT

- Adult-onset Still disease is an inflammatory disease characterized by polyarthritis and fever that spikes once or twice daily.

Bibliography

Efthimiou P, Paik PK, Bielory L. Diagnosis and management of adult onset Still's disease. Ann Rheum Dis. 2006;65(5):564-572. [PMID: 16219707]

Item 36   Answer: A

Educational Objective: Manage scleroderma renal crisis.

This patient most likely has scleroderma renal crisis (SRC), and the most appropriate management for this patient is to begin captopril. SRC is a complication of systemic sclerosis that most commonly affects patients with diffuse cutaneous disease within the first 48 months after diagnosis. The use of corticosteroids (usually more than 15 mg/d) in the preceding 6 months increases the risk for SRC, and particularly normotensive renal crisis, in patients with diffuse cutaneous systemic sclerosis.

SRC classically is characterized by the acute onset of severe hypertension, renal failure, and microangiopathic hemolytic anemia. Patients who develop this condition as a result of corticosteroid use often are normotensive but may have blood pressures higher than their normal baseline levels. Prompt initiation of therapy with an angiotensin-converting enzyme inhibitor such as captopril is the treatment of choice for SRC. This therapy should be continued even in patients with significant renal insufficiency, as renal function has been shown to improve even after months of dialysis. Before the advent of these agents, mortality was an almost universal outcome in patients with SRC.

Case reports suggest that cyclosporine may worsen renal disease in patients with systemic sclerosis. Therefore, cyclosporine, a renal vasoconstrictor, is not the most appropriate therapeutic agent for SRC, which is characterized by narrowing and obliteration of the vascular lumen of the renal arteries.

Thrombotic thrombocytopenic purpura and the hemolytic uremic syndrome (TTP-HUS) are thrombotic disorders characterized by microangiopathic hemolytic anemia and thrombocytopenia. Other manifestations may include neurologic abnormalities (headache, mental status changes, seizures), renal dysfunction, and fever.

Distinguishing TTP-HUS from SRC can be difficult but is critical. Plasma exchange often benefits patients with TTP-HUS but not those with SRC and may delay appropriate therapy. However, this patient developed the abrupt onset of renal failure and has a recent diagnosis of diffuse sclerosis and exposure to high-dose corticosteroid therapy; this clinical presentation is therefore more characteristic of SRC, and plasma exchange is not indicated.

Corticosteroid use is associated with an increase in risk for SRC and, when used, should be administered at the lowest possible effective dose for the shortest period of time compatible with resolution of the treated condition. Corticosteroid use is not indicated as a treatment for normotensive SRC.

KEY POINT

- **Prompt initiation of therapy with an angiotensin-converting enzyme inhibitor such as captopril, regardless of the serum creatinine concentration, is the treatment of choice for scleroderma renal crisis.**

Bibliography

Teixeira L, Mouthon L, Mahr A, et al; Group Français de Recherche sur le Sclérodermie (GFRS). Mortality and risk factors of scleroderma renal crisis: a French retrospective study of 50 patients. Ann Rheum Dis. 2008;67(1):110-116. [PMID: 17557890]

Item 37   Answer: D
Educational Objective: Diagnose septic arthritis in a patient with Crohn disease arthropathy.

This patient has acute monoarticular arthritis associated with warmth and swelling of the involved joint, an inflammatory synovial fluid, and fever. This clinical presentation raises strong suspicion for septic arthritis. A diagnosis of septic arthritis should be considered in any patient who presents with the sudden onset of monoarthritis or the acute worsening of chronic joint disease and an increase in the synovial fluid leukocyte count.

The synovial fluid leukocyte count in patients with septic arthritis is usually higher than 50,000/µL. In adults presenting with acute mono- or oligoarthritis, the probability of septic arthritis increases directly with the synovial fluid leukocyte count. For example, the positive likelihood ratio for patients with a synovial fluid leukocyte count between 25,000/µL and 50,000/µL is 2.9, whereas this value for patients with a synovial fluid leukocyte count between 50,000/µL and 100,000/µL is 7.7. In patients with a synovial fluid leukocyte count higher than 100,000/µL, the positive likelihood ratio is 28.

A negative Gram stain does not exclude a diagnosis of septic arthritis. In addition, patients who are immunocompromised due to use of agents such as infliximab also have an increased risk for infection, including septic arthritis. Because of this patient's recent flare of bowel disease, infection with gram-negative bacteria must particularly be considered. In this patient, treatment of this type of infection should include the immediate initiation of empiric antibiotics (for example, vancomycin and ceftriaxone), repeated joint fluid drainage via arthrocentesis or surgical joint débridement, and discontinuation of infliximab.

Avascular necrosis may be associated with the use of corticosteroids but usually manifests as a subacute or chronic condition. Synovial fluid in patients with this condition is usually noninflammatory.

This patient has Crohn disease associated with musculoskeletal involvement. Crohn disease arthropathy may manifest as spondylitis accompanied by sacroiliitis. This condition also may be associated with two types of peripheral arthritis. In type I arthropathy, the peripheral arthritis is acute, affects six or fewer joints, and is associated with joint inflammation that tends to correlate with the activity of the bowel disease. Type I arthropathy also occurs early in the course of the bowel disease and may precede the onset of bowel disease. Type II arthropathy is characterized by polyarticular or migratory arthritis that is chronic and recurrent and does not parallel the activity of the bowel disease. Onset of type II arthropathy rarely precedes the diagnosis of inflammatory bowel disease. However, neither type of Crohn disease arthropathy manifests as acute monoarthritis, and the synovial fluid in patients with Crohn disease arthropathy is rarely markedly inflammatory.

This patient's musculoskeletal symptoms and elevated synovial fluid leukocyte count are consistent with crystal-induced arthritis, but this condition is unlikely in the absence of crystals in polarized light microscopy of the synovial fluid.

- A diagnosis of septic arthritis should be considered in patients who present with the sudden onset of monoarthritis or the acute worsening of chronic joint disease and an increase in the synovial fluid leukocyte count.

Bibliography

Strangfeld A, Listing J. Infection and musculoskeletal conditions: Bacterial and opportunistic infections during anti-TNF therapy. Best Pract Res Clin Rheumatol. 2006;20(6):1181-1195. [PMID: 17127203]

Item 38   Answer: D

Educational Objective: Manage osteoarthritis of the knee.

This patient has osteoarthritis of the knee. The most appropriate next step in her management is referral for physical therapy, which is an appropriate first-line management option for patients with this condition. Quadriceps muscle training in particular has been shown to reduce pain in this population group. Use of over-the-counter acetaminophen or an NSAID on an as-needed basis also may benefit this patient.

Arthroscopy and MRI of the knee would most likely reveal abnormalities of the articular cartilage not visible on plain radiography but are not needed to establish the diagnosis of osteoarthritis. Similarly, aspiration of the knee joint would be warranted in patients with an effusion to obtain a synovial fluid leukocyte count but is not needed to establish a diagnosis; furthermore, this patient does not have an effusion.

- Physical therapy is an appropriate first-line management option for patients with osteoarthritis of the knee, and quadriceps muscle training in particular has been shown to reduce pain in this setting.

Bibliography

Bennell KL, Hinman RS, Metcalf BR, et al. Efficacy of physiotherapy management of knee joint osteoarthritis: a randomised, double blind, placebo controlled trial. Ann Rheum Dis. 2005;64(6):906-912. [PMID: 15897310]

Item 39   Answer: C

Educational Objective: Treat psoriatic arthritis.

This patient has psoriasis, dactylitis, and symmetric peripheral polyarthritis involving the small joints. This constellation of symptoms raises strong suspicion for psoriatic arthritis. Methotrexate is the most appropriate treatment for this patient.

Psoriatic arthritis affects 20% to 40% of patients with psoriasis and is most likely to develop in patients with psoriasis who have extensive skin involvement. Patients with psoriatic arthritis also may have arthritis solely involving the distal interphalangeal joints; asymmetric oligoarthritis; arthritis mutilans; spondyloarthritis that is often associated with peripheral joint disease; spinal involvement that manifests as inflammatory pain and stiffness of the neck and lower back; and tendinitis of the Achilles tendon, flexor tendons of the fingers, and tendons around the ankles.

Despite an absence of evidence obtained from clinical trials, methotrexate has dominated therapy in patients with psoriatic arthritis for many years and is effective in those who have low risk for bone marrow or liver toxicity. In patients with psoriatic arthritis, methotrexate helps to control cutaneous and musculoskeletal manifestations; long-term therapy with this agent also is well tolerated.

Hydroxychloroquine would be helpful in a patient with rheumatoid arthritis, and this patient's pattern of musculoskeletal involvement is somewhat consistent with this condition. However, rheumatoid arthritis usually spares the distal interphalangeal joints and involves the proximal interphalangeal joints. This patient also has dactylitis, which is characterized by inflammation of the whole digit resulting from joint and tendon inflammation that is typical for psoriatic arthritis but not associated with rheumatoid arthritis. Furthermore, hydroxychloroquine has been associated with severe flares of psoriasis and should be avoided in patients with this condition.

Prednisone therapy may help to relieve this patient's joint symptoms. However, tapering of corticosteroids in patients with psoriatic arthritis may be associated with dramatic flares in skin disease; these agents therefore should be used with caution in this population group. NSAIDs such as ibuprofen may help to alleviate this patient's pain and swelling involving the joints but are believed to similarly exacerbate psoriasis. Furthermore, neither prednisone nor ibuprofen would slow the progression of this patient's articular damage.

Sulfasalazine has modest efficacy in the treatment of joint disease in patients with psoriatic arthritis, and a meta-analysis showed that it may help to relieve skin disease, as well. However, this agent is less effective than methotrexate for both skin and joint disease associated with psoriatic arthritis.

- In patients with psoriatic arthritis, methotrexate helps to control cutaneous and musculoskeletal manifestations, slows the progression of joint destruction, and is considered first-line therapy for this condition.

Bibliography

Jones G, Crotty M, Brooks P. Interventions for psoriatic arthritis. Cochrane Database Syst Rev. 2000;(2):CD000212. [PMID: 10796328]

Item 40　　Answer:　B

Educational Objective: Diagnose mixed connective tissue disease.

This patient most likely has mixed connective tissue disease, which is a specific disorder that combines clinical findings of systemic lupus erythematosus, systemic sclerosis, and polymyositis and is characterized by high titers of anti-ribonucleoprotein antibodies. This patient's long-standing Raynaud phenomenon with associated digital ulcerations, arthralgia, myositis (characterized by proximal muscle weakness and elevated muscle enzyme levels, including alanine and aspartate aminotransferase and creatine kinase levels), and pleuritic chest pain compatible with serositis is consistent with mixed connective tissue disease.

Antiribonucleoprotein antibodies may be present in patients with systemic lupus erythematosus (SLE), particularly those whose manifestations include Raynaud phenomenon and mild myositis. Furthermore, SLE may be associated with pleuritis and antinuclear antibodies. However, this patient does not have additional features associated with SLE, including malar or discoid rash, oral ulcers, or renal or neurologic involvement. This patient's prominent muscle weakness and Raynaud phenomenon also are more consistent with mixed connective tissue disease than SLE. Anti-Smith antibodies are highly specific for SLE but are associated with glomerulonephritis and central nervous system disease, which also are absent in this patient.

Antimitochondrial antibodies are present in approximately 95% of patients with primary biliary cirrhosis, which occasionally may manifest as slightly elevated alanine and aspartate aminotransferase levels. However, elevated alkaline phosphatase levels are more typical of this condition, which also usually is associated with fatigue, pruritus, and hepatosplenomegaly.

Patients with Sjögren syndrome often have anti-Ro/SSA antibodies, but this patient does not have the symptoms of keratoconjunctivitis sicca (dryness of the eyes and mouth) that characterize this condition. Anti-Ro/SSA antibodies also may be associated with SLE, particularly subacute cutaneous disease. Subacute cutaneous SLE manifests as a papulosquamous or annular rash that typically involves the neck, trunk, and extensor surfaces of the arms, which this patient does not have.

Systemic sclerosis may manifest as Raynaud phenomenon associated with digital ulcerations. Antitopoisomerase I (anti–Scl-70) antibodies are present in approximately 30% of patients with systemic sclerosis and are particularly associated with diffuse skin disease. However, this patient has no additional signs of skin thickening characteristic of this condition or additional manifestations of systemic sclerosis, such as gastroesophageal involvement or basilar fibrosis visible on chest radiography. Furthermore, this patient's arthritis, serositis, and myositis are more suggestive of mixed connective tissue disease than systemic sclerosis.

> **KEY POINT**
>
> - Mixed connective tissue disease is characterized by Raynaud phenomenon, arthralgia, and myositis accompanied by high titers of antiribonucleoprotein antibodies.

Bibliography

Venables PJ. Mixed connective tissue disease. Lupus. 2006;15(3):132-137. [PMID: 16634365]

Item 41　　Answer:　B

Educational Objective: Manage osteoarthritis of the knee in an elderly patient.

In patients with osteoarthritis of the knee, intra-articular hyaluronan injections have been shown to be superior to placebo and comparable to other active interventions, such as physical therapy, NSAIDs, and intra-articular corticosteroids. This therapy may be considered in patients with osteoarthritis of the knee in whom NSAIDs are either contraindicated or do not provide adequate pain relief. The treatment consists of three or more hyaluronan injections administered 1 week apart, depending on the preparation. Hyaluronan injections can provide pain relief for at least 6 months but may not become effective until several weeks after an injection is administered. This intervention is effective in only a small number of patients, but those in whom this therapy is effective experience significant benefits.

NSAIDs have been shown to be more effective than acetaminophen in relieving pain associated with osteoarthritis. However, neither selective nor nonselective NSAIDs would be indicated for an elderly patient with chronic kidney disease. These agents also should be used with caution in patients with heart failure and hypertension.

Like hyaluronan injections, narcotic analgesics may benefit patients in whom NSAIDs are contraindicated or for whom NSAIDs do not sufficiently relieve pain. However, a narcotic analgesic is not appropriate in a patient with a history of severe constipation caused by previous narcotic treatment.

Total knee arthroplasty is warranted only when no further medical therapy is available and the patient decides that the impairment caused by his or her condition warrants this intervention. Because of this patient's comorbidities, her functional status is most likely not sufficiently impaired to warrant the risk of surgery, and most importantly, the patient has indicated a preference for medical therapy.

> **KEY POINT**
>
> - Hyaluronan injections may be considered in patients with osteoarthritis of the knee in whom NSAIDs are either contraindicated or do not provide adequate pain relief.

Bibliography

Bellamy N, Campbell J, Robinson V, Gee T, Bourne R, Wells G. Viscosupplementation for the treatment of osteoarthritis of the knee. Cochrane Database Syst Rev. 2006;(2):CD005321. [PMID: 16625635]

Bibliography

Guillevin L, Mahr A, Callard P, et al; French Vasculitis Study Group. Hepatits B virus-associated polyarteritis nodosa: clinical characteristics, outcome, and impact of treatment in 115 patients. Medicine (Baltimore). 2005;84(5):313-322. [PMID: 16148731]

Item 42   Answer: D

Educational Objective: Treat polyarteritis nodosa.

This patient's constitutional symptoms, abdominal pain, symptoms of peripheral neuropathy, and skin biopsy specimen showing necrotizing vasculitis are consistent with polyarteritis nodosa. Testicular tenderness also is a particularly specific finding for polyarteritis nodosa. The most appropriate treatment for this patient is prednisone, 60 mg/d tapered over 2 weeks, plus lamivudine, 100 mg/d.

Additional features of polyarteritis nodosa may include renovascular hypertension, and cutaneous polyarteritis nodosa may manifest as nodules, ulcers, purpura, or livedo reticularis. Anemia, leukocytosis, and an elevated erythrocyte sedimentation rate are typical laboratory findings in patients with polyarteritis nodosa. Involvement of the renal arterioles, gastrointestinal tract, and heart may occur. This patient also has hepatitis B virus infection, which is present in approximately 50% of patients with polyarteritis nodosa; rarely, patients with infection with hepatitis C virus or HIV may have polyarteritis nodosa.

In patients with polyarteritis nodosa who do not have active hepatitis B virus infection, high-dose corticosteroid therapy is indicated. The presence of systemic involvement is a poor prognostic sign and typically warrants treatment with cyclophosphamide, as well.

In patients with polyarteritis nodosa who have concomitant active hepatitis B virus infection, however, the use of potent immunosuppressive agents can increase the viral load and worsen viral infection. Therefore, these agents should be avoided if possible. Patients with polyarteritis nodosa in the acute setting who also have hepatitis B virus infection should undergo only short-term (typically 2 weeks) high-dose corticosteroid therapy in order to help decrease inflammation and relieve symptoms. Because patients with both polyarteritis nodosa and hepatitis B virus infection typically achieve remission of their vasculitis when seroconversion from hepatitis B e antigen positivity to hepatitis B e antibody positivity occurs, short-term high-dose corticosteroid therapy should be accompanied by long-term treatment with an antiviral agent, such as lamivudine.

> **KEY POINT**
>
> - **Patients with polyarteritis nodosa in the acute setting who also have hepatitis B virus infection should undergo short-term high-dose corticosteroid therapy accompanied by long-term treatment with an antiviral agent.**

Item 43   Answer: D

Educational Objective: Diagnose parvovirus B19 infection.

This patient most likely has parvovirus B19 infection. This condition commonly develops in outbreaks in children that manifest as erythema infectiosum, and adults usually acquire this infection from infected children; parents of young children and childcare workers are therefore more likely to develop this condition than the general population. Parvovirus B19 infection in children characteristically manifests as fever and an erythematous malar rash known as the "slapped cheek" rash, whereas infected adults are more likely to develop joint involvement.

In adults, parvovirus B19 infection typically initially manifests as constitutional symptoms such as fever, myalgia, fatigue, and nausea. Approximately 70% of patients also develop an erythematous rash that may involve the face, trunk, or extremities. These symptoms are followed by the onset of symmetric arthritis that usually involves the small joints of the wrists, hands, and feet as well as the knees that typically resolves within weeks to months. IgM antibodies against parvovirus B19 would confirm the presence of this condition; these antibodies would be detectable 7 to 10 days after exposure to this virus and can be measured for several months after this time.

This patient's pattern of joint involvement is compatible with early rheumatoid arthritis and systemic lupus erythematosus (SLE). However, caution is warranted before diagnosing this patient with either of these conditions because of the short duration of her symptoms.

Rheumatoid arthritis is associated with anti–cyclic citrullinated peptide antibodies and may be present in patients who do not have rheumatoid factor; conversely, some patients with parvovirus B19 infection have positive titers of rheumatoid factor and antinuclear antibodies. A diagnosis of rheumatoid arthritis would not explain this patient's rash.

Anti–double-stranded DNA antibodies are an insensitive but highly specific marker for SLE, which usually affects women in their 20s to 30s and also may manifest as constitutional symptoms. However, this patient does not have additional signs or symptoms consistent with SLE, such as serositis, anemia, or kidney disease. In addition, SLE is associated with a photosensitive malar or discoid rash, which is not consistent with this patient's cutaneous manifestations.

Antitopoisomerase I (anti–Scl-70) antibodies are a specific marker for diffuse cutaneous systemic sclerosis. This condition may manifest as acute polyarthritis in patients with early disease, but musculoskeletal involvement in patients with systemic sclerosis is almost always preceded by Raynaud phenomenon. Systemic sclerosis also would be associated with characteristic skin thickening and would not explain this patient's erythematous rash.

> **KEY POINT**
>
> - **Parvovirus B19 infection in adults typically initially manifests as constitutional symptoms and an erythematous rash followed by the onset of symmetric arthritis of the small joints that may mimic rheumatoid arthritis.**

Bibliography

Franssila R, Hedman K. Infection and musculoskeletal conditions: Viral causes of arthritis. Best Pract Res Clin Rheumatol. 2006;20(6):1139-1157. [PMID: 17127201]

Item 44   Answer: D

Educational Objective: Manage rheumatoid arthritis in a patient with chronic hepatitis C virus infection.

Despite the modest duration of his morning stiffness, this patient has chronic symmetric polyarthralgia, tenderness around the joints, positive rheumatoid factor, and the presence of periarticular osteopenia on radiography. This clinical presentation is compatible with a diagnosis of rheumatoid arthritis. However, patients with hepatitis C virus (HCV) infection may have arthritis that mimics rheumatoid arthritis. Furthermore, even in the absence of arthritis, patients with HCV infection frequently have positive titers of rheumatoid factor because of the presence of circulating cryoglobulins. An anti–cyclic citrullinated peptide (CCP) antibody assay is therefore warranted to determine whether this patient's symptoms are caused by rheumatoid arthritis; these antibodies have a 95% specificity for rheumatoid arthritis and are not associated with HCV infection. Concomitant rheumatoid factor and anti-CCP antibody positivity are highly specific for rheumatoid arthritis.

Differentiating between HCV infection–associated arthritis and rheumatoid arthritis is essential, because treatment of these conditions differs greatly. Initiation of effective antiviral treatment is indicated for HCV infection–associated arthritis, whereas careful selection and early initiation of disease-modifying antirheumatic drug therapy is indicated for rheumatoid arthritis.

Therapy with prednisone would most likely help to control this patient's joint symptoms but would not help to establish a diagnosis. More importantly, patients with HCV infection treated with corticosteroids typically experience an increase in HCV viral load. Short courses of corticosteroids probably do not greatly impact the natural history of HCV infection, but the effect of long-term treatment is unknown.

Rheumatoid arthritis often affects the feet, and radiographs of this patient's feet may show evidence of joint inflammation even in early disease. Radiographic changes typical of rheumatoid arthritis include erosions or unequivocal bony decalcification adjacent to the involved joints. Although the presence of these radiographic findings may support the diagnosis of rheumatoid arthritis, these findings are not diagnostic nor does their absence exclude this diagnosis. In addition, these findings are not likely to be present in a patient without symptomatic involvement of the feet. Therefore, radiographs of the feet would be unlikely to support a diagnosis of rheumatoid arthritis.

Because methotrexate can cause hepatotoxicity, fibrosis, and cirrhosis, usually after prolonged use, use of this agent in a patient with pre-existing liver disease is contraindicated.

> **KEY POINT**
>
> - **Anti–cyclic citrullinated peptide antibodies are a more specific marker for rheumatoid arthritis than rheumatoid factor.**

Bibliography

Liu FC, Chao YC, Hou TY, et al. Usefulness of anti-CCP antibodies in patients with hepatitis C virus infection with or without arthritis, rheumatoid factor, or cryoglobulinemia. Clin Rheumatol. 2008;27(4):463-467. [PMID: 17876647]

Item 45   Answer: D

Educational Objective: Diagnose pulmonary arterial hypertension associated with systemic sclerosis.

This patient most likely has pulmonary arterial hypertension (PAH) associated with collagen vascular disease related to systemic sclerosis. Pulmonary disease is the primary cause of morbidity in patients with systemic sclerosis; PAH is among the most common manifestations of lung involvement in these patients, particularly in those with limited cutaneous disease. This patient's worsening fatigue and dyspnea on exertion in the presence of clear lung fields are consistent with PAH.

Physical signs of elevated pulmonary artery pressure include a loud P_2, fixed split S_2, pulmonic flow murmur, and tricuspid regurgitation. Chest radiographs are usually normal in early disease but may show enlarged pulmonary arteries, right atrium, and right ventricle. Electrocardiographs in these patients may show right ventricular strain or hypertrophy.

Pulmonary function studies in patients with PAH usually reveal an isolated decreased DLCO in the setting of normal airflow and lung volumes (excluding restrictive lung disease). Echocardiography is an early diagnostic test for patients with signs and symptoms of PAH. This study is used to exclude congenital heart disease, such as atrial septal defect, and valvular heart disease, such as mitral stenosis, that may manifest as PAH. Echocardiography may be used to estimate peak right ventricular systolic pressure if tricuspid regurgitation is noted on examination.

Atrial septal defects are the second most common form of congenital heart disease in adults. The characteristic physical examination finding in patients with an atrial septal defect is related to the development of PAH. This patient's limited systemic sclerosis and normal cardiopulmonary evaluation 3 years ago makes atrial septal defect a much less likely cause of her findings.

Interstitial lung disease (ILD) is a common pulmonary manifestation in patients with systemic sclerosis who also have dyspnea and fatigue, and patients with ILD also usually have dry cough. The absence of late inspiratory crackles on pulmonary examination and the presence of normal lung volumes on pulmonary function testing further argue against this condition. In patients with ILD, the lung volumes are less than 80% of predicted.

Left ventricular failure may manifest as dyspnea and fatigue and may be associated with cardiac murmurs. However, this condition is unlikely in the absence of additional abnormal cardiopulmonary examination findings, such as an S_3 or S_4 gallop and pulmonary crackles. In addition, chest radiographs in patients with left ventricular heart failure usually demonstrate pulmonary vascular congestion.

KEY POINT

- **Pulmonary arterial hypertension is among the most common manifestations of lung involvement in patients with systemic sclerosis.**

Bibliography

Highland KB, Garin MC, Brown KK. The spectrum of scleroderma lung disease. Semin Respir Crit Care Med. 2007;28(4):418-429. [PMID: 17764059]

Item 46   Answer: A

Educational Objective: Diagnose antisynthetase syndrome.

This patient most likely has the antisynthetase syndrome. Polymyositis and dermatomyositis are inflammatory myopathies that typically present with the gradual onset of symmetric proximal weakness over weeks to months. This weakness causes progressive difficulty with rising from a chair, climbing stairs, or hair combing. Nearly one third of patients with an inflammatory myopathy have the antisynthetase syndrome. This condition can have an acute or subacute onset and is characterized by fever; fatigue; Raynaud phenomenon; synovitis; interstitial lung disease; and scaly, rough, dry, darkened, cracked horizontal lines that develop on the palmar and lateral aspects of the fingers that are known as "mechanic's hands."

Patients with antisynthetase syndrome have antisynthetase antibodies that are specific for an inflammatory myopathy. The most common antisynthetase antibody is the anti–Jo-1 antibody. Not all patients with anti–Jo-1 antibodies develop the antisynthetase syndrome and not all patients with this syndrome have all of its manifestations, but patients who have anti–Jo-1 antibodies typically have several features of the antisynthetase syndrome in addition to their muscle disease. The greatest concern in patients with this syndrome is the risk for developing interstitial lung disease.

Idiopathic pulmonary fibrosis (IPF), the most common of the idiopathic interstitial pneumonias, is a fibrosing interstitial pneumonia. This condition manifests as slowly progressive dyspnea and a chronic, nonproductive cough. Pulmonary examination in patients with IPF reveals end-inspiratory crackles, and chest radiograph performed on presentation nearly always reveals decreased lung volumes and basal reticular opacities. However, IPF is not associated with extrapulmonary involvement.

Patients with systemic lupus erythematosus (SLE) may have fever, arthralgia or arthritis, Raynaud phenomenon, and very rarely, an acute interstitial pneumonia (lupus pneumonitis). However, SLE usually affects women in their 20s and 30s and is often associated with additional manifestations such as serositis, aphthous ulcers, malar or photosensitive rash, and specific autoantibodies including anti–double-stranded DNA and anti-Smith antibodies. SLE is an unlikely diagnosis based upon the extent of muscle weakness, degree of elevation of the creatine kinase level, absence of specific antibodies, and presence of anti–Jo-1 antibodies.

Systemic sclerosis most frequently develops in patients between 30 and 50 years of age and has a 3:1 female predominance. Diagnosis may be established in patients who present with two of the following features: sclerodactyly, digital pitting, and basilar fibrosis visible on chest radiography. Antinuclear antibodies are present in more than 95% of patients with systemic sclerosis. Patients with anti–Scl-70 antibodies are at increased risk for developing diffuse cutaneous disease and interstitial lung disease. Systemic sclerosis is unlikely in the absence of sclerodactyly or digital pitting. Furthermore, this condition would not explain this patient's proximal muscle weakness.

KEY POINT

- **Nearly one third of patients with inflammatory myopathy have the antisynthetase syndrome, which is characterized by an acute or subacute onset, fever, fatigue, Raynaud phenomenon, "mechanic's hands," synovitis, and interstitial lung disease.**

Bibliography

Tillie-Leblond I, Wislez M, Valeyre D, et al. Interstitial lung disease and anti-Jo-1 antibodies: difference between acute and gradual onset. Thorax. 2008;63(1):53-59. [PMID: 17557770]

Item 47   Answer: C

Educational Objective: Manage severe osteoarthritis of the knee.

Trials of acetaminophen and two NSAIDs did not relieve this patient's pain, tramadol provided only modest pain relief, and an intra-articular corticosteroid injection only alleviated her pain for 1 week. Moreover, the presence of bone-on-bone contact on radiography and pain even on rest suggests that she is unlikely to achieve significant pain relief from additional nonsurgical therapy. The most appropriate next step in this patient's management is total knee arthroplasty, which is appropriate only when no further medical therapy is available and the patient decides that the impairment caused by his or her condition warrants this procedure.

Diclofenac is unlikely to effectively manage this patient's pain. Previous trials of several NSAIDs have not been beneficial. Furthermore, this patient's age and comorbidities pose the potential for complications associated with NSAID use, including the risk for renal and gastrointestinal toxicity. These agents also may exacerbate heart failure and should be used with caution in patients with hypertension.

The American College of Rheumatology guidelines recommend opioid analgesics as second-line agents in the treatment of osteoarthritis. These agents are particularly useful in patients with osteoarthritis of the hip or knee who are intolerant of or who do not achieve adequate pain control using acetaminophen and/or NSAIDs. However, tramadol was already tried in this patient and was not beneficial.

Repeat administration of intra-articular corticosteroid injection would be unlikely to sufficiently benefit a patient with such severe osteoarthritis. In addition, a previous intra-articular corticosteroid injection provided only transient relief.

KEY POINT

- **Total knee arthroplasty is warranted only when no further medical therapy is available and the patient decides that the impairment caused by his or her condition warrants this procedure.**

Bibliography
Hawker GA, Guan J, Croxford R, et al. A prospective population-based study of the predictors of undergoing total joint arthroplasty. Arthritis Rheum. 2006;54(10):3212-3220. [PMID: 17009255]

Item 48   Answer: A
Educational Objective: Diagnose bacterial overgrowth associated with systemic sclerosis.

This patient most likely has small-bowel bacterial overgrowth. Gastrointestinal involvement is common in both limited and diffuse cutaneous systemic sclerosis, and dysfunctional motility in this setting may cause bacterial overgrowth. This patient's chronic diarrhea, abdominal pain, tender and distended abdomen, and hypoalbuminemia consistent with malabsorption raise suspicion for this condition. Although the gold standard is aspiration of duodenal luminal contents for quantitative culture at the time of upper endoscopy, this study is available at only a limited number of centers. A less invasive and more readily available

screening test is the hydrogen breath test. Many clinicians simply recommend an empiric trial of antibiotics to evaluate whether the patient's symptoms improve.

Clostridium difficile–associated colitis manifests as loose, watery stools; lower abdominal cramping; low-grade fever; and leukocytosis. Affected patients often have a history of antibiotic use or nosocomial exposure. *Clostridium difficile*–associated colitis is unlikely in a patient with symptoms suggestive of malabsorption and no recent hospitalization or antibiotic exposure.

Irritable bowel syndrome is characterized by pain relieved with defecation. This condition initially manifests as a change in stool frequency or in the consistency of stool in the absence of hematochezia, unintentional weight loss, fever, or anemia. Irritable bowel syndrome could be responsible for this patient's chronic diarrhea and abdominal distention but would not explain the presence of greasy stools, weight loss, and hypoalbuminemia.

Microscopic colitis is characterized by chronic diarrhea that is often accompanied by abdominal pain and mild weight loss. This condition most often affects otherwise well middle-aged to elderly patients. Microscopic colitis typically manifests as chronic or intermittent nonbloody watery stool. A syndrome of formed or semiformed greasy stools with evidence of malabsorption is not compatible with microscopic colitis.

KEY POINT

- **Gastrointestinal involvement is common in both limited and diffuse cutaneous systemic sclerosis and may manifest as bacterial overgrowth.**

Bibliography
Ebert EC. Gastric and enteric involvement in progressive systemic sclerosis. J Clin Gastroenterol. 2008;42(1):5-12. [PMID: 18097282]

Item 49   Answer: B
Educational Objective: Treat polymyalgia rheumatica.

The most appropriate management in this patient is to increase the prednisone dosage to 7.5 mg/d and add methotrexate, 10 mg weekly. Typically, patients with polymyalgia achieve resolution of their symptoms with low-dose prednisone (10 to 20 mg/d); once these symptoms are controlled, the prednisone dosage can then be tapered. However, polymyalgia rheumatica commonly recurs when the prednisone dosage is being tapered. During flares, the prednisone dosage should be increased to the minimum amount needed to provide symptomatic relief; once symptoms subside, slower tapering of the dosage is warranted.

Because two previous attempts to taper this patient's prednisone dosage below 7.5 mg/d have been unsuccessful, the addition of a steroid-sparing agent as well as an increase in her prednisone dosage is warranted. Methotrexate in particular has been shown to be an effective steroid-sparing agent in patients with polymyalgia rheumatica.

This patient's prednisone dosage should be increased to the minimum dosage needed to control her symptoms, which in this individual has been shown to be between 7 and 7.5 mg/d. Increasing this patient's prednisone dosage to 20 mg/d would unnecessarily place her at greater risk for corticosteroid toxicity. Infliximab has not been shown to be an effective steroid-sparing agent in patients with polymyalgia rheumatica and therefore would not be indicated for this patient.

KEY POINT

- **Methotrexate is an effective steroid-sparing agent in the treatment of polymyalgia rheumatica.**

Bibliography

Caporali R, Cimmino MA, Feraccioli G, et al; Systemic Vasculitis Study Group of the Italian Society for Rheumatology. Prednisone plus methotrexate for polymyalgia rheumatica: a randomized, double-blind, placebo-controlled trial. Ann Intern Med. 2004;141(7):493-500. [PMID: 15466766]

Item 50   Answer: D

Educational Objective: Evaluate a persistently elevated serum creatine kinase level.

MRI of the thigh muscles is warranted for this patient. For more than 6 months, this patient has had minor myalgia and a mildly elevated creatine kinase level despite discontinuation of atorvastatin. Statin-related myopathy usually begins within weeks to months after starting the inciting medication and may manifest as myalgia, weakness, and an elevated creatine kinase level. Some affected patients develop myalgia without elevations of the creatine kinase level. In most cases, the symptoms and laboratory abnormality associated with this condition resolve within a few days or weeks of stopping the inciting medication. Approximately 95% of cases of this condition resolve within 6 months.

This patient discontinued atorvastatin 6 months ago and does not have a history of excessive alcohol use, which may cause myopathy. Her normal thyroid-stimulating hormone level excludes hypothyroidism. In this setting, MRI of the proximal muscles, particularly the thighs, would help to assess whether muscle inflammation is present and to help localize a biopsy site.

Unlike electromyography, MRI can screen only a limited number of muscle groups. Nevertheless, MRI of the involved muscle groups, particularly the thighs, is being increasingly employed to initially evaluate a suspected myositis and to monitor disease progression. On MRI, actively inflamed muscle groups demonstrate increased edema within the muscle; this finding is not specific for myositis but does suggest a myopathic process. MRI also is a noninvasive means of localizing a muscle for biopsy. However, the role of MRI in patients with an inflammatory myopathy is still being defined, and the results of this study should be interpreted within the clinical context and should be considered complementary to results of electromyography and nerve conduction velocity studies.

Patients with active muscle disease may have an elevated aldolase level, but this enzyme is less specific for muscle damage than creatine kinase. Furthermore, the results of aldolase measurement would not influence the need to evaluate this patient for inflammatory muscle disease.

Approximately 80% of patients with an inflammatory myopathy have positive titers of antinuclear antibodies. Therefore, the absence of these antibodies would not exclude myositis, and the presence of antinuclear antibodies is not diagnostic of active muscle disease.

Similarly, patients with myositis may have an elevated erythrocyte sedimentation rate, but this finding is a nonspecific marker of inflammation and is not used to diagnose an inflammatory myopathy or to monitor disease activity.

KEY POINT

- **MRI of the proximal muscles, particularly the thighs, is helpful in patients with persistently elevated creatine kinase levels to assess whether muscle inflammation is present.**

Bibliography

Baer AN, Wortmann RL. Myotoxicity associated with lipid-lowering drugs. Curr Opin Rheumatol. 2007;19(1):67-73. [PMID: 17143099]

Item 51   Answer: E

Educational Objective: Treat osteoarthritis in a patient with concomitant coronary artery disease.

This patient's clinical presentation is consistent with osteoarthritis, and the most appropriate next step in his treatment is to begin tramadol. Osteoarthritis is characterized by pain on activity that is relieved with rest. This condition also is associated with a painful, limited range of motion and the presence of joint-space narrowing, subchondral sclerosis, and osteophyte formation on radiography. Tramadol is an appropriate second-line agent in the treatment of osteoarthritis and is particularly useful in patients with osteoarthritis of the knee or hip who are intolerant of or who do not achieve adequate pain control using NSAIDs.

Arthroscopic lavage and/or débridement is not indicated for osteoarthritis of the knee. A randomized controlled trial comparing arthroscopic lavage and arthroscopic lavage plus débridement compared with a sham procedure for knee osteoarthritis showed no benefit of the intervention compared with sham arthroscopy. Patients with hip and knee osteoarthritis who have not responded to conservative therapy and who have functional limitations should be referred to an orthopedic surgeon for consideration of arthroplasty. However, this patient is not severely incapacitated, and other medical options are available to manage his knee pain.

Use of an NSAID such as celecoxib or ibuprofen would be appropriate in a patient with moderate to severe osteoarthritis or a patient with osteoarthritis in whom acetaminophen did not provide sufficient pain relief. However, both selective and nonselective NSAIDs are associated with an increased risk of cardiovascular disease and should be avoided in patients with cardiovascular conditions. Finally, coadministration of an NSAID with aspirin also may inhibit the antiplatelet effects of aspirin.

> **KEY POINT**
>
> • **Tramadol is an appropriate second-line agent in the treatment of osteoarthritis and is particularly useful in patients with osteoarthritis of the knee who are intolerant of or who do not achieve adequate pain control using NSAIDs.**

Bibliography

McGettigan P, Henry D. Cardiovascular risk and inhibition of cyclooxygenase: a systematic review of the observational studies of selective and nonselective inhibitors of cyclooxygenase-2. JAMA. 2006;296(13):1633-1644. [PMID: 16968831]

Item 52   Answer: E

Educational Objective: Diagnose systemic lupus erythematosus.

This patient most likely has systemic lupus erythematosus (SLE). Her extraintestinal manifestations consist of butterfly rash, physician-confirmed arthritis, pancytopenia including Coombs-positive hemolytic anemia, serositis, pleuritis, renal insufficiency, and urine sediment findings suggestive of glomerulonephritis. She also has antinuclear antibodies, anti–double-stranded DNA antibodies, and hypocomplementemia. This constellation of features is consistent with SLE.

This patient also has abdominal pain, nausea, vomiting, and blood per rectum. Her imaging studies are consistent with bowel ischemia. Mesenteric vasculitis is the most likely cause of this clinical presentation. Approximately one third of patients with active SLE who have abdominal pain have mesenteric vasculitis. This condition typically warrants immediate treatment with high-dose corticosteroids and intravenous cyclophosphamide; occasionally, surgical intervention is indicated.

Patients with Crohn disease may present with fever, weight loss, abdominal pain, nausea, vomiting, or diarrhea. Extraintestinal manifestations of this condition include arthralgia and arthritis, pyoderma gangrenosum, or erythema nodosum. Inflammation in patients with Crohn disease involves the bowel mucosa; endoscopic examination may show aphthous ulcers or large ulcers that can coalesce and cause a "cobblestone" appearance. Rectal sparing is common, and areas of disease activity may be separated by areas of normal mucosa ("skip areas"). Bowel ischemia is

rare in these patients. Anemia is a common manifestation of Crohn disease but usually is caused by iron deficiency or chronic disease, not hemolysis. Pancytopenia, glomerulonephritis, anti–double-stranded DNA antibodies, hypocomplementemia, and high titers of antinuclear antibodies also are not associated with this condition.

Hemolytic uremic syndrome (HUS) is characterized by acute kidney injury accompanied by microangiopathic hemolytic anemia and thrombocytopenia. This condition also may manifest as painful bloody diarrhea. HUS would be unlikely in the absence of schistocytes on a peripheral blood smear and would not explain this patient's positive results on a direct antiglobulin (Coombs) test, antinuclear and anti–double-stranded DNA antibodies, or hypocomplementemia.

Bowel ischemia and glomerulonephritis should raise strong suspicion for Henoch-Schönlein purpura (HSP). HSP is a systemic IgA-mediated vasculitis that may involve the skin, joints, gastrointestinal tract, and kidneys. This condition most commonly affects children and usually is associated with a purpuric rash. HSP also would not explain this patient's pancytopenia, hypocomplementemia, or autoantibodies.

Polyarteritis nodosa is a medium-sized vessel vasculitis that may manifest as arthritis and, occasionally, as a vasculitic rash; affected patients also may develop involvement of the renal arteries and arterioles, which may cause hypertension. Suspicion for polyarteritis nodosa always should be raised in patients who present with mesenteric ischemia. However, polyarteritis nodosa would not cause glomerulonephritis or pancytopenia and would not be associated with autoantibodies.

> **KEY POINT**
>
> • **Approximately one third of patients with active systemic lupus erythematosus who have abdominal pain have mesenteric vasculitis.**

Bibliography

Hallegua DS, Wallace DJ. Gastrointestinal manifestations of systemic lupus erythematosus. Curr Opin Rheumatol. 2000;12(5):379-385. [PMID: 10990173]

Item 53   Answer: D

Educational Objective: Diagnose myositis associated with mixed connective tissue disease.

This patient's elevated creatine kinase level and proximal muscle weakness are consistent with an inflammatory muscle disease. She also has arthritis, Raynaud phenomenon with digital pitting, pancytopenia, and high titers of antinuclear and antiribonucleoprotein antibodies. This clinical presentation is consistent with mixed connective tissue disease, and the most appropriate next step in this patient's management is initiation of prednisone therapy.

Treatment in patients with mixed connective tissue disease involves managing the specific visceral manifestations.

High-dose oral corticosteroid therapy is the standard first-line treatment for active inflammatory muscle disease and is warranted particularly in a patient with muscle weakness of this severity.

This patient's pancytopenia is most likely associated with mixed connective tissue disease features consistent with systemic lupus erythematosus, and bone marrow biopsy is unlikely to provide additional information that would alter the diagnosis or treatment options. Although the complete blood count in this patient should be monitored closely, corticosteroid therapy initiated to treat the muscle disease is likely to also help to treat her hematologic abnormalities.

The inflammatory myopathies are associated with malignancy, particularly in older patients. However, malignancy associated with a myopathy is rare in patients under 30 years of age and in those whose myositis is associated with a systemic connective tissue disease. Therefore, evaluation for malignancy, including screening CT of the chest, abdomen, and pelvis, is not indicated in this patient.

Liver biopsy would be beneficial in a patient with elevated liver enzyme levels of unknown origin. However, active muscle disease is associated with an increase in aspartate and alanine aminotransferase levels, and this patient's liver enzyme study results are most likely related to her underlying muscle disease.

KEY POINT

- **Patients with an inflammatory myopathy and features of systemic sclerosis, systemic lupus erythematosus, and rheumatoid arthritis accompanied by high titers of antiribonucleoprotein antibodies often have mixed connective tissue disease.**

Bibliography

Hall S, Hanrahan P. Muscle involvement in mixed connective tissue disease. Rheum Dis Clin North Am. 2005;31(3):509-517, vii. [PMID: 16084322]

Item 54   Answer: A

Educational Objective: Manage scleroderma renal crisis in a pregnant patient.

The most likely diagnosis is scleroderma renal crisis (SRC), and the most appropriate management for this patient is initiation of captopril. Patients with early diffuse systemic sclerosis have an increased risk for developing SRC.

The differential diagnosis of a pregnant patient with diffuse cutaneous systemic sclerosis who presents with acute kidney injury, proteinuria, thrombocytopenia, and a microangiopathic hemolytic anemia includes SRC and preeclampsia, eclampsia (preeclampsia with seizures), HELLP (hemolysis, elevated liver function tests, low platelets) syndrome, and thrombotic thrombocytopenic purpura (TTP). Differentiating among these conditions is often extremely difficult but critical. SRC occurs almost exclusively in patients with diffuse cutaneous systemic sclerosis, particularly those with skin fibrosis that develops within 3 years of disease onset. In this patient, the abrupt onset of the signs and symptoms of hypertension and renal failure in the presence of diffuse systemic sclerosis during early gestation supports the diagnosis of SRC and helps to exclude the other entities in the differential diagnosis. Angiotensin-converting enzyme inhibitor therapy with aggressive upward titration is indicated in patients with SRC to reduce mortality. Therefore, captopril must be used in this patient to preserve renal function, control blood pressure, and reduce mortality despite being associated with an increased risk to the fetus.

Preeclampsia is most commonly characterized by the gradual onset of hypertension, proteinuria, and edema. Symptoms typically develop in the late third trimester and rarely as early as the late second trimester. Some patients experience the onset of symptoms after delivery, but the presence of signs and symptoms of this condition before 20 weeks of gestation is unusual and argues strongly against this diagnosis. HELLP syndrome develops only in women whose pregnancies are complicated by preeclampsia. Delivery of the fetus is curative for patients with preeclampsia, eclampsia, or HELLP syndrome. Because this patient is symptomatic during the twelfth week of pregnancy, preeclampsia, eclampsia, and the HELLP syndrome are unlikely and delivery of the fetus is not appropriate.

Methyldopa is an appropriate treatment for chronic hypertension in a pregnant patient, but chronic hypertension would not explain this patient's acute kidney injury and microangiopathic anemia. Methyldopa also does not alter outcome in patients with SRC and is therefore not indicated for this patient.

TTP is characterized by thrombocytopenia, microangiopathic hemolytic anemia, acute kidney injury, fever, and neurologic symptoms; however, hematologic and renal manifestations are usually predominant. TTP is a much more rare complication of pregnancy compared with preeclampsia and tends to present at midpregnancy or later. Like preeclampsia, the occurrence of TTP before 20 weeks would be very unusual. In addition, the lactate dehydrogenase level is often markedly elevated in TTP secondary to both hemolysis and widespread tissue ischemia. The treatment of choice for TTP is plasma exchange. Because TTP is an unlikely diagnosis in this patient based upon the timing of the symptoms, treatment with plasma exchange would not be warranted.

KEY POINT

- **Therapy with an angiotensin-converting enzyme inhibitor is indicated for scleroderma renal crisis in pregnant patients despite being associated with an increased risk to the fetus.**

Bibliography

Steen VD. Pregnancy in scleroderma. Rheum Dis Clin North Am. 2007;33(2):345-358, vii. [PMID: 17499711]

Item 55   Answer: B

Educational Objective: Manage dermatomyositis.

This patient has dermatomyositis, which initially responded well to high-dose prednisone therapy. However, now that her prednisone dosage has been decreased, her elevated creatine kinase and aspartate and alanine aminotransferase levels indicate that she again has active disease. She also is now experiencing hyperglycemia, a complication of high-dose corticosteroid therapy. The addition of methotrexate is indicated for this patient.

Because an increase in creatine kinase levels often precedes a decrease in muscle strength, this patient's normal results on muscle strength testing do not preclude active myositis. Unless additional immunosuppressive therapy is instituted in this patient, she most likely will develop muscle weakness. Methotrexate is a commonly used adjunctive immunosuppressive agent in patients undergoing long-term corticosteroid therapy and will help to treat this patient's myositis and allow for further tapering of her corticosteroid dosage over time. This patient's elevated alanine and aspartate aminotransferase levels most likely reflect muscle injury rather than a liver abnormality. When using methotrexate in patients with myositis, liver toxicity due to use of this agent should only be suspected when these enzyme levels increase in the presence of a stable or decreasing creatine kinase level. This agent can be used safely in this setting with appropriate monitoring. Azathioprine, individually and in combination with methotrexate, also has been shown to be an effective steroid-sparing agent in the treatment of inflammatory myositis.

Further decreasing this patient's prednisone dosage without adding additional therapy would place her at risk for worsening of her myositis and therefore would not be appropriate.

The initiation of cyclosporine may be considered as an adjunct or substitute for methotrexate and azathioprine if these agents are ineffective in the treatment of myositis or cannot be tolerated. This agent may be effective but in some patients is associated with an increase in blood pressure and a reduction in renal function, which has limited its use as a first-line steroid-sparing agent.

Uncontrolled studies support the effectiveness of rituximab in the treatment of myositis, but this agent is considered a third-line treatment after failure of methotrexate or azathioprine.

KEY POINT

- In patients with myositis undergoing long-term corticosteroid therapy, the addition of methotrexate helps to control muscle disease and allow for further tapering of the corticosteroid dosage over time.

Bibliography
Iorizzo LJ III, Jorizzo JL. The treatment and prognosis of dermatomyositis: an updated review. J Am Acad Dermatol. 2008;59(1):99-112. [PMID: 18423790]

Item 56   Answer: D

Educational Objective: Treat osteoarthritis in a patient with compromised renal function.

This patient's clinical presentation is consistent with osteoarthritis of the hip, and the most appropriate treatment for his groin pain is tramadol. Pain associated with osteoarthritis of the hip is often referred to the groin and medial thigh and, less frequently, the knee and/or buttocks. Patients with this condition also often experience pain on passive range of motion of the hip joint at the extremes of flexion, extension, or internal and external rotation.

NSAIDs such as celecoxib, ibuprofen, or sulindac are indicated for patients with osteoarthritis who have moderate-to-severe disease or who have achieved inadequate pain relief with acetaminophen. However, this patient has chronic kidney disease. In patients with compromised renal function, prostaglandin inhibition associated with ibuprofen can lead to frank renal failure, particularly in patients already taking an angiotensin-converting enzyme inhibitor.

The most appropriate therapy for this patient's pain, therefore, is tramadol, which would not be expected to have any effect on renal function. The American College of Rheumatology guidelines recommend tramadol as a second-line agent in the treatment of osteoarthritis. This medication is considered particularly useful in patients with osteoarthritis of the hip or knee who are intolerant of or who do not achieve adequate pain control using acetaminophen and/or NSAIDs. Tramadol is a centrally acting analgesic, and the most common adverse effects associated with this agent are nausea and dizziness.

KEY POINT

- Both selective and nonselective NSAIDs have been shown to cause acute kidney injury in patients with chronic kidney disease and should not be used in this setting.

Bibliography
Gooch K, Culleton BF, Manns BJ, et al. NSAID use and progression of chronic kidney disease. Am J Med. 2007;120(3):280.e1-7. [PMID: 17349452]

Item 57   Answer: B

Educational Objective: Treat joint manifestations in a patient with systemic lupus erythematosus.

This patient's arthralgia and arthritis, malar rash, oral ulcers, symptoms of pleuritis, positive titers of antinuclear and anti-Ro/SSA antibodies, and hypocomplementemia are consistent with systemic lupus erythematosus (SLE). This condition also may be associated with low titers of rheumatoid factor and tendon laxity that results in reducible joint deformities that mimic those in patients with rheumatoid arthritis but are not erosive; the development of these deformities is known as Jaccoud arthropathy.

NSAIDs help to relieve pain in patients with SLE who have serositis or joint manifestations but do not alter disease progression or prevent disease flares. Therefore, these agents are not typically used as monotherapy for SLE.

Hydroxychloroquine is usually effective in managing mild manifestations of SLE, including cutaneous and joint involvement. This medication also is an extremely effective disease-modifying agent in SLE and helps to prevent disease flares. Rarely, hydroxychloroquine causes an irreversible retinopathy, and regular ophthalmologic screening is indicated in patients using this agent.

The tumor necrosis factor α inhibitor etanercept may worsen disease activity in patients with SLE and is generally not used in this patient population.

Methotrexate is indicated for patients with active rheumatoid arthritis. This patient has positive titers of rheumatoid factor, but this finding alone is not diagnostic of rheumatoid arthritis. In addition, although this patient's joint deformities are suggestive of erosive joint disease associated with rheumatoid arthritis, they are in reality caused by tendon laxity. Methotrexate can be used in patients with SLE whose arthritis is unresponsive to hydroxychloroquine and is indicated for rare patients with SLE who have erosive joint disease.

KEY POINT

- Hydroxychloroquine is usually effective in managing mild manifestations of systemic lupus erythematosus and helps to prevent disease flares.

Bibliography

Reeves GE. Update on the immunology, diagnosis and management of systemic lupus erythematosus. Intern Med J. 2004;34(6):338-347. [PMID: 15228395]

Item 58   Answer: A

Educational Objective: Manage corticosteroid-induced myopathy in a patient with dermatomyositis.

This patient most likely has corticosteroid-induced myopathy, and the most appropriate next step in his management is to decrease the prednisone dosage. He has progressive muscle weakness, but the significant decrease in his creatine kinase level suggests that his dermatomyositis is well controlled. Improvement in muscle strength typically is preceded by improvement in the creatine kinase level, but the discrepancy between this patient's findings on laboratory studies and symptoms is highly suggestive of a secondary cause for his weakness.

Corticosteroid-induced myopathy should be suspected in patients with polymyositis or dermatomyositis treated with corticosteroids who develop progressive weakness despite significant improvement in muscle enzyme levels. This patient's cushingoid features also are consistent with this condition.

The most appropriate management of a patient whose clinical presentation raises concern for corticosteroid-induced myopathy is to decrease the corticosteroid dosage and closely monitor the creatine kinase level for elevations. If corticosteroid-induced myopathy is causing this patient's symptoms, his muscle weakness should begin to resolve 3 to 4 weeks after his prednisone dosage is decreased.

Increasing the azathioprine dosage would not be warranted in a patient with dermatomyositis whose creatine kinase level is not significantly elevated. Furthermore, this intervention would not directly address this patient's underlying corticosteroid-induced myopathy.

Cyclosporine is an adjunct or substitute for methotrexate and azathioprine in patients in whom these agents are ineffective in the treatment of myositis or in those who cannot tolerate these agents. This patient is tolerating azathioprine, and there is therefore no need to add or substitute cyclosporine.

Methotrexate is effective in the treatment of inflammatory myositis and is an alternative steroid-sparing drug to azathioprine. However, the patient's condition is responsive to his current medication regimen of corticosteroids and azathioprine, and substituting methotrexate is not likely to offer any advantage to a patient with corticosteroid-induced myopathy.

KEY POINT

- Corticosteroid-induced myopathy should be suspected in patients with polymyositis or dermatomyositis treated with corticosteroids who develop progressive weakness despite significant improvement in muscle enzyme levels.

Bibliography

Schakman O, Gilson H, Thissen JP. Mechanisms of glucocorticoids-induced myopathy. J Endocrinol. 2008;197(1):1-10. [PMID: 18372227]

Item 59   Answer: B

Educational Objective: Treat rheumatoid arthritis in a patient with melanoma.

There is evidence that tumor necrosis factor α (TNF-α) is active against some forms of cancer and that TNF-α inhibitors may increase the risk of cancer, particularly lymphoma, some solid cancers, and skin cancer. Patients with rheumatoid arthritis also have an increased risk of developing certain cancers, including leukemia and lymphoma, even in the absence of therapy with a TNF-α inhibitor. Therefore, establishing a causal relationship between cancer and TNF-α inhibitors is difficult.

Studies attempting to demonstrate a relationship between TNF-α inhibitors and lymphoma and solid malignancies have yielded mixed results. In a study that used the National Data Bank for Rheumatic Diseases, the odds ratio for developing melanoma while taking a TNF-α inhibitor was approximately 2 but did not reach statistical significance.

Nevertheless, standard practice based on expert opinion is to discontinue TNF-α inhibitor therapy in patients who develop cancers, including melanomas.

The addition of leflunomide or an increase in the prednisone dosage would be warranted in a patient with rheumatoid arthritis who had signs or symptoms of disease activity, such as prolonged morning stiffness, fatigue, loss of function, swelling and tenderness of numerous joints, elevated levels of acute phase reactants, or progressive erosive changes visible on radiography. However, this patient's disease appears to be well controlled on her current medication regimen, and additional therapy would not be warranted.

KEY POINT

- Standard practice is to discontinue tumor necrosis factor α inhibitors in patients who develop cancers, including melanomas.

Bibliography

Wolfe F, Michaud K. Biologic treatment of rheumatoid arthritis and the risk of malignancy: analyses from a large US observational study. Arthritis Rheum. 2007;56(9):2886-2895. [PMID: 17729297]

Item 60   Answer: A

Educational Objective: Diagnose ankylosing spondylitis in a patient with anterior uveitis.

The patient has anterior uveitis with a hypopyon, and the associated systemic disease is most likely ankylosing spondylitis. The classic triad for acute anterior uveitis is pain, sensitivity to light, and blurred vision; headache, tenderness, and tearing may also occur. Photophobia during penlight examination has a positive predictive value of 60% for severe eye disease and a negative predictive value of 90%.

Prospective studies have documented systemic illness in 53% of patients with anterior uveitis. Patients with uveitis associated with systemic disease usually have a history or physical examination findings that suggest an underlying disorder. The most commonly diagnosed systemic illnesses in this setting are reactive arthritis, ankylosing spondylitis, and sarcoidosis.

Acute anterior uveitis, particularly unilateral presentations that fluctuate between both eyes over time, is strongly associated with the HLA-B27–related arthropathies, including ankylosing spondylitis. In addition, this patient's chronic back stiffness is highly suggestive of ankylosing spondylitis. Furthermore, in up to 65% of patients with uveitis, spondyloarthropathy remains undiagnosed until these patients present with uveitis.

Posterior uveitis may be related to sarcoidosis or vasculitis but is not typically associated with pain or redness of the eye. Patients with posterior uveitis also often have decreased visual acuity and floaters, which is not consistent with this patient's presentation. Furthermore, sarcoidosis is an unlikely cause of this patient's chronic low back pain.

Sicca syndrome manifests as dryness of the mouth, eyes, and vagina and variable enlargement of the parotid glands in association with concomitant redness and gritty irritation of the eyes. This condition is suggestive of primary or secondary Sjögren syndrome. However, Sjögren syndrome would not cause anterior uveitis and also would not explain the presence of chronic low back pain in a young man.

Anterior uveitis is associated with psoriasis and, in rare cases, Whipple disease, systemic lupus erythematosus, and the systemic vasculitides. However, the patient's long history of back pain in the absence of cutaneous and other manifestations of systemic lupus erythematosus makes this diagnosis unlikely.

KEY POINT

- The most commonly diagnosed systemic illnesses in patients with anterior uveitis are reactive arthritis, ankylosing spondylitis, and sarcoidosis.

Bibliography

Sampaio-Barros PD, Conde RA, Bonfiglioli R, Bértolo MB, Samara AM. Characterization and outcome of uveitis in 350 patients with spondyloarthropathies. Rheumatol Int. 2006;26(12):1143-1146. [PMID: 16957887]

Item 61   Answer: B

Educational Objective: Treat suspected lupus glomerulonephritis.

This patient's hypertension, ankle edema, hematuria, proteinuria, hypoalbuminemia, and erythrocyte casts on urinalysis are highly suggestive of lupus nephritis despite the absence of renal insufficiency. To prevent irreversible renal damage, early treatment with a high-dose corticosteroid such as prednisone is indicated for patients whose condition raises strong suspicion for lupus nephritis. Whether renal biopsy is necessary in this clinical situation in order to establish a diagnosis remains uncertain, and treatment with high-dose corticosteroids would not significantly alter subsequent biopsy results.

Initiation of antihypertensive therapy would benefit this patient but is not the most appropriate next step in the management of her condition; treatment of her nephritis takes precedence and may itself help to control her hypertension. Instead of a calcium channel blocker such as amlodipine, angiotensin-converting enzyme inhibitors are the antihypertensive drugs of choice in patients with lupus nephritis because these agents help to control proteinuria.

Ibuprofen may help to control this patient's arthralgia. However, NSAIDs can significantly worsen renal function in patients with lupus nephritis and are therefore contraindicated in this patient population.

Low-dose prednisone may help to alleviate this patient's arthralgia and rash but would not treat her lupus nephritis.

- **Early treatment with high-dose corticosteroids is indicated in patients whose condition raises strong suspicion for lupus nephritis.**

Bibliography

Buhaescu I, Covic A, Deray G. Treatment of proliferative lupus nephritis—a critical approach. Semin Arthritis Rheum. 2007; 36(4):224-237. [PMID: 17067659]

Item 62   Answer: B

Educational Objective: Manage reproductive health in a patient with systemic lupus erythematosus.

This patient has active systemic lupus erythematosus (SLE), lupus nephritis, antiphospholipid antibodies, and a history of recurrent fetal loss. The most appropriate management option for this patient is to start monthly leuprolide acetate injections.

Pregnancy outcomes in pregnant women with recently or currently active SLE at the time of conception tend to be poor, and pregnancy in this setting is associated with an increased risk of intrauterine growth restriction and premature birth. Furthermore, pregnant patients with SLE, particularly those with renal manifestations, have an increased risk of preeclampsia. Active SLE is therefore a relative contraindication to pregnancy.

Cyclophosphamide therapy, when combined with high-dose corticosteroids, is the treatment of choice in patients with lupus nephritis. However, this drug is a U.S. Food and Drug Administration category D agent in pregnancy, and conception should be avoided during its use. In addition, a course of cyclophosphamide is likely to cause infertility in a 31-year-old patient. Therefore, effective management of this patient's reproductive health consists of trying to avoid pregnancy during cyclophosphamide therapy and while SLE is active as well as trying to maintain fertility.

In patients with mildly to moderately severe SLE, dehydroepiandrosterone has been shown to lower disease activity. However, this therapy has not been shown to be beneficial in patients with lupus nephritis. This therapy also does not preserve fertility or provide contraception.

Monthly leuprolide acetate injections administered 2 weeks before administration of each cyclophosphamide dose will induce a temporary menopause and have been shown to protect the ovaries from the effects of cyclophosphamide. This treatment will maintain fertility and provide contraception, although use of a nonhormonal form of contraception, such as a barrier method or placement of an intrauterine device, is recommended to further ensure that pregnancy does not occur. Leuprolide acetate therapy can be discontinued once remission of this patient's renal disease has been achieved and she is switched from cyclophosphamide to mycophenolate mofetil (generally after 3 to 6 months).

Use of a nonhormonal form of contraception alone would not prevent cyclophosphamide-induced infertility in this patient.

Mycophenolate mofetil therapy does not have a detrimental effect on fertility and is an appropriate alternative to cyclophosphamide to induce and maintain remission of lupus nephritis. However, mycophenolate mofetil has been associated with birth defects and is therefore contraindicated during pregnancy. Women of child-bearing age should use effective contraception while taking this agent because of the risk of congenital malformation and pregnancy loss.

Oral contraceptives increase the risk of thrombosis and are generally avoided in patients with antiphospholipid antibodies. These agents also may exacerbate activity of SLE and are therefore contraindicated in patients with SLE who have active and/or unstable disease. However, recent studies have shown that oral contraceptives can be used in patients with mild, stable SLE without inducing a flare.

- **In women treated with cyclophosphamide, coadministration of leuprolide acetate helps to maintain fertility and provide contraception.**

Bibliography

Somers EC, Marder W, Christman GM, Ognenovski V, McCune WJ. Use of a gonadotropin-releasing hormone analog for protection against premature ovarian failure during cyclophosphamide therapy in women with severe lupus. Arthritis Rheum. 2005;52(9):2761-2767 [PMID: 16142702]

Item 63   Answer: E

Educational Objective: Diagnose ankylosing spondylitis.

This patient most likely has ankylosing spondylitis, and MRI of the sacroiliac joints is most likely to establish a diagnosis. Radiographic evidence of sacroiliitis is required for definitive diagnosis and is the most consistent finding associated with this condition. Onset of ankylosing spondylitis usually occurs in the teenage years or 20s and manifests as persistent pain and morning stiffness involving the low back that are alleviated with activity. This condition also may be associated with tenderness of the pelvis. Ankylosing spondylitis in women may have a less aggressive disease course than in men.

Typically, the earliest radiographic changes in affected patients involve the sacroiliac joints, but these changes may not be visible for several years; therefore, this patient's normal radiographs of the pelvis do not exclude sacroiliitis. MRI, especially with gadolinium enhancement, is considered a sensitive method for detecting early erosive inflammatory changes in the sacroiliac joints and spine and can assess sites of active disease and response to effective therapy.

Anti–cyclic citrullinated peptide antibodies are highly specific for rheumatoid arthritis. However, rheumatoid arthritis does not involve the sacroiliac joints or lumbar spine, and testing for this condition in this patient is therefore not indicated.

Increased radionuclide uptake of the sacroiliac joints on a bone scan would be consistent with but not specific for ankylosing spondylitis and would not confirm this diagnosis. Furthermore, assessing uptake of the sacroiliac joint on a bone scan may be difficult, because an increased signal usually exists in this site and differentiating normal uptake from abnormal uptake is not precise.

An elevated erythrocyte sedimentation rate would raise suspicion for an inflammatory process but would not help to establish a specific diagnosis. In addition, the erythrocyte sedimentation rate does not correlate with disease activity in patients with ankylosing spondylitis, and measurement of this value is therefore not useful in diagnosing or monitoring patients with this condition.

HLA-B27 positivity is a strong risk factor for ankylosing spondylitis. However, less than 5% of patients who have this allele develop this condition. In addition, not all patients who have ankylosing spondylitis have this allele. Therefore, it is neither 100% sensitive nor 100% specific for the diagnosis of ankylosing spondylitis.

KEY POINT

- MRI, especially with gadolinium enhancement, is a sensitive method for detecting early erosive inflammatory changes in the sacroiliac joints and spine.

Bibliography

Zochling J, Baraliakos X, Hermann KG, Braun J. Magnetic resonance imaging in ankylosing spondylitis. Curr Opin Rheumatol. 2007 Jul;19(4):346-352. [PMID: 17551364]

Item 64 Answer: A

Educational Objective: Treat early rheumatoid arthritis.

This patient has rheumatoid arthritis, and the most appropriate treatment patient is the addition of hydroxychloroquine, 400 mg/d. Prominent morning stiffness that usually lasts for more than 1 hour and fatigue are consistent with early presentations of rheumatoid arthritis. This condition most often involves the small joints of the hands and feet in a symmetric pattern, but involvement of the large joints also may occur. The presence of both rheumatoid factor and anti–cyclic citrullinated peptide antibodies is highly specific for rheumatoid arthritis, and radiographic manifestations of affected patients include periarticular osteopenia and, eventually, articular erosions.

In patients with rheumatoid arthritis, early, aggressive disease control is critical and should be instituted as soon as the diagnosis is established. Experts recommend that affected patients begin disease-modifying antirheumatic

drug (DMARD) therapy within 3 months of the onset of this condition. Hydroxychloroquine is warranted in a patient with early, mild, and nonerosive rheumatoid arthritis and is well tolerated.

Methotrexate is often used as an initial DMARD in the treatment of rheumatoid arthritis. However, this agent is associated with hepatotoxicity, and risk for this condition is increased in patients who regularly consume alcoholic beverages; therefore, methotrexate is not indicated for these patients. The amount of alcohol that can safely be consumed in patients who use methotrexate has not yet been determined, but daily consumption of alcoholic beverages while using this agent is not recommended and most experts advise against the use of methotrexate for patients who regularly consume alcohol.

The biologic DMARD etanercept would be an appropriate adjunct medication in a patient with rheumatoid arthritis in whom oral DMARD therapy has not provided adequate disease control. Etanercept and other tumor necrosis factor α inhibitors have greater efficacy when used in combination with methotrexate. However, there is currently insufficient evidence showing that single-agent use of a biologic DMARD is an appropriate initial treatment for this condition.

Combination therapy with an NSAID and a DMARD has been shown to reduce joint pain and swelling in patients with rheumatoid arthritis. However, increasing this patient's ibuprofen dosage in the absence of DMARD therapy would not help to control her disease progression or prevent radiographic damage.

KEY POINT

- In patients with rheumatoid arthritis, disease-modifying antirheumatic drug therapy should be initiated as soon as the diagnosis is established.

Bibliography

American College of Rheumatology Subcommittee on Rheumatoid Arthritis Guidelines. Guidelines for the management of rheumatoid arthritis: 2002 Update. Arthritis Rheum. 2002;46(2):328-346. [PMID: 11840435]

Item 65 Answer: C

Educational Objective: Diagnose relapsing polychondritis associated with respiratory failure.

This patient most likely has relapsing polychondritis, an inflammatory disorder of the cartilage. Diagnosis of this condition is based on the presence of inflammation in at least two cartilaginous sites (such as the ears, nose, or trachea) or the presence of inflammation at one site accompanied by at least two of the following features that need not be present at the same time: ocular inflammation, audiovestibular manifestations, and/or inflammatory arthritis. Typical laboratory abnormalities in patients with relapsing polychondritis include an elevated erythrocyte sedimentation rate and C-reactive protein level.

This patient's respiratory failure is consistent with one of the most severe forms of relapsing polychondritis, large-airway disease. Large-airway disease that includes the larynx, trachea, and bronchi may begin subtly and, if undiagnosed, may evolve into life-threatening disease. His tracheal tenderness and stridor are suggestive of tracheal inflammation and subglottic stenosis, which often cause tracheal and/or airway collapse in patients with severe manifestations of relapsing polychondritis. In addition, this patient's eye redness that resolved with eye drops is most likely a manifestation of inflammatory eye disease, which develops in up to 50% of patients with relapsing polychondritis.

Goodpasture syndrome is a pulmonary-renal syndrome characterized by the presence of anti–glomerular basement membrane antibodies. Affected patients commonly develop pulmonary hemorrhage and a rapidly progressive glomerulonephritis. Goodpasture syndrome may manifest as acute respiratory failure and may be associated with an elevated erythrocyte sedimentation rate and leukocyte count. However, this condition typically causes cough, hemoptysis, and fever and is unlikely in a patient with a normal chest radiograph and an absence of renal involvement.

Patients with rheumatoid arthritis can present with respiratory manifestations, and involvement of the cricoarytenoid joint in particular may cause hoarseness, stridor, and potential upper-airway respiratory distress. However, extra-articular disease is not usually the presenting manifestation of rheumatoid arthritis.

Systemic sclerosis is characterized by visceral fibrosis and vascular manifestations such as Raynaud phenomenon, whereas polymyositis is an inflammatory muscle disease characterized by proximal muscle weakness. One of the leading causes of mortality in patients with systemic sclerosis is pulmonary involvement, which most commonly manifests as interstitial lung disease (ILD) or pulmonary artery hypertension; polymyositis also may be associated with ILD. However, this patient does not have features compatible with ILD, such as dry cough, crackles heard on pulmonary examination, or bibasilar infiltrates visible on chest radiographs. His presentation also is not consistent with pulmonary artery hypertension, which may manifest as fatigue, dyspnea, syncope, a loud P_2 on cardiac auscultation, and central pulmonary artery enlargement seen on chest radiographs. In addition, pulmonary involvement in a patient with systemic sclerosis or polymyositis would have a more gradual onset and would not cause acute respiratory failure.

KEY POINT

- **Relapsing polychondritis may manifest acutely as respiratory failure associated with tracheal and/or airway collapse.**

Bibliography

Letko E, Zafirakis P, Baltatzis S, Voudouri A, Livir-Rallatos C, Foster CS, Relapsing polychondritis: a clinical review. Semin Arthritis Rheum. 2002;31(6):384-395. [PMID: 12077711]

Item 66   Answer: D

Educational Objective: Manage systemic lupus erythematosus in a pregnant patient.

This patient has systemic lupus erythematosus (SLE) and is in her first trimester of pregnancy, but her disease is well controlled with hydroxychloroquine. No change in treatment is warranted. She has had no symptoms of SLE for 10 months and currently has no signs of active disease, such as anemia, leukopenia, thrombocytopenia, hypocomplementemia, or anti–doubled-stranded DNA antibodies. She does have antinuclear, anti-Smith, and anti-Ro/SSA antibodies, but the presence of these autoantibodies does not vary with disease activity. Anti-Ro/SSA antibodies may be associated with congenital heart block in the fetus, and pregnant patients with these antibodies should undergo fetal echocardiography starting at 16 weeks of pregnancy.

Hydroxychloroquine is a U.S. Food and Drug Administration category C agent in pregnancy. However, this agent is useful for preventing SLE flares, and expert opinion considers use of this agent to be appropriate during pregnancy because the benefits outweigh the risks. Discontinuation of this agent is therefore not needed in this patient.

Patients with SLE whose disease has been quiescent for at least 6 months, during which time they either did not use medications for SLE or used medications that can safely be continued during pregnancy, generally have positive pregnancy outcomes. Therefore, there is no need to recommend termination of this patient's pregnancy.

Pregnancy may trigger SLE flares, and, if needed, prednisone can be used during pregnancy. However, the addition of prednisone would not be warranted in a patient with no signs of active SLE, and corticosteroids generally are not used prophylactically.

KEY POINT

- **Hydroxychloroquine is safe to use in pregnancy and is useful for preventing systemic lupus erythematosus flares.**

Bibliography

Clowse ME. Lupus activity in pregnancy. Rheum Dis Clin North Am. 2007;33(2):237-252, v. [PMID: 17499705]

Item 67   Answer: A

Educational Objective: Diagnose disseminated gonococcal infection.

This patient most likely has disseminated gonococcal infection (DGI). Bacterial arthritis is classified as gonococcal or nongonococcal; gonococcal infection is associated with a better outcome. Gonococcal arthritis is the most common form of bacterial arthritis in young sexually active adults and is most likely to develop after menstruation in young sexually active women.

DGI typically manifests as moderate fever and chills, subacute migratory polyarthralgia and arthritis, and tenosynovitis. Patients with this condition also may have tender pustular or vesiculopustular lesions on an erythematous base that usually develop on the distal extremities. DGI frequently involves the knees, hips, and wrists but not the spine. Synovial fluid analysis in patients with DGI usually reveals inflammatory synovial fluid, and microorganisms are rarely seen on Gram stain.

Genitourinary symptoms associated with DGI usually are absent in women, and genital infection in women may have occurred long before systemic dissemination. Rectal and pharyngeal colonization of *Neisseria gonorrhoeae* in the setting of DGI is commonly asymptomatic. In all patients with clinical suspicion for DGI, routine culture of the rectum, cervix, and pharynx, as well as the blood and the joints, is indicated.

More than 40% of patients with nongonococcal septic arthritis present without fever, and rigors infrequently occur in this setting. Nongonococcal septic arthritis usually manifests as acute monoarthritis and is not associated with pustular or vesiculopustular dermatitis. Gram staining of the synovial fluid is approximately 60% sensitive for bacteria in patients with nongonococcal septic arthritis. Synovial fluid culture is the gold standard for diagnosing nongonococcal joint infection in patients who have not undergone previous antibiotic therapy.

Parvovirus B19 infection is a viral condition that commonly develops in children, and adults often acquire this condition from infected children. Affected adults usually present with nonspecific symptoms such as malaise, myalgia, and fever. Parvovirus B19 infection may manifest as acute symmetric polyarthritis involving the hands, wrists, knees, and feet that is indistinguishable from rheumatoid arthritis or systemic lupus erythematosus. This patient's migratory arthritis is not compatible with this diagnosis.

Rheumatic fever is usually a disease of childhood but may present in adults as a migratory polyarthritis and fever. The knees, ankles, elbows, and wrists are affected most commonly. Arthritis might be the only initial symptom, but other manifestations may include carditis and chorea. Most importantly, patients with rheumatic fever do not have pustular skin lesions. Cutaneous findings in patients with rheumatic fever manifest as erythema marginatum, an evanescent, pink macular rash that affects the trunk and sometimes the limbs but not the face. This rash tends to expand centrifugally with clearing in the center.

Bibliography

Rice PA. Gonococcal arthritis (disseminated gonococcal infection). Infect Dis Clin North Am. 2005;19(4):853-861. [PMID: 16297736]

Item 68   Answer: D

Educational Objective: Diagnose Takayasu arteritis.

This patient's hypertension is most likely caused by renal artery stenosis. Her clinical presentation is strongly suggestive of Takayasu arteritis, a disease of the large arteries that most commonly affects young women. Typical initial manifestations of Takayasu arteritis include fever, arthralgia, myalgia, fatigue, and weight loss. Affected patients also commonly have elevated acute phase reactants, such as the erythrocyte sedimentation rate, and a normocytic, normochromic anemia.

After several weeks or months, patients with Takayasu arteritis develop symptoms of vascular insufficiency, such as arm and leg claudication, or hypertension that is usually caused by renal artery stenosis that is often bilateral. Affected patients also commonly have diminished, often asymmetric arterial pulses in the extremities.

Takayasu arteritis commonly causes stenoses in the aorta and its branches. Significant stenosis of one of the subclavian arteries, which is suggested by this patient's left subclavian bruit, results in decreased blood pressure in the ipsilateral arm. In patients with a discrepancy in blood pressure between the arms, the higher measurement is considered the most accurate. Blood pressure also can be measured in the legs, but some patients may have artificially low blood pressure in all four limbs because of large-vessel stenoses.

High-dose corticosteroids often help to resolve hypertension associated with Takayasu arteritis. However, renal artery bypass grafting or angioplasty may be needed if hypertension in patients treated with these agents persists.

Glomerulonephritis is unlikely in the absence of significant hematuria, proteinuria, or erythrocyte casts on urinalysis. In addition, although Takayasu arteritis may cause inflammation of the renal arteries, this condition does not cause glomerulonephritis.

Screening for pheochromocytoma is often performed in young patients with new-onset hypertension, but this patient's constitutional symptoms and elevated erythrocyte sedimentation rate are more consistent with an inflammatory process.

Polyarteritis nodosa is a necrotizing vasculitis of the medium-sized arteries that commonly involves the intrarenal and renal arteries. Aneurysmal beading of these vessels can be seen on angiography, and hypertension is common in affected patients. Signs and symptoms of large-vessel stenosis, such as claudication, bruits, or absence of peripheral pulses, are not consistent with polyarteritis nodosa.

KEY POINT

- The initial manifestations of Takayasu arteritis include fever, arthralgia, myalgia, fatigue, and weight loss and may precede the development of signs and symptoms of large-vessel narrowing by several months.

Bibliography

Samarkos M, Loizou S, Vaiopoulos G, Davies KA. The clinical spectrum of primary renal vasculitis. Semin Arthritis Rheum. 2005;35(2):95-111. [PMID: 16194695]

Item 69   Answer: B

Educational Objective: Manage suspected reactivation tuberculosis.

Adverse effects of tumor necrosis factor α (TNF-α) inhibitors include the risk for serious infection. Infliximab, adalimumab, and etanercept are associated with an increased incidence of reactivation tuberculosis, particularly extrapulmonary tuberculosis. Therefore, all patients being considered for such therapy should undergo screening for latent tuberculosis infection, which includes a full medical history, physical examination, tuberculin skin testing with purified protein derivative (PPD), or an interferon-γ release assay. If screening is positive, appropriate treatment for the patient's tuberculin status is indicated before beginning therapy with a TNF-α inhibitor. The Centers for Disease Control and Prevention recommends treatment of latent tuberculosis infection for all patients planning to take a TNF-α inhibitor who have a PPD result of 5 mm or more of induration or a positive interferon-γ release assay. Therefore, the most appropriate treatment for this patient is isoniazid for 9 months. Although the most appropriate duration of treatment with isoniazid before beginning infliximab is unknown, most experts recommend at least 2 months of isoniazid therapy before initiating a TNF-α inhibitor.

The finding of a normal PPD reaction does not rule out the possibility of latent tuberculosis infection, as rheumatoid arthritis may be associated with false-negative results, particularly in patients taking immunosuppressive drugs. Whenever infliximab or another TNF-α inhibitor is initiated, a high index of suspicion for reactivation tuberculosis must be maintained even after negative screening for latent tuberculosis. Therefore, initiation of infliximab without isoniazid therapy or initiation of infliximab concomitantly with isoniazid therapy would not be recommended in a patient with positive results on PPD testing.

Four-drug antituberculous therapy is indicated for active tuberculosis when a patient's drug resistance status is unknown but is not appropriate for this patient, who has no evidence of active tuberculosis.

KEY POINT

- The Centers for Disease Control and Prevention recommend treatment of latent tuberculosis infection for all patients planning to take a tumor necrosis factor α inhibitor who have a tuberculin skin test result of 5 mm or more of induration or a positive interferon-γ release assay.

Bibliography

Ponce de León D, Acevedo-Vásquez E, Sánchez-Torres A, et al. Attenuated response to purified protein derivative in patients with rheumatoid arthritis: study in a population with a high prevalence of tuberculosis. Ann Rheum Dis. 2005;64(9):1360-1361. [PMID: 16100342]

Item 70   Answer: D

Educational Objective: Diagnose prosthetic joint infection.

This patient most likely has prosthetic joint infection, which may occur at any time in the postoperative period. Prosthetic joint infections that occur after the first postoperative year are most frequently caused by hematogenous spread of organisms to the prosthetic joint. The source of infection in this setting is often obvious and includes skin or genitourinary tract infection or, as in this patient, an abscessed tooth. Pain is the predominant or only symptom in patients with prosthetic joint infection, and fever and leukocytosis are frequently absent. Patients with prosthetic joint infection usually have an elevated erythrocyte sedimentation rate. Radiography may reveal prosthetic loosening, but hardware loosening may occur in patients without infection, as well.

The gold standard for diagnosing prosthetic joint infection is arthrocentesis or intraoperative tissue sampling with culture before antibiotic therapy is initiated. The synovial fluid leukocyte count in patients with prosthetic joint infection is usually lower compared with that in patients with other forms of septic arthritis.

Aseptic loosening refers to loss of fixation of the arthroplasty components, which is a major long-term complication of hip arthroplasty. The most striking manifestation of this condition is pain in the proximal and medial aspect of the thigh that is worse with weight bearing. Osteolysis is typically seen on radiographs of affected patients, which this patient does not have. Aseptic loosening also would not explain this patient's inflammatory synovial fluid.

This patient's elevated synovial fluid leukocyte count with a predominance of neutrophils is suggestive of gout, but this condition does not have a subacute onset and does not commonly affect the hips. An acute attack of gout also would be associated with crystals visible on polarized light microscopy of the synovial fluid.

organism is not identified in an inflammatory synovial fluid or when empiric antibiotic therapy does not cause a response. Suspicion for viral, fungal, or mycobacterial infection requires further specialized laboratory investigations to establish the diagnosis. However, fungal arthritis is unlikely in the absence of signs and symptoms of inflammation. In addition, the synovial fluid in a patient with fungal arthritis would most likely be inflammatory and have a predominance of neutrophils.

KEY POINT

- Avascular necrosis is associated with systemic lupus erythematosus and with long-term use of high doses of corticosteroids and may manifest as chronic monoarticular arthritis in the absence of signs and symptoms of inflammation.

Bibliography

Margaretten ME, Kohlwes J, Moore D, Bent S. Does this adult patient have septic arthritis? JAMA. 2007;297(13):1478-1488. [PMID: 17405973]

Item 73   Answer: A

Educational Objective: Manage fibromyalgia.

This patient most likely has fibromyalgia, which typically affects women and most commonly occurs in patients between 40 and 60 years of age. The most appropriate next step in this patient's management is participation in a graded low-impact aerobic exercise program.

Fibromyalgia is characterized by chronic widespread musculoskeletal pain above and below the waist of at least 3 months' duration. Additional manifestations of fibromyalgia include fatigue and difficulty sleeping. This patient does not have constitutional symptoms or inflamed joints, which would suggest a systemic inflammatory condition.

The most appropriate initial management for fibromyalgia is regular participation in a graded low-impact aerobic exercise program. This intervention has been shown to benefit physical capacity in affected patients and to control the symptoms of this condition. Aerobic exercise is safe for patients with fibromyalgia but should be increased slowly, aiming for moderate intensity (at least 20 minutes per day 2 to 3 days weekly). If symptoms worsen, patients should decrease exercise until symptoms improve.

The only approved agents for fibromyalgia are pregabalin and duloxetine, which have been shown to help alleviate pain and fatigue and improve sleep quality. Off-label use of antidepressant drugs even in the absence of depressive symptoms may be helpful for mood, pain, and sleep symptoms associated with this condition but have limited effect on overall health outcomes.

An antinuclear antibody assay would be appropriate in a patient whose clinical presentation is suggestive of systemic lupus erythematosus. This condition is associated with polyarthralgias and fatigue but is unlikely in a patient who has no additional features associated with lupus, such as serositis, rash, and mucosal ulcerations.

Electromyography would be warranted in a patient whose clinical presentation raises suspicion for polymyositis. This condition affects the proximal and truncal muscles and may involve the neck but usually manifests as muscle weakness; if present, pain in this setting is usually mild. Patients with polymyositis also usually have elevated muscle enzyme levels, which are absent in this patient.

There are no data suggesting that off-label use of NSAIDs alone is effective in the treatment of fibromyalgia, but these agents may be beneficial in treating fibromyalgia when combined with amitriptyline (also off-label use).

Prednisone would be indicated for a patient with polymyalgia rheumatica, which may manifest as chronic pain involving the neck and shoulders and may be associated with fatigue. However, polymyalgia rheumatica exclusively affects patients over 50 years of age and is almost always associated with an elevated erythrocyte sedimentation rate. In addition, polymyalgia rheumatica would not explain this patient's lower back symptoms. Corticosteroids have not been shown to be effective in fibromyalgia.

KEY POINT

- Pregabalin and duloxetine are approved for the management of fibromyalgia.

Bibliography

Abeles M, Solitar BM, Pillinger MH, Abeles AM. Update on fibromyalgia therapy. Am J Med. 2008;121(7):555-561. [PMID: 18589048]

Item 74   Answer: D

Educational Objective: Treat septic arthritis in a patient with chronic gout.

This patient may have septic arthritis and should begin treatment with intravenous vancomycin. He has a history of chronic tophaceous gout but also has a history of cellulitis and the new onset of acute monoarthritis of the knee, fever, peripheral leukocytosis, and a markedly elevated synovial fluid leukocyte count. This constellation of symptoms is consistent with an acute flare of gout but also raises strong suspicion for septic arthritis. A diagnosis of septic arthritis should be considered in any patient who presents with the sudden onset of monoarthritis or the acute worsening of chronic joint disease. In patients with gout or pseudogout, the presence of crystals on polarized microscopic analysis of the synovial fluid does not exclude a concomitant infection. Therefore, until culture results are available, empiric antibiotic treatment is indicated for this patient.

Infection with gram-positive pathogens such as staphylococci or streptococci is the most common cause of septic arthritis in older patients. Therefore, vancomycin, which has broad gram-positive coverage, is the empiric therapy of choice in patients with suspected septic arthritis whose Gram stain reveals gram-positive organisms. Furthermore, many experts recommend empiric antibiotic therapy with vancomycin for immunocompetent patients with suspected septic arthritis and a negative Gram stain, whereas vancomycin and a third-generation cephalosporin such as ceftriaxone are recommended for patients who are immunocompromised or have trauma-associated infection. In addition, experts suggest careful joint management with repeated arthrocenteses or drainage until the inflammatory component of this condition is resolved.

If disseminated gonococcal infection is included in the differential diagnosis, ceftriaxone may be added to vancomycin.

Gram-negative organisms account for 9% to 20% of cases of septic arthritis, and certain pathogens occur more frequently in specific patient groups. For example, *Salmonella* infection has been reported in patients with systemic lupus erythematosus, AIDS, or sickle cell anemia, whereas patients who use illicit injection drugs often have infection with *Pseudomonas aeruginosa*. Comorbid medical conditions, a history of antibiotic use, and extra-articular infections (particularly urinary tract infections and decubitus ulcers) predispose patients to gram-negative septic arthritis.

Neither prednisone nor intra-articular corticosteroids are effective for treating infections.

KEY POINT

- **Pending culture results, empiric vancomycin is recommended for patients with suspected septic arthritis whose synovial fluid Gram stain reveals gram-positive organisms and for immunocompetent patients with a negative synovial fluid Gram stain.**

Bibliography
Mathews CJ, Coakley G. Septic arthritis: current diagnostic and therapeutic algorithm. Curr Opin Rheumatol. 2008;20(4):457-462. [PMID: 18525361]

Item 75 Answer: C
Educational Objective: Diagnose reactive arthritis.

This patient most likely has reactive arthritis, which may be associated with plantar fasciitis and Achilles tendinitis. Reactive arthritis is characterized by the presence of inflammatory arthritis that manifests within 2 months of an episode of bacterial gastroenteritis or nongonococcal urethritis or cervicitis in a genetically predisposed patient. This patient's history of conjunctivitis preceding her musculoskeletal symptoms is also consistent with this condition. Historically, what is now called reactive arthritis was previously called Reiter syndrome, which referred to the co-incidence of arthritis, conjunctivitis, and urethritis (or cervicitis). However, only one third of affected patients have all three symptoms. Reactive arthritis usually has an asymmetric

oligoarticular pattern and involves the lower extremities; inflammatory back pain also may be present. Reactive arthritis also may be associated with enthesitis, which commonly manifests as Achilles tendinitis (as seen in this patient), plantar fasciitis, and spondylitis. Reactive arthritis also is associated with numerous cutaneous manifestations, including keratoderma blenorrhagicum, oral ulcerations, and circinate balanitis.

Up to 20% of patients with Crohn disease or ulcerative colitis develop inflammatory joint disease. Polyarthritis that resembles seronegative rheumatoid arthritis develops in 20% of these patients, whereas 10% to 15% of these patients develop spondylitis. Joint involvement also may manifest as chronic or intermittent asymmetric oligoarthritis. Risk for inflammatory joint disease associated with Crohn disease or ulcerative colitis increases in patients with more advanced colonic conditions and additional concomitant extraintestinal manifestations, including abscesses, erythema nodosum, uveitis, or pyoderma gangrenosum. The course of peripheral arthritis parallels intestinal involvement except in those with spinal disease. The absence of bowel symptoms except for the initial infection, stable weight, and lack of cutaneous manifestations argue against enteropathic arthritis as the cause of this patient's findings.

Psoriatic arthritis is a systemic chronic inflammatory arthritis associated with numerous clinical manifestations. Asymmetric oligoarthritis of the large joints of the lower extremities is present in 40% of patients with this condition, whereas 25% of these patients develop small-joint polyarthritis similar to rheumatoid arthritis. Psoriatic arthritis also may manifest as uveitis, tendinitis, and enthesitis. Cutaneous involvement may be limited to nail pitting and commonly precedes joint inflammation, although 15% of affected patients develop joint inflammation first. However, in the absence of skin findings, this patient's preceding gastrointestinal infection most strongly suggests the diagnosis of reactive arthritis.

Rheumatoid arthritis is a symmetric polyarthritis that involves the small joints of the hands and feet as well as other joints throughout the body. The subacute onset of asymmetric oligoarthritis following a gastrointestinal infection is not characteristic of this condition.

KEY POINT

- **Reactive arthritis is characterized by the presence of inflammatory arthritis that manifests within 2 months of an episode of bacterial gastroenteritis or nongonococcal urethritis or cervicitis in a genetically predisposed patient.**

Bibliography
Carter JD. Reactive arthritis: defined etiologies, emerging pathophysiology, and unresolved treatment. Infect Dis Clin North Am. 2006;20(4):827-847. [PMID: 17118292]

Item 76   Answer: C

Educational Objective: Diagnose relapsing polychondritis.

This patient most likely has relapsing polychondritis. This condition is characterized by inflammation of the cartilage that commonly involves the nose, ears, trachea, and joints. Auricular involvement typically manifests as redness, swelling, and tenderness; rarely, hearing loss also may occur. Local trauma associated with cartilage piercing infrequently may trigger chondritis in these patients.

Relapsing polychondritis may have a relapsing-remitting disease course with self-limited episodes that often resolve without specific therapy and are often misdiagnosed as infection. In this patient, corticosteroids would help to manage her auricular symptoms. Relapsing polychondritis also may manifest as large-airway disease, which has an acute, severe presentation and can cause airway collapse and respiratory failure. Therefore, patients with relapsing polychrondritis should undergo evaluation for end-organ involvement, including upper-airway, and valvular manifestations. Screening for upper-airway involvement should include spirometry and flow volume loop, whereas echocardiography would help to evaluate for valvular manifestations.

Churg-Strauss syndrome and Wegener granulomatosis are small- to medium-vessel granulomatous vasculitides. Although Churg-Strauss syndrome may cause destruction of the nasal cartilage and Wegener granulomatosis frequently causes nasal cartilage inflammation resulting in saddle nose deformity, auricular cartilage involvement is not typical of either of these conditions.

Cogan syndrome is an autoimmune inflammatory disorder characterized by nonsyphilitic keratitis and audiovestibular dysfunction that results in progressive hearing loss. However, this condition is not characterized by inflammation of the cartilage.

KEY POINT

- Relapsing polychondritis is characterized by inflammation of the cartilage that commonly involves the nose, ears, trachea, and joints.

Bibliography
Kent PD, Michet CJ Jr, Luthra HS. Relapsing polychondritis. Current Opin Rheumatol. 2004; 16(1):56-61. [PMID: 14673390]

Item 77   Answer: B

Educational Objective: Diagnose gastric antral vascular ectasia (GAVE) in a patient with systemic sclerosis.

This patient most likely has gastric antral vascular ectasia (GAVE), also known as watermelon stomach. Patients with systemic sclerosis may develop cutaneous telangiectasias as well as mucosal telangiectasias that involve the upper and lower gastrointestinal tract; the development of telangiectasias in the stomach is known as GAVE and is associated with chronic blood loss. Most cases of GAVE are idiopathic and occur in elderly women, but this condition may occur secondary to systemic sclerosis or cirrhosis.

The presence of fatigue and iron deficiency anemia in a patient with systemic sclerosis should raise suspicion for GAVE. A diagnosis of GAVE is established if upper endoscopy shows telangiectasias in the antrum. In patients with this condition, endoscopic laser coagulation and obliteration of vascular ectasias is then indicated to decrease the risk of gastrointestinal bleeding.

The hallmark of erosive gastropathy is the development of erosive lesions or superficial ulcers due to a direct action of NSAIDs or alcohol, mucosal hypoxia, or a combination of factors. Erosions in this condition tend to be multiple and shallow and are usually located in the corpus and fundus. This patient has no apparent risk factors for erosive gastropathy, and the endoscopic appearance of her gastric mucosa is not consistent with this diagnosis.

Patients with gastric lymphoma may present with pain, anorexia, weight loss, and occult gastrointestinal bleeding. Most cases occur in individuals who are 50 to 60 years of age. On endoscopy, the appearance is varied and may include a gastric mass with or without ulceration, an ulcer, or nodular thickened gastric folds. This patient's endoscopic findings are incompatible with gastric lymphoma.

A condition similar to GAVE known as portal hypertensive gastropathy may develop in patients with cirrhosis and portal hypertension. In this condition, the severity of the gastropathy is related to the degree of portal hypertension, and there are diffuse antral angiomas rather than the classic linear pattern seen in GAVE. Portal hypertensive gastropathy is unlikely in a patient with no history of liver disease, hepatosplenomegaly, or ascites. In addition, the appearance of the gastric mucosa on endoscopy in this patient is not characteristic of this condition.

KEY POINT

- The presence of fatigue and iron deficiency anemia in a patient with systemic sclerosis should raise suspicion for gastric antral vascular ectasia.

Bibliography
Burak KW, Lee SS, Beck PL. Portal hypertensive gastropathy and gastric antral vascular ectasia (GAVE) syndrome. Gut. 2001;49(6): 866-872. [PMID: 11709525]

Item 78   Answer: A

Educational Objective: Treat Henoch-Schönlein purpura.

This patient most likely has Henoch-Schönlein purpura (HSP), a typically self-limited condition that is characterized by purpuric rash, arthralgia, abdominal pain, and renal involvement that may manifest as hematuria and proteinuria.

His skin biopsy shows leukocytoclastic vasculitis accompanied by perivascular IgA deposition, which is characteristic of HSP. The most appropriate management for this patient is short-term treatment with a corticosteroid such as prednisone in order to provide symptomatic relief.

There is no evidence showing that infliximab, rituximab, cyclophosphamide, or plasmapheresis is beneficial in patients with HSP. Furthermore, no agent has yet been found that modifies the natural history of renal disease in HSP.

KEY POINT

- Management of Henoch-Schönlein purpura may include short-term corticosteroids, which provide symptomatic relief but do not alter the course of the disease.

Bibliography

Gedalia A. Henoch-Schönlein purpura. Curr Rheumatol Rep. 2004;6(3):195-202 [PMID: 15134598]

Item 79   Answer: A

Educational Objective: Diagnose Sjögren syndrome–associated lymphoma.

This patient's symptoms of keratoconjunctivitis sicca (dry eyes and dry mouth); the presence of antinuclear, anti-Ro/SSA, and anti-La/SSB antibodies; and an elevated rheumatoid factor level are characteristic of primary Sjögren syndrome. Her fatigue, arthralgia, Raynaud phenomenon, and low-grade fever also are consistent with this condition. Sjögren syndrome also may occur secondary to another autoimmune disease, such as rheumatoid arthritis or systemic lupus erythematosus.

Patients with primary Sjögren syndrome have up to a 44-fold increased incidence of lymphoma, particularly non-Hodgkin lymphoma, and should be monitored closely for lymphadenopathy. This patient's firm enlarged left axillary lymph node and pancytopenia particularly raise suspicion of lymphoma, and an excisional axillary lymph node biopsy is the most appropriate next step in this patient's management.

A minor (labial) salivary gland biopsy would help to confirm the diagnosis of Sjögren syndrome and would reveal increased lymphocytic infiltration. Because this patient has clinical evidence of Sjögren syndrome, salivary gland biopsy is not necessary; furthermore, this study would not help to evaluate this patient's enlarged axillary lymph node.

Prednisone may help to treat constitutional symptoms associated with Sjögren syndrome but would not address this patient's more urgent enlarged left axillary lymph node. In addition, her constitutional symptoms may be manifestations of malignancy and not Sjögren syndrome.

Infective endocarditis may manifest as fever, fatigue, and lymphadenopathy, and transthoracic echocardiography can help to diagnose this condition. However, infective endocarditis is unlikely in a patient with no cardiac abnormalities; negative blood culture results; and an absence of associated vascular phenomena or risk factors for this condition. Therefore, transthoracic echocardiography would not be warranted in this patient.

KEY POINT

- Patients with primary Sjögren syndrome have up to a 44-fold increased incidence of lymphoma and should be monitored closely for lymphadenopathy.

Bibliography

Voulgarelis M, Dafni UG, Isenberg DA, Moutsopoulos HM. Malignant lymphoma in primary Sjögren's syndrome: a multicenter, retrospecive, clinical study by the European Concerted Action on Sjögren's Syndrome. Arthritis Rheum. 1999;42(8):1765-1772. [PMID: 10446879]

Index

Note: Page numbers followed by f and t denote figures and tables, respectively. Test questions are indicated by a Q.

for systemic lupus erythematosus, 11, 40
Hypertension, pulmonary, in systemic sclerosis, 45, 46, Q45
Hyperuricemia, 49–53, 50t. *See also* Gout
    treatment of, 52–53
Hypocomplementemia, in rheumatic disease, 7

Idiopathic inflammatory myopathies. *See* Inflammatory myopathies
Immune globulin, for inflammatory myopathies, 63
Immunization
    in immunosuppression, 14
    in systemic lupus erythematosus, 40
Immunosuppression
    antibiotic prophylaxis for, 14
    immunization in, 14
    for inflammatory myopathies, 63
    reactivation tuberculosis and, 14, Q69
    for rheumatic disease, 11–12, 14
Inclusion body myositis, 59–63, 60t, Q31. *See also* Inflammatory myopathies
Infectious arthritis. *See* Septic arthritis
Inflammatory bowel disease
    arthritis in, 7, 31t, 32
    joint involvement in, 2t
Inflammatory myopathies, 59–63
    cancer and, 63
    classification of, 59, 60t
    clinical features of, 59–60, 60t
    diagnosis of, 60–62, Q50
    epidemiology of, 59
    pathophysiology of, 59
    prognosis of, 63
    treatment of, 62–63
Infliximab
    for rheumatic disease, 13
    for rheumatoid arthritis, 13, 20
Influenza, immunization for, in immunosuppression, 14
Interstitial lung disease
    anti–Scl-70 antibody in, 8
    in inflammatory myopathies, 60
    in rheumatic disease, 6–7
    in systemic sclerosis, 43, 45
Intestinal pseudo-obstruction, in systemic sclerosis, 45
Intravenous immune globulin, for inflammatory myopathies, 63
Isoniazid, prophylactic, in immunosuppression, 14

Jobe test, 4
Joint aspiration, 9
    for septic arthritis, 58
Joint infections, prosthetic, 57, Q70
Joint pain. *See* Pain, joint
Juvenile dermatomyositis, 59–63, 60t. *See also* Inflammatory myopathies

Kawasaki disease, 64t
Keratoconjunctivitis sicca, in Sjögren syndrome, 47–48
Keratoderma blennorrhagicum, 6
Kidney disease. *See under* Renal
Knee
    bursitis of, 3
    crepitus of, 22, 23
    effusion in, 5, 5f
    examination of, 5, 5f
    instability of, 23, 24f
    osteoarthritis of, 22–26. *See also* Osteoarthritis
    pain in, differential diagnosis of, 1–3
    total arthroplasty for, 26
        infection in, 57

Lactation, disease-modifying antirheumatic drugs and, 21
Lateral epicondylitis, 3
Leflunomide
    for psoriatic arthritis, 34
    for rheumatoid arthritis, 12, 20
Leukocytes, in synovial fluid, 9
Leukopenia, in systemic lupus erythematosus, 38
Lifestyle modification, in rheumatic disease, 14
Livedo reticularis, 6
    in cutaneous leukocytoclastic vasculitis, 70, 70f
Low-purine diet, for gout, 52
Lung disease. *See also under* Pulmonary

interstitial
    in inflammatory myopathies, 60
    in systemic sclerosis, 43
    in rheumatic disease, 6–7
    in systemic lupus erythematosus, 37–38
Lupus erythematosus
    discoid, 36, Q18, Q20
    drug-induced, 39, 40t
    neonatal, 8, 41
    subacute cutaneous, 36, 37f
    systemic. *See* Systemic lupus erythematosus
Lupus glomerulonephritis, 37, Q61
Lupus nephritis, 36–37
    membranous, 37
    mycophenolate mofetil for, 12
    proliferative, 36–37
    treatment of, 41, Q27
Lupus pneumonitis, 37–38
Lyme disease
    joint involvement in, 2t
    rash in, 5, 6f
Lymphoma, in Sjögren syndrome, 48, Q79

Macular toxicity, of hydroxychloroquine, 11
Magnetic resonance imaging
    in musculoskeletal disorders, 9
    in rheumatic disease, 9
Malar rash, in systemic lupus erythematosus, 4, 35–36, 36f, 37f
Mechanic's hands, 5, 8
    in dermatomyositis, 59, 61t
Medial epicondylitis, 3
Membranoproliferative glomerulonephritis, 37, Q61
Membranous lupus nephritis, 37
Methotrexate
    for ankylosing spondylitis, 34
    for reactive arthritis, 34
    for rheumatoid arthritis, 11, 12–13, 20
    for Wegener granulomatosis, 68
Microscopic polyangiitis, 8, 64t, 67, 68–69
Milwaukee shoulder, 54
Miscarriage, in antiphospholipid syndrome, 38, 41
Mixed connective tissue disease, 8, 48–49, Q40
Monoclonal antibodies, for rheumatic disease, 12–13
Mononeuritis multiplex, in rheumatoid arthritis, 19
Morphea, 46
Mouth. *See under* Oral
Muscle biopsy, in inflammatory myopathies, 62
Muscle inflammation. *See* Myositis
Muscle weakness, in inflammatory myopathies, 59
Musculoskeletal examination, 4–5, 5f
    imaging studies in, 8–9
    joint aspiration in, 9
    laboratory findings in, 7–8
    physical findings in, 4–5, 5f
Mycobacterial arthritis, 55t, 56
Mycophenolate mofetil
    for lupus nephritis, 12
    for systemic lupus erythematosus, 41
Myositis, 59–63, 60t. *See also* Inflammatory myopathies
    inclusion body, 59–63, 60t, Q31
    in mixed connective tissue disease, 48, 49, Q53
    systemic sclerosis and, 44
Myxoma, vs. vasculitis, 65t

Nails, in psoriatic arthritis, 32–33, 33f, 34f
Neonatal lupus erythematosus, 8, 41
Nephritis, lupus, 36–37, Q27
    mycophenolate mofetil for, 12
    treatment of, 41
Nephrogenic systemic fibrosis, 47t
Nephrolithiasis, in gout, 50t, 52
Neuropathic arthropathy, vs. calcium pyrophosphate deposition disease, 53
Nodules, rheumatoid, 16, 17f
Nonsteroidal antiinflammatory drugs (NSAIDs)
    for gouty arthritis, 51
    for osteoarthritis, 25
    proton pump inhibitors with, 10
    for rheumatic arthritis, 10, 20